AF605903

# WOMEN'S SPACE

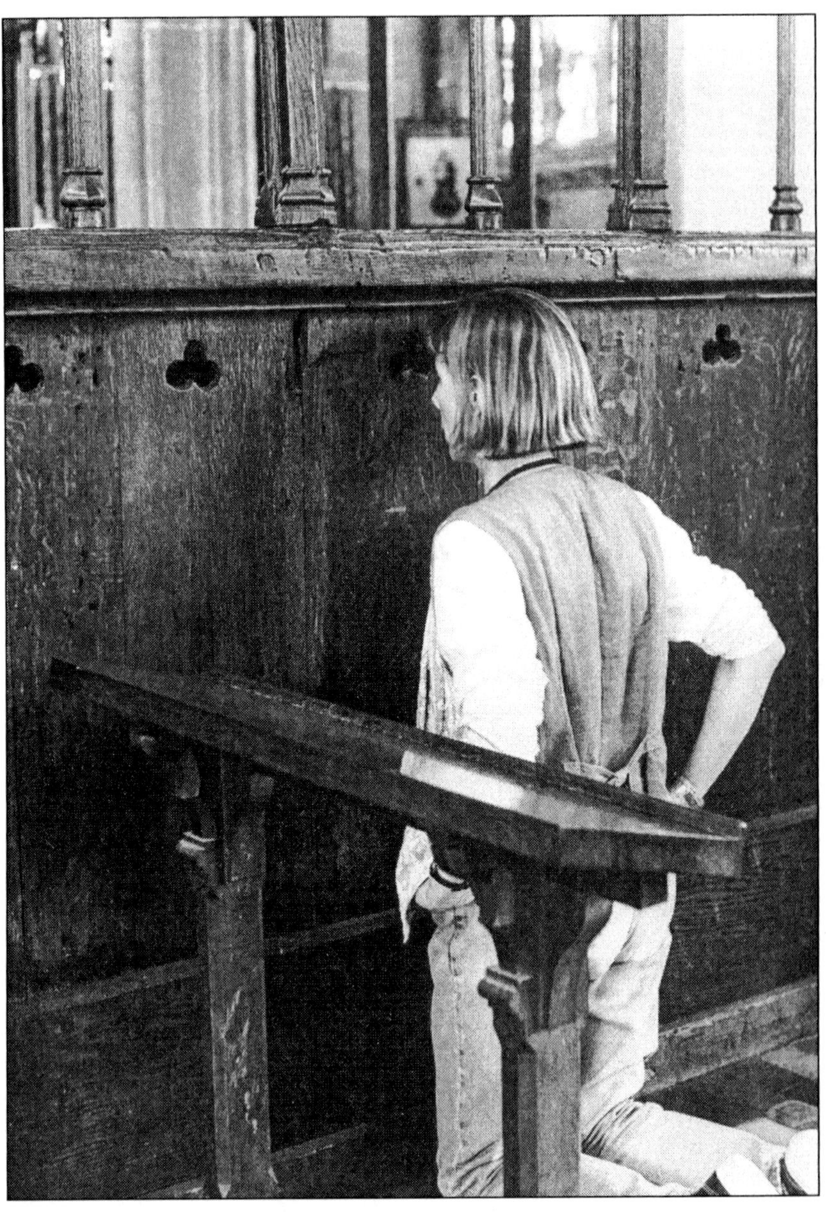

Squints in rood screen at church of St. Peter and St. Paul, Lavenham. Photo Virginia Raguin.

SUNY series in Medieval Studies

*Paul E. Szarmach, editor*

# WOMEN'S SPACE

## *Patronage, Place, and Gender in the Medieval Church*

EDITED BY

VIRGINIA CHIEFFO RAGUIN

AND

SARAH STANBURY

STATE UNIVERSITY OF NEW YORK PRESS

Published by
State University of New York Press, Albany



Printed in the United States of America



For information, address the State University of New York Press,
90 State Street, Suite 700, Albany, NY 12207

Production, Laurie Searl
Marketing, Susan Petrie

**Library of Congress Cataloging-in-Publication Data**

Women's space : patronage, place, and gender in the medieval church / edited by Virginia Chieffo Raguin and Sarah Stanbury.
p. cm. — (SUNY series in medieval studies)
Includes bibliographical references and index.
ISBN 0-7914-6365-6 (alk. paper)
1. Women—Religious life—History. 2. Church history—Middle Ages, 600–1500. I. Raguin, Virginia Chieffo, 1941– II. Stanbury, Sarah. III. Series.

BR163.W66 2005
274'.052'082—dc22 2004048159

10 9 8 7 6 5 4 3 2 1

# CONTENTS

List of Illustrations vii

Introduction 1
*Sarah Stanbury and Virginia Chieffo Raguin*

1 Signs of the Body: Gender, Sexuality, and Space in York and the York Cycle 23
*Ruth Evans*

2 Ely's St. Æthelthryth: The Shrine's Enclosure of the Female Body as Symbol for the Inviolability of Monastic Space 47
*Virginia Blanton*

3 Margery Kempe and the Arts of Self-Patronage 75
*Sarah Stanbury*

4 Real and Imaged Bodies in Architectural Space: The Setting for Margery Kempe's *Book* 105
*Virginia Chieffo Raguin*

5 The Seat under Our Lady: Gender and Seating in Late Medieval English Parish Churches 141
*Katherine L. French*

6 Access to Salvation: The Place (and Space) of Women Patrons in Fourteenth-century Florence 161
*Ena Giurescu Heller*

7 Gender, Celibacy, and Proscriptions of Sacred Space: Symbol and Practice 185
*Jane Tibbetts Schulenburg*

8 Men on the Right—Women on the Left: (A)symmetrical Spaces and Gendered Places 207
*Corine Schleif*

List of Contributors 251

Index 253

# ILLUSTRATIONS

Frontispiece. Squints in rood screen at Church of St. Peter and St. Paul, Lavenham.

2.1. *Miracle of Æthelthryth's Resistance to Ecgfrith's Desire*, 1330s? Octagon Capital, Ely Cathedral, Ely, England. 59

3.1. Flint inscription, ca. 1496, "Pray for ye sowle of William Clopton esqwyer . . . ," Lady Chapel, Holy Trinity Church, Long Melford. 81

3.2. Elizabeth Talbot and Elizabeth Tilney, late fifteenth century, Holy Trinity Church, Long Melford. 82

3.3. Lady of Pity, with donor, late fifteenth century, Holy Trinity Church, Long Melford. 87

3.4. Trinity, late fifteenth century, Holy Trinity Church, Long Melford. 92

3.5. Alabaster Trinity, 1400–1450, Museum of Fine Arts, Boston. 93

3.6. Trinity Man of Sorrows with donor John Walker, late fifteenth century, Holy Trinity Goodramgate, York. 95

4.1. King's Lynn, St. Margaret's, exterior, south side. After William Taylor, *The Antiquities of King's Lynn* (London, 1844). 106

4.2. King's Lynn, St. Margaret's, plan 1102–1481, length 236 feet. After E. M. Beloe, F.S.A., *Our Borough: Our Churches: King's Lynn, Norfolk* (Cambridge, 1899). 107

4.3. King's Lynn, St. Margaret's, interior of choir, south side. After William Taylor, *The Antiquities of King's Lynn* (London, 1844). 108

4.4. Mary of Burgundy at Prayer, *Hours of Mary of Burgundy*, ca. 1477, Vienna Österreichische Nationalbibliothek, Cod. Vind. 1857, fol. 14v. 110

4.5. Philip the Good Attending Mass, *Traité sur l'oraison dominicale*, trans. Jean Miélot, Lille(?), ca. 1460, Brussels, Royal Library, MS 9092, fol. 9. 111

4.6. Margaret Tudor at Prayer, *Book of Hours of James IV*, ca. 1503, Vienna Österreichische Nationalbibliothek, Cod. 1897, fol. 243v. 112

4.7. Christ the Good Shepherd, Ebsdorf, Benedictine nunnery, Cloister window, 1400–1410. 118

4.8. Parable of Vine-dressers, *Speculum humanae salvationis*, ca. 1360, Darmstadt, Hessische Landes und Hochschulbibliothek Hs 2505, fol. 41. 120

4.9. Parable of Vine-dressers, Ebsdorf, Benedictine nunnery, Cloister window, 1400–1410. 121

4.10. Brass of Adam de Walsoken and wife Margaret, 1349, St. Margaret's, King's Lynn, Detail of bottom, men carry grist to mill and carry Walsoken in litter over stream. After John Sell Cotman, *Engravings of Sepulchral Brasses in Norfolk* (London: Bohn, 1838). 127

4.11. Brass of Robert Braunche with Leticia, first, and Margaret, second wife, 1364, St. Margaret's, King's Lynn, Detail of bottom, Peacock Feast. After John Sell Cotman, *Engravings of Sepulchral Brasses in Norfolk* (London: 1838). 128

6.1. Santa Maria Novella, Florence, facade of the church. 162

6.2. Santa Maria Novella, Florence, plan of the church in the fourteenth century. After James Wood Brown, *The Dominican Church of Santa Maria Novella of Florence* (Edinburgh, 1902). 163

6.3. Sacristy, interior view, Santa Maria Novella, Florence. 164

6.4. Giovanni del Biondo, *Annunciation and Saints*, ca. 1385, tempera on panel, Accademia, Florence. 165

6.5. Italian School, *Apparition of St. Michael* (detail), 1330s, fresco, Velluti Chapel, Santa Croce, Florence. 170

8.1. Jan van Eyck, *Altarpiece of the Lamb*, closed, 1432, Cathedral of St. Bavo, Ghent. After Hermann Beenken, *Hubert und Jan Van Eyck*. (Munich: Bruckman, 1941). 208

8.2. Jan van Eyck, *Altarpiece of the Lamb*, open, 1432, Cathedral of St. Bavo, Ghent. 209

8.3. Rogier van der Weyden, *Last Judgment Altarpiece*, closed, after 1433, Musée de l'Hôtel Dieu, Beaune. 209

8.4. Rogier van der Weyden, *Last Judgment Altarpiece*, open, after 1433, Musée de l'Hôtel Dieu, Beaune. 210

8.5. *Crucifixion*, Herrad of Hohenbourg's *Hortus deliciarum*. Nineteenth-century copy of destroyed original, ca.1180–95. After A. Straub and G. Keller, *Herrade de Landsberg, Hortvs Delictarvm* (Schlesier and Schweikhardt: Strasbourg, 1879–99). 214

8.6. Attributed to Hans Schäufelein, *Crucifixion*, 1520, oil on panel, Collegiate Church, Tübingen. 215

8.7. *Wise and Foolish Virgins*, ca. 1130, stone sculpture, archivolts over the central west portal, Saint-Pierre, Aulnay. 216

8.8. Jakob Elsner, miniature showing the Synthronoi Trinity, Kreß Missal, 1513. Germanisches Nationalmuseum, Nuremberg, Hs 113264, fol. 2v. 217

8.9. *Christ and Six Apostles*, north choir enclosure, ca. 1200, stucco, Liebfrauenkirche, Halberstadt. 218

8.10. *Virgin and Six Apostles*, south choir enclosure, ca. 1200, stucco, Liebfrauenkirche, Halberstadt. 218

8.11. *Virgin and Apostles with Saint Benedict*, north choir enclosure, ca. 1200, stucco, St. Michaelskirche, Hildesheim. 219

8.12. Male and Female Martyrs, ca. 490, mosaic, Sant' Apollinare Nuovo, Ravenna. 219

8.13. Gregor Erhart, *Madonna Misericordia*, 1510–14, stone sculpture, Wallfahrtskirche, Frauenstein (Austria). 221

8.14. *Emperor Justinian with Entourage*, ca. 547, mosaic, north side of choir, San Vitale, Ravenna. 222

8.15. *Empress Theodora with Entourage*, ca. 547, mosaic, south side of choir, San Vitale, Ravenna. 223

8.16. *Savonarola Preaching in Florence Cathedral*, 1496, woodcut illustration from *Compendio di Revelatione dello inutile servo di Iesu Cristo Frate Hieronymo da Ferrara*. 227

8.17. Sano di Pietro, *San Bernardino Preaching in Piazza San Francesco in Siena*, 1444–50, tempera on panel, Siena Cathedral. 228

8.18. Sano di Pietro, *San Bernardino Preaching in the Piazza del Campo*, 1444–50, tempera on panel, Siena Cathedral. 229

8.19. Bernd Notke, Crucifixion Group, 1477, wood sculpture, Lübeck Cathedral. 231

8.20. Wipplar Epitaph, ca. 1420, tempera on panel, St. Lorenzkirche, Nuremberg. 232

8.21. *Queen Aelfgifu (Emma) and King Cnut Presenting a Cross to New Minster*, 1031, Winchester, *Liber vitae*, London, British Library, Stowe MS 944, fol. 6r. 232

8.22. *Margarete of Holland and Ludwig the Bavarian with the Virgin and Child*, 1321–24, stone relief, Bayerisches Nationalmusem, Munich. 233

8.23. *Emperor Charles IV and Anna von Schweidnitz Venerating the Virgin and Child*, 1355, fresco, Karlstein. 234

8.24. Piero della Francesca, Portrait of Battista Sforza, after 1472, oil on panel, Uffizi Gallery, Florence. 234

8.25. Piero della Francesca, Portrait of Federico da Montefeltro, after 1472, oil on panel, Uffizi Gallery, Florence. 235

8.26. *Abbess Hitda Presenting Gospel Book to Saint Walburga*, ca. 1000, Hitda Codex, Darmstadt, Landesbibliothek, cod. 1640, fol. 6r. 236

8.27. *Mystical Marriage of St. Catherine*, 1491, Antiphonal, Regensburg, Bischöfliche Zentralbibliothek. 237

8.28. *St. Anne Altarpiece*, 1510–23, St. Lorenzkirche, Nuremberg. 238

8.29. *Last Judgment with Charles IV and Elizabeth of Pomerania*, 1370, mosaic, Golden Portal, St. Vitus Cathedral, Prague. 240

8.30. Bumper Sticker, *Links tut gut* (Left feels good or Left does well), late 1990s. 242

# INTRODUCTION

Sarah Stanbury and Virginia Chieffo Raguin

THIS INTERDISCIPLINARY COLLECTION of essays addresses the location of women and their bequests within the single most important public and social space in pre-Reformation Europe: the church. As Virginia Woolf eloquently phrased the dilemma of women's spaces in *A Room of One's Own*, female autonomy has always been closely linked to resources. Room in the church was similarly a question of the power to pay. Focusing on women as donors and as "paying customers" in a world of art and ritual, this volume explores definitions of strategies of empowerment, addressing questions of class—both mercantile and noble—and of acquired as well as inherited wealth.[1] When we examine village and urban life in the Middle Ages, we often turn to gifts to the parish as key records of the social and economic power of the local families and individuals. What were the strategies for demonstrating or acquiring power through largess? How did women, as well as men, define their status not only by the giving of gifts to the church, but also by the artistic quality of their gifts? And most germane to the concerns of this volume, how did the placement of those bequests—and of living bodies—in religious buildings define the identity of the giver? In a media culture the choice of dress, so vividly affirmed in the display of the Hollywood pecking order on Oscar night, is a means of claiming one's own space, one's right to be present and be seen by others. In a parish culture, the most visible way to project and commemorate family and self is through acts of donation, specifically through the donation of named gifts to the church.

The parish is conceptually central to this volume, for it was in the medieval parishes, not the great cathedrals, that most people in the Middle Ages experienced daily and weekly religious ritual and the landmark ceremonies marking individual and community life, such as baptism, marriage, and death. Medieval parish space incorporated a richness of display now deeply compromised by later usage. Complex imagery in stained glass and wall painting represented both the eternal, in its panoply of saints, and the mundane, in the invariable donor petition and image. Tomb monuments in private chapels and in floor slabs resonated with both piety and self-advertisement. Space within the church articulated the lay practice of the sacraments: baptismal fonts conspicuously displayed town wealth and armorials of prominent families, confessional pews localized the administration of penance, and elaborate porches formed backdrops to the ceremonials of churching and marriage. Medieval churches, few now intact but many more reconstructed with their furnishing from composite sources, are microcosms of the life of the village. In architectural studies, however, which routinely pass over the parish to focus their gaze on the great cathedrals, the ritual and design of the medieval parish have been historically neglected. One important contribution of this collection will be to redress that neglect and focus attention on the uses of parish space in the material, cultural, and imaginative life of medieval women.

The chapters in this volume also contribute to our understanding of the gendered uses of space in medieval monasteries. Given the restricted nature of parish documentation, especially for the earlier Middle Ages, historians have continued to study monastic chroniclers to find records of women's interaction with privileged, sacred space. Until the development of the primacy of the urban community in the thirteenth century, the centers of power were the great landed estates and the monasteries. Indeed, because the nobility comprised most of the monastic population, especially the offices of abbots, the monastery was an extension of a class. Emerging thus from patterns of family alliances and systems of gift exchange (the spiritual for the material), documents from these sites describe both consolidation of wealth and negotiated access, invariably linked to gender prohibitions. Historians have also found documentation of attempts to limit the access and influence of real women, even as these documents construct elaborate systems of symbolic gender privilege—as, for instance, when the "physical" woman, especially in her role as a producer of offspring, is elided to prioritize the virginal state. The position of the virgin, at the same time, could be constructed as one demanding shelter, seclusion, and protection, effectively grouping women as a class as either too polluted for sacred space or too fragile to be given access to social spaces where they might be contaminated by others. Using such metaphoric shifts between the real and the ideal, the literature and chronicles of this time set the groundwork for the later parsings of space by gender that come to organize the physical life of the parish.

*Women's Space* engages in dialogue with studies that have considered the ways that space articulates the psychic and material demands of a community.[2] Architectural history and cultural studies have increasingly paid attention to the complex tissue of social threads that connect buildings with the people that commission them and use them. In 1956 Otto Von Simpson wrote *The Gothic Cathedral: Origins of Gothic Architecture and the Medieval Concept of Order*, in which he characterizes Gothic form as reflection of "the medieval mind" and the "Christian imagination" in an attempt to find in an architectural form the mirror of a generalized intellectual consciousness.[3] Postmodern work on space, suspicious of the grand récit, has attempted to dismantle holistic projects and master narratives such as Von Simpson's in order to consider economic or political forces that produce ideologies and their ideograms, such as "the" Gothic cathedral. Forty-five years after Von Simpson's landmark book, analyses of medieval religious architecture are much more likely to be site-specific and attentive to the political and ideological agendas that commissioned and paid for the construction of buildings: how did families with the means to endow them make key choices about the placement and decoration of private chapels within a church; or, more broadly, how did the screens separating chancel from nave reinforce social hierarchies separating lay parishioners from the clergy?

Perhaps the most influential recent work to consider the integration between space and community is the writing of French anthropologist Pierre Bourdieu, whose work is best known for the theories of habitus and field, theories of social behavior that grew from his fieldwork among the Berbers in Morocco. "Field" may be understood as the site of play and "habitus" as the rules of game or, as Bourdieu puts it, "history turned into nature."[4] Actions or practices of the habitus are those we attribute to "nature," whether that nature is imagined as custom or as biology (as in "human nature") but that nevertheless owe their apparent logic or rightness to conditions of production shared, however unconsciously, by a group. The spaces we inhabit, embodied projections of the habitus, represent and also enact the laws of community organization and the deep structures of community psyche. In his well-known analysis of a Kabyle house, Bourdieu reads its organization as a mirror of oppositions that its inhabitants perceive as fundamental to the organization of the universe. Opposing the public domain, the home is structured by public/private contraries that take as their organizing principle the male/female divide: the lower part of the house, which is kept for livestock and is damp, dark, generative, and private, corresponds to the female, whereas the upper section, which is dry, bright, and public as the space for visitors, corresponds to the male. By mimicking in its boundaries the divides that structure society, the house reifies a perception of the world as organized by male/female opposition, for it requires that we repeat and live out the opposition between the "male discontinuous and the female continuous" in everyday practices of inhabitation.[5] As Bourdieu's reading of the house makes clear, the gendered divide is so deeply etched as to make the divisions of domestic space seem a principle of nature or even of cosmic and biological law. Behaviors are practices that come to seem like natural law as we repeat them; the house affirms the logic not only of the social body but of nature itself.

Bourdieu's influence has been increasingly felt in studies of performance and space, for both provide a clearly defined "field" or place of play articulated by specific and apparently "doxic" or naturalized practices. While Bourdieu's writing on gender has been limited, his work has consistently argued that all aspects of culture, high or low, participate in the process of legitimizing structures of power in a process that simultaneously renders those structures invisible.[6] In an analysis of Bourdieu's importance for feminists, Toril Moi argues that while Bourdieu has been critiqued for essentialism, his persistent attention to the everyday, coupled with his anti-essentialist position that all systems of power are both constructed and arbitrary, offers important methodological tools for feminist scholars engaged in the work of revisiting the traditional or, as Bourdieu might say, doxic accounts of cultural productions.[7]

Feminist studies of space have consistently argued a position similar to Bourdieu's in addressing the systems of power that gird what appear to be culturally naturalized oppositions—which is to say, the practices of gender and the buildings that underwrite them. As feminist geographer Doreen Massey puts it, "geography matters"[8]—understanding geography to be a discipline engaged in the semiotics of materiality and embodiment. Voicing as a global truth the mantra of the real estate broker (location, location, location), the title of Massey's essay collection, *Geography Matters!* directs attention to the crucial function of spatial coordinates. As this and other recent work in cultural and feminist geography demonstrates, the "mattering" of the map comes from social and cultural codes that place differing values on bodies; it comes from the fact that the history of human habitation, or geography, is a social history nuanced by the workings of power and exclusion.[9] Events occur, things happen, because of the actions of bodies, human or inanimate, in mappable spaces. Objects and landforms created by human bodies generally do not appear because of chance (being at the right place at the right time) but more often because of desire, will, and status. The all-important ability to be at the right place is largely determined by modalities of identity that limit and parse access; "being there" is rarely serendipitous but a function of forms of privilege and exclusion—religion, race, age, class, or gender—that allow one to get in the door.

When we look at medieval religious buildings, how, we might ask, did the public/private divide, structurally instituted through interior screening such as partitions, dados, and rood screens, represent or even contribute to the dynamics of social power and of gendered identities of the lay community? Anthropological and geographical studies of private and public domains have illustrated the extraordinary complexity with which "private" and "public" must be understood, however, since most political and social ordering depends on variable spatial technologies of display.[10] In twenty-first-century America, the "public" is often figured as the place of power; "high visibility" in a media culture codes for influence, whereas the private is most often imagined as the place of domestic life and of women and hence as that which is less critical for the general good. An invasion might be understood to threaten national security and the public welfare, whereas an "invasion of privacy" is "just" an ethical violation and like rape, often difficult to prosecute. Yet the technologies of power are far more complex than this simple public/private binary would suggest, as Foucault has demonstrated in his important work on visibility and surveillance. Private space in the contemporary West has increasingly become the locus of high-impact decision making—behind closed doors, where the back-room boys do their work, and hence often the place of clandestine control.[11] In a similar ironic twist, visibility in a media culture is often synonymous with our most common and egregious practices of objectification; as Peggy Phelan puts it, "if representational visibility equals power, almost-naked white women should be running Western culture."[12] Often the very opposition "public" and "private" generates a dialectical system of responses and resistances. In certain regimes, notably formerly Communist Eastern Europe, the home came to be the place for political resistance, with the public the space of surveillance and overt compliance.[13] The uses of private and public space, this is to say, may be highly variable but consistently generate a powerful symbolism that both represents as well as organizes the movement of bodies.

Studies of the medieval parish most directly influenced by Bourdieu's concepts of 'field' and 'habitus' would certainly include the 1989 essay by C. Pamela Graves, "Social Space in the English Medieval Parish Church," which has laid a foundation for considering the architecture of the parish as an important social document.[14] Although she does not take up questions of gender, Graves outlines a cultural and theoretical framework for developing a taxonony of the spatial use of the medieval parish, especially by class. The medieval parish, she suggests, can be read as a locus for the inscription of cultural norms as well as for the dynamic production of social and individual identities.

Recent work addressing how lay parishioners used the spaces of the medieval parish, whether it adopts Bourdieu's hermeneutic or not, has benefited greatly from the monumental work of Eamon Duffy, particularly *The Stripping of the Altars*. Duffy's scholarship not only has directed attention to the parish but also has provided a massive amount of information about the ways that the material culture of parishes, from liturgical vessels to wall paintings to internal walls and screens, would have been experienced in daily and festival ritual in the fifteenth century.[15] The most important interior divisions in medieval churches separated the chancel, the place of a male clergy, from the nave, the far more public space of the congregation. Medieval instructions for uses of parochial space in general forbid all lay parishioners entrance to the chancel during the Mass but single out women with particular directness for this prohibition.[16] We might approach questions of the impact of internal screening of medieval churches by considering how parish space, internally divided by screens, parcloses, private chapels, and pews, helped to codify group or familial identities. Many of the chapels in medieval parishes were endowed by single families and intended for private use. What were the negotiations when the construction of a chantry by the endowment of a female testator staked a public claim through the construction of a familial space within a public building?

Formal divisions between public and private space in medieval churches may also mime fundamental gendered epistemes, particularly the enduring hierarchy in Western culture that has distinguished body, often coded as female, from the often male mind or soul. [17] This divide, which has persisted from the classical era to contemporary life, is deeply etched into the structure of church architecture, schematized as a human corporeal form, with the chancel, the locus of the male clergy, understood to be the head, and the nave figured as the body.[18] The church as a human body even takes specifically gendered form in many accounts; in medieval allegorical and exegetical texts, the church, *ecclesia*, is consistently described as the bride of Christ, female and material consort to the male *noumen*.

The importance of the body/mind division for the replication of patriarchial social organizations can hardly be overstated. Contemporary feminist theory has taken the male/mind versus female/body division, an organizing philosophical principle in Western thought, as one of its chief targets, mapping the cultural history of the female body and calling for a reconfigured set of principles and epistemes. Indeed, a critique of boundaries—the boundaries that have historically split private from public, body from mind, inner from outer—has been foundational to the work of feminist spatial semiotics. This critique has also emerged as an important issue in postcolonial studies, which have interrogated the ways national boundaries gird territorial imperatives through both exclusion and domination.[19] The boundary excises the other as "not us," even as it permits mastery of colonized or racially excluded others by us and "for us." In relation to the parish—the one space shared by men and women, the high and the low, the clerical and the lay in pre-Reformation Europe—internal boundaries are richly coded signs for a community's social organization. Where women sat or positioned themselves within church space and where and how they placed their gifts to the church can offer a great deal of information about the social dynamics of the parish community. How were women, and women from a variety of social and economic backgrounds, able to claim space within or around an edifice where they were segregated by gender and whose very architecture reinforced essentialized divisions of a male and female body politic?

A single curious feature of the medieval English parish church can illustrate some of the possibilities that a geographic analysis brings to a social study of gender and architecture. This is the squint, also called the "elevation squint," the term for apertures in the internal screening that allow one to see into the chancel. Extant in many English churches from the thirteenth century to the Reformation, squints often take the form of small windows in the wall separating side chapels or the nave from the chancel. Sometimes squints are located on the exterior of a church and appear as small windows on the outside wall; squints such as these may have originally connected the chancel with a now-absent anchorhold or a vestry.[20] Numerous squints survive in the form of small "peepholes," quatrefoil, trefoil, or loophole in character, cut through the dados or wooden screens that separate nave from chancel. What all squints share is a view of an altar. Placed to provide a view either of a secondary altar but more often the high altar, squints enabled parishioners as well as secondary priests a view of the elevation of the host and operated architecturally as lenses for the visual coordination of the Mass.[21] Offering testimony to the central importance of the elevation of the host during the Mass, squints also provide us tantalizing but uncertain hints about the visual organization and delineation of ritual life in the medieval parish.

How were these squints used? While many squints survive in pre-Reformation churches, little remains in the form of textual or visual evidence to indicate how parishioners actually positioned themselves to see through the apertures or precisely who those parishioners were that would have access to the openings. Would hangings within the parcloses or the chancel screens have served at times to isolate even more completely these spaces as privileged and secret? In a recent review essay on the medieval English parish, Paul Binski suggests that the image of St. John peering through a window at the enthroned Christ in medieval illuminated Apocalypse manuscripts extrapolates from the visual experience of a parishioner peering through an elevation squint, looking at Christ in the form of his liturgical incarnation, the elevated wafer.[22] It is not clear, however, exactly what we learn about ordinary or everyday ritual experience from these illustrations. Certainly images of St. John peering through a door (or squint) at the sights of his vision in deluxe Apocalypse manuscripts suggest that the experience of revelatory seeing was a coveted visual privilege. John, after all, is the preeminent representative of visionary, revelatory knowledge; John sees God. Yet how were squints actually used by parishioners during daily liturgical ritual? Did they offer privileged points of visual access to the chancel, as the Apocalypse illustrations imply? During the service of a Mass, either the daily service, the Sunday service, or special feast-day services, which members of the congregation had access to them? And more pertinent to the questions of this book, what women, if any, would get to position themselves with a view?

On a recent tour of East Anglian churches, we kneeled before small keyhole squints that pierced the dado of the parish church at Lavenham (see frontispiece). The positioning created a curious feeling of both exposure and voyeuristic pleasure, for we could only see through the openings while pressed up against the screen, in effect "being first" and leading the (imaginary) congregation in our proximity to the chancel. At the same time, however, everything in the nave space was at our back, out of sight and temporarily out of mind. The viewer projects visually into the space beyond; squints work something like binoculars, and though they do not magnify they give you sense of being an intimate participant. The fifteenth-century viewer, peering through the squints into the chancel, would have the sense of a private viewing of the Mass. The show would unfold for the viewer alone.

If we had been among the congregation in the fourteenth or fifteenth century when these holes in the screens were pierced, would we, as women, have been able to look through them during the Mass? Or would they have been the privilege of prominent male parishioners? Scholars have as yet little information about their actual use. Nevertheless, information about access to squints could reveal a good deal about the social structure of parish community. By their very form elevation squints, visual penetrations in the material body of the church, can also serve as a fascinating site for inquiry into theoretical problems of psycho/social space that have been articulated in geographic, anthropological, and psychoanalytic discourses. Visual access to a space is, of course, a way of laying claim to that space—whether the claim we stake operates on a "first come, first served" basis or, as would have been far more likely the case in late medieval parishes, through customary practices that governed the placement of people. Dividing the chancel from the more public space of the nave, squints provided a sidelong look across the instituted divide, offering a means of laying claim on the privileged space of the chancel; at the same time squints may have served to institute a new form of internalized privacy through the creation of the viewing subject as a single voyeur, as Paul Binski has provocatively suggested, and hence could be understood through a broader discourse of space and the history of selfhood.[23] The squint, that is, invites us to consider the very nature of private and public as constructs in late medieval life.

Acts of peeking into privileged spaces and maneuvers to control the gaze appear throughout medieval church practice and document strategic uses of space and visibility. In the *Hours of Mary of Burgundy*, Bruges, about 1477 (Raguin, Figure 4.4), the noble patron reads her hours within a well-appointed oratory complete with shutters equipped with a bulls-eye glass lattice, where she is surrounded by objects of luxury such as blown glass vessels, flowers, and a lap dog. She views the spacious setting of the choir of a church through shutters she is privileged to open or close. She controls what she sees, while in the recess of her space she is not subjected to viewing by others. Similar withholding and granting of the privilege of viewing can be seen in the real-life practice of parishes, such as the great urban churches of fifteenth-century Nuremberg. St. Lorenz, spared Reformation iconoclasm that destroyed so many monuments, preserves the quintessence of the late-medieval sacral ambiance. A wide circle of affluent citizens from various levels of society had competed to furnish the structure within and without. In St. Lorenz, as in many churches in the late Middle Ages, the themes and the placement of monuments reflected the donors' deep conviction of the importance of sacred space. Corine Schleif has documented how donors accrued special merit via the images with which they were associated.[24] These monuments were systematically presented or removed from view. Dust covers, folding shutters, Lenten veils, and textiles were opened and shut, or draped over the sculptures and images depending on times of the year.

The control of the gaze through the placement of elevation squints, veils, and shutters also raises an important set of questions about what we might call "visual epistemes," the construction of visual knowledge, particularly if we articulate those questions across discourses in feminist film theory. Film theory has amassed a great deal of evidence to suggest that how we see and receive knowledge is contoured for us in a myriad of ways that include both the oedipal structure of the psyche and gendered social hierarchies. We might suggest that the peephole gaze of a male or female viewer through an elevation squint at the Mass can be read not only through discourses of private and public access but also through discourses of reception that take into account the gender of the viewer and the performance that is viewed. The Mass, as a ritual performance, provides medieval culture perhaps its most distilled and most familiar experiences of somatic continuity; bread turns into body in a performance whose salient characteristic is its iterability as a transformation that takes place and can be seen many times a day.[25] The Mass, we might even suggest, produces for display a living body in mimicry of life-producing processes of childbirth, although the receiving of Christ in the wafer is a birth orchestrated by a wholly male community. We can only imagine a female parishioner as spectator at the peephole squint, and about that spectator, we can only speculate about her pleasures in the private viewing of this transformed space of parturition.[26]

The transcending of human limitation through radical paradox is, of course, a paradigmatic structure of medieval thought and structures both the symbolism and the physical space of the church. Christ as mother, and Mary, mother and virgin, are among the many transformative concepts enabled by church doctrine.[27] Gender, male or female, is also a human limit that can be transcended through celibacy, where one can be free from the vagaries of procreation and obligations of family. The liturgical calendar of the church community also allows for transcendence of time and space, as, for example, in rituals of liturgical commemoration of Holy Week, where the space of Jerusalem becomes coexistent with the space of the parish, and the organization of the cloister and refectory obviate space and time for the clergy to make their fellowship an extension of the apostolic circle around Christ. Male clerical control of the body, birthing Christ in the consecration, performs a similar paradox. In the Apocalypse manuscripts John looks through a window to see Christ enthroned in a posture of regal majesty; when a female parishioner witnessed the sacrament through a squint, she may have seen in it a very different kind of drama.

We offer these speculations about the elevation squint to suggest just a few directions that a gendered analysis of church space might lead. The gendered uses of space in medieval Europe have only recently begun to receive the attention of scholars, with most of this new work addressing the articulations between female bodies and spaces marked and structured through devotional practices. With disciplinary debts to both anthropology and geography, a few studies have begun to map out the ways that devotional spaces in medieval Europe not only mirrored gendered identities but also constructed those identities—or, we might say, articulated with an embodied female semiotic. As Bourdieu suggests in his reading of a Kabyle house, buildings are, in a sense, the bodies that build and use them; and indeed, the female body itself has been read as a kind of stage for the performance of devotional identity, most notably in the important work by Caroline Walker Bynum.[28] In a recent study of pilgrimage Susan Signe Morrison, drawing broadly on anthropological discourse on place and space, argues that pilgrimage routes were marked as liminal zones between public and private, spaces in which women could move with exceptional public freedom and visibility but in which they were still constrained by gendered modalities. Morrison's study has also contributed to the archival documentation of "women's space" by documenting pilgrimage sites that forebade women access to certain privileged shrines.[29] Perhaps the richest field for studies of gender and space in the Middle Ages has been the anchoritic enclosure. As Elizabeth Robertson and Jocelyn Wogan-Browne have noted, the body of the anchoress and the cell of her anchorhold were often imagined and described in synonymous terms in *regulae* by contemporary male writers, an overlap that used spatial language not only to describe the female recluse but also to control her bodily actions.[30]

Gendered analyses of devotional space would turn above all to two studies of East Anglia, both of which focus with particular clarity on the ways that women participated in the architectural history of their communities in late medieval England: Gail McMurray Gibson's landmark study, *The Theater of Devotion: East Anglian Drama and Society in the Late Middle Ages* (1989), and *Gender and Material Culture: The Archaeology of Religious Women* (1994), by Roberta Gilchrist. Gibson takes a distinctly sociological approach to late medieval dramatic performance in England, reading fifteenth-century dramatic performance and East Anglian parishes both as ritual "texts" expressing the interests of an engaged lay population—with women an important interest group.[31] As Gibson amply documents, women were substantial contributors to the fifteenth-century building boom in East Anglia, leaving their own names and inscribing images of favorite saints and devotional programs in the stained glass and tombs of their parishes.

In an archaeological study, Roberta Gilchrist has examined female nunneries in medieval England for evidence of how the buildings were used, analyzing the layout of buildings for information about how social arrangements were forged and articulated.[32] Gilchrist, as does Pamela Graves, follows the work of Bourdieu to understand space as a habitus, a socially constructed articulation whose meaning is constituted in the interplay between repeating, ritualized human practices and the spaces that both enable and constrain those practices. Bourdieu defines habitus as "principles which generate and organize practices and representations that can be objectively adapted to their outcomes without presupposing a conscious aiming at ends. . . . Objectively 'regulated' and 'regular' without being in any way the product of obedience to rules, they can be collectively orchestrated without being the product of the organizing action of a conductor."[33] Such an explanation elucidates female status and spatial positioning in the Middle Ages as well as the modern difficulties in interpreting records from the past. There need be no explicit or identifiable causality for phenomena; structures and behaviors that seemed as natural as winter snow within the habitus of the Middle Ages can appear quite different to a new set of "transposable dispositions" or habitus.

Gilchrist's argument that medieval East Anglian nunneries operated as a habitus that has been reinterpreted by the habitus of twentieth-century scholars reflects her understanding of Bourdieu's principles of "harmonization" by which cultural agents reinforce each others' practices.[34] Claiming that scholars have misunderstood medieval nunneries by contrasting them to male monastic establishments, Gilchrist argues that the spatial design of East Anglian nunneries should be understood in the context of networks of social arrangements that link them to the community at large. The relative poverty and structural simplicity of nunneries does not reflect devaluation or inferior status, as most scholars of medieval monasticism have believed, but rather a very different habitus or set of practices. Nunneries were much more fully engaged in the outside community than were monasteries and hence did not require such a large and self-contained design.[35] Only by understanding the network of social relations that connects a building to its community, she suggests, can we "read" the evidence left from archaeological remains; and only by understanding the economic lives of women can we understand women's roles in the design and use of medieval religious buildings.

The essays in *Women's Space* contribute to this developing archive on the gendered organization of medieval religious buildings, taking as their particular focus the uses of walls, chapels, tombs, commemorative objects, and pew arrangements as sites for the inscription of female identities. Offering materially grounded analyses of specific architectural and decorative forms, these chapters ask how religious spaces, particularly parish buildings, impeded or facilitated the movement of lay women within parish enclosures and how female parishioners claimed and used the architectural design of church buildings to their advantage. These chapters ask, "who was where?" to consider the relationship between the territorial divides of religious buildings and the construction of identities. Where did women sit in the church? How did women "lay claim" and gain visibility through gifts and testamentary bequests?

All the pieces in this collection evidence the interdisciplinary tendencies in current scholarship. Confronted with largely undocumented questions about practices of donation and access to spaces in religious buildings, the authors have assembled and read nontraditional sources. Scholars of literature look to visual paradigms as sources for a text's imaginative construction of space, as does Sarah Stanbury, or to legal records, as does Virginia Blanton and Ruth Evans. Virginia Chieffo Raguin, researching building history, turns to mystical biography, whereas Corine Schleif, examining donor imagery, looks to anthropology. Yet these chapters have been selected precisely because they represent, as well, classic methodologies for their disciplines. For the text-based studies, the text is above all a construction rather than a literal record of lived "reality." The first three chapters, all by scholars in literature, examine medieval texts as archives of material culture, loci for the play of identity, and also performatives within the social sphere. Ruth Evans's analysis of the play-text of the York cycle, Virginia Blanton's examination of the historical charter of Ely Cathedral, and Sarah Stanbury's study of the *Book of Margery Kempe* read texts as fictive spaces, we might say, in which the writers have moved around the furniture for strategic and even playful positioning. Texts work as records of gendered spatial arrangements in society; but even more important, they serve as stages for the orchestration of new and desired modalities of gender, power, belief, and identity.

Bringing the tensions among space, play, and gendered performance into particularly sharp focus is the textual study by Ruth Evans, "Signs of the Body: Gender, Sexuality and Space in York and the York Cycle," which examines the apportioning of space by gender in the theatrical installations of the York religious cycle. Arguing that cross-dressing is a notable feature of the York drama, a cycle of biblical plays staged outside the church in the zones of urban life, Evans hypothesizes that the spaces in which drama is performed shape the possibilities of gender; most striking, she argues that transgressive play with gender in these texts requires performance outside church space. Her study evokes for the modern reader the indissoluble flow of the spaces of inhabitation, ritual, and passage of the medieval town. She notes that spaces are never neutral, but carry with them inherited resonances, "palimpsests of already-scripted symbolic meanings." Her work also opens an important theoretical dimension in addressing questions about how the physical uses of space reinforce or subvert the ways that men and women inhabit their bodies as gendered identities. Her study invites us to consider how performances within the church, such as Kempe's highly theatrical self-fashioning, were influenced by the very structure of the building.

In her exploration of cross-dressing and theatrical space, Evans draws on the work of Judith Butler, whose theories of gender as performance have sparked a paradigm shift in gender theory. Following Butler, a rapidly growing body of work has examined both masculinity and femininity as carefully scripted cultural performances. Religious spaces, designed for ritual, offer a fascinating ground for questions about the ways that reiterated performances institute social identities. While public ritual such as the Mass, with its theatricality and manipulation of the potentials of dramatic space, was overtly the domain of an entirely male clergy, performances of female identity have also left their traces in archaeological and textual records: pew arrangements, donor images, tomb monuments, and relics, as other essays in this volume delineate. Evans's essay shares with many of these studies an invitation to consider performances of identity that are not stage-managed by the clergy but occur rather inside (or outside) spaces defined for lay use.

Analyzing a text that would seem to have little to do with "performance," Virginia Blanton's chapter, "Ely's St. Æthelthryth: The Shrine's Enclosure of the Female Body as Symbol for the Inviolability of Monastic Space," takes a little-known document, the *Liber Eliensis*, and demonstrates that it is a highly dramatic and interactive historical charter with profound political—and territorial—consequences for the monastery at Ely. In this text, a 1134 monastic compilation of deeds and monastic privileges of Ely that includes a vita of its founding patron, the twice-married virgin Æthelthryth, the compilers troped the imagery of rape and family to shape a persuasive political argument for Ely's natal purity and independence from outside jurisdiction, Blanton argues. By using the bones of Æthelthryth, preserved in Ely's sacristy at the heart of the monastic establishment, as evidence of her virginity, the *Liber Eliensis* transformed earlier versions of the life of Æthelthryth to dramatize in the vita both her risks of violation and her powers of vengeance, exploiting the story's potential as politico-domestic drama. The political autonomy of Ely, a male community, was signified by the revirgined female body at its architectural and figurative core.

Although grounded in historic fact, the narratives constructed by the monks at Ely freely restructure and invent in order to establish an image of Ely never invaded as well as consistently independent of episcopal and royal power. Addressing the ways that a female writer could describe her own access to sacred space are chapters by the editors, who contribute paired studies of *The Book of Margery Kempe*. As Sarah Stanbury argues in "Margery Kempe and the Arts of Self-Patronage," the *Book* structures an account that, like the *Liber Eliensis*, manipulates chronology and remembrance to make the constructed text the ultimate "reality," one that shows the author as an intimate of Christ. Exploring how Kempe creates a public persona in her autobiography, Stanbury argues that Kempe models her interaction with Christ on contemporary donor images, even donor images that would have been present in churches that she visited. Kempe fashions not only a theatrical devotional self but also a public self defined by strategic spatial placement, giving to the church to buy a vivid immediate memorial and purchase her way through purgatory. This chapter examines Kempe's extraordinary attention to location in her explicit naming of churches and awareness of where she is—at the high altar, in a particular chapel—within them. "Being there" defines the persona of Margery Kempe.

Arguing that Kempe's vocal outbursts and prostrating of herself on the floor of her church were specific responses to clerical ritual and local patronage, Virginia Chieffo Raguin, "Real and Imaged Bodies in Architectural Space: The Setting for Margery Kempe's *Book*," explores the ways that Kempe uses her body to compete vocally with clerical sound and to compete posturally with local patrons, members of mayoral families like her own who had their brasses etched into the very floor on which Kempe prostrated herself. Operating at the unusual intersection between literate and oral recall, Kempe uses buildings as locations for memories of events; she also fully embodies their spatial mappings as she turns her own body and vocalizations into monument and liturgy. A key issue addressed in the two studies on Margery Kempe in this volume is the interplay between material culture and narrative, between valued objects or places and the story a writer tells to bring objects and places into a personal orbit.

Raguin, like Ena Giurescu Heller, builds on research of the site itself, including evaluation of the physical evidence, often stylistic and archeological, in an attempt to establish the "authentic" text of the building. This evaluation is a frequent initial phase of art historical study. For Raguin, the establishment of the environment of St. Margaret's of Lynn in the first quarter of the fifteenth century has been frustrated by massive losses and alterations to the building. Indeed, since no single church mentioned by Kempe has survived sufficiently intact to act as a case study, Raguin and Stanbury have developed a website, Mapping Margery Kempe, as a means of presenting the visual context through comparative study of other buildings. Raguin's study thus forms a bridge between text-based studies and the following chapters, which address both history and art history. Whereas Stanbury envisions the literary construction as primary, Raguin focuses more on architectural space and the placement of the body within the built environment.

Katherine L. French's research, referring like Raguin's to the specifics of material culture, such as pews and church arrangement, also addresses the crucial importance of primary research in building an archive about how spaces were used in medieval churches, archives that are central to all interpretive modeling. Her scholarship involves groundbreaking perusal of wills, donations, and other records. Unlike the chapters on Kempe or on the York play-text, which build on established and well-edited texts, French's scholarship exemplifies the essential gathering of primary sources in historical work. Her study of pew arrangements in fifteenth-century English churches, "The Seat under Our Lady: Gender and Seating in Late Medieval English Parish Churches," examines archival documents to evaluate the effect of pew arrangements on female communities. As does Corine Schleif, French addresses the left/right, or in this case, north/south, division between men and women. The development of fixed and purchased pew seating in the fifteenth century, French argues, was a significant force in the development of various female subcultures, linking women together in shared class units and also by shared interests in the life of the parish. Parishioners considered proximity to the chancel, to a cult image, or to a specific side altar when purchasing a seat. Accounts also suggest that complex issues, not simply gender segregation for moral rectitude, conditioned placement. Women's seating could shift due to changes in financial status as well as to change in marital status from single, to married, or to widowed. Women are even recorded as purchasing new seats for the rite of churching, indicating that a shift in maternal status might occasion relocation within the church.

Ena Giurescu Heller's chapter, like French's, is also the result of exhaustive archival research, examining data from the time of the building construction of Santa Maria Novella in Florence as well as records of subsequent historians. Noting, as does Corine Schleif in her earlier work on patronage in Nuremberg, that it was obligatory for the laity to engage in largess directed toward religious edifices, Heller, "Access to Salvation: The Place (and Space) of Women Patrons in Fourteenth-century Florence," also shows how the record of that largess has been skewed through later assumptions about gendered practices of donors and patrons. Although she makes little explicit reference to theoretical work on space, Heller demonstrates that the habitus can elucidate practices of patronage in fourteenth-century Florence as well as later paradigms for reading the historical records, which would take as axiomatic that important gifts are perforce male. In the early records of Santa Maria Novella, Heller has discovered significant documentation of female presence in civic and religious spheres. However, visible public markers and later historical records—from the seventeenth century to the present—have systematically overlooked the role played by women, such as Monna Andrea Acciaiuoli, widow of Mainardo Cavalcanti, who was the effective patron in the building of a new sacristy in the Church of Santa Maria Novella in Florence. Most documents mention only the founders of chapels or monuments and rarely mention the contributions of widows who went on to execute the legacy after the founders' death; and even where the contribution is documented, public acknowledgment of the gift, both contemporary and later, invariably highlights male patronage. The evidence Heller has assembled, dramatizing the importance of reexamining historical documents, offers a compelling case study of ways that historical records have significantly misrepresented women's gifts and women's lives.

Historical archives also provide important information about the access of women to shrines, as is demonstrated by the contribution by Jane Tibbetts Schulenburg, "Gender, Celibacy, and Proscriptions of Sacred Space: Symbol and Practice." Schulenburg provides a synthetic overview noting the growth of the cult of relics and the restrictions to access that disproportionally marginalized women. Indeed, access of women to religious or clerical space in premodern Europe is one of the key questions addressed in this volume. Might these records, however, describe an official account of female exclusion perhaps at great variance with practice? In the United States, for example, as we write, the Roman Catholic hierarchy forbids almost all methods of contraception currently practiced by the vast majority of Catholics. As has been well documented with sumptuary laws, do prohibitions come into being precisely because they are being transgressed? Are prohibitions selectively constructed or recalled in order to provide more leverage to the controller to negotiate waivers of restriction for his advantage? Heller suggests that a woman's intense involvement with the decoration and funding of a Florentine chapel would certainly have implied some element of access. Schulenburg documents how monasteries granted permission to enter the sanctuary or proximity to healing relics—for a price. The miraculous cure of Adela, countess of Flanders, as she prayed before the altar at St. Bertin in a "unique" privilege, resulted in her making many donations to the monastery. When we hear of special treatment of noblewomen such as Adela, we need to remember that at this time only noblewomen were abbesses, making them valuable for their access to powerful family ties.

The control exercised over women's wealth by males and strategies adopted by nonrelatives to gain influence resonate through all these chapters. Schulenburg shows that donations proffered through a male intermediary could obtain the saint's intercession for miraculous cures, thus augmenting the male role of mediator. Heller, similarly, mentions Monna Gemma Velluti, the documented patron of the St. Michael chapel in Santa Croce. At the death of her husband and son, she retired to live in proximity to the church as a Franciscan tertiary, ultimately building and decorating a chapel in memory of her son. In the 1320s, widowed and without male relatives, she was able to take the personal initiative to build a chapel for herself and her descendants. Yet, since she was living next to the Franciscans, what influence did the friars have on her choice of disposable wealth and her inability to place herself as the focus of intercessory prayers and remembrance after her death?

"Gender, Celibacy, and Proscriptions of Sacred Space" reiterates many of the points taken up in previous chapters. Schulenburg, like Heller, demonstrates the male control of the written text, both in the creation of the contemporary document and in its survival. We are not privileged to know the actual negotiations that resulted in the tomb of St. Romanus being located not in the male house where he lived, but in the women's convent where his sister was abbess. This situation, as expected, was later textualized by Gregory of Tours as a male decision: Romanus himself *chose* to be buried outside of the monastery to allow general public access to his tomb. Both Schulenburg and Blanton describe how documents often work to embellish an underlying purpose—territorial inviolability of the monastic site or female exclusion—through the documentation of miracles. A catalog of vivid transgressions and punishments is then created by male communities to demonstrate that their rules—whether transgressed in ignorance or by ruse—will be punished by God' power. The standard nature of the stories betray their common origin of equating practice (Bourdieu's habitus) with an external and ineluctable order.

In marked contrast with this record of cooption of female interests, however, Schulenburg also notes that female houses were structured by radically different principles. Unlike male institutions, women's houses made provisions for the laity to be allowed in churches and shrines that they controlled. Such a conclusion calls to mind Roberta Gilchrist's studies that demonstrate that in the later Middle Ages there were a great variety of female religious communities interacting in various ways with the lay population. Many, because they did not fall within the canonically recognized religious institutions for women, were ignored by clerical chroniclers. Their existence and their work in the community is testified through archeological evidence as well as wills of townspeople and clerics.[36]

The final chapter in the volume, perhaps most wide-ranging in its demonstration of connections between control of money and the symbolic uses of spaces, buildings, and images, is Corine Schleif's study, "Men on the Right—Women on the Left: (A)symmetrical Spaces and Gendered Places." Schleif, like Schulenburg, presents an extensive survey of material encompassing a large historical and geographic spread. She lays out the intertwining of political and religious mentalities that encouraged polarity. Documenting insistent construction of female as opposed to male, she links the polarized concepts of 'strong' and 'weak,' 'dominant' and 'submissive,' even 'good' and 'bad' that then carry over to definitions of gender. Why is it, Schleif asks, that women in donor images always are placed on the left? Her observations, which draw on anthropology, phenomenology, art history, and feminist theory to situate the representation of donor images within a larger cultural history of the left/right divide, are far-reaching and resonate with observations within this collection. Ena Heller's study of the decoration of a fourteenth-century chapel at Santa Maria Novella notes the patron's arms. Those of the male donor, Mainardo Cavalcanti, are closest to the prestigious iconography of the Passion, whereas those of the female patron, Monna Andrea Acciaiuoli, appear at the side, flanking her husband's, in the traditional dexter and sinister positions. And as Katherine French points out, seating positions within medieval English parishes conventionally conformed to the left/right distinction.

Schleif's chapter and others in this collection foreground, indeed, the intimate connections among money, space, and visibility to the construction and practices of gender. These pieces especially invite us to consider the space of pre-Reformation churches as a dynamic site for the performance of identity through the legacy of material objects. As these chapters show, women signed themselves in church space in dynamic and highly assertive ways. Bodies operate in spaces that are prearticulated, coded in their design for the management of persons; and medieval religious architecture reinforced binary divisions of male/female through material practices of reiteration, designing identities through conventional, and strategic, placement of screens and pews. Yet as these chapters also show through a synergy among discourses in history, art history, and literature, a woman's place within the church was often material ground for re-negotiation—and re-negotiation that continued, or even still continues, long after habitation or bequest. The structural and textual records examined here document a dynamic world of female testamentary bequests and even territorial occupations, in spite of spatial divisions and historical practices that would keep women "in their place."

## NOTES

1. Recent studies on conspicuous display and gender include *Heraldry, Pageantry and Social Display in Medieval England*, ed. Peter Coss and Maurice Keen (Woodbridge, Suffolk, and Rochester, N.Y.: Boydell and Brewer, 2002), and Loveday Lewes Gee, *Women, Art and Patronage from Henry III to Edward III, 1217–1377* (Woodbridge, Suffolk, and Rochester, N.Y.: Boydell and Brewer, 2002).

2. For a valuable recent volume on space in medieval culture, see *Medieval Practices of Space*, ed. Barbara A. Hanawalt and Michael Kobialka (Minneapolis: University of Minnesota Press, 2000).

3. Otto Von Simpson, *The Gothic Cathedral: Origins of Gothic Architecture and the Medieval Concept of Order*, Bollingen Series 48 (Princeton: Princeton University Press, 1956), xviii, 11.

4. Pierre Bourdieu, *Outline of a Theory of Practice*, trans. Richard Nice (Cambridge: Cambridge University Press, 1977), 78.

5. Pierre Bourdieu, *The Logic of Practice*, trans. Richard Nice (Stanford: Stanford University Press, 1990), 218.

6. Bourdieu's most fully developed analysis of gender relations appears in *Masculine Domination*, trans. Richard Nice (Editions de Seuil, 1998; Stanford: Stanford University Press, 2001).

7. Toril Moi, "Appropriating Bourdieu: Feminist Theory and Pierre Bourdieu's Sociology of Culture," *New Literary History* 22 (1992): 1017–49.

8. Dorreen Massey and J. Allen, eds., *Geography Matters!* (Cambridge: Cambridge University Press, 1984).

9. See, for instance, *BodySpace: Destabilizing Geographies of Gender and Sexuality*, ed. Nancy Duncan (London and New York: Routledge, 1996); *Sexuality and Space*, ed. Beatriz Colomina, Princeton Papers on Architecture, I (Princeton: Princeton University Press, 1992); Daphne Spain, *Gendered Spaces* (Chapel Hill: University of North Carolina Press, 1992); and Henrietta Moore, *Space, Text and Gender: An Anthropological Study of the Marakwet of Kenya* (Cambridge: Cambridge University Press, 1986).

10. Nancy Duncan, "Renegotiating Gender and Sexuality in Public and Private Spaces," in *BodySpace*, 127–45.

11. Michel Foucault, *Discipline and Punish: The Birth of the Prison*, trans. Alan Sheridan (New York: Pantheon Books, 1977), 191–92.

12. Peggy Phelan, *Unmarked: The Politics of Performance* (London and New York: Routledge, 1993), 10.

13. Joanne Sharp, "Gendering Nationhood: A Feminist Engagement with National Identity," in *BodySpace*, 101.

14. C. Pamela Graves, "Social Space in the English Medieval Parish Church," *Economy and Society* 18 (1989): 297–322

15. Eamon Duffy, *The Stripping of the Altars: Traditional Religion in England 1400–1580* (New Haven: Yale University Press, 1992).

16. Margaret Aston, "Segregation in Church," *Women in the Church*, Studies in Church History, Vol. 27, ed. W. J. Sheils and Diana Wood. (Oxford: Blackwell, 1990), 244.

17. Linda Martin Alcoff, "Feminist Theory and Social Science: New Knowledges, New Epistemologies," in *BodySpace*, 14–17.

18. Kevin Marti, Body, *Heart and Text in the Pearl-Poet* (Lewiston: Mellon, 1991), 41.

19. Homi Bhabha, *The Location of Culture* (London and New York: Routledge, 1994), 219; "Of Mimicry and Man: The Ambivalence of Colonial Discourse," *October* 28 (Spring 1984): 126–29; Anne McClintock, *Imperial Leather: Race, Gender and Sexuality in the Colonial Contest* (London and New York: Routledge, 1995), ch. 1, "The Lay of the Land: Genealogies of Imperialism."

20. Francis Bond, *The Chancel of English Churches* (New York: Oxford University Press, 1916), 250.

21. Duffy, *Stripping of the Altars*, 97.

22. Paul Binski, "The English Parish Church and Its Art in the Later Middle Ages: A Review of the Problem," *Studies in Iconography* 20 (1999): 14.

23. Ibid.

24. Corine Schleif, *Donatio et Memoria, Stiftung, Stifter, und Motivationen an Beispiele aus der Lorenzkirche in Nürnberg* (Munich: Deutscher Kunstverlag, 1990). See a similar study for England, but where the objects themselves have disappeared: Judith Middleton-Stewart, *Inward Purity and Outward Splendor: Death and Remembrance in the Deanery of Dunwick, Suffolk, 1370–1547* (Woodbridge, Suffolk, and Rochester, N.Y.: Boydell and Brewer, 2001).

25. On desire for bodily continuity in the high Middle Ages, see Caroline Walker Bynum, *The Resurrection of the Body in Western Christianity, 200–1336* (New York: Columbia University Press, 1995), 122–54, 213–20.

26. Id., *Holy Feast and Holy Fast* (Berkeley and Los Angeles: University of California Press, 1987). The importance of food to medieval women is detailed, especially in "Woman as Body and as Food" and "Women's Symbols," 260–96.

27. Id., *Jesus as Mother: Studies in the Spirituality of the High Middle Ages* (Berkeley and Los Angeles: University of California Press, 1982).

28. Bynum directly engages with questions of gender and spatiality in her critique of the paradigms of liminality developed by Victor and Edith Turner in *Fragmentation and Redemption: Essays on Gender and the Human Body in Medieval Religion* (New York: Zone Books, 1991), 32.

29. Susan Signe Morrison, *Women Pilgrims in Late Medieval England: Private Piety and Public Performance* (London and New York: Routledge, 2000), esp. ch. 3, "Gender, Pilgrimage and Medieval Perceptions of Space," 83–105; on pilgrimage sites with restricted access, see pp. 89–90. See for contemporary writing about pilgrimage,

Dee Dyas, *Pilgrimage in Medieval English Literature, 700–1500* (Woodbridge, Suffolk, and Rochester, N.Y.: Boydell and Brewer, 2001).

30. See especially Elizabeth Robertson, "The Rule of the Body: The Feminine Spirituality of the *Ancrene Wisse*," in *Seeking the Woman in Late Medieval and Renaissance Writers*, ed. Sheila Fisher and Janet E. Halley (Knoxville: University of Tennessee Press, 1989), and Jocelyn Wogan-Browne, "Chaste Bodies: Frames and Experiences," in *Framing Medieval Bodies*, ed. Sarah Kay and Miri Rubin (Manchester: Manchester University Press, 1994), 24–42; see also Ann K. Warren, *Anchorites and Their Patrons in Medieval England* (Berkeley and Los Angeles: University of California Press, 1985); Jocelyn Price, "Inner and Outer: Conceptualizing the Body in *Ancrene* Wisse and Aelred's *De Institutione Inclusarum*," in *Medieval English Religious and Ethical Literature: Essays in Honour of George Russell* (Cambridge: Brewer, 1986), 192–208; Gail Ashton, *The Generation of Identity in Late Medieval Hagiography: Speaking the Saint* (London and New York: Routledge, 2000), esp. ch. 2, "A Concept of Space and a Notion of Identity."

31. Gail McMurray Gibson, *The Theater of Devotion: East Anglia Drama and Society in the Late Middle Ages* (Chicago: University of Chicago Press, 1989).

32. Roberta Gilchrist, *Gender and Material Culture: The Archaeology of Religious Women* (London and New York: Routledge, 1994), 150. Gilchrist also addresses the gendered space of medieval castles in "Medieval Bodies in the Material World: Gender, Stigma, and the Body," in *Framing Medieval Bodies*, 49–58.

33. Bourdieu, *The Logic of Practice*, 53.

34. Ibid., 80.

35. Gilchrist, *Gender and Material Culture*, 191.

36. Roberta Gilchrist, *Contemplation and Action: The Other Monasticism* (London and New York: Leicester University Press, 1995), 148–51.

## FURTHER READING

Binski, Paul. "The English Parish Church and Its Art in the Later Middle Ages: A Review of the Problem." *Studies in Iconography* 20 (1999): 1–25.

Bourdieu, Pierre. *The Logic of Practice*. Trans. Richard Nice. Stanford: Stanford University Press, 1990.

Duncan, Nancy, ed. *Body/Space: Destabilizing Geographies of Gender and Sexuality*. London and New York: Routledge, 1996.

Duffy, Eamon. *The Stripping of the Altars: Traditional Religion in England 1400–1580*. New Haven: Yale University Press, 1992.

Gibson, Gail McMurray. *The Theater of Devotion: East Anglian Drama and Society in the Late Middle Ages*. Chicago: University of Chicago Press, 1989.

Gilchrist, Roberta. *Gender and Material Culture: The Archaeology of Religious Women*. London and New York: Routledge, 1994.

Graves, C. Pamela. "Social Space in the English Medieval Parish Church." *Economy and Society* 18 (1989): 297–322.

Hanawalt, Barbara, and Michael Kobialka, eds. *Medieval Practices of Space*. Medieval Cultures Series, vol. 23. Minneapolis: University of Minnesota Press, 2000.

Morrison, Susan Signe. *Women Pilgrims in Late Medieval England: Private Piety as Public Performance*. New York: Routledge, 2000.

Stanbury, Sarah, and Virginia Raguin. *Mapping Margery Kempe*. www.holycross.edu/kempe.

Wogan-Browne, Jocelyn. "Chaste Bodies: Frames and Experiences." In *Framing Medieval Bodies*. Eds. Sarah Kay and Miri Rubin. Manchester: Manchester University Press.

ONE

# SIGNS OF THE BODY: GENDER, SEXUALITY, AND SPACE IN YORK AND THE YORK CYCLE

Ruth Evans

HENRI LEFEBVRE ARGUES THAT "every society produces . . . its own space."[1] What the Middle Ages produces, he claims, is the space of towns, a novel locus shaped by the scandalously liberating forces of markets and commodities: "deconsecrated, at once spiritual and material, intellectual and sensory, and populated by signs of the body" (264). Lefebvre could easily be describing both the densely packed city spaces of medieval York and the complex topographies of its great Corpus Christi Play, the cycle of pageants re-enacted annually from 1377 (the date of the earliest record) to 1569 (the date of the last performance).[2] Within the new space of the medieval town, Lefebvre continues, "[r]eligious space did not disappear with the advent of commercial space; it was still . . . the space of speech and knowledge." But alongside parish and devotional space there were other spaces: "the space of exchange, . . . the space of power" (266). Exchange and power: the terms here belong not only to trade but also to social anthropology and sexual politics. What then of Lefebvre's "signs of the body"? How do gendered bodies figure within this innovatory urban space?[3] And, given the concerns of this volume, how do women's bodies figure? Who occupies York's various urban localities (parishes, streets, marketplaces) and playing spaces (the pageant wagons, the "stations" along the route where the play was performed, the spectators' scaffolds)? Who is excluded from them? What institutions sponsor these occupations and exclusions? These are "historico-political" questions that touch on women's access to and ownership of the spaces of Corpus Christi.

Toward the end of this chapter I address some of these important questions. But the very nature of the York Play as a complex set of signifying practices challenges the apparently stable and transparent identities of both "women" and "space" to which this volume's title alludes. The male impersonation of women on the late medieval stage and the concomitant performance of gender roles as an oscillation between human embodiment and a fugitive textuality point to sex, gender, and the body as objects that can never be looked at directly but only perceived through and as a structure of representation. As Lefebvre suggests, urban spaces are peopled by "*signs* of the body": disruptive and heterogeneous signifiers rather than material essences. Moreoever, the mobile nature of York's urban drama greatly enhances our sense of its gender performances as provisional, intermittent, fluid.

Nor do these signs of the body simply act themselves out in pregiven spaces. Bodies do of course take up space, but they also transform spaces, just as spaces transform them. This reciprocal transformative effect is crucial: the meanings of gender and sexuality are spatially produced and productive of space. I begin by arguing that the question of human sexuality is central to an understanding of the Play's salvific dynamic: the shameful "discovery" of sexual difference in Eden is the powerful originary myth that underwrites the redemptive drama of the Play. But what has this to do with space? A dominant medieval view holds that the fall constructs fixed, heteronormative gender roles for men and women. On one level, it is easy to read the representations of Adam and Eve in the York Play as upholding that fixity of gender. Yet the performance of gender roles on the stage is not underpinned by a stable, material binary sexual difference. That very stability is itself an effect. So also is the fixity of places (Eden, earth, Pilate's wife's bedroom) an effect. During the time of theatrical performance the meanings of both gender and space are produced from moment to moment to moment and from locale to locale, queering the signs of the body and allowing the audience a glimpse of desires and identities beyond the binary frame. To some extent the pleasures and provocations of such queer transgressions might appear to depend on the prior existence of binary oppositions (male/female, here/there). But such binaries are, as I have said, an effect, and the Play often confronts its audience with their constructed nature.

A crowd of corporeal signifiers throngs the streets of York and its play text: orderly and disorderly social bodies, the bodies of the guildsmen-performers, the bodies represented on the stage—all cohering in the dynamic and polyvalent symbol of *corpus* Christi: the body of Christ. These are all bodies marked in one way or another by gender difference (though not necessarily, as I shall argue, by a gendered binary). They are also bodies of ambiguous and varied status: imaginary, historical, social. As Sarah Beckwith observes, the business of the Corpus Christi procession and dramatic performances in York was to "mould and recreate urban topography in ways both fantastical and material."[4] But the dramatic performances themselves also mold and recreate the many imaginary topographies of the play text: heaven, the Garden of Eden, the hills of Armenia, Egypt, Mary's inviolate body, Herod's palace, Procula's chamber, Pilate's seat of judgment, the gates of hell. These sites are perambulated annually through York's streets on pageant wagons, stopping to perform at the approved "stations" along a specified route. These myriad spatializations include distinctive gynotopias (spaces associated with women) and androtopias (those associated with men). But some of them constitute what Foucault terms "heterotopias": "other places," where sex, gender, sexuality, and bodies appear unstable and uncertain.[5] Practices such as cross-dressing and the locomotion of "displaced" sites (bedrooms, courtrooms, Calvary itself) through the public places of York play havoc with established bodily norms, creating new heterotopias: risky spaces of pleasure and desire. The feast of Corpus Christi is itself an "other space": what Foucault calls "the heterotopia of the festival" (26).

Like the other great civic "mystery" plays, the York cycle is a sacramental and redemptive drama that explores the consequences for humanity of the Fall of Adam and Eve. This is a drama initiated by the shocking recognition of sexual difference and by the troubling knowledge that it brings. Although Foucault argues that the conceptual alliance of knowledge and sex only reaches back to the late eighteenth century, the locus classicus of the link is Genesis, where Eve's first disobedience is to persuade Adam to eat the apple of the tree of knowledge.[6] What we know now as sexuality, Eve Sedgwick reminds us, "is fruit—apparently the only fruit—to be plucked from the tree of knowledge."[7]

Within the Christian hermeneutic tradition, it is St. Augustine in the early fifth century who makes sexuality so decisively the sign of humanity's fallen state. In his *Concerning the City of God against the Pagans*, he relates how after their transgression Adam and Eve become suddenly aware of shame attaching to their organs. They feel, he says, "a novel disturbance in their disobedient flesh."[8] The "novel disturbance" that Augustine refers to is sexual excitation, although it is unclear if he means specifically the male capacity for erection (making the male body the paradigm for human sexuality), or if he includes female arousal. Despite the ambiguities here, the effect of Augustine's commentary is to make sexuality the only fruit of knowledge in a postlapsarian world. This projection of the Garden of Eden as the originary locus of sex knowledge is one that haunts the medieval imaginary of the York Play. I will argue that the shameful (and pleasurable) secret of sexuality is a powerful shaping force within the Play, interpellating and constructing the subjectivities of both actors and audiences: as fallen human beings in need of salvation, as ethical subjects of the sacraments, and (important) as desiring bodies marked by the awareness of sexuality.

But in arguing for the centrality of postlapsarian sexuality to the redemptive project of the drama, I also want to rethink the relationship between space and sexuality. For the Play does not simply imagine the Garden of Eden as an established place of innocence in which the drama of sex-knowledge takes place. If Foucault's *History of Sexuality* (volume 1) teaches us that there is no before of sexuality, that sexuality is a discursive effect, then it is also the case that Eden (like other spaces in the York Play) is produced as a contingent space: an effect of other discourses (the body, sex, gender, and sexuality). What the Play demonstrates is that sexuality and space in effect depend upon each other. As Beatriz Colomina observes, "It is not a question of looking at how sexuality acts itself out in space, but rather to ask: How is the question of space already inscribed in the question of sexuality?"[9] Colomina is certainly not suggesting that we reverse our traditional priorities, that we look at how space is anterior to sexuality. Reversal is not what is at stake, since the "question" in the first part of her sentence can work both ways (sexuality precedes space, space precedes sexuality) because it assumes that such categories operate as independent, bounded entities (and indeed Colomina critiques this assumption). Rather she is posing a different question: in what ways is sexuality (understood as a category of knowledge-power at a specific point in history and produced within specific discourses) linked to the production of a certain understanding of space? One way of answering this is to return to Augustine's influential commentary on the Fall, and to note that a theological construction of sexual difference as a binary is simultaneously a binary construction of space that opposes a place of innocence to a place of knowledge.

In one of the early pageants of the cycle, the Coopers' *Fall of Man*, these binaries of space and gender are simultaneously inscribed through Eve's predictably disruptive femininity, which brings about the expulsion from Eden.[10] If Eden was (initially, at least) an idealized place lacking in self-consciousness of the body and knowledge of sexual difference, then the new space of earth to which Adam and Eve are banished is thoroughly imbued with awareness of sex. This is what it means to be fallen. In the following pageant, the Armourers' *Expulsion*, Adam blames Eve's feeble intellect for their expulsion: "We bothe þat were in blis so brighte, / We mon go nakid euery ilke a nyghte, . . . Allas, what womans witte was light!" (130–33). The ensuing argument between Adam and Eve presents in vernacular terms the theology of Adam's role in the Fall, but it also constructs and makes visible the gendered norms of social behavior. Eve defends herself against Adam's accusation of female stupidity by manipulating the very hierarchical categories that have been used to define her female inferiority: "Bot sethyn that woman witteles ware / Mans maistrie shulde haue bene more / Agayns þe gilte" (136–38). If men are naturally sovereign, then they should be more able than feeble-minded women to withstand temptation. Adam's riposte—that Eve refused to heed his "biddyng"—reinforces the bleak misogyny of the Fall or more accurately reinforces the Fall's condemning of both men and women to the effects of gendered stereotypes: "Now God late never man aftir me / Triste woman tale" (149–50). Women's fate is to be never believed;

men's never to believe them. The gender roles that each performs are here apparently underwritten by a traditional, stable binary sexual difference.

I want to suggest some of the ways in which their representations resist the binary inscriptions of gender and space. This resistance happens at both the level of the text and the level of embodied performance. In *The Fall of Man* Adam's bite of the apple produces acute self-consciousness of the body: "Me shames with my lyghame" (110). Overwhelmed with shame, he is anxious to hide the evidence of sexual difference: "Oure shappe for doole me defes, / Wherwith þay shalle be hydde" (129–30). Eve suggests they resort to "fygge-leves" (131). The double meaning of Augustine's term *pudenda*—"organs of shame" / "sexual organs"—articulates this double knowledge. Richard Beadle's glossary to his edition of the York Play does not give the definition "genitals" for "shappe," but this is what Adam means. Augustine's commentary brings this out: "Their organs were the same as they were before, but previously there was no shame attaching to them" [s.v. *MED* shape n. 6 (a)]. As John Mirk observes in his sermon for the Feast of the Innocents (c. 1415), "Bot as sone as þay haden synned, þay seen hor schappe, and wern aschamet þerof, and hydden hit wyth leues of fygge-tre."[11] Here "schappe" must mean "genitals" because the fig leaves would be insufficient to cover their whole bodies. When Adam is first created he is made in "schape [likeness] of man" (Play 3, the Cardmakers' *The Creation of Adam and Eve*, 36), an ambiguous phrase that may or may not point to Adam's distinctively male sexual characteristics, but which may be an echo of its use in the earlier pageant. In *The Creation* Eve's construction from Adam's "lyft rybe" (38) focuses the audience's attention on another part of Adam's body (one that is nevertheless sexualized) and on questions of woman's "natural" subordination.

Sexual difference is not decisively born until the fateful moment in the Garden of Eden. The covering with fig leaves is, as Sarah Beckwith observes, an instance that "everything has changed in a new postlapsarian world, a world where costume and covering are an intrinsic part of human appearance."[12] The fig-leaf "aprons" are an attempt to hide sexual difference, but their role is ambivalent. The idea that a fixed gender identity can be read off the body starts to undo itself. "Shappe" does not only mean "genitals": it can also mean a fashion of dress or the make or cut of a garment [s.v. *MED* shape n. 4]. The related adjective *shaply* can mean "[of] clothes: well fitting on" [*MED* 5]. "Shappe," then, points both to the visible signs of sexual difference and to their opposite: the coverings that mask or deny that difference. This linguistic play is one of the means whereby the York dramatist calls attention to the artifice of a transvestite theater and so to the artifice of gender identity. If the male actor playing Eve were dressed in a close-fitting suit of white leather or cloth (though we do not know what costume "Eve" wore at any point during the history of the Play's performance, since there is scant evidence about costumes in the York records), then the action of putting on the fig leaves would draw attention to the ambiguities of "her" sex, as well as to the ambiguities of covering up. "Shappe," like the fig leaves, performs a paradoxical linguistic striptease, simultaneously revealing and concealing, making uncertain the biological signs of sexual difference as well as the supposed gender identity that accompanies them. This uncertainty, produced somewhere between the verbal signifier and the practice of cross-dressing, is decidedly queer, in the sense that Eve's gender and sexuality, in Sedgwick's words, "aren't made (or *can't be* made) to signify monolithically."[13] The text does not here draw explicit attention to the fact that "Eve" is a man impersonating a woman. But later pageants in the cycle, as I will demonstrate, do make conscious play with the undecidability that cross-dressing can produce.

If we glimpse gender identity as an effect, not an essence, in the oscillation between words and performance, then so too does the Play produce the opposition between innocent and sexualized space (Eden versus earth) as an effect. Eve's desire to eat the apple initiates a pattern that inscribes the question of space in the question of sexuality. By expelling Eve (and Adam) from paradise, York's God preserves it as an idealized, desexualized, or presexualized place. Earth, by contrast, is now charged with potentially shameful and eroticized meanings. The movement from Eden to earth enacts and reinforces the notion of Eve's female sexuality as errant, transgressive, dangerously mobile. But we might also see this as her resistance to categorization, and to the fixed categorization of spaces. For the knowledge of sexuality that her transgressive desire ushers in is associated with the fugitive: with the idea of the escape out of or away from one space into another. Similarly, the Play imagines spaces not as already fixed but as capable of transformation. In a sense, sexuality never takes up a single place but is the very figure of that which escapes localization and the very figure of the play of signifying differences that constitutes its meaning: always mobile, never fully present or absent.

Today sex and sexuality have a vast array of topographies, physical, geographical, textual, somatic, psychic, and virtual: the confessional, the bedroom, Bangkok, the top shelf, the closet, the drive-in, the singles bar, the analyst's consulting room, the bathhouse, the public school, the street corner, the *Jerry Springer Show*, the motel, Freud's "erogenous zones," the internet chat room.[14] The later Middle Ages shares some of these sexualized spaces (the confessional, the bedroom) but generates its own topographical set: the Garden of Eden, the garden of medieval romance, the merchant's house of fabliau, the stews, church and temporal courts, the Temple of Venus, the monastic dormitory, the virgin martyr's body, Mary's belly in the York cycle. Some critics deny that these medieval places are loci of erotic pleasure, insisting on the period as one of sexual innocence or refusing altogether the historical validity of the category of the erotic by claiming that sex and sexuality are simply aspects of sinful humanity's "natural" fallen state. But we make such historical distinctions at our peril. As I have suggested, Augustine's account of the Fall inscribes the question of space in the question of sexuality, and in ways that make it the source of erotic meanings as well. I have argued that the question of sexuality makes space itself deviant, mobile, and heterotopic: queer rather than fixed. But alongside the overtly eroticized spaces of the postlapsarian Garden of Eden and of an earth newly colonized by Adam and Eve, there are deviant spaces that can signify erotically because of how they are *practiced*.

Margery Kempe's parish church of St. Margaret temporarily becomes such a deviant space when she makes an agreement there with a man to meet him after evensong for sex (though he turns out to be tricking her): "whan euensong was do, sche went to þe man befor-seyd þat he xuld haue hys lust, as sche wend þat he had desyred, but he made swech symulacyon þat sche cowd not knowe his entent, & so þei partyd a-sondyr for þat nygth."[15] If it is true, as Virginia Raguin argues in this volume, that Kempe understands the church floor as a space of privilege, then her trysting plans might be viewed as a challenge (perhaps an unconscious one) to the clerical control of the meanings of space. Kempe's strategy of self-revelation is clearly allied to the anxious presentation of what Sarah Stanbury, also in this volume, terms an "autobiographical self," but it is a self also constituted through the queering of space.

The case of the London transvestite "prostitute" John/Eleanor Rykener also illustrates this production of deviant and sexualized parish and urban spaces.[16] Rykener is "detected in women's clothing" by officials of the city of London one December night in 1395, "lying by a certain stall in Soper's Lane" (111). He is caught "committing that detestable, unmentionable and ignominious vice" with one John Britby. Britby (who, significantly perhaps for the purposes of this chapter, comes from "the county of York," even if not actually from the city of York) is of unknown profession. Britby too is pursuing a London itinerary with a definite sexual purpose when, having accosted Rykener on "the high road of Cheap, . . . thinking he was a woman, [he] ask[s] him as he would a woman if he could commit a libidinous act with her." Rykener's busy sexual perambulations take in not only the Cheapside area, but also Bishopsgate, a marsh in Oxford, the Swan inn in Burford, Oxfordshire, somewhere in Beaconsfield, and "the lanes behind St. Katherine's Church by the Tower of London" (112).

This temporary transformation of public city and parish spaces into "queer" heterotopias can also be illustrated by reference to events in early modern York. The York House Books for 15 May 1536 (within the history of the Corpus Christi cycle) document the "Confessyon" of one "Alexander Mason, smyth," that Ralph (Rauff) Walker, a shoemaker, took part in a riotous assembly protesting against the enclosure of Knavesmire, an area of common pasturage just outside York, and "was also then and ther in womens clothyng with a muffell over his face."[17] It is not clear if Walker's accomplices were also cross-dressed, but no sexual intrigue of the sort Rykener practiced seems to be at stake. Walker's ritualized drag invokes the sexual and transgressive power of the unruly woman to enact a political protest by a man of the laboring classes against the restricting of access to common land, a clear encroachment on the rights of York's less prosperous citizens.[18] But did Walker intend to conceal his identity? Though there are certainly many precedents of men concealing their identity in order to escape criminal detection, disguise (as Claire Sponsler observes) may not have been the point: drag was meant to be looked at and hence was productive of identity. Both Rykener and Walker confront the authorities with a challenge to normative versions of masculinity, by suggesting that sex/gender roles do not proceed from stable gender identities. Walker's playing with the visible trappings of gender calls in question the firm boundary between the inner and outer topographies of the body (outward appearance as a map of the contours of the inner self) in a manner analogous to the rioters' overturning of gates and ditches on the boundaries of Knavesmire. On the phantasmatic spaces of his body Walker figures the disruption of the material spaces of the city, just as his transvestite behavior (like Rykener's) transforms the meaning of the spaces through which he temporarily passes.

For the citizens of York, urban spaces were neither new territories to be discovered nor blank pages to be written on, but palimpsests of already-scripted symbolic meanings. Like mirrors set at angles to each other, these spaces reflected a series of repetitions, correspondences, resemblances, and analogies that articulated authoritative relationships between God and the World, and between the World and the Body. To its citizens, medieval York was also Jerusalem, the holy city.[19] In the annual performance of Play 25, the Skinners' *Entry into Jerusalem*, the city of York is coterminous with Jerusalem, site of sorrow and celebration. As Christ dismounts from the ass, he proclaims to the treacherous Peter, "I murne, I sigh, I wepe also / Jerusalem on þe to loke" (470–71). But when he enters the city he is hailed as a secular king, in formulas typical of a royal entry. City space and symbolic space are not simply here superimposed. Rather, sacred meanings exist alongside the nonsacred significations established through York's position as a trading center and (to evoke again Lefebvre's terms) through the various spaces of exchange and power associated with that. As Paul Strohm observes, "the peculiarity of medieval space involves the extent to which it is already symbolically organized by the meaning-making activities of the many generations that have traversed it."[20] But the peculiarity of drama lies in the practical difficulties it faces in attempting to preserve the illusion that one place can simply represent another through relations of similitude. The meanings of symbolic locations can always escape their presignifications, shifted by the activities of their temporary inhabitants. In this sense (a perverse one, perhaps), I understand the spaces of medieval York and its Corpus Christi play in terms of Michel de Certeau's reversal of the established hierarchy of space and place. Traditionally, space is seen as the location for place, as a prior "site," a topographical *tabula rasa* that needs to be filled with meaning in order to attain the status of place. But de Certeau upends this, reading space and spaces as the products of an activity: "space," he says, "is a *practiced place*."[21]

Space therefore also has a temporal and dynamic dimension.[22] This dimension is marked by what de Certeau calls "spatial stories": the stories that found and narrate spaces, delinquent stories that escape official "mapping." The York Corpus Christi procession produced its version of a nonofficial spatial story as it "perambulated the host around the boundaries of the city, blessing and delineating its borders" in a manner similar to that of the Rogationtide ridings.[23] At York, the form of "true processional staging" of the Corpus Christi cycle recreated the processional impulse of the sacred perambulation of the host by constantly moving the pageants from station to station.[24] And as Sarah Rees Jones observes, civic propaganda in York was managed through the physical design of York's civic space and through elaborate civic ceremonial.[25] In Beckwith's words, "[T]he ritualization of the city is not about the imposition of a homogeneous kind of unity onto the city but rather an implication of its webs of signification. . . . . The politics we need to talk about, then, will not be those of dominance and subversion or resistance and containment, but rather the politics of mobility and access"[26]—and I would add, the politics of sex, gender, and sexuality insofar as those categories are necessarily implicated in York's webs of signification.

De Certeau's "spatial stories" are not essentialized but made up from moment to moment and from locale to locale. I have already suggested how the performance of gender in the *Fall of Man* is also made up, rather than presented as a given. Now I want to suggest some of the ways in which the Play challenges the official understanding of spaces as saturated with pregiven symbolic meanings. I suggest that the destabilizing of prescribed gender roles in the *Fall of Man* pageant is repeated in the Play's larger structures, especially those that concern the delineation of space. In the opening pageant of the cycle, the Barkers' *Fall of Lucifer*, God's first words, "Ego sum Alpha et O: vita, via, veritas, primus et nouissimus," present his very being as the official map for the coming journey. It is not simply that he will act as guide for the route (*via*, "road") down which the good Christian will travel. He *is* that route: "I am lyfe and way" (3). God goes on to found "a place," somewhere "full of plenté to my plesyng at ply" (12), which he miraculously makes out of "noghte" (16). His words offer the audience an apparently authoritative view of space as already charged with symbolic meaning: the World as Book, created *ex nihilo* as a place of plenitude that delights its creator. This is God as Author, fully in control of meanings of his creation.

But as God simultaneously names the world and brings it into being, his language is less of the order of the "map," defining the visible, flat plane projection of Renaissance perspectival space, and more of the order of the "tour," to borrow de Certeau's distinction between the orders of *seeing* and *going*. In de Certeau's words, "description [deriving from New Yorkers' oral accounts of their apartments] oscillates between the terms of an alternative:

either *seeing* (the knowledge of an order of places) or *going* (spatializing actions). Either it presents a *tableau* ("there are . . ."), or it organizes *movements* ("you enter, you go across, you turn . . ."). . . . How are *acting* and *seeing* coordinated in this realm of ordinary language in which the former is so obviously dominant? The question ultimately concerns the basis of the everyday narrations, the relation between the itinerary (a discursive series of operations) and the map (a plane projection totalizing observations)."[27] The stasis of the map is "official" and modern, the mobility of the tour is "unofficial" and postmodern. While de Certeau's distinctions offer a problematic reinscription of binary categories, they also open up a space that allows me to continue rethinking the question of the representation of space in the York Play. To what extent does York's God offer a totalizing view of space?

In the *Fall of Lucifer*, God gives directions as if he were offering a guided tour. Or more accurately, the space he summons up—microcosmically, the place of the pageant wagon with its three tiers corresponding to heaven, earth, and hell; macrocosmically, the city of York as a phantasmatic representation of the heavenly Jerusalem—is conditioned by the rhetoric of the *tour*, not that of the *map*: "Here vndernethe me nowe a nexile I neuen, / Whilke ile sall be erthe. Now all be at ones / Erthe haly, and helle, þis hegheste be heuen, / And that welth sall welde sall won in þis wones" (25/28). What is most interesting is that the "tour" language ("Here vndernethe me . . . ; þis hegheste be heuen") marks out a series of spatializing operations that not only conjure up places but also make available their history, by not effacing—as maps do—the operations that brought those places into being.[28] The subsequent pageants also present a series of locations that are marked by movement and symbolic history, by the condition of their possibility, just as the "stations" where the Play is played are also marked by this historical fluxity: premodern versions of "spatial stories."

In his analysis of spatial epistemes, Foucault argues that medieval space is the "space of emplacement," a space characterized by a complete hierarchy of places and by localization. By contrast, the Renaissance is the space of "extension," of Galileo's "constitution of an infinite and infinitely open space," and the modern period is that of the "site": of "relations of proximity between points or elements."[29] While it must be conceded that Foucault's essay attempts to rethink the historical categories of periods by presenting the disruptive force of heterotopias that can disrupt any of these period boundaries, it is also true that his characterization of medieval space presents it as monolithic: hierarchic and localized. This does scant justice to the extraordinarily mobile locometries of the York Corpus Christi play. And his "troop of epochal figures" (in Margreta de Grazia's sardonic phrase) is problematically inadequate for describing a drama that is still performed well into the early modern period.[30]

Just as spaces do not preexist location and localized activity (even when they are caught up in preexisting webs of signification), neither does a body already marked for gender difference straightforwardly inhabit those spaces. Rather, physical spaces and spatial practices *produce* the effects of gender. They do so precisely because they inscribe preexisting gendered meanings that serve to coconstruct the bodies that come to inhabit them. As Charles Zika argues, albeit in relation to a different cultural event, the placing of women at the back of the Corpus Christi procession in Germany signals a "liturgical marking-out of space, an identification of individuals and local groups with a certain territory."[31] The position at the back constructs for those placed there a gender identity (as female) as well as an inferior or less powerful subjectivity. Corine Schleif, in this volume, suggests that the placement of male and female donors of sacred art to the right and left in pictorial space is gendered, inscribing a sense of both divine complementarity and gendered hierarchy. As I suggested earlier, space constructs gender. But if gender constructs space, and space constructs gender, rather than *acting itself out* in space, then the question is how bodies marked for gender difference and sexuality produce particular spatial narratives and are in turn produced by those narratives. York's practice of processional staging, on pageant wagons, is not just a material practice but also a system of representation. Although it is true, as Beckwith argues, that space comes to have meaning through bodily practices, the categories of "space" and "bodily practices" are not separate from each other but continually redefine the borders of each other, through a complex interplay of cultural signification and coconstruction.[32]

I have been focusing on the representational aspects of gender because biological women are scarcely present in the surviving records of dramatic activity in York. But there is evidence that women did play active roles in the patronage of city spaces, independent of their husbands. In a manner analogous to the control of female saints' cult sites within male monastic space (as Jane Tibbetts Schulenburg elaborates in this volume), women in York did gain access to male-dominated spaces and laid claim to their own memorial identity within those spaces. Yet at first glance it might appear that the "stations" (places for hearing the Play) along the route of the Corpus Christi cycle constitute androtopias: places associated exclusively with men. For example, in 1398 and 1399 the pageant wagons stop to perform before the houses of a number of prominent York men: Robert Harpham (identity unknown), John Gysburn (Mayor in 1370, 1371, and 1379), Henry Wyman (merchant and goldsmith), and Adam del Brigg (a wealthy mercer and close friend of John Gysburn).[33] Control of these stations appears to have been in the hands of a tiny "city merchant elite," intent on protecting its commercial interests by deriving profit from a paying audience. By 1454, the number of names of stationholders has increased, numbering twenty-two citizens and three ecclesiastical institutions (Fountains Abbey, St. Leonard's Hospital, the Augustinian Friary), in addition to other anonymous persons connected with the lease of five stations. All the names are male. The records of 1569, the date of the last performance of the Play, only mention "stations" controlled by men: Mr. Henrison, Mr. Paycock, Mr. Appleyard, Mr. Fawkes, Christopher Willoughby, Mr. Birnand, John Chamber, William Beckwith, Mr. Herbert, the sheriff, Mr. Allen, and a certain "Hutton."[34]

But the records obscure some "facts" about female patronage of these important sites. For example, John Gysburn died in 1390. It is possible that his wife, Elene (d. 1407), and his two daughters continued to be stationholders of his very substantial dwelling between 1390 and 1399 and into the fifteenth century. Both daughters married into powerful families. Alice, the elder, married Sir William Plumpton. Isabella, the younger, married Sir William Frost, who was nine times lord mayor of York. In the later fifteenth century, a few women were stationholders in their own right, often as widows. In 1468 the widow of John Toller rented a station in Micklegate with unnamed others ("*et aliis*," a common formula in the records at this date) and again in 1475 (this time apparently on her own, though by 1486 the station is leased to a man, Adam Barbour). The lady mayoress, Katherine Lam, a very wealthy mercer of the parish of St. Crux, also rented a station at the Pavement in 1475 (her husband William Lam was lord mayor in 1475; she is the Lady Lambe who in 1487, as a widow, is "discharged" from acting as pageant master for the ironmongers).[35] But David Crouch points out that the practice of the lady mayoress renting a station in her own name became common after 1522, "when the Mayoress and her ladies often took rooms separately from the mayoral party" (93). In 1499, the wife of William Sharp, a tapiter (tapestry weaver), and the wife of a certain unidentified "Thuaytes" (no first name), rented the ninth station. According to Crouch, John Elys, who in 1499 and 1508 rented a station now identified as the Three Kings inn, bequeathed it to his wife in 1510 (89). The York stations were not the exclusive property of men: women too were patrons.

Additionally, the areas of the city through which the route passed have gender (and class) implications, insofar as concerns the distribution of women in households and in trades. Households along the route were generally wealthier and larger than those in the outlying, poorer suburbs. The route at the beginning of the fifteenth century passed through some of the most affluent parts of the city. The most expensive shops were concentrated in the Ousebridge area and in the upper part of Stonegate. Mercantile quarters were in the parishes of St. Martin and St. John, Ousebridge, and along Coney Street, Daveygate, and Petergate. And from 1450 through 1500 the commercial sector, though diminished, was concentrated in a smaller and more defined space and may by this time have numbered far fewer women in the guilds of mercers and drapers, with consequently less opportunity for women manufacturers to offer their goods for sale at prime sites on the route. During the later fifteenth century, women's role in guilds and in the household economy upon which they were predicated was in decline.[36] Gender relations and gender difference order the very operations and the conditions of reception of the Corpus Christi processions and the play performances.

But in the practices of transvestism we see a radical reordering of established sex/gender systems. What is the historical evidence for men playing women's roles in late medieval, Tudor, and Elizabethan productions of the York cycle? And what are the implications (necessarily changing in significance over the Play's lifetime) of men impersonating women on the English stage? Although the York Play (in common with the other mystery plays) has few women's parts (Eve; Noah's Wife; Mary; the anonymous Mothers of the Innocents; the woman taken in adultery; Pilate's wife, Procula; Mary Magdalene), a single production of the cycle might nevertheless include as many as thirty different Maries. This is a statistically significant display of transvestite "signs of the body."

Overwhelmingly, the evidence points to male actors in these roles.[37] But from time to time theater historians have questioned this basic assumption, cautiously suggesting that things may not be that simple.[38] Jeremy Goldberg argues that lack of evidence does not preclude the possibility—in York, at any rate—that women *might* have acted in the guild drama at the end of the fourteenth century and during most of the fifteenth century. This is because of their integral role within the crafts and their associated guilds during that period. As women's standing in the York crafts and guilds was gradually eroded by the late fifteenth century, men would have taken over women's roles.[39] Given that the earliest recording (in Coventry guild accounts) of a man playing a female role only dates from 1496, this allows for the possibility that *women* could have played women's roles in the earlier period in any of the urban centers with a biblical drama.

Some support for this view may be provided by evidence from Beverley (not far from York), although it concerns ritual rather than drama (a distinction that is often difficult to maintain). The 1389 guild returns for the Purification of the Blessed Virgin Mary indicate women as participants in the dramatic action and even suggest that a woman took the part of Mary in the patronal procession.[40] The early date of this guild return is consistent with Goldberg's suggestion that evidence of female actors is more likely to be found in the early part of the period of the urban civic drama, rather than later, when the position of women in guilds was in decline. However, the 1389 guild return for St. Helen and Mary, Beverley, offers contradictory evidence. It unequivocally states that a very beautiful young man played the part of Queen Helen in the patronal procession: "pulcherrimus iuvenis."[41] So women *did* play women in the early part of the period—but equally men took female roles. That women did occasionally play the parts of women in religious ritual at an early date may not, in any case, have a bearing on Goldberg's argument, since we lack conclusive evidence that the Corpus Christi Play was even acted in York before the early fifteenth century. At the most we can only be sure that women's roles in the biblical drama were taken by men at the very end of the fifteenth and throughout the sixteenth century. Despite the occasional presence of women actors, it is not quite the case, as Stephen Orgel airily declares, that "until the 1530s, at least, women seem to have performed unproblematically in guild and civic theatrical productions" (5). Orgel's comment is misleading: it suggests (on the basis of very little evidence) that women were everywhere on the medieval stage and that, by implication, men did not take women's roles until the Reformation. Behind this view lies the familiar assumption that the Middle Ages is less complex, less exciting, and less peculiarly *other* than the early modern period. And not at all queer.

But even if we do accept the current view (among medievalists, at least) that male impersonation of women on the stage was the norm throughout the lifetime of the religious drama, this does not mean that it has no implications. For too long medieval transvestite theater has been persistently regarded as unproblematic, with the consequence that the politics of male impersonation of women is often left unexplored.[42] This is symptomatic of what Jane Tolmie describes as "the assumption that cross-dressing in medieval drama is a simple function of a male-dominated society and as such can be construed as a stepping stone for later and more exciting Renaissance innovations."[43] Unlike Shakespearean drama there are no moments in the mystery plays when a cross-dressed man points at himself: Look at me; I am not a woman, but a man; in fact, I may be something else altogether. Without this impersonatory deixis, we have to look elsewhere in the biblical drama for a conscious play with transvestism.

We might begin with Tolmie's observation that female parts and aspects are "made up" on the stage: that sexual identity is never regarded as a given (251). Cross-dressing transforms women on the stage into "absent" presences: male actors can never make sex, gender, or the body fully present, for what is the ontological status of the body that we see before us or of the gender identity that is being performed? And since the "female" characters cannot be said to inhabit their gender identities in any straightforward way, the male characters with whom they interact (sometimes in a highly sexualized way) are reconfigured to produce moments of "queer" undecidability. I must emphasize that it is not cross-dressing per se that produces these effects, since transvestism occurs everywhere in medieval culture (in medieval fabliaux and in saints' lives, for example) and does not always provoke a sense of the uncanny. Rather, cross-dressing must be put into play in specific texts and with specific effects for it to have the capacity to destabilize fixed categories of sex, gender, and the body.

As Tolmie remarks, the ease of passing as a woman is "an uncertain proposition for medieval drama" (256). Men are taller than women, and performance is a risky business. Somewhere in the interplay between language and the presence of actual bodies moving from locus to *platea*, from pageant wagon to street playing area, illusion is broken (if it was ever established in the first place), giving rise to moments of self-consciousness. Stable patterns of familial and genealogical relations are disturbed by the absence of actual women on the stage. The resulting confusion of categories operates not only to produce (on occasions) a homoerotic dynamic within the performance but also to render unstable the categories of masculinity and femininity, insofar as they cannot be fixed in relation to the body. Claire Sponsler, following Marjorie Garber, suggests that cross-dressing is a figure of "category-crisis," but I propose in addition that it be understood as a spatial story—like those of John/Eleanor Rykener and Ralph Walker—where errant sexualities are constructed through the production of deviant social spaces.[44]

Play 30, the Tapiters' and Couchers' *Christ before Pilate I: The Dream of Pilate's Wife*, does not even attempt to produce the illusion that Procula, Pilate's sexy wife, is a "real" woman. The action takes place in Pilate's chamber and in his wife's bedroom. "[D]ame precious Percula" is a boy/man dressed as a high-ranking, sexual woman, and the audience is never allowed to forget it. Both the stage business and dialogue constantly draw attention to the artificiality of her gender identity. First Pilate introduces her: "Lo sirs, my worthely wiffe, þat sche is, / So semely, loo, certayne scho schewys" (26–27). Beautiful, yes, but only on the outside: Pilate's use of "schewys" teases the audience with what might lie below the elaborate costume. Procula responds by similarly highlighting the discrepancy between her male body and her outward appearance: "All welle of all womanhede I am, wittie and wise, / Consayue [Perceive] now my countenaunce so comly and clere. / The coloure of my corse is full clere / And in richesse of robis I am rayed" (39–42). The invitation to "[c]onsayue" her physical attractions is given further point by the use of "corse," here meaning (innocently enough) "complexion" but picked up several lines later by Pilate with a sexual innuendo to refer directly to his "body": "Yhitt for to comforte my corse me must kisse you madame" (48). "Corse," of course, can just mean "self." But its use signals the gap between signifier and signified, playing on the ludic possibilities of an unfixed corporeal identity.

Though Pilate and Procula's inordinate desire for each other establishes the pair's inherent pride and evil sensuousness, we might also want to acknowledge another dynamic. For the scene does more than draw attention to Procula's made-up gender. As a male transvestite she may have been unconcerned about passing as female (difficult to sustain on the stage in any case, as I have said). Taller and broader (possibly) than a woman, perhaps smoothing her hands over "her" padded and hyperfeminized feminine body, Procula is a gloriously camp figure. And in "her" lewd interactions with her husband there is the suggestion that she harbors homoerotic desires. When she pushes her lips forward for Pilate to kiss them, his jocular aside to the audience—"Howe, howe, felawys! Nowe in faith I am fayne / Of theis lippis so loffely are lappid / In bedde is full buxhome and bayne" (50–52)—emphasizes the pleasures of her dubiously gendered body. But what is the nature of

Pilate's desire for his wife? Is it same-sex desire? A transvestite Procula casts doubt on the security of Pilate's gender identity, deranging normative sexual taxonomies. This scene suggests at the very least that we need to rethink the view of cross-dressing on the medieval stage as unproblematic.

What then of space? Procula and Pilate are represented here enacting an extraordinarily intimate moment in the public street. But the aristocratic or bourgeois bedroom in the fifteenth century cannot be described as a private space in any twenty-first-century sense. As Norbert Elias observes, in medieval society amongst the secular upper classes the bed was not "privatized and separated from the rest of social life."[45] Beds might be shared with strangers. People within lay society slept naked (138). Shame, Elias notes, comes later, along with other tools of civilization (139). But did the actors playing Pilate and Procula undress completely in their bedchambers? How much we would like to know about actions and costumes! I think we are meant to see husband and wife here as an ironic counterpoint to Adam and Eve, shamelessly ignorant of the lesson of sexual difference so forcefully delivered in the *Fall of Man* pageant.

But the presence of beds as essential props in this pageant does not automatically connote feminized privacy or luxurious sinfulness. It is true that within the monastic tradition, from the eleventh century onward, the bed is "a zone of danger," because of its association with the polluting effects of wet dreams.[46] Beds can be dangerous in other ways, too: when Chrétien's Lancelot sleeps in the wrong bed he has to dodge a flaming lance.[47] But beds were not necessarily primarily associated with sex. They were also feudal rewards within a "use economy," their prestige value related to their opulence, as when the narrator in Chaucer's *Book of the Duchess* makes a comic present of his "alderbeste / Yifte," a deluxe "fether-bed," to Morpheus, the god of sleep (246–51).[48]

It is the prestige value of the beds in Play 30 that make this pageant so appropriate for its guild sponsors. The tapiters were workers of figured clothes, and the couchers, makers of bedding and bedhangings. Even in a precommercial theater, they could still benefit economically by displaying samples of their goods on the "couche" in Pilate's chamber and on the "bedde arayed of the beste" (153) in Procula's bedroom. We know that tapestries were hung out on the occasion of Henry VII's royal entry to York in 1486.[49] And in 1544 the York House Books record a council decision that all householders on the route of the Corpus Christi procession should hang out mattresses and bed coverings: "[E]very howseholder that dwellith in the hye way ther as the sayd procession procedith, shall hang before ther doores & forefrontes beddes [i.e., mattresses] & Coverynges of beddes of the best that thay can gytt . . . for the honour of god[d] & worship of this Citie." This agreement was enforced by a forfeit of 3s 3d for noncompliance.[50] Because the practice of hanging out bed coverings was standard for royal entries throughout the medieval period, the York city council's decision may signal its desire to dignify the route of the Play by giving it associations with a royal occasion.[51] But equally, as Duffy suggests, it may represent a desire for greater visibility of householders' wealth.[52]

Doubtless the tapiters and couchers were canny enough to exploit this desire in the props they provided for their pageant. But the household spaces represented on the stage are far from straight. The homoerotic overtones of the first exchange between Pilate and Procula are continued in the scene between Pilate and his Beadle, as the servant prepares him for sleep. He assures Pilate: "þis nyght sir, newe [annoyance] schall ye noght, / I dare laye, fro ye luffly be layde" [when you are laid down in a seemly manner? with a pun on "laye" [wager] and "laye" [to lie down]?] (130–131). Sexual innuendoes surface again when Pilate commands the Beadle to carry him across to his couch but warns him: "loke þat þou tene me not with þi tastyng, but tendirly me touche" (134). "Tastyng" can mean not only "touching" but also "feeling" or even "groping." This homoeroticized undercurrent serves to disrupt the traditional hierarchical master-servant relationship along axes of both gender and social class. This disturbance of the household hierarchy is further reinforced by Procula's Boy, who when commanded to awaken Pilate to tell him the content of her dream, responds with sly insolence: "Madame, I am dressid to þat dede—/ But first will I nappe in þis nede" (193–94). The Boy's comic insubordination draws attention to the elaborate performances of bodily acts that confer (incoherent) social and sexual identifications.

In this pageant a certain transformation of the meanings of the bedroom takes place, deranging the discrete topographies of inside and outside. The spatial practices of the processional performance also preclude any easy distinction between public and private, house and street, judgment room and bedchamber. The street setting transforms the intimate bedroom into a public space, just as the bedroom transforms the open-air spaces of the "stations" into a cozy, domestic theater. We can only speculate about the kinds of unofficial meanings that might have been produced for both performers and audiences in acting out these sexually disruptive scenes at, say, the politically charged and conflicted space of the Minster Gates or the Pavement, a place of public punishment.[53]

Although the York cycle occupies and moves across parish locations, it is by no means exclusively identified with them. Instead it traverses city spaces that are simultaneously sacred, civic, domestic, and commercial, "populated by signs of the body," and offering a complex set of transformations of the "parish," "civic," "domestic," and "commercial" identities associated with them. The building of the first public theater in London, in 1576 (seven years after the York Play "closed down"), is often held to mark an epochal moment: the birth of the commercial theater and of a fixed place for the drama. Spaces cease to be mobile. Instead space becomes an abstract category, infinitely expandable and existing not in a material location but in consciousness—the very sign of modernity. Like Hamlet, we become kings of infinite space, in our heads.[54] But the medieval stage does not, as De Grazia points out, "enframe" (20) meaning, so it militates against presenting what can be readily perceived or known. By its very itinerant nature, the York Play offers a series of spatializations that question the bounded categories of sex, gender, and the body, exposing the divisions between private and public spaces, upper and lower social ranks, as performative rather than essential. Queer play indeed.

## NOTES

I would like to thank Mark Amsler, John Arnold, Jeremy Goldberg, Pamela King, Sarah Rees Jones, Felicity Riddy, Paul Strohm, and Jane Tolmie. I am grateful to Theresa Coletti, Ad Putter, and Sarah Stanbury for their helpful and informative comments. Versions of this chapter were given as papers at the University of York, the University of Delaware, the University of Wales Conference Center at Gregynog, and the University of Oxford.

1. Henri Lefebvre, *The Production of Space*, trans. Donald Nicholson-Smith (Oxford and Malden, Mass.: Blackwell, 1991), 53.

2. For studies of the York Corpus Christi cycle and the politics of city space, see Martin Stevens, "The York Cycle: City as Stage," in *Four Middle English Mystery Cycles: Textual, Contextual and Critical Interpretations* (Princeton: Princeton University Press, 1987), 17–87; Martin Stevens, "From *Mappa Mundi* to *Theatrum Mundi*: The World as Stage in Early English Drama," in *From Page to Performance: Essays in Early English Drama*, ed. John A. Alford (East Lansing: Michigan State University Press, 1995), 25–49; Sarah Beckwith, "Making the World in York and the York Cycle," in *Framing Medieval Bodies*, ed. Sarah Kay and Miri Rubin (Manchester and New York: Manchester University Press, 1994), 254–76; Sarah Beckwith, "Ritual, Theater, and Social Space in the York Corpus Christi Cycle," in *Bodies and Disciplines: Intersections of Literature and History in Fifteenth-Century England*, ed. Barbara Hanawalt and David Wallace (Minneapolis: University of Minnesota Press, 1995), 63–86.

3. On the sexual politics of embodiment in the York cycle, see Katie Normington, "Dreams Made Public? Juliana of Mont Cornillon and Dame Procula," in *New Trends in Feminine Spirituality: The Holy Women of Liège and Their Impact*, Medieval Women: Texts and Contexts, vol. 2, ed. Juliette Dor, Lesley Johnson, and Jocelyn Wogan-Browne (Turnhout: Brepols, 1999), 251–67; Ruth Evans, "Body Politics: Engendering Medieval Cycle Drama," in *Feminist Readings in Middle English Literature: The Wife of Bath and All Her Sect*, ed. Ruth Evans and Lesley Johnson (London and New York: Routledge, 1994), 112–39; Ruth Evans, "When a Body Meets a Body: Fergus and Mary in the York Cycle," *New Medieval Literatures* 1 (1997): 193–212; Theresa Coletti, "Purity and Danger: The Paradox of Mary's Body and the En-gendering of the Infancy Narrative in the English Mystery Cycles," in *Feminist Approaches to the Body in Medieval Literature*, ed. Linda Lomperis and Sarah Stanbury (Philadelphia: University of Pennsylvania Press, 1993), 65–95.

4. Beckwith, "Making the World," 254.

5. Michel Foucault, "Of Other Spaces," *Diacritics* 16 (1986): 22–27.

6. Michel Foucault, *The History of Sexuality*, vol. 1 [1976], trans. Robert Hurley (Harmondsworth: Penguin, 1990).

7. Eve Kosofsky Sedgwick, *Epistemology of the Closet* (Harmondsworth: Penguin, 1994), 73.

8. Augustine, *Concerning the City of God against the Pagans*, ed. David Knowles, trans. Henry Bettenson (Harmondsworth: Penguin, 1972), book 13, chapter 13.

9. Beatriz Colomina, ed., *Sexuality and Space* (Princeton: Princeton Architectural Press, 1992), iv.

10. Richard Beadle, ed., *The York Plays* (London: Edward Arnold, 1982). All subsequent line references are to the individual pageants in this edition and appear in parentheses in the text. There is only one extant copy of the Play (known as the "York Register"), in British Library MS Additional 35290, dating from 1463–77. This unique copy, which preserves only one version of the text at one particular moment in its evolution, gives little sense of the diachronic changes affecting the Play during its lifetime of nearly two centuries, nor of the dynamic conditions of its performance. See Richard Beadle, "The York Cycle," in *The Cambridge Companion to Medieval English Theatre*, ed. Richard Beadle (Cambridge: Cambridge University Press, 1994), 85–108, at 89–92.

11. *Mirk's Festial: A Collection of Homilies*, ed. Theodor Erbe, EETS e.s. 96 (London: Kegan Paul, Trench, Trübner, 1905, reprint 1973), 35/20.

12. Beckwith, "Making the World," 257.

13. Eve Kosofsky Sedgwick, *Tendencies* (London and New York: Routledge, 1994), 8.

14. On the sexualization and eroticization of spaces, see Lefebvre, *The Production of Space*, 166–67, 309–10.

15. Margery Kempe, *The Book of Margery Kempe*, ed. Sanford Brown Meech and Hope Emily Allen, EETS o.s. 212 (London: Oxford University Press, 1940), 14/26–15/28, at 15/12–16.

16. Ruth Mazo Karras and David Lorenzo Boyd, " '*Ut cum muliere*': A Male Transvestite Prostitute in Fourteenth-Century London," in *Premodern Sexualities*, ed. Louise Fradenburg and Carla Freccero (New York and London: Routledge, 1996), 99–116.

17. *York Civic Records*, 4 vols, ed. Angelo Raine (Wakefield: Yorkshire Archaeological Society, 1941–45), 4: 3. I am grateful to Chris Humphrey for this reference. According to the *OED*, "muffel" (muffle sb.[1], "Something that muffles or covers the face or neck") is not recorded before 1570, but this sense of disguise is clearly intended by the 1536 York entry.

18. Claire Sponsler, "Outlaw Masculinities: Drag, Blackface, and Late Medieval Laboring-Class Festivities," in *Becoming Male in the Middle Ages*, ed. Jeffrey Jerome Cohen and Bonnie Wheeler (New York: Garland, 1996), 1–27. See also Natalie Zemon Davis, "Women on Top," in *Society and Culture in Early Modern France* (Stanford: Stanford University Press, 1975), 124–51.

19. See Stevens, "The York Cycle," 52; Beckwith, "Ritual, Theater, and Social Space," 65–66.

20. Paul Strohm, "Three London Itineraries: Aesthetic Purity and the Composing Process," in *Theory and the Premodern Text*, Medieval Cultures, vol. 26 (Minneapolis and London: University of Minnesota Press, 2000), 3–19.

21. Michel de Certeau, "Spatial Stories," in *The Practice of Everyday Life*, trans. Steven F. Rendell (Berkeley, Los Angeles, and London: University of California Press, 1984), 115–130, at 117.

22. See Michael Camille, "Signs of the City: Place, Power, and Public Fantasy in Medieval Paris," in *Medieval Practices of Space*, ed. Barbara A. Hanawalt and Michal Kobialka, Medieval Cultures, vol. 23 (Minneapolis and London: University of Minnesota Press, 2000), 1–36, at 9.

23. Beckwith, "Making the World," 25; for accounts of the procession, see Miri Rubin, *Corpus Christi: The Eucharist in Late Medieval Culture* (Cambridge: Cambridge University Press, 1991), 243–71; on the Rogationtide ridings, see Eamon Duffy, *The Stripping of the Altars: Traditional Religion in England c.1400–c.1580* (New Haven and London: Yale University Press, 1992), 138.

24. The form of true processional staging for York is now generally accepted by theater historians. See Eileen White, "Places to Hear the Play: The Performance of the Corpus Christi Play at York," *Early Theatre*, Special Volume: *The York Cycle Then and Now* 3 (2000): 49–78.

25. Sarah Rees Jones, "York's Civic Administration, 1354–1464," in *The Government of Medieval York*, ed. Sarah Rees Jones (York: Borthwick Institute of Historical Research, 1997), 109–139, at 137.

26. Beckwith, "Ritual, Theater, and Social Space," 76.

27. De Certeau, "Spatial Stories," 119.

28. On the differences between space-time correlations in the mapping practices of the Western medieval and early modern worlds, see David Harvey, *The Condition of Postmodernity: An Enquiry into the Origins of Cultural Change* (Oxford: Blackwell, 1989), 240–45.

29. Foucault, "Of Other Spaces," 22–23.

30. Margreta de Grazia, "World Pictures, Modern Periods, and the Early Stage," in *A New History of Early English Drama*, ed. John D. Cox and David Scott Kastan (New York: Columbia University Press, 1997), 7–21.

31. Charles Zika, "Hosts, Processions and Pilgrimages: Controlling the Sacred in Fifteenth-Century Germany," *Past and Present* 118 (1988): 25–64, at 42–44.

32. Beckwith, "Ritual, Theater, and Social Space," 81.

33. See Anna J. Mill, "The Stations of the York Corpus Christi Play," *Yorkshire Archaeological Journal* 37 (1948–51): 492–502. For a detailed chronological account of the changing history of the York stations see David Crouch, "Paying to See the Play: The Stationholders on the Route of the York Corpus Christi Play in the Fifteenth Century," *Medieval English Theatre* 13 (1991): 64–111: 7. See also David Crouch, "Paying to See the Play: The Stationholders on the Route of the York Corpus Christi Play in the Fifteenth Century," master's thesis, University of York, Center for Medieval Studies, 1990. On the stations as contested social space, see Beckwith, "Ritual, Theater, and Social Space," 71–75.

34. White, "Places to Hear the Play," 54–55.

35. Crouch, "Paying to See the Play," 86. For Lady Lambe, see *REED: York* 1.153.

36. P. J. P. Goldberg, *Women, Work, and Life Cycle in a Medieval Economy: Women in York and Yorkshire c. 1300–1520* (Oxford: Clarendon, 1992), 200–02, 333–61. Jeremy Goldberg, "Craft Guilds, the Corpus Christi Play and Civic Government," in *The Government of Medieval York*, ed. Rees Jones,141–163, at 147; Beckwith "Ritual, Theater, and Social Space," 75–76; Martha C. Howell, "Citizenship and Gender: Women's Political Status in Northern Medieval Cities," in *Women and Power in the*

*Middle Ages*, ed. Mary Erler and Maryanne Kowaleski (Athens and London: University of Georgia Press, 1988), 37–60.

37. Meg Twycross, " 'Transvestism' in the Mystery Plays," *Medieval English Theatre* 5 (1983): 123–180, at 127; Richard Rastall, "Female Roles in All-Male Casts," *Medieval English Theatre* 7 (1985): 25–50.

38. Twycross " 'Transvestism,' " 124–28; Stephen Orgel, *Impersonations: The Performance of Gender in Shakespeare's England* (Cambridge: Cambridge University Press, 1996), 4–5; Glynne Wickham, *Early English Stages 1300–1660*, vol. 1 (London and New York: Routledge and Kegan Paul, 1959), 271–72; Rosemary Woolf, *The English Mystery Plays* (London and New York: Routledge and Kegan Paul, 1972, rpr. Berkeley: University of California Press, 1980), 410; Clifford Davidson, "Women and the Medieval Stage," *Women's Studies* 11 (1984): 99–113; James Stokes, "Women and Mimesis in Medieval and Renaissance Somerset (and Beyond)," *Comparative Drama* 27 (1993): 176–96. One example of the problematic nature of the evidence is the ambiguity of names, cf. "Frauncys Cocckes," playing Salome in *The Destruction of Jerusalem* in 1584 in Coventry, might have been male (Davidson, "Women," 103).

39. Goldberg, "Craft Guilds," 147.

40. PRO C47/46/448: see also H. F. Westlake, *The Parish Guilds of Mediaeval England* (London: SPCK; New York: Macmillan, 1919): "Yearly on the Feast of the Purification the brothers and sisters meet in a fitting place from which to make procession to the church. One of them is clad as a queen to represent the B.V.M. with the appearance of a son in her arms. . . . The sisters follow the Virgin, and then come the brothers" (233). See also *English Gilds*, ed. Toulmin Smith, with introduction and notes by Lucy Toulmin Smith and a preliminary essay by Lujo Brentano, EETS o.s. 40 (London: Trübner, 1870), 149.

41. PRO C47/46/446, and Toulmin Smith, *English Gilds*, 148. I am grateful to Cordelia Beattie for this information.

42. Claire Sponsler, "Counterfeit in Their Array: Cross-Dressing in Robin Hood Performances," in *Drama and Resistance: Bodies, Goods, and Theatricality in Late Medieval England* (Minneapolis and London: University of Minnesota Press, 1997), 24–49, at 26. See also Catherine Normington, "Holy Women/Vulgar Women: Women and the Corpus Christi Cycles," Ph.D. diss., University of Exeter, 1999, 9.

43. Jane Marianna Tolmie, "Performing Eve in the Medieval Theatre," D. Phil. diss., Oxford, 2001, 249.

44. Sponsler "Counterfeit in Their Array," 27. Marjorie Garber, *Vested Interests: Cross-Dressing and Cultural Anxiety* (New York and London: Routledge, 1992), 16.

45. Norbert Elias, *The Civilizing Process: Sociogenetic and Psychogenetic Investigations*, trans. Edmund Jephcott, rev. edn, ed. Eric Dunning, Johan Goudsblom, and Stephen Mennell (Oxford: Blackwell, 2000), 136–42, at 138.

46. Dyan Elliott, *Fallen Bodies: Pollution, Sexuality, and Demonology in the Middle Ages*, The Middle Ages Series (Philadelphia: University of Pennsylvania Press, 1999), 31.

47. Chrétien de Troyes, "The Knight of the Cart," in *Arthurian Romances*, trans. D. D. R. Owen (London: Dent, 1987), lines 514–23.

48. *The Riverside Chaucer*, 3rd edn., ed. Larry D. Benson (Oxford: Oxford University Press, 1988).

49. *REED: York*, 2 vols., Records of Early English Drama, vol. 2, ed. Alexandra Johnston and Margaret Rogerson (Toronto and Manchester: University of Toronto Press and University of Manchester Press, 1979), 1.137–43; John Leland, *J. Lelandi Antiquarii de Rebus*, 6 vols. (Sheldonian Theatre: Oxford, 1715; London: Richardson, 1770; London: White, 1774; Farnborough: Gregg International Publishers, 1970), "In divers Places of the Citie was hanging oute of Tapestry, and other Clothes" (4:190). I am grateful to Chris Humphrey for these references.

50. *REED: York* 1.283.

51. On royal entries, see Gordon Kipling, *Enter the King: Theatre, Liturgy, and Ritual in the Medieval Civic Triumph* (Oxford: Clarendon, 1998). The practice of hanging out tapestries from windows is a feature of the celebrations in Arthurian romances, for example in Chrétien de Troyes' *Erec et Enide* (2354), *Guillaume de Palerne* (2921), *Raoul de Cambrai* (8184), and the *Histoire des ducs de Normandie* (196). I am grateful to Ad Putter for these references.

52. "[T]he display of piety [was] an opportunity for the display of the worship and the social clout of those involved." In late-fifteenth-century Hull, "testators left sumptuous bed-hangings to drape their hearses on their anniversary obsequies," and these were then displayed annually in Holy Trinity Church on St. George's Day (Duffy, *Stripping*, 44).

53. The York House Books record several instances of disputes between the city and the minister over the rights of common lands: these are especially prevalent in the late fifteenth century: see *York Civic Records*, ed. Raine, 2: viii, and E. Miller, "Medieval York," in *A History of Yorkshire*, ed. P. M. Tillott, *The City of York, The Victoria History of the Counties of England*, ed. R. B. Pugh (London: Institute of Historical Research, University of London, Oxford University Press, 1961), 25–113, at 83.

54. De Grazia, "World Pictures," 20.

## FURTHER READING

Beadle, Richard. "The York Cycle: Texts, Performances, and the Bases for Critical Enquiry." In Tim William Machan, ed., *Medieval Literature: Texts and Interpretation*. Binghamton: MRTS, 1991.

Beadle, Richard, ed. *The Cambridge Companion to Medieval English Theatre*. Cambridge: Cambridge University Press, 1994.

Beckwith, Sarah. "Making the World in York and the York Cycle." In Sarah Kay and Miri Rubin, eds., *Framing Medieval Bodies*. Manchester and New York: Manchester University Press, 1994.

———. "Ritual, Theater, and Social Space in the York Corpus Christi Cycle." In Barbara Hanawalt and David Wallace, eds., *Bodies and Disciplines: Intersections of Literature and History in Fifteenth-Century England*. Minneapolis: University of Minnesota Press, 1995.

Best, Sue. "Sexualising Space." In Elizabeth Grosz and Elspeth Probyn, eds., *Sexy Bodies: The Strange Carnalities of Feminism*. New York and London: Routledge, 1995.

Colomina, Beatriz, ed. *Sexuality and Space*. Princeton: Princeton Architectural Press, 1992.

Davidson, Clifford. "Women and the Medieval Stage." *Women's Studies* 11 (1984): 99–113.

*Early Theatre*. Special Volume: *The York Cycle Then and Now* 3 (2000).

Goldberg, P. J. P. *Women, Work, and Life Cycle in a Medieval Economy: Women in York and Yorkshire c. 1300–1520*. Oxford: Clarendon, 1992.

Hanawalt, Barbara A., and Michal Kobialka, eds. *Medieval Practices of Space*. Medieval Cultures Series, vol. 23. Minneapolis and London: University of Minnesota Press, 2000.

King, Pamela M. "Spatial Semantics and the Medieval Theatre." In *Themes in Drama, the Theatrical Space*, vol. 9. Ed. J. Redmond. Cambridge: Cambridge University Press, 1987.

Lefebvre, Henri. *The Production of Space*, trans. Donald Nicholson-Smith. Oxford and Malden, Mass.: Blackwell, 1991.

Lomperis, Linda. "Bodies That Matter in the Court of Late Medieval England and in Chaucer's *Miller's Tale*." *Romanic Review* 86 (1996): 243–64.

Normington, Catherine. "Holy Women/Vulgar Women: Women and the Corpus Christi Cycles." Ph.D. diss., University of Exeter, 1999.

Rees Jones, Sarah, ed. *The Government of Medieval York*. York: Borthwick Institute of Historical Research, 1997.

Rubin, Miri. *Corpus Christi: The Eucharist in Late Medieval Culture*. Cambridge: Cambridge University Press, 1991.

Spain, Daphne. *Gendered Spaces*. Chapel Hill and London: University of North Carolina Press, 1992.

Sponsler, Claire. *Drama and Resistance: Bodies, Goods, and Theatricality in Late Medieval England*. Minneapolis and London: University of Minnesota Press, 1997.

Tolmie, Jane Marianna. *Performing Eve in the Medieval Theatre*. D. Phil. diss., Oxford, 2001.

Twycross, Meg. " 'Transvestism' in the Mystery Plays." *Medieval English Theatre* 5 (1983): 123–80.

TWO

# ELY'S ST. ÆTHELTHRYTH: THE SHRINE'S ENCLOSURE OF THE FEMALE BODY AS SYMBOL FOR THE INVIOLABILITY OF MONASTIC SPACE

Virginia Blanton

Ibi est unum feretrum sub quo clauditur vas marmoreum continens sancte Ædeldrede corpus virgineum, versus altare proprium, sicut precellens domina, tota integra, tota incorrupta, quiescit in tumulo, quod Dei iussione angelicis ei, ut credimus, parabatur manibus.

[There is one shrine, within which the marble sarcophagus containing the virgin body of St. Æthelthryth is enclosed, turned in the direction of her own altar, just as the exalted lady, entirely whole, entirely uncorrupted, rests in the tomb which, we believe, had been prepared for her at God's command by the hands of angels.]

THIS DESCRIPTION OF THE SHRINE of Æthelthryth, Anglo-Saxon queen and abbess, comes from an inventory list assembled in 1134 and documented in the *Liber Eliensis*, which is a compilation of deeds, charters, privileges, and estate litigation designed to recount the history of the Benedictine monastery at Ely, England.[1] This chronicle begins with a book-length vita of Æthelthryth, who is the house's founder and patron saint, and it features, interspersed throughout the collected documents, a number of miracle stories associated with the twice-married virgin and her shrine.[2] In effect, the compilation highlights the life of the monastery's royal patron and documents the significant events at Ely subsequent to her death. The story of Æthelthryth's life and of the entombment of her incorruptible corpse figure largely in this monastic narrative, for the shrine—as a material extension of the founder's preserved corporeality—is invoked as the organizing symbol for the community's identity. In describing the shrine as an enclosure, one that protects the incorrupted body of the saint and one over which the monks swear oaths of allegiance (and thus form a collective body), the chronicle indirectly associates the shrine with the architectural space of the monastery, even as it suggests the imagery of enclosure for the spiritual body represented by the group of monks. As a symbol of permanence and purity, the dead saint's corporeality is manifested in the materiality of her resting place, for the shrine carries the multivalent attributes associated with the woman's life—she is royal, chaste, monastic, abbatial, sovereign—and the values directly tied to her post mortem physicality—the body is pure, virginal, incorruptible, inviolable, impenetrable, immutable.

Drawing upon the work of cultural anthropologists, Sarah Beckwith has argued forcefully for an understanding of how symbols are culturally contingent, "signifying devices which provide the communicative context through which social worlds are imagined, invented and changed."[3] Her analysis of the ambiguity of meaning associated with Christ's body in the late medieval period provides a theoretical framework for investigating how Æthelthryth's uncorrupted corpse is situated as a prominent symbol in the *Liber Eliensis*. In repeatedly underscoring the elements of royalty, chastity, inviolability, and immutability, the chronicle's description of the enshrined body establishes a recurring symbol of power through which the monks assert their sovereignty over the Isle of Ely and their autonomy in the monastery's governance. Thus, not only does the construction of the chronicle draw on the institution's traditions to present an image of the saint in which the monks glory, but it also illustrates how the monks want themselves to be understood. At times, they indicate that the saint risks violation because of her purity; at others, they illustrate how her sovereignty affords her the right to defend her properties, even through violence. By aligning themselves with the royal saint, whether she is imagined as a victim or as an aggressor, the monks present a careful rhetorical record of their institution, a record that allows them to assert either their victimization or their aggression in the face of external threat. As the second wealthiest monastery at the time of the Conquest, Ely had every reason to be concerned about its future under a Norman administration.[4]

In order to legitimize the monastery's representation of its history, the text draws largely on the most authoritative account of the queen and abbess's life, which appears in Bede's *Historia Ecclesiastica Gentis Anglorum* (completed in 731). Nearly Æthelthryth's contemporary, Bede relies on firsthand testimony to prove that the East Anglian princess insisted upon conjugal chastity when married the first time to an ealdorman of her father's kingdom and again when she was married to King Ecgfrith of Northumbria. After living twelve years in chastity, Ecgfrith, who had struggled with the proviso, finally agreed that his wife could become a nun at Coldingham, a royal monastery governed by his aunt. Bede indicates that one year later (673) Æthelthryth left Northumbria and founded a double house at Ely, an island in her natal fenlands, where she governed the women and men as abbess. Sixteen years after her death in 679, her sister and successor, Sexburg, discovered that the founder's body would not decay, a sign to the community that Æthelthryth had preserved her virginity throughout her marriages. Following this revelation, Bede describes how the uncorrupted corpse was placed within a stone sarcophagus and conducted with ceremony into the monastic church.[5]

The twelfth-century *Liber Eliensis* augments Bede's eighth-century narrative to illustrate the events following the founder's death and translation. Book 2 of the chronicle indicates that while the monastery at Ely was destroyed during the Danish invasions, Æthelthryth's corporeal purity remained undisturbed within the sanctity of her sarcophagus. When King Edgar and Bishop Æthelwold refounded Ely in 970, expelling the clerics living there and repopulating it with Benedictine monks, the *Liber Eliensis* indicates that the tomb was intact and that "nemo inspicere presumpsit" [no one dared to inspect it] (229). Based upon now-lost vernacular documents, the chronicle illustrates that Æthelwold carefully orchestrated the Anglo-Saxon refoundation, for alongside his many gifts to the house, he rebuilt the complex and with great ceremony enshrined Æthelthryth's sarcophagus within the church, placing alongside it the relics of her sisters: Wihtburg, abbess of her own foundation at East Dereham, and Sexburg, queen of Kent and founder/abbess of Minster-in-Sheppey. In addition, Æthelwold enshrined there the relics of Sexburg's daughter, Eormenild, queen of Mercia and mother to Werburg, nun of Ely and later founder of several monasteries and patron of Chester. While no early documents survive to indicate the history of Ely after the Æthelthryth's death and translation, the twelfth-century chronicle provides an elaborate account that claims Eormenild and Werburg succeeded Sexburg as abbess of Ely.

Likewise, another element is added to the *Liber Eliensis* that suggests how the gathering of the sororal family was important to the establishment of this cult center. The chronicle describes how Wihtburg's relics were brought by stealth from the monastery at East Dereham and that, when inspected, they too were found incorrupted (120–23). Christine Fell has demonstrated that Wihtburg's identity is likely a fabrication, since no records of her life survive before the tenth century.[6] It appears, then, that during the translation ceremony honoring this East Anglian royal family, a visual demonstration of incorruptibility was necessary. Since the community did not dare to examine Æthelthryth's body for fear of compromising its purity, Wihtburg's corporeality is substituted. The demonstration of her incorruptibility increases the magnificence of Ely's holy family; in effect, a sister's corporeal purity lends authenticity to the narrative claim that Æthelthryth's preserved body continues to rest within the sarcophagus.[7] The result is that the tombs of the four royal women—two virgins and two mothers who produced yet more nuns for this royal house—form a nexus of royal and abbatial power. Royal position and abbatial service are highlighted here as the dominant elements leading to the sanctity of these Anglo-Saxon women, and these terms are important to the claim of sovereignty made by the twelfth-century monks. What is more, the narrative of the *Liber Eliensis* illustrates these events as a deliberate staging of power, showcasing how gender, wealth, position, and authority converge to demarcate Ely as a distinctly royal, feminized monastic space.

Material objects, ones that can be seen, inspected, touched, venerated, are essential to Ely's monastic identity; these objects—the shrine and the sarcophagus, and even Wihtburg's body—are the means by which the saint's potency can be demonstrated. As Judith Butler illustrates, "signs work *by appearing* (visibly, aurally), and appearing through material means."[8] If the corpse cannot be displayed, then it cannot signify. These material objects, therefore, operate as a remapping of the virgin's post mortem corporeality, and they are encoded with the meanings associated with the virgin's body. The result is that the material goods are conflated with the saint's body and become interchangeable signs in the monastic narrative. Indeed, the chronicle endeavors to establish the presence of the body through these objects, even as the material goods simultaneously render the visualized corpse unnecessary.

The convergence of corporeality and materiality imagined in the body/shrine conflation was first introduced in the *Liber Eliensis*, but the idea draws on Bede's description of the sarcophagus as a complement to the saint's physical perfection. The translation of the saint in 695, as he relates in the *Historia*, revealed three miraculous aspects of her body: the corpse was incorrupt; the tumor on her neck that had caused her death had been perfectly healed; and the Roman sarcophagus found nearby perfectly fit the contours of the saint's remains (394–97). Bede's account stresses that the sarcophagus was made expressly to fit her body, although its manufacture predates Æthelthryth's life. This miraculous revelation begins the discourse of the body's association with an architectural enclosure, but only in the *Liber Eliensis* is this connection made explicit. As the epigraph specifies, the monks believe God ordered the sarcophagus made for Æthelthryth's body, an assertion that lends legitimacy to the imagery of enclosure in the text. The enclosures presented, moreover, are multiple in that the sarcophagus holds the body, the shrine contains the sarcophagus, the church surrounds the shrine, and the monastic close envelops the church. Ely, an island in the East Anglian fenlands, was, at that time, completely surrounded by marshes. Thus, the body, which Bede had characterized as sealed off by God, is described in the *Liber Eliensis* as being enclosed by a number of architectural and geographic elements. The narrative capitalizes on this imagery to suggest that just as the body of the saint is paralleled by the monastic body, the multiple enclosures of her body are symbols for the institution's boundaries, both architectural and geographical. Enveloped within the fenland waters, the monastery on the Isle of Ely is represented as a bounded space protected by God.

In imagining this sacred space, the twelfth-century Ely monks present themselves as an integral part of this holy body. Following established devotional practice, the gifts offered to Æthelthryth were called her "possessions." In her extensive examination of pre-Conquest cult rituals, Jane Tibbetts Schulenburg finds that threatened female communities often supported the belief that their founding abbess-saints were formidable protectors and that their bodily residence within the monasteries allowed them to watch over and protect their properties.[9] Adopting this ideology, the Ely monks describe themselves as custodians of Æthelthryth's estates on her behalf, and as such they see themselves as responsible for maintaining her holdings. Susan Ridyard has shown that a number of Anglo-Saxon monasteries envisioned themselves as caretakers of a patron saint, and at Ely Æthelthryth's incorrupt body symbolized the institution's legitimate and permanent privileges so that "guardianship of her relics conferred 'guardianship' of the same church and lands."[10] Drawing upon the scholarship of the chronicle's editor, E. O. Blake, Ridyard demonstrates the monks' rationale for their presentation: the loss of lands and wealth associated with the emergence of the diocese in the early twelfth century and the civil strife experienced as Stephen and Matilda struggled for the throne.[11]

While Ridyard's analysis of Ely's twelfth-century history is compelling, I would like to suggest that the narrative of the *Liber Eliensis* serves also as a rhetorical maneuver by which the community defines its identity as a sovereign and autonomous political entity. The monks deliberately rewrite their situation, illustrating their community as a physical part of the saint's corporate body in order to appear to be the victims of aggression during the Norman invasion. This stance allows them to produce a history that reflects their needs as an institution, positions them to claim their liberty from external governance, and establishes an identity of sovereign authority over the Isle of Ely.

This authority is clearly vulnerable, as Monika Otter finds. In discussing a symbolic rape of the saint's shrine, Otter examines the monks' relation to a female "communal body," suggesting that the female body enclosed within a male house sets up a sexualized tension between the monks and their female patron, one that renders the virginal body a tangible, rapable woman.[12] She demonstrates that the *Liber Eliensis* allegorizes this tension when a Danish invader foolishly makes an opening in the saint's sarcophagus and places a stick inside. The consequence of this highly transgressive act (the man is blinded) provides a definitive moral for the audience of monks: "noli me inspicere" (do not look at me). As Otter asserts, living daily alongside the sarcophagus would create a strong temptation to examine the saint's uncorrupted body, but the monks insist that they have not, a claim that "allows the community continually to stage its own purity."[13] The episode seems to indicate that, prior to Æthelwold's refoundation of Ely and the enclosure of the tomb within the shrine, the sarcophagus (and thus, the saint's corporeality) was vulnerable to violation. This detail underscores the importance of the shrine's protection by a legitimate monastic community. After the clerics are expelled and the monastery is repopulated with Benedictine monks, the community envelops the sarcophagus within a shrine. All the while, the monks insist that the saint's body remained "intentata et inconspecta" (229) [intact and unseen]. A very neat rhetorical move, the suggestion of poor guardianship allows the monastic community to assert that the saint had not been violated on their watch and that their stewardship led to further protections for their patron's continued purity. Their assertion, moreover, indicates that a true rape would include a visual violation of the physical body, not an assault on the sarcophagus as a material extension of that body. Since there is no ocular transgression, the saint's corporeal purity is maintained. It is important that the identification of looking as transgressive behavior indicates how dependent the narrative is upon the saint's preserved corporeality. If the body were to be discovered corrupted, the symbolic system constructed within the chronicle would break apart, so the narrative must reflect the importance of defending the body from intrusion and punishing those who transgress. Thus, the violator is blinded, a fitting punishment for his attempted infringement, and the monks adamantly refuse to open the sarcophagus of their patron.

The imagery of the safeguarded body, therefore, leads to the ideology of body at risk, and significantly, physical violence against the saint is recast in other episodes not considered by Otter, ones that illustrate how the monastic writers are playing with the rhetorical imagery of purity and rape, victim and aggressor. The *Liber Eliensis* details several episodes of violence against the saint's physical and material bodies; each time, the narrative carefully negotiates the difficult line between inviolability and invasion, whether it be a transgression against the shrine or against the patron's holdings. Certainly, the description of sexual violation places Æthelthryth in a decidedly useful position as victim, for it calls on early hagiographical narratives of the virgin martyr who successfully evades a tyrant's ardent advances. The monks' use of this image, moreover, suggests that if the purity of their patron is compromised, so too is their autonomy as guardians of her body and of her holdings. The narrative illustrates these transgressions against the saint as potential rapes, but the text repeatedly denies that the saint is violated physically, even if the shrine itself undergoes attack.

The alignment of the monastic body with the saint's body appears at moments of crisis throughout the *Liber Eliensis*. While Ridyard's analysis of the political tensions at twelfth-century Ely and Otter's critique of the monks' anxiety regarding their patron provide important ground work for the present study, neither identifies the *Liber Eliensis* as a rhetorical document that establishes the saint's body and shrine as multivalent symbols designed to elucidate the monks' situation. Indeed, Otter examines the narrative as an authentic report of the monks' lived experience with the body of a female in their midst. While the proximity of the female body might indeed be a cause for sexual tension for the monks, I posit that the chronicle is actually a construction that illustrates monastic anxieties in the midst of a major political and cultural shift. While the Norman administration had been in place for some sixty years before the chronicle was begun, undoubtedly there were adjustments, especially when the new diocese of Ely was formed in 1109 and when the war between Stephen and Matilda developed. Most important, the chronicle seems to indicate that the monastery was concerned about its political and economic fortunes, which could rest on the new king's favor, and as Ridyard suggests, on the benevolence of their new bishop. By invoking the hagiographical trope of the rape narrative, and by positioning the saint's body as rapable, the monks are able to imagine themselves as victims of royal rapaciousness during the Norman invasion, especially when the monastery's lands had been unjustly seized by the king's officials after the Conquest and again during the formation of the diocese. This strategy is particularly useful for asserting their rights to estates lost through encroachment. The monks identify the monastic holdings with the body of the saint, and thus their narrative situates the erotic body as an economic body that can be plundered. In effect, Æthelthryth's enshrined corporeality represents the economic wealth of the institution, and thus violation does not destroy sexual purity per se, but instead threatens the monastery's economic sovereignty. As the images of purity and sovereignty become coterminous, the narrative issues a direct challenge to anyone who attempts to compromise the monastic holdings. By placing this narrative during the Norman invasion, moreover, the monks avoid a risky direct accusation about the current political tensions, rewriting their past history in terms that support their present concerns. The description of retribution exacted from invaders, whether Danish or Norman, poses an indirect but clear warning to those who threaten the monastic space at Ely.

The remainder of this chapter, then, explores the chronicle's representations of sexualized violence against the saint's body, against the shrine, and against the monastery to illustrate how the monks handled their anxieties by positioning themselves within a female-gendered space and by imagining themselves as economic victims of the Norman invaders. But before turning to a consideration of these rhetorical constructions, I want to distinguish the narrative strategies by which the *Liber Eliensis* is fabricated as a vehicle for preserving the monastery's economic rights. Using not only traditional documents of history, such as charters, deeds, and records of estate litigation, but also hagiographical elements, such as a book-length vita and miracle stories, the monastic community signals its desire to create a rhetorical narrative in which the imagery invoked by Æthelthryth's incorrupted body is integral to the monks' economic and political existence. A brief discussion of the structural elements in the *Liber* positions us to understand more fully how the episodes of violence, which are miracles staged as historical acts, are written to legitimize monastic autonomy and to protect the institution from significant economic loss. It is significant that each of the three episodes of violence discussed thereafter depicts a physical assault on the monastery by royal power; by positioning the aggression as royal, each story reminds us of the hagiographical tradition invoked by the imagery used, for the violation of a virgin, who had dedicated herself to God, warranted a bad end for the tyrant kings depicted in early martyr narratives, but the violation of a royal virgin whose miracles prove her sanctity escalates the nature of the assault. In effect, the narrative situates the powerful imagery of a royal saint against the secular powers exercised by a monarch, even as it amplifies the punishment that a king might receive for interfering with this divinely sanctioned body politic.

## HISTORY AND HAGIOGRAPHY AS RHETORICAL HYBRID

The *Liber Eliensis* demonstrates how a monastery's historical documents can be successfully interwoven with a hagiographical narrative and, likewise, how hagiography supports the historical tradition of a monastic institution.[14] The text is drawn from a collection of vernacular and Latin documents, which were compiled between 1131 and 1174 following the formation of the Ely diocese. This reorganization from Benedictine abbey to cathedral church, which included a division of properties between bishop and monks, reflects the monastery's need to identify itself as a distinct political and economic entity.[15] As a response to the apportionment of revenues by a new bishop, the monastic community compiled records that detailed the rights given them by their founder. One privilege in particular is highlighted: Æthelthryth's royal status meant that the institution was exempt from external influence or control (72–76). This assertion is supported by Edward the Confessor's royal charter and by papal bull (161–64). Following the Norman invasion, moreover, such documentation was imperative, particularly because a monastery could then legitimately argue for the same privileges it had previously enjoyed under the Saxon kings.[16]

The monastic chronicle relies heavily on Ely's historical tradition to qualify its position: it includes a significantly augmented life of Æthelthryth to illustrate the house's foundation (book 1), it incorporates a history of the monastery from the time of its refoundation until its reorganization as an episcopal see (book 2), and it details the reigns of the first two bishops of Ely (book 3). Interspersed throughout the second and third portion of this narrative are charters, documents of estate litigation, and several miracle stories illustrating Æthelthryth's personal intercession on behalf of the house. Compared to more traditional Anglo-Latin *libelli* designed to honor a saint (which usually comprise a *passio* and a collection of miracles associated with a patron that are not necessarily appended to a chronicle manuscript), the *Liber Eliensis* differs somewhat in that it not only includes the life of the saint as an integral part of the chronicle, but it also features miracle narratives about the saint's benefaction alongside the documents of historical record in books 2 (210–17) and 3 (263–83). The result is a rhetorical narrative designed to lend historical authority to the saint's legend, even as the saint's posture as intercessor provides a direct warning against encroachment, should the validity of the historical documents be doubted. Granted, this hybridization of historical and hagiographical matter is one made by writers at other institutions, but few seem to have interlaced the documents of record with miracle stories in the manner described here.[17]

Since the miracles included in the *Liber Eliensis* are distributed among charters and descriptions of lawsuits (rather than collected in a separate *libellus*), they figure prominently among the royal, episcopal, and papal charters of privilege as a counterpoint to the authority of these documents. The compilation of historical and hagiographical material suggests that we are to read the life and miracles of Æthelthryth as historical events and therefore to regard them in the same light as we might a charter, a papal privilege, or a record of estate litigation. The assertion of the saint's governance of the isle is forefronted in the narrative, for it is the introduction to the vita that emphasizes Æthelthryth held the Isle of Ely through her first marriage: "accepta iure dotis insula a Tonberto primo sponso suo, postquam illic mansionem elegit, prope fluentis alveum in loco eminentiore habitacula posuit" (4).[18] [having accepted the isle by right of dower from her first husband Tonbert, she selected a house there, and afterward, she put a more distinguished dwelling in the place near the bed of the river.] This claim carefully defines Ely's ancient sovereignty, and positioned at the beginning of this long monastic narrative, it becomes the basis for the house's claim of independence.[19]

The structural and material evidence of the *Liber Eliensis* suggests further that the compilation provided both a defensive and an offensive strategy for the twelfth-century community. By positioning themselves within the sanctity of an ancient Anglo-Saxon foundation, the monks use this monastic history to lay claim to an older tradition of institutional liberty, and in so doing, they place themselves securely within that privilege by defining the institution and its holdings as a body politic (3–4, 32–34). Akin to the idea of the king's body as a symbol of the secular polity he governs, the *Liber Eliensis* presents the royal founder's body as a symbol of the monastic polity she founded and governed as abbess.[20] The monks' responsibility as guardians of the dead woman's body and her domain situates them as active participants in this polity, ones who carefully encode the saint's body with meaning. The saint's body comes to represent not just a set of ideological ideals but also a physical space: the virgin's corpse denotes the monastic holdings, landed estates, and revenues associated with the body politic.

These representations are rhetorical conventions of miracle writing worthy of close textual examination. In their discussion of the miracles of St. Foy, for instance, Kathleen Ashley and Pamela Sheingorn illustrate how such narratives operate, observing that "[i]n analyzing these miracle narratives as semiotic entities we must simultaneously attend to three aspects of the texts; we must see them as rhetorical structures (a set of internally related signs), as historically contingent constellations of signs, and as sign systems designed to have historical agency."[21] Examining how and where miracle stories are presented in the *Liber Eliensis* positions us to scrutinize how a pseudo-history is created to represent the house's conception of itself and its traditions. It is meaningful that the chronicle employs the miraculous in its account of the Norman invasion explicitly to document Æthelthryth's continued purity, her powerful protection of the monastic properties against royal interference, and her vengeance on those who appropriate her lands. These stories of physical violence, moreover, indicate a strong rationale for the monks' identification with this distinctly female space: having re-created Ely's pre-Conquest history, the chronicle asserts the monks' liberty by establishing the power of virginity in the face of potential rape. Whether it be a violation of the virginal body or of the monastic properties, the community defines economic violation as a physical, a spiritual, and most certainly, a political mistake.

## THE SAINT'S BODY AS INVIOLABLE SYMBOL

The first narrative to be considered here is a miracle story that describes the conjugal conflict between Æthelthryth and her second husband, King Ecgfrith of Northumbria. Using the imagery of rape, the Ely monk employs a conventional topos of medieval hagiography, yet the depictions of violence in the *Liber Eliensis* do not follow the idealized pattern of saints such as Agatha who endure the tortuous cruelty of non-Christian rulers.[22] Typically, hagiographical representations of rape exist solely in relation to the ideal of *integritas*—complete chastity for a woman in imitation of both Christ and the Virgin Mary.[23] The essential plot of a female saint's life consists of the following: a pagan man desires a Christian virgin; he attempts to violate the virgin; God saves the pious woman from the impurities of sex and from pollution by the non-Christian; and thus both carnality and paganism are defeated by the virgin.[24] The repetition of this theme shows that attempted rape is the test by which many female religious enter the community of faith; surviving this trial becomes a type of initiation rite, a rite of passage into true purity.[25]

Following a hagiographical tradition that demanded that a virgin's purity be tested, the *Liber Eliensis* amplifies Bede's account of the conjugal conflict between Æthelthryth and Ecgfrith with a story of sexualized violence. Bede says that the king unsuccessfully pressed Æthelthryth to submit to his conjugal demands, even trying to gain the York bishop's support by offering him money and lands; but when Wilfrid refused the bribe, the king agreed that Æthelthryth could become a nun.[26] In the Anglo-Saxon analog, there is no attempted rape, whereas the Ely chronicle describes Ecgfrith's attempted abduction of his wife from Coldingham, a royal Northumbrian monastery.

> (Ecgfrith) de monasterio illam, licet iam sanctitatis velamine obtectam, eripere conabatur. Nec mora, ad monasterium ubi virgo sancta degebat cum furore et fremitu festinanter ascendit. (27–28)
>
> [(Ecgfrith) tried to abduct her from the monastery, although she was now covered by the veil of sanctity. And without delay, he went up quickly, with fury and clamor, to the monastery where the holy virgin was living.]

The strength of this passage illustrates the power of the husband: he plans to seize her, or in the Latin, *eripere*, and he comes in a rage to get her. His anger here foreshadows the intended sexual violence, yet the king's desire is juxtaposed with God's protection.

> Instat enim rex, in matrimonio cupiens eam resumere, non omittens persequi, si forte valeat comprehendere. . . . cum duabus Dei ancillis Sewenna et Sewara collem eminentem prope, qui Coldeburcheshevet, quod Latine caput Coldeburci dicitur, adiit et ascendit. Sed Deus, qui ventis et mari imperat et obediunt ei, non derelinquit sperantes in se, illius iussu credimus fieri, quod mare, suum alveum egrediens nunc aquas multipliciter effundens, locum in quem sacre virgines ascenderant circumdedit et . . . per septem continuos dies sine cibo et potu in oratione consistentes eas occuluit et . . . quamdiu rex illic aut penes locum morabatur. (27)
>
> [The king persistently chased her, desiring to take her back in marriage, not omitting to pursue her, if by chance he might be able to take hold of her. . . . [W]ith the two handmaidens of God, Sewenna and Sewara, she approached and ascended a prominent hill nearby, one Coldeburcheshevet that is called in Latin the head of Coldeburchus. But God, who commands the winds and the sea and they obey him, did not abandon those hopeful in him, the sea—which we believe was made at the command of that one—surrounded the place onto which the holy virgins had ascended and . . . forgetting its customary ebbing, it hid them for seven continuous days while they remained steadfast in prayer without food or drink . . . as long as the king remained there or near the place.]

This passage can be rendered mildly or can be translated with expressions of violence, but each meaning suggests a threat to Æthelthryth's monastic vow, and potentially, to her chastity. The verb *eripere* can be rendered in several ways: the king wanted "to pursue" or "to threaten" her, "to take vengeance upon" or "to chase after" her, "to snatch her away with violence" or "to free" her. The term's multiple meanings, couched in violence, come from *rapere* (*ex* + *rapio*), which is "to seize and carry off," "to snatch," "to tear," "to wrench off." In both *eripere* and *rapere*, the idea of pursuit merged with violence is represented by the terms of capture. Kathryn Gravdal observes that early translations of *rapere* implied only seizure, not necessarily sexual violence, but by the twelfth century, when this miracle scene was inserted into the chronicle, abduction was so often followed by intercourse that the two concepts had become nearly linguistically synonymous: "Some of the more common meanings of *rapere* are to carry off or seize; to snatch, pluck, or drag off; to hurry, impel, hasten; to rob, plunder; and, finally, to abduct (a virgin). . . . But as early as 1155, the Latin *raptus* in the sense of abduction brings about the shift toward a sexual meaning: *rap* (ca. 1155) or *rat* (ca. 1235) designates abduction by violence or by seduction, for the purposes of forced coitus."[27] Further, Christopher Cannon's discussion of rape illustrates that in the twelfth century English law made a careful distinction between abduction and forcible sex so that "in *Glanvill* (ca. 1187–89) *raptus* was defined as forced coitus."[28] Despite a clear distinction between the two twelfth-century legal terms, the Ely monk did not use a noun when describing this attempt, preferring instead an infinitive-plus-verb construction: *eripere conabatur*. By choosing the infinitive construction, the writer establishes a gap between the king's desire for his wife and the act of seizing her, which would be a specific act of rape. In so doing, the chronicle establishes an elision between the idea of rape and the execution of the act. As Gravdal observes, this elision is characteristic of rape terminology; it "favors periphrasis, metaphor, and slippery lexematic exchanges, as opposed to a clear and unambiguous signifier of sexual assault."[29]

The chronicler's decision to utilize more elusive language suggests, too, that the assault is intentionally metaphoric and that direct terminologies of rape cannot be used to describe the king's act. In her discussion of rape and power, Brenda Silver defines periphrasis "as a figure that both opens up and exists in a gap or space between sign and meaning."[30] The periphrastic representation of rape in the *Liber Eliensis* does not state clearly that the king is a rapist, but this indirect language allows the monastic community to critique royal aggression without the reprisal that a direct accusation might have. Periphrastic language also positions the virgin's symbolic body as a site of potential (but not realized) violence. In other words, the rape is attempted, but not completed, which is an essential element of this story: the monks must position themselves so that the shrine remains sanctified and the saint remains a virgin, and in so doing, they underscore the continuing process of potentiality.[31] As long as the saint remains virginal, there is the possibility of violation; by positioning themselves within this gendered space, moreover, they illustrate how the isle continues as a protected site that is always threatened by pollution.[32]

Anthropological research like Mary Douglas's has provided an avenue for scholars to examine medieval bodies as metaphoric or symbolic spaces.[33] Important recent work on gender and enclosure in medieval studies has pointed to the ways that ideologies of the body mirror the social and political uses of architectural space.[34] As Roberta Gilchrist illustrates, "Space forms the arena in which social relationships are negotiated, expressed through the construction of landscapes, architecture and boundaries. The resulting spatial maps represent discourses of power based in the body."[35] Architectural space as an extension of the body is a valuable framework within which to explore the social relationship between the monastery of Ely and its patron saint. The narrative emphasizes how nature will support the besieged. The saint's ability to withstand physical assault, particularly the threat posed by royal power, is emphasized further by the passage's detailed description of natural elements: the women remain on the hill, surrounded by water without food or drink. Enclosed by the rising waters, the isle on which the women kneel is created and sanctified by God, and it is geographical space that protects the saint and renders her inviolable.[36] Previous hagiographical narratives about Æthelthryth had always intimated that her conjugal chastity made her a closed vessel, but here the *Liber Eliensis* expands this theme to show that, encapsulated by the waters, she and her properties, as extensions of her chaste body, are completely protected from penetration.

The twelfth-century miracle story, which so clearly articulates Æthelthryth's continued purity in the face of aggression, is recalled by a pictorial cycle on the eight stone supports that surrounded the monks' choir.[37] Added to the cathedral two centuries after the *Liber Eliensis* was written, the grouping includes a representation of the miracle of the rising waters (figure 2.1). Three women,

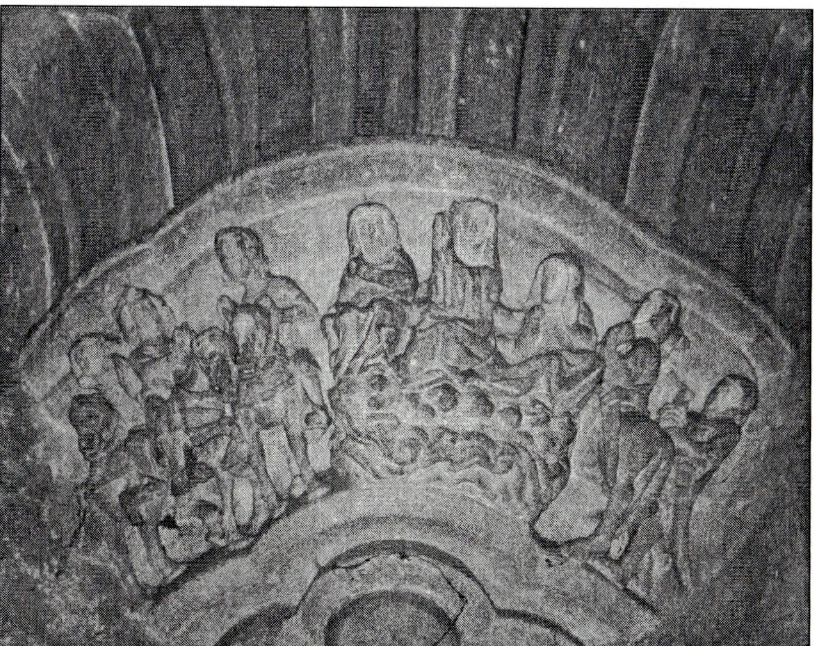

**Figure 2.1.** *Miracle of Æthelthryth's Resistance to Ecgfrith's Desire*, 1330s?, Octagon Capital, Ely Cathedral, Ely, England. Photo Blanton.

Æthelthryth and her two servants, Sewenna and Sewara, kneel on a hill surrounded by churning waters. Æthelthryth is at the center, crowned, with her clasped hands raised high in prayer. Her servants raise their hands as if to ward off the attack of the five men who surround them, four on horseback, all of whom are kept back by the waves. The two on the viewer's right are armed with an axe and a sword. On the left, the men are shown controlling their mounts, which are stamping and prancing, as if the raging waters have surprised them. Two of the men face away, but the third, crowned, is Ecgfrith, who faces his wife, seemingly intent on taking her from the small island, but as the *Liber Eliensis* attests, "Taliter ancilla Christi munita presidio, evasit minas regis nec sensit quandoque lesionem ab eo" (27). [In this way the handmaiden of Christ, protected in that citadel, evaded the threats of the king, and not at any time did she suffer harm from him.] Æthelthryth kneels on the island, which becomes a physical extension of her chaste body. This image of the female saint's body as sacred space extends the familiar topos of the feminized personification of *Ecclesia*, or Mother Church. Yet in this case, Æthelthryth is presented specifically as virginal, not maternal, a categorization that changes the ecclesiastical discourse about the church and locates it specifically within the Isle of Ely and its monastic institution. The turbulent water around the shrine, moreover, provides a geographic boundary of defense and a demarcation of symbolic sanctity.

The metaphoric violence illustrated in this miracle scene is suggestive about the problems the Ely monastery encountered just as the *Liber Eliensis* was compiled in the midtwelfth century. The turbulence of Stephen and Matilda's war sets the stage for understanding the reasons behind the illustration of this miracle, particularly since the Ely bishop used the shrine's decorations to support Matilda initially and, after switching sides, to pay his fine of contrition to Stephen (321–35). Yet the chronicle also apportions a significant number of chapters to the political problems associated with the Norman invasion, and in the context of William's conquest, the compiler argues for Æthelthryth's continued sovereignty. Specifically, the *Liber Eliensis* uses the imagery of this miracle story when it records William's siege at the Isle of Ely and the monks' resistance to him.

## HISTORICIZING ELY'S RESISTANCE TO THE NORMAN CONQUEST

If we examine the account of the Norman Conquest chronicled in book 2 of the *Liber Eliensis*, we find clear echoes of the writer's presentation of Æthelthryth's resistance to royal aggression in book 1. It seems as if the chronicler is intentionally drawing parallels between the two parts of his narrative and asking his reader to remember the monastery's position in relation to royal power. Specifically, the narrative describes Ely as the site of a seven-year resistance against William's forces, led by several Anglo-Saxon noblemen and the famed Hereward (173–95).[38] In 1071, as the new king attempted to bring more of England under his control, the monastic community sided with the Saxon rebels in repudiating William's attempts to invade the fenlands. The justification for their resistance lay in the ancient monastic privilege known as the "Liberty of Ely."[39] As I have detailed above, the monks' liberty was based on Æthelthryth's royal position as the original proprietor of the isle. This declaration is coupled in book 1 with their insistence that they are free of external episcopal authority, an important claim following the division of the abbey lands between bishop and monastery:

> Ab omnium namque iudicio et potestate insula admodum libera est, quo neque episcopus neque alicuius exactionis minister sine advocatione fratrum se intromittat vel rem sancte inquietare presumat. (4)

> [For indeed, the isle is quite free from all jurisdictional power and control, into which neither bishop nor any agent of supervision will be allowed to pass without a brother's support for him nor will he presume to disturb the holy property.]

This claim is enlarged in book 2, when the chronicle describes the Norman siege at Ely, saying all will be denied entrance, including secular officials: "sine aliqua exceptione secularis vel ecclesiastice iustitie" (181) [without any exception for secular or ecclesiastical authority]. The monk clarifies the ambiguous "neque alicuius exactionis minister" of the preceding passage, specifically affixing a reference to secular authority. Inserted directly within the narrative of William's offenses against the monastery, this embellishment permits the monks to stage their position within this conflict: here, they are the victims of the Norman king's unjust attempt to subdue them. This posture makes the allusions to the miracle story more direct, reminding the reader that God's benefaction for Æthelthryth's sovereignty extends to their guardianship of the isle. Membership within this elite group, moreover, was determined by one's loyalty to the saint: "Sed neque aliquem in suo contubernio admittebant, nisi prius fidelitatem supra corpus sacratissime virginis Æðeldreðe iureiurando" (176). [But by no means did they admit anyone into their band of retainers, without his first having sworn an oath over the body of the most holy virgin Æthelthryth.]

The two episodes of assault, one hagiographical and one historical, illustrate how hagiographical tropes are used to write the monastery's version of events during the siege. Using allusions to the miracle scene allows the monastic community to assert that, even though the narrative events differ considerably, the monks will challenge invaders because an assault on the isle is a transgression against the saint and her body politic. As a symbol of immutability, the saint's body recalls the previous narratives of aggression, including the violation of the Danish soldier who so foolishly inserted a stick in the sarcophagus. Furthermore, the invocation of the body at this moment demonstrates that whenever the monks feel threatened, this symbol of their autonomy will be presented.

While it is known that all of England eventually came under Norman rule by force, the *Liber Eliensis* maintains that the Isle of Ely was never overrun, reporting that the monks only negotiated for peace when, after seven years, their food reserves were depleted (189). The text then details the agreement made with the king, a result that differs considerably from the miracle of the rising waters. The description of the Norman advance into the Isle of Ely intimates that the monks are forced into submission, but the chronicle writer is careful to specify that William only comes to Ely because he was invited.

By comparison, the *Gesta Herewardi*, a chronicle produced by the same Ely monk before he wrote the history of the siege in the *Liber Eliensis*, illuminates a different reason for the community's submission.[40] In describing the deeds of Hereward, the *Gesta Herewardi* presents the siege in much different terms, maintaining the monks' prowess as soldiers and explaining that surrender came only when William allowed his noblemen to seize many of the Ely properties that lay outside the Isle of Ely.[41] This document admits what the *Liber Eliensis* cannot: through force, the community was subjected to the king's command because Ely was economically threatened. Although the two accounts differ regarding the reason for the monks' capitulation (starvation versus land seizure), both maintain that the monks invite William into their community. The invitation is significant because it sanctions his access, which is in keeping with their claim that none will enter the isle without a brother's approbation, and it negates the imagery of violation. The narrative adds a second crucial element to the agreement; it records that when William arrived, he entered the church to visit Æthelthryth's shrine, and the king's behavior there indicates his knowledge of the saint's power:

> Ad monasterium denique veniens, longe a sancto corpore virginis stans, marcham auri super altare proiecit, propius accedere non ausus; verebatur sibi a Deo iudicium inferri pro malis que sui in loco patrarunt. (194)
>
> [Finally, having come to the monastery and standing a distance from the holy body of the virgin, he threw a mark of gold onto the altar, not daring to come nearer; he feared judgment from God to be brought upon him because of the evils that they had perpetrated in that place.]

The gift to the shrine, depicted as a grudgingly ungracious gesture on the part of the vanquished king, also connotes the community's new compact with him. Drawing upon Gayle Rubin's well-known essay "The Traffic in

Women," Margaret Brose has demonstrated that the "profound implication of [women's cultural position as a commodity] . . . is that the fundamental alliances in culture are those that unite or bond male to male—alliances in which the female is coined as the lucre to purchase such alliances."[42] The imagery here suggests that William has debased himself before Æthelthryth, yet his public demonstration shows that an economic agreement has been made over her body.

The account of the surrender, as represented in the *Liber Eliensis*, suggests that the monks are able to force some degree of submission from William and that the alliance does not come totally at their expense. Other historical accounts recount the rebellion differently. The *Anglo-Saxon Chronicle* records that William handily subjugated the Ely community within a year.[43] Florence of Worcester includes a more detailed account in which William's flotilla encircles the Isle of Ely and ends the siege quickly.[44] In contrast to these independent accounts, the *Gesta Herewardi* shows that, after a long and difficult siege in which the rebels and monks always maintain the upper hand, William forced the monks to capitulate, not through military force, but through estate seizure.[45] By rewriting the history of the rebellion in the *Liber Eliensis*, an account that does not tally with the reports of other narratives, the monks could continue to assert the isle's purity as a direct extension of Æthelthryth's chastity, while suggesting that their invitation to William and his gift to the shrine demonstrates his subjection to their patron.

While the *Liber Eliensis* describes the monks' subordination as an economic transgression, it glosses over the violation by hiding the terms of the surrender. In warfare, rape is often the final subjugation of a people.[46] It destroys family relationships, and if the result of sexual violence is children, the race of people can be assimilated into the conquering one. The community of monks, however, is significantly different. The rebels within the isle are specifically gendered as male—monks and soldiers—within a female space. No women exist to be raped, except the virginal patron, but by identifying with the saint's vulnerability, the rebels could envision themselves as a community capable of being victimized by the king.[47] The exchange of money for land, however, refocuses the settlement and makes the community members part of an economic exchange among men, not victims of the king's aggression.

Perhaps initially designed to conceal any form of violation, the episode closely mirrors the first image of violent transgression in the chronicle: the three virgins are protected from Ecgfrith, who lays siege to the isle on which they pray for seven days. Seven days in the miracle scene is amplified to seven years in the description of the Norman siege, but it is clear why the hagiographical record insisted that Æthelthryth was accompanied by Sewenna and Sewara: the servants symbolize the community yet to be established at Ely, and as virgins they literally participate in the threat against their leader. Likewise, then, the monks can position themselves as virginal followers of Æthelthryth, threatened by the king's assault. In both narratives, therefore, the besieged endure starvation but are protected from seizure by the watery enclosure. The similarities between these accounts also suggest that the two were written at the same time, for if we ignore the information provided by the *Gesta Herewardi*, we see that the monks wanted their surrender to be read as a result of starvation, not of rape or military conquest. By adding the detail of William's subjection, the chronicle reestablishes the monks' position as authoritative agents on behalf of the saint, despite the fact that they use Æthelthryth's shrine in the transaction.

The *Liber Eliensis*, therefore, glosses over the subjugation of Ely, but the narrative acknowledges that part of the properties must be compromised in order to satisfy William's anger. This forfeiture is illustrated in a highly visual way: instead of the loss of land, "imagines sanctarum virginum multo ornatu auri et argenti" (195) [images of holy virgins ornamented in gold and silver] are stripped of their treasure to pay William's fine. Material figures that stand in for the body of Ely's patron are uncovered and humiliated to spare the physicality of the landed estates. The chronicle describes several statues, including "imaginem sancte Marie cum puero suo" (195) [an image of holy Maria and her son] being disfigured to pay this fine. It is telling that the statue of Mary is specifically identified as depicting the holy mother, whereas the other figures are not distinguished; they are simply "images of the holy virgins." While these statues are not specified, internal evidence identifies them with the four women enshrined at Ely: Æthelthryth, her sisters Sexburg and Wihtburg, and her niece, Eormenild.[48] The exchange of figurative bodies for physical bodies of land, therefore, allowed the Ely community to insist that the literal body of the virgin remained intact within its shrine and, as a consequence, that their liberties and properties should also remain unmolested.

After peace was made between William and the monks, the king placed Norman soldiers and monks at Ely and eventually appointed a Norman abbot. In the chronicle, the new members are described as strong advocates for Ely, which leads to a close relationship between Saxons and Normans in this united community (195).[49] Hereafter, the *Liber Eliensis* illustrates a marked difference in the way the saint is depicted; her symbolic value as the inviolable, passive virgin shifts starkly. Once the Normans are depicted as the authoritative guardians of Ely, the chronicle then begins to illustrate Æthelthryth as a virago, a masculinized fighter who wreaks vengeance on those who abuse her properties. This shift makes the saint (and by consequence, the monks) immune to the threat of sexual violence, because, as the next section demonstrates, she becomes the perpetrator of violence and vengeance against those who appropriate her properties.

## THE SAINT AS VIRAGO

Because the Normans recognized the saint's authoritative power, they adopted Ely's patron, and they employed the symbol of purity in a continued effort to protect the Ely properties. The monks altered the portraiture of the inviolable virgin to an image of an indomitable virago capable of defending her properties through force, an image played out in a series of miracle stories. One episode recounts that Gervase, a Norman and servant of the county sheriff, Picot, seized some of the monastery's properties during the invasion but had not returned them as William had ordered.[50] The Ely land pleas illustrate that despite William's ruling in favor of the churches, individuals could petition to keep their estates (212–13).[51] Following the king's decree, therefore, Gervase initiates a lawsuit against Ely in 1081, but the day before the court litigation is to be heard, the *Liber Eliensis* records that Æthelthryth and her sisters appear to him, saying:

> "Tune es ille, qui homines meos, quorum patrona sum ego, me contempta totiens vexasti nec adhuc ab ecclesie mec inquietatione desistis? Habebis igitur istud pro mercede, ut alii per te discant familiam Christi non vexare." Tulitque baculum quem gerebat graviterque aculeum eius loco cordis, tanquam eum perfossurus, inseruit. Deinde sorores eius sancta Withburga et sancta Sexburga, que simul cum ipsa venerant, duris baculorum suorum stimulis eum pupugerunt. (212)
>
> ["Are you not he who, in contempt of me, has so many times vexed my men whose patron I am, and who has not yet desisted from troubling my church? Therefore you will have this for a reward, so that others through you will learn not to vex the household of Christ." And she brandished the staff she carried and violently implanted the point of it into the place of his heart as if it was about to pierce him. Then her holy sisters Wihtburg and Sexburg who had come together with her stung him with hard pricks of their own staffs.]

Gervase then cries out, and when others come running, he barely has enough time to describe his vision before dying. Other accounts, by contrast, suggest Gervase expired from a heart attack before the court date.[52] At his death, the monastery was awarded the disputed properties.

The report of his vision shows that the monks are deliberately reconfiguring the terms by which the saint's body is understood. Instead of focusing on the shrine as a material body that keeps the corpse from view, the narrative now imagines the saint's corporeality as viable, active matter; visualized as living and mobile, Æthelthryth leads the defense of her monastic community. Because this scene engenders the saint as a masculinized warrior, it redirects the description of the monks' agency and masculinity: if Æthelthryth is a virago, they can leave off their identification with the passive female body and adopt a masculinist stance of aggression.

In describing Ely's patron saint as a symbol of military power, the chronicler invokes a different topos of hagiographic discourse, the *miles*

*Christi.*[53] The image of the militant saint is an old tradition in hagiographic texts, especially those about virgin saints. Specifically, the rape plot is consistently used to glorify virginity by making the literary motif of the *miles Christi* available to females, as Gravdal argues: "Under physical assault, the female saint becomes the soldier of Christ in the early days of Christian militancy. The threat of rape thus opens a space for female heroism."[54] The category of "woman" is exchanged for the virgin who is saved from "the inferior female nature by renouncing sexuality and becoming like a man, *vir*, through virginity."[55] Regendering the saint, furthermore, erases the tension Otter describes between the monks and their female patron; it allows them to assert their own masculinity as soldier/monks. The chronicle sharply delineates this characterization, recording that she will protect her properties "manfully," or as the text reads, *viriliter*:

> Fit timor sancte per omnes vicinos multoque tempore nullus procerum, iudicum, ministrorum et cuiuscumque potestatis hominum quicquam audebat preripere in Elyensem possessionem, sancta virgine res suas viriliter ubique protegente. (213)[56]
>
> [Fear of the saint spread through all the neighbors and for a long time not one of the nobles, judges, servants, and powerful men dared to seize anything within Ely's possession, the holy virgin manfully protecting her properties everywhere.]

In describing the saint's masculinity, the writer employs here "preripere," the same Latin word used in his description of Ecgfrith's attack on Æthelthryth. Perhaps designed as an intentional reversal, the invocation of the word redirects the potential threat and allows the Anglo-Norman community to reimagine its association within the body politic.

The change in Æthelthryth's signification relocated Ely's monastic identity from a corporate body under siege to an institutional power whose privileges were diligently recorded and militantly defended.[57] This posturing shows why it was necessary to bring Ely's hagiographical tradition to bear on its historical documentation: without Æthelthryth's legacy, the monks had no authoritative position in the midst of upheaval in the twelfth century. Certification of privileges and ownership must have seemed a shaky protection for Ely's temporalities, especially when we know that some of the pivotal charters are forgeries. The compilation of the *Liber Eliensis* and the inclusion of vengeance miracles speaks to the anxiety over documentation and suggests the necessity of miracles in bolstering Ely's historical narrative.[58] As Schulenburg has found, "*vitae* served as propaganda for the expansion or promotion of the cult of the saint and the exaltation of a religious center."[59] The expanded vita of Æthelthryth and the series of miracle stories illustrate that twelfth-century Ely was actively promoting its saint as a symbol of sovereignty for very specific reasons. In providing a narrative history of the foundation and its liberties, *tota integra, tota incorrupta*, the monastery could stage a rhetorical defense against encroachment that would be useful in estate litigation and, at the same time, broaden the awareness of the cult center at Ely. The compilation of materials, moreover, provided a discourse through which the monks could critique contemporary forms of violation, such as Bishop Nigel's stripping of the shrine to pay his fines to King Stephen. Hagiographical accounts, especially when intertwined with historical narratives, therefore, could be important rhetorical instruments of communication, and in this case, proved to be imperative to the composite monastic record as a challenge to king, bishop, and laity.

## NOTES

A longer version of this chapter entitled "*Tota integra, tota incorrupta*: The Shrine of St. Æthelthryth as Symbol of Monastic Autonomy" first appeared in the *Journal of Medieval and Early Modern Studies* 32/2 (2002): 227–67. It is reprinted here by permission of Duke University Press.

1. *Liber Eliensis*, edited by E. O. Blake, Camden Third Series, no. 92 (London: Royal Historical Society, 1962), 289, hereafter cited parenthetically in the text by page numbers. Translations of the *Liber Eliensis* are my own.

2. Three Ely cartularies have also survived, and each was inserted into a codex containing the *Liber Eliensis*. In his introduction to the edition (xxxix–xli), Blake indicates that manuscript G demonstrates the most overlap between chronicle and cartulary, but the three cartularies are often redundant catalogs of the evidence marshaled together in the *Liber Eliensis*.

3. Sarah Beckwith, *Christ's Body: Identity, Culture, and Society in Late Medieval Writings* (New York: Routledge, 1993), 2.

4. See David Knowles, *The Monastic Order in England: A History of Its Development from the Times of St. Dunstan to the Fourth Lateran Council, 940–1216*, 2nd. ed. (Cambridge and New York: Cambridge University Press, 1966), 102.

5. *Bede's Ecclesiastical History of the English People*, ed. Bertram Colgrave and R. A. B. Mynors (1969, reprint Oxford: Clarendon, 1992), 390–401, hereafter cited in the text parenthetically by page numbers.

6. Christine Fell, "Saint Æðelþryð: "Historical-Hagiographical Dichotomy Revisited," *Nottingham Medieval Studies* 38 (1994): 18–34, at 32.

7. In a private communication, Stephanie Hollis first suggested to me that the translation of Wihtburg's relics demonstrates Ely's concern with material bodies. Her comment points to the monastic desire to use the bodies in a highly ceremonial demonstration of power. Wihtburg's identity as Æthelthryth's sister, though likely specious, recalls Bede's description of this family in the *Historia Ecclesiastica*; he describes the body of another sister, Æthelburg, who was an abbess at Faremoûtier-en-Brie, which was found incorrupted (238–39).

8. Judith Butler, *Bodies That Matter: On the Discursive Limits of "Sex"* (New York: Routledge, 1993), 68.

9. Jane Tibbetts Schulenburg, "Female Sanctity: Public and Private Roles, ca. 500–1100," in *Women and Power in the Middle Ages*, ed. Mary Erler and Maryanne Kowaleski (Athens: University of Georgia Press, 1988), 102–25, at 113.

10. Susan Ridyard, *The Royal Saints of Anglo-Saxon England: A Study of West Saxon and East Anglian Cults* (Cambridge and New York: Cambridge University Press, 1988), 191. See also her discussion of the Norman appropriation of Anglo-Saxon cults in "*Condigna Veneratio*: Post-Conquest Attitudes to the Saints of the Anglo-Saxons," *Anglo-Norman Studies* 9 (1986): 179–206.

11. In his edition (xlix), Blake was the first to posit these anxieties as being tied to the civil war between Stephen and Matilda, a civil dispute during which a large portion of the *Liber Eliensis* was produced. The chronicle does include descriptions of the difficulties faced during the political turmoil of Matilda's claim to the throne, but it focuses more directly on the ways in which the Ely bishop abused the monastery by taking its properties and stripping the shrine's ornaments to pay fines for his support of Matilda over Stephen. This argument has become standard for understanding the chronicle's production.

12. Monika Otter, "The Temptation of St. Æthelthryth," *Exemplaria* 9 (1997): 139–63, at 161. See *LE*, 55–56 and 229, for the episode she describes, which is recounted twice in the chronicle.

13. Otter,"Temptation of St. Æthelthryth," 163.

14. Despite the many insights the text offers into pre- and post-Conquest England and the availability of Blake's edition, the *Liber Eliensis* has received little attention. In addition to Ridyard's work, the following discuss Ely's productions in the tenth and eleventh centuries: Henry Wharton, *Anglia Sacra, sive Collectio Historiarum, Partim Antiquitus, Partim recenter Scriptarum, de Archiepiscopis et Episcopis Angliae*, vol. 1 (London, 1591); James Bentham, *The History and Antiquities of the Conventual and Cathedral Church of Ely: From the Foundation of the Monastery, A.D. 673, to the Year 1771* (1771, reprint Cambridge, 1812); William Dugdale, *Monasticon Anglicanum: A History of the Abbies and Other Monasteries, Hospitals, Frieries, and Cathedral and Collegiate Churches with Their Dependencies in England and Wales* (London, 1817); D. J. Stewart, ed., *Liber Eliensis*, vol. 1 (London, 1848); *The Victoria History of the County of Cambridgeshire and the Isle of Ely*, vols. 1–4, ed. L. F. Salzman, J. P. C. Roach, and R. B. Pugh (1930–59, reprint London: Dawsons, 1967); Edward Miller, *The Abbey and Bishopric of Ely* (1951; repr. Cambridge and New York: Cambridge University Press, 1969); Edward Miller, "The Ely Land Pleas in the Reign of William I," *English Historical Review* 62 (1947): 438–56; Christine Wille Garrison, "The Lives of St. Ætheldreda: Representation of Female Sanctity from 700 to 1300," Ph.D. diss., University of Rochester, 1990; and Virginia Blanton-Whetsell," St. Æthelthryth's Cult: Literary, Historical, and Pictorial Constructions of Gendered Sanctity," Ph.D. diss., Binghamton University, 1998.

15. For a discussion of the problems between monastery and bishop precipitated by the creation of the Ely diocese, see Miller, *Abbey and Bishopric of Ely*; Seiriol Evans, *The Medieval Estate of the Cathedral Priory of Ely: A Preliminary Survey* (Ely: Dean and Chapter of Ely, 1973); Everett U. Crosby, *Bishop and Chapter in Twelfth-Century England: A Study of the* Mensa Episcopalis (Cambridge and New York: Cambridge University Press, 1994), 151–74; and E. G. Wood, "On the Formation of the Ancient Diocese of Ely," *Proceedings of the Cambridge Antiquarian Society*, n.s. 7 (1893): 157–68. While the entirety of book 3 discusses these problems, the relevant passages

in the *Liber Eliensis* are chapters 25 and 26 of book 3 (*LE* 261–63). A contemporary account of these events is Eadmer's *Historia Novorum in Anglia*, ed. Martin Rule, Rerum Britannicarum Medii Ævi Scriptores, vol. 81 (1884, reprint Vaduz: Kraus, 1965), 195–96.

16. Miller has written prolifically about Ely's difficulties and the monastery's response to them: see "The Liberty of Ely," in *Victoria History of Cambridgeshire*, 4:1–27; "Ely Land Pleas"; and *Abbey and Bishopric of Ely*.

17. For a contemporary monastic chronicle, see Hugh of Poitiers, *The Vézelay Chronicle*, ed. John Scott and John O. Ward (Binghamton, N.Y.: Medieval and Renaissance Texts and Studies, 1992). The Vézelay chronicle, however, is distinctly separate from the monastic cartulary and a *passio* for Mary Magdalene, but the chronicle, like the *Liber Eliensis*, is written to document the political strife of the house. Similarly, a thirteenth-century English chronicle produced at Bury St. Edmunds is distinct from a cartulary in that it is laid out much like the *Anglo-Saxon Chronicle*: information is presented for each year, and not all data is specific to the institution. See *The Chronicle of Bury St. Edmunds, 1212–1301*, ed. Antonia Gransden (London: Thomas Nelson and Sons, 1964). A chronicle more similar in style to the *Liber Eliensis* is *The Chronicle of Battle Abbey*, ed. and trans. Eleanor Searle (Oxford: Clarendon, 1980). Like the Ely chronicle, it is a twelfth-century document written by the Normans to document ownership of land. Even still, this chronicle does not foreground hagiographical data as does the *Liber Eliensis*. By contrast, Ely's geographical neighbors, Croyland Abbey and Ramsey Abbey, share a common history, and the chronicles produced there in the twelfth century are much like the *Liber Eliensis*, blending cartulary and monastic history. See *Ingulph's Chronicle of the Abbey of Croyland*, trans. Henry T. Riley (London, 1854); and *Chronicon Abbatiæ Rameseiensis*, ed. W. Dunn Macray, Rerum Britannicarum Medii Ævi Scriptores (London, 1886).

18. This passage comes from the introduction to book 1, which is comprised entirely of the vita. In the saint's life proper, 32, the monk is explicit about Tonbert's dower gift and Æthelthryth's perpetual ownership of the isle after their marriage.

19. Blake, *Liber Eliensis*, xxviii–xlii.

20. The imagery of the body politic was often used to describe the relationship between the king and his kingdom in the secular world, as well as to describe the position of Christ's body in the spiritual world. Several scholars have remarked on this ideology, including Beckwith, *Christ's Body*, 22–44; and Michael Camille, "The Image and the Self: Unwriting Late Medieval Bodies," in *Framing Medieval Bodies*, ed. Sarah Kay and Miri Rubin (Manchester: Manchester University Press, 1994), 62–99. See also Louise Olga Fradenburg, "Introduction: Rethinking Queenship," in *Women and Sovereignty*, ed. Louise Olga Fradenburg (Edinburgh: Edinburgh University Press, 1992), 1–13; Jocelyn Wogan-Browne, "Queens, Virgins and Mothers: Hagiographic Representations of the Abbess and Her Powers in Twelfth- and Thirteenth-Century Britain," in *Women and Sovereignty*, 14–35; and Peggy McCracken, "The Body Politic and the Queen's Adulterous Body in French Romance," in *Feminist Approaches to the Body in Medieval Literature*, ed. Linda Lomperis and Sarah Stanbury, New Cultural Studies (Philadelphia: University of Pennsylvania Press, 1993), 38–64.

21. Kathleen M. Ashley and Pamela Sheingorn, *Writing Faith: Text, Sign, and History in the Miracles of Sainte Foy* (Chicago: University of Chicago Press, 1999), 20.

22. Kathryn Gravdal, *Ravishing Maidens: Writing Rape in Medieval French Literature and Law* (Philadelphia: University of Pennsylvania Press, 1991), 22.

23. R. Howard Bloch, *Medieval Misogyny and the Invention of Western Romantic Love* (Chicago: University of Chicago Press, 1991).

24. Karen A. Winstead, *Virgin Martyrs: Legends of Sainthood in Late Medieval England* (Ithaca: Cornell University Press, 1997), 5–10.

25. Jane Tibbetts Schulenburg, "The Heroics of Virginity: Brides of Christ and Sacrificial Mutilation," in *Women in the Middle Ages and the Renaissance*, ed. Mary Beth Rose (Syracuse: Syracuse University Press, 1986), 29–72, at 31.

26. Bede, *Historia Ecclesiastica*, 390–93.

27. Gravdal, *Ravishing Maidens*, 4. See also James A. Brundage, "Rape and Seduction in the Medieval Canon Law," in *Sexual Practices and the Medieval Church*, ed. Vern L. Bullough and James Brundage (Buffalo, N.Y.: Prometheus Books, 1982), 141–48.

28. Christopher Cannon, "*Raptus* in the Champagne Release and a Newly Discovered Document concerning the Life of Geoffrey Chaucer," *Speculum* 68 (1993): 74–94, at 79. Carolyn Dinshaw has also described the changing value of *raptus* in fourteenth-century England, in *Chaucer's Sexual Poetics* (Madison: University of Wisconsin Press, 1989), 7–14.

29. Gravdal, *Ravishing Maidens*, 2.

30. Brenda R. Silver, "Periphrasis, Power, and Rape in *A Passage to India*," in *Rape and Representation*, ed. Lynn A. Higgins and Brenda R. Silver (New York: Columbia University Press), 115–37, at 115.

31. Otter's discussion highlights this continual potentiality ("Temptation of St. Æthelthryth," 163).

32. Linda Woodbridge, "Palisading the Elizabethan Body Politic," *Texas Studies in Literature and Language* 33 (1991): 327–54, at 331. See also Judith Williamson, "Woman Is an Island: Femininity and Colonization," in *Studies in Entertainment: Critical Approaches to Mass Culture*, ed. Tania Modleski (Bloomington: Indiana University Press, 1986), 99–118.

33. Mary Douglas, *Purity and Danger: An Analysis of Concepts of Pollution and Taboo* (1966, reprint New York: Praeger, 1970), 115. Another anthropological discussion of spatial institutions is Daphne Spain, *Gendered Spaces* (Chapel Hill and London: University of North Carolina Press, 1992). See also *Medieval Practices of Space*, ed. Barbara Hanawalt and Michal Kobialka (Minneapolis: University of Minnesota Press, 2000); and Kathleen Ashley and Pamela Sheingorn, "*Discordia et lis*: Negotiating Power, Property, and Performance in Medieval Sélestat," *Journal of Medieval and Early Modern Studies* 26 (1996): 419–46.

34. See Sarah Beckwith, "Passionate Regulation: Enclosure, Ascesis, and the Feminist Imaginary," *South Atlantic Quarterly* 93 (1994): 803–24; Roberta Gilchrist, "Medieval Bodies in the Material World: Gender, Stigma, and the Body," in *Framing Medieval Bodies*, 43–61; Jane Tibbetts Schulenburg, "Strict Active Enclosure and Its Effects on the Female Monastic Experience (ca. 500–1100)," in *Distant Echoes*, vol. 1 of *Medieval Religious Women*, ed. John A. Nichols and Lillian Thomas Shank (Kalamazoo, Mich.: Cistercian, 1984), 51–86; and Shari Horner, *The Discourse of Enclosure: Representing Women in Old English Literature* (Albany: State University of New York Press, 2001).

35. Roberta Gilchrist, *Gender and Material Culture: The Archaeology of Religious Women* (New York: Routledge, 1994), 43. The connection between female bodies and landed bodies has also been discussed by Margaret Brose, who demon-

strates how Petrarch's poem "Italia mia" fetishizes Italy as a female body; see "Petrarch's Beloved Body: Italia mia," in *Feminist Approaches to the Body*, 1–20.

36. This imagery foreshadows the forms of self-enclosure enacted by medieval women mystics, as the following have demonstrated: Elizabeth Robertson, "Medieval Medical Views of Women and Female Spirituality in the *Ancrene Wisse* and Julian of Norwich's *Showings*," in *Feminist Approaches to the Body*, 142–67; Robertson, *Early English Devotional Prose and the Female Audience* (Knoxville: University of Tennessee Press, 1990); and Jocelyn Wogan-Browne, "Chaste Bodies: Frames and Experiences," in *Framing Medieval Bodies*, 24–41.

37. The cycle includes eight scenes from the *Liber Eliensis*, carved onto columns that support the cathedral octagon at the crossing. Carved in high relief, this visual cycle illustrates the important moments in the life, including several miracles that attest to her power as saint: (1) Æthelthryth's marriage to Ecgfrith; (2) her acceptance into the monastery at Coldingham; (3) her escape from Ecgfrith; (4) the miracle of her budding staff while she sleeps; (5) her consecration as abbess of Ely by Bishop Wilfrid; (6) her death and burial; (7) her translation; and (8) the posthumous miracle of Brystan. Several art and architectural historians have discussed this cycle, including T. D. Atkinson, *An Architectural History of the Benedictine Monastery of Saint Etheldreda at Ely* (Cambridge and New York: Cambridge University Press, 1933); Anne Rudloff Stanton, "On the Lady Chapel of Ely Cathedral," Ph.D. diss., University of Texas at Austin, 1987; Phillip Lindley, "The Imagery of the Octagon at Ely," *Journal of the British Archaeological Association* 139 (1986): 75–99; and Nicola Coldstream, "Ely Cathedral: The Fourteenth-Century Work," in *Medieval Art and Architecture at Ely Cathedral*, ed. Nicola Coldstream and Peter Draper (Leeds: BAR, 1979), 28–46.

38. Blake discusses the *Liber Eliensis* representation of the siege in relation to other historical accounts and finds that it adds much detail and generally is unreliable (*LE*, liv–lviii).

39. Miller describes the "liberty of Ely" as giving the monastery immunity from a sheriff's intervention ("Liberty of Ely," 6).

40. See Blake's comparison of the two texts, including his identification of the *Liber Eliensis* author (*LE*, xxxiv–xxxvi and liv–lviii).

41. Ibid., xxxv; and cf. *LE*, 191–93, and the *Gesta Herwardi Incliti Exulis et Militis* in *Lestoire des Engles Solum La Translacion Maistre Geffrei Gaimar*, ed. T. D. Huffy and C. T. Martin, vol. 1 (London, 1888), 381–82, at 390–91. See also Michael Swanton, trans., *Three Lives of the Last Englishmen* (New York: Garland, 1984); Trevor Bevis, ed., *Hereward: The Siege of the Isle of Ely and Involvement of Peterborough and Ely Monasteries. Together with De Gestis Herewardi Saxonis* (March, Cambridgeshire: Westrydale, 1982).

42. Brose, "Petrarch's Beloved Body," 16.

43. *The Anglo-Saxon Chronicle*, ed. George Garmonsway (London: Dent, 1954), 206.

44. *The Chronicle of Florence of Worcester*, trans. Thomas Forester (London, 1854), 177.

45. Following the invasion, estate disputes were commonplace between ecclesiastical communities and the Conqueror's knights. When the Ely community complained that its properties were being unlawfully held, William's response was divided: the king expressed outward support for the monks' claims but did not evict his

Norman followers from properties awarded for their service. This attitude forced the monks to negotiate for estates improperly seized, but the estate problems detailed in the *Liber Eliensis* suggest that recovering alienated property was far more difficult than it appeared. Their complaints, then, were included to document the economic wrongs. See Blake's discussion of these events in his introduction (xlix–liv); and Marjorie Chibnall's discussion of William's decisions, in *Anglo-Norman England, 1066–1166* (1986, reprint Oxford: Blackwell, 1993), esp. 30–31.

46. Susan Brownmiller, *Against Our Will: Men, Women and Rape* (New York: Fawcett Columbine, 1975), 38.

47. John Boswell indicates that Roman soldiers were known to exploit the males under their power, and rape was a common act of aggression. While it is not clear that Norman soldiers raped Anglo-Saxon men during the Conquest, Boswell's findings are suggestive about the metaphoric image through which power relations are demonstrated in the *Liber Eliensis*. See Boswell, *Same-Sex Unions in Premodern Europe* (New York: Villard Books, 1994), 54.

48. Ridyard, "*Condigna Veneratio*," 180–81.

49. See Ridyard's discussion of amelioration, ibid., 186–87.

50. In *Royal Saints* (198–210), Ridyard discusses this episode and several others in which violators die as a result of Æthelthryth's protection of monastic properties.

51. Picot is often identified in the chronicle as the enemy, particularly for appropriating Ely properties and not returning them. The *Liber Eliensis* (210–11) records that when pressured to forfeit the lands of Æthelthryth, he insulted the saint by denying knowledge of her. Eventually Picot did acknowledge that "he held of the abbot and convent by knight service" in exchange for the Ely properties even if he continued not to recognize their patron. See also *Victoria History of Cambridgeshire*, 2:202.

52. Ridyard, "*Condigna Veneratio*," 206.

53. Bede includes this image in a hymn to Æthelthryth included in the *Historia Ecclesiastica* (400–01).

54. Gravdal, *Ravishing Maidens*, 23. For a broader discussion of virginity and the *miles Christi*, see John Bugge, *Virginitas: An Essay in the History of a Medieval Ideal* (The Hague: Martinus Nijhoff, 1975), esp. 47–58. See also Barbara Newman, *From Virile Woman to Woman Christ: Studies in Medieval Religion and Literature* (Philadelphia: University of Pennsylvania Press, 1995).

55. Gravdal, *Ravishing Maidens*, 22.

56. In "Female Sanctity," Schulenburg observes that women were often praised "for acting *non mulieriter sed viriliter*" in public church roles (114, my emphasis).

57. Pauline Thompson and Elizabeth Stevens have observed a similar representation of Æthelthryth's role as avenger in Gregory of Ely's verse life, (1116 X 1131), which prefigures the account in the *Liber Eliensis* (1131 X 1174) and is more vehement in its claims about Æthelthryth's vengeance on those who appropriate the monastery's lands. Gregory's representation, moreover, of the isle as an enclosed space that protects the monks from their enemies is striking. See Thompson and Stevens, "Gregory of Ely's Verse Life and Miracles of St. Æthelthryth," *Analecta Bollandiana* 106 (1988): 333–90.

58. On the authority of the documents, see Blake, *LE*, xlix–liv.

59. Jane Tibbetts Schulenburg, "Saints' Lives as a Source for the History of Women, 500–1100," in *Medieval Women and the Sources of Medieval History*, ed. Joel. T. Rosenthal (Athens: University of Georgia Press, 1990), 285–320, at 287.

## FURTHER READING

Ashley, Kathleen M., and Pamela Sheingorn. *Writing Faith: Text, Sign, and History in the Miracles of Sainte Foy*. Chicago: University of Chicago Press, 1999.

Beckwith, Sarah. *Christ's Body: Identity, Culture, and Society in Late Medieval Writings*. London and New York: Routledge, 1993.

Gilchrist, Roberta. *Gender and Material Culture: The Archaeology of Religious Women*. London and New York: Routledge, 1994.

Gravdal, Kathryn. *Ravishing Maidens: Writing Rape in Medieval French Literature and Law*. Philadelphia: University of Pennsylvania Press, 1991.

Horner, Shari. *The Discourse of Enclosure: Representing Women in Old English Literature*. Albany: State University of New York Press, 2001.

*Liber Eliensis*, ed. E. O. Blake. Camden Third Series, no. 92. London: Royal Historical Society, 1962.

Miller, Edward. *The Abbey and Bishopric of Ely*. Cambridge: Cambridge University Press, 1969.

Otter, Monika. "The Temptation of St. Æthelthryth." *Exemplaria* 9 (1997): 139–63.

Ridyard, Susan. *The Royal Saints of Anglo-Saxon England: A Study of West Saxon and East Anglian Cults*. Cambridge: Cambridge University Press, 1988.

Schulenburg, Jane Tibbetts. "Female Sanctity: Public and Private Roles, ca. 500–1100." In *Women and Power in the Middle Ages*. Ed. Mary Erler and Maryanne Kowaleski. Athens: University of Georgia Press, 1988). 102–25.

THREE

# MARGERY KEMPE AND THE ARTS OF SELF-PATRONAGE

SARAH STANBURY

ONE OF THE LINCHPINS in arts programming in the tweny-first century is the benefactor list. Discreetly tucked away toward the end of the program, this list nonetheless draws the eye through its conspicuous ordering, a hierarchical ranking that brackets orders of patronage with clear dollar amounts. It might begin in the thousands, with the Seraphim—as in "Seraphim (gifts of fifty thousand dollars or more: Bill and Melinda Gates)"; followed by Cherubim, perhaps, with then the Angels, and finally the Patrons and then the Friends—gifts of one hundred dollars or less. This list clearly serves its cause through its polite and careful acknowledgment of material gifts. Equally clearly, the list serves the benefactors by circulating their names and dollar attachments among a select readership, in a strategic network. If we are among this celestial hierarchy, we would be likely to look and find our own name and scan the list to see what company we keep. The benefactor list, taking up its pages in the program, also claims public space for its patrons, transforming the private individual into a nominal corporate identity. In this translation from the private self into a named entity endowed with the power to give, the benefactor list also constructs identity, in a sense institutionalizing the performance (the play, the symphony, the opera) as a cultural space within the community. At the very least it requires that the individual take on a public name that claims performance space through the metonymic ownership of space in the program.

But what if we are not on the list? This list, like all roll calls, serves to mark who is in and who is out, or we might say, states of being or nothingness. A mechanism of cultural envy, the patronage list suggests, with a curious reverse turn, that those who are named have been chosen and leaves us feeling that we are excluded from the circle even if we have never considered giving to this cause. Or it might do so, I would qualify, if the names on the list had the potential to include me: a neighbor on the list, and my name is absent.

For women, the claiming of a public name and public space has historically involved a complex negotiation between private and public identity. To have one's name recorded as the patron of a public space or building is also to leave a record of one's influence in the public sphere, to announce the material purchase power of a female self, with a name becoming a form of enduring symbolic capital. Increased opportunities for public roles for women in the recent past have led, of course, to sometimes traumatic, often comic confrontations with the politics of self-naming: what do I even call myself? A recent program from the Boston Symphony Orchestra, reflecting changing protocols that themselves signify a profound transition in the terms in which women claim public space, allows a variety of ways for female patrons to name themselves: Ms. Ruth Russel Smith, Mrs. Joan D. Wheeler; William and Deborah Elfers; Joseph Hearne and Jan Brett, and the conventional and still most common form in the BSO program, Mrs. George R. Rowland, Mr. and Mrs. Peter Brooke, wives whose gifts are recorded through the patronymic.

Certainly some of the anxieties about naming arise from genre, and in this case the genre of named donation with its subtle protocols. A group of women that I know started meeting together as a support/consciousness raising group in the early 80s and has continued to meet to this day. A few years ago a member of the group, a dancer, died, and the group as a whole decided to give a joint gift in her memory to a local arts center. Their gift of money was to be acknowledged by a plaque on a wall. The problem they faced with the plaque, however, was how to record their identity. They had always called themselves by the name *Stitch and Bitch*. Should Stitch and Bitch be etched on the plaque, the enduring bronze record of donation?

I do not know how the plaque was finally printed. I tell this story, however, because it seems to illustrate the tentative, often transitional claims women continue to have on public space. In the case of the Stitch and Bitch, anxieties about public naming were not only recorded in the question over the plaque but also in the very choice of a name to begin with, which itself playfully acknowledged the group's transitional identity in between a woman's sewing circle and something very different, and in a time of unparalleled change in the visibility of women in public roles: Stitch, the private life; Bitch, the complaints about it.

While the benefactor list and the conventions for recording the names of its patrons, both male and female, have developed (or deconstructed) their own protocols in recent years, they have deep affiliations with forms of conspicuous patronage in the late Middle Ages. Studies of lay patronage of fifteenth-century churches reveal a remarkable record of lavish endowments to rebuild church roofs and to glaze windows, of legacies outlining monetary gifts either for the saying of prayers for the dead or of endowments for chantries, with much of the evidence stamped in the physical fabric of the church building. Tangible evidence of patronage in the forms of inscribed names and coats of arms suggests that we might speak of the fifteenth century in terms borrowed from later accounts of the "cult of the artist" as the "cult of the patron" and often of a patron who was female. As studies by Gail McMurray Gibson and others have demonstrated, in many respects the fifteenth-century English parish would have appeared as a vital memorial register of local family history, with names and portraits of both male and female benefactors appearing in the glass, their effigies and inscriptions etched on the bronzes, their paid priests offering masses for their souls.[1] Indeed, the devotional ornament and furnishings in fifteenth-century parishes might be described as signally entailed, marked by the incision of a self, whether named or painted, or emblemized with a coat of arms, in a passion for self-portraiture.

## SELF, SPACE, AND THE DONOR IMAGE

This chapter focuses on a quixotic and highly localized fifteenth-century benefactor list, *The Book of Margery Kempe*. It is of course a curious list, for one name appears over and over in all the categories, and that is Kempe's ("this creature"); and the amounts of her gifts are registered not in dollars or pounds but in hundreds of thousands of souls she saves with her prayers.[2] Kempe's *Book*, a hybrid between autobiography and spiritual or mystical memoir, also borrows conventions from the saint's life and spiritual confession, constructing a personal history defined, in part, by the worldly pleasures she has come to renounce. One of the continuing pressures of her autotext, however, is the need to have a public self, even though she claims to renounce that goal; and it is a public self that also is deeply indebted, I will argue, to contemporary donor images, themselves signs of subtle but crucial shifts in attitudes toward self-representation in fifteenth-century England. The Creature whose life story Kempe recounts, as Virginia Raguin describes in this volume, makes astonishingly territorial claims over public space, demanding audience with powerful clerics and interrupting church services repeatedly with her crying and weeping. As recent criticism has ably demonstrated, Margery Kempe was acutely a woman of her time, conscious of her social position and strategically invested in creating an enduring public image.[3] In the mystical portions of her text, Kempe equally claims material space, for in her visions she imagines herself in a complex set of postures as a donor of means, envisioning herself in a sense in the very fabric of the buildings themselves.

It has been widely recognized that Kempe's visions are contoured by contemporary iconography—both as transmitted through the *Meditations on the Life of Christ* and through the drama.[4] The debts of her visions to images that she would have seen in Lynn, Norwich, York, and elsewhere have been less fully addressed, in part because her *Book*, in spite of its detailed mapping of her travels, offers few concrete details about the spaces she inhabited and visited, either in England or in her pilgrimages. Certainly she responds energetically to images. In the few references to images or devotional objects that she does provide, she indicates that they produce powerful, even visceral reactions. She marvels at a vision of the host and chalice trembling during a Mass (ch. 20), weeps at the stations of the cross in Jerusalem, and collapses in a fit at Calvary (ch. 28). She sobs and cries out when she sees the Virgin's kerchief in Assisi (ch. 31), when she looks at a crucifix in Leicester (ch. 46), or when she sees a pietà at a church in Norwich (ch. 60).

Nevertheless, as readers have noted, there is an absence of descriptive detail and attention to place in Kempe's *Book*, and although she tells us a great deal about where she goes and with whom she talks, she gives us little information about the surface texture of either people or places.[5] Repeatedly she locates herself within clerical spaces that would certainly have been, in the fifteenth century, richly or even lavishly ornamented: the Prior's Chapel in Lynn (ch. 56),[6] the Chapterhouse at Beverly (ch. 54),[7] the high altar at St. Stephen's in Norwich (ch. 60) and at All Saints in Leicester (ch. 48),[8] the choir (ch. 23) and the Chapel of the Gesine in her home church of St. Margaret's (ch. 63);[9] Nonetheless, she does not explicitly catalog the rich surfaces of these sites, which would have been filled with retables, windows, statuary, and textiles describing sacred history. Rather, she appears to interiorize this complex and absorbing imagery.

As she narrates her visions and dialogues with Christ, however, Kempe repeatedly constructs tableaux that can be said to flesh out the spaces that she has visited. Certainly on one level Kempe transposes the exterior to an interior life, one that authenticates her sanctity through her imagined participation in important moments of Christ's life as she would have seen those events represented in alabasters, glazing, and panel painting. This feature of style, which may well represent her deployment of a strategic choice made in the interests of constructing an "authoritative" visionary history, may be driven in part by late medieval aesthetic practice, and specifically a generalized prohibition on description of devotional objects. In fifteenth-century England, writers did not casually describe "works of art" or devotional objects—since indeed, they were usually one and the same thing.[10] Yet the dual pressure of her meditations not just to take in the image and place the self within its frame but also to reconstruct in the meditation a kind of public devotional art with herself as donor or key player, constitutes an extraordinarily complex act of border crossing. Ingesting an image and its animus in a move pitched toward the dynamic and embodied experience of a spiritual life, Kempe also uses her visions to textualize a self within a picture frame, turning self into object and image into text. As has long been recognized, the elision of mental and material images characterizes medieval devotional imagery;[11] recent studies of female piety have also recognized the particularly concrete quality of the meditations of medieval women, which often expressed itself through images that were themselves even explicitly based on material objects.[12] The ekphrastic and self-dramatizing form of Kempe's meditations, however, allows her to use images in ways that are even more materially efficacious than has been suggested. Kempe's incorporation of iconographic schema and of devotional images in her text opens up in fact important questions about the currency of visual objects as they circulate through language and are claimed and publicized through personal use.

Margery Kempe's textual imaging may use "art" in ways similar to familiar arts of social connoisseurship, in which one can claim social status through the very knowledge of high art, though for Kempe, the contingencies of value are social rather than aesthetic.[13] Certainly her text, which has been repeatedly called the first autobiography in English, becomes, through her own localized narration, a form of cultural capital; her constant self-aggrandizement, her repeated references to her intimate contract with Christ, and her detailed accounts of interviews with the powerful ecclesiastics of her time all contribute to turning her *Book* into an accreditation or deed, a document legitimizing Kempe's purchase on the world as she has inhabited it and, as a kind of set of chantry prayers, a missal insuring her well-being in the afterlife.

This chapter raises questions about the role of matter in the materializations of her text, the role of absent things that take on life when they are transformed into visions. To what extent does Margery Kempe borrow from emerging traditions of visual signatures to describe a self that is both donor and self-portrait, creating a kind of autoportrait?[14] To what extent, I want to ask, does the textual materializing of Kempe's life also depend on contemporary arts of patronage and in effect transform the material culture of fifteenth-century East Anglian churches into the very fabric of her text itself?

The pressure to exhibit the self in the act of supporting the material life of the parish was certainly a familiar and sanctioned social impulse in the late Middle Ages, one that has been the subject of increasing attention by the work of art historians interested in the interplay between images and their local production and use.[15] In England, the impulse to exhibit the self in the form of a name, coat of arms, or portrait has left its traces widely on objects that have survived Reformation iconoclasm. A signal feature of fourteenth-century East Anglian manuscript illumination, for instance, is the display of heraldic ornament, visible, for instance, in the *Gorleston Psalter*, a richly illustrated early fourteenth-century manuscript from the Norwich region. The coats of arms in the four corners of the border of the *Domine exaudi* page, most likely displaying the arms of important local families, are typical of the uses of armorial signatures throughout the manuscript, and indeed, in East Anglian manuscript illumination in general.[16] In the *Despenser Retable* in Norwich Cathedral, an East Anglian work that that has been dated in the late fourteenth century and may have been given to the cathedral in acknowledgment of the help of local families in suppressing the 1381 rebellion, coats of arms of local families are included prominently in the frame. Coats of arms also appear prominently in fifteenth-century East Anglian glass; in his study of the Norwich school of glass painting, Christopher Woodforde lists more than 130 identifiable coats of arms appearing in the glazing.[17]

While coats of arms display the patronage and power of noble families, names and portraits of donors commemorate the gifts of individuals and families of merchant classes. Recent work on lay patronage and devotion in the late Middle Ages has increasingly drawn attention to the deeply imbricated relationships among laity, clergy, and material culture, such that fifteenth-century East Anglia was, as Gail McMurray Gibson puts it, a highly material "theater of devotion," with the emphasis on theatricality and display. Certainly Kempe, who repeatedly recounts events in her home parish of St. Margaret's in Lynn, would have seen the huge commemorative brasses marking the tomb of Robert Braunche, mayor of Lynn in 1349 and 1359, and his wives Leticia and Margaret and of Adam de Walsoken, Mayor in 1334 and 1342 and his wife Margaret, as Virginia Raguin points out in this volume. We can only speculate how Kempe might have responded to these larger-than-life memorials to mayor's wives when her family, and she herself, a mayor's daughter, left no such records in the material life of the parish. Gail Gibson's discussions of John Baret of Bury St. Edmunds, John Clopton of Long Melford, and Ann Harling of East Harling are illuminating in this regard for their assessment of strategically visible patronage in fifteenth-century East Anglia. The name of John Clopton, a wealthy clothier who helped finance the rebuilding of Long Melford Church from the 1460s to the 1490s, appears repeatedly in inscriptions around the exterior walls of the church and lady chapel, in effect emblazoning the church with the name of its principle sponsor (figure 3.1).[18] Illustrating the power that women could wield as patrons in fifteenth-century Norfolk, Ann Harling of East Harling left a highly visible legacy in the beautiful parish Church of St. Peter and St. Paul. Ann Harling donated its windows, which remain some of the finest examples of fifteenth-century glass work in England, contributed to the rebuilding of the steeple of the parish in 1449 and in the 1460s founded a chantry chapel dedicated to St. Anne in the north aisle.[19]

Patronage in fourteenth- and fifteenth-century English cathedrals and parishes was at its most strategically visible in the use of donor portraits. Richard Marks' work on patronage in glazing indicates that images of donors most commonly appear in medieval stained glass from the thirteenth to the fifteenth century as small figures, hands pressed in prayer, kneeling below or beside a devotional scene.[20] The spectacular fourteenth- and fifteenth-century windows at York—some of which Kempe may well have seen and noted, since she recounts, in chapter 50, spending fourteen days in the minster—display numerous donor figures not only from the elite estates, but also from

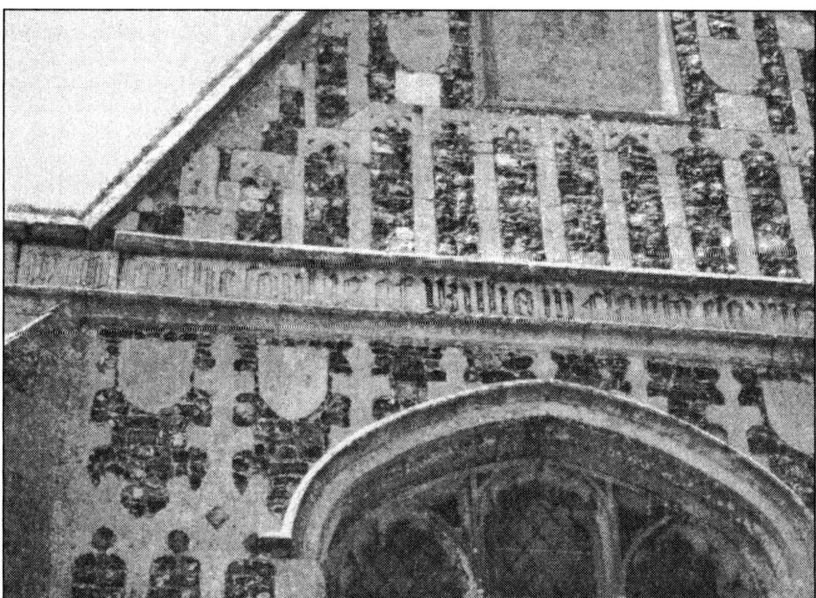

**Figure 3.1.** Flint inscription, ca. 1496, "Pray for ye sowle of William Clopton esqwyer . . . ," Lady Chapel, Holy Trinity Church, Long Melford. Photo Virginia Raguin.

the merchant class, a relationship strikingly illustrated in a window in the nave north aisle, which depicts goldsmith Richard Tunnoc presenting his window to St. William of York. [21]

The line between venerator and venerated, perhaps always flexible in a picture where both are represented, becomes even hazier in the windows in Holy Trinity Church at Long Melford (Suffolk), which are packed with figures representing members of the Clopton family and people connected to them by important social links.[22] The extant images, originally from the clerestory, have been relocated to the north aisle. Suggestive for Margery's localization of herself within the space of the church, these donor images represent both men and women, offering a striking visual record of female patronage and influence in a late fifteenth-century Suffolk town. Members of the Clopton family, their heraldry constructing the very fabric of their dress in a public display of familial networks, make a commanding frieze across the fifteenth-century glazing. Images of family members include Anne Danvers, Elizabeth Fray, Margaret Fray, Catherine Mylde, Elizabeth Tilney, and Elizabeth Talbot (figure 3.2)—the source, so it is said, for the Duchess in Teniel's illustrations for Lewis Carroll's *Alice and Wonderland.* In these windows the object of veneration is even absent, beyond the parameters of the picture, allowing the images to suggest in part that the gift and object of veneration is the Clopton family network itself or even the sanctuary that the figures face.

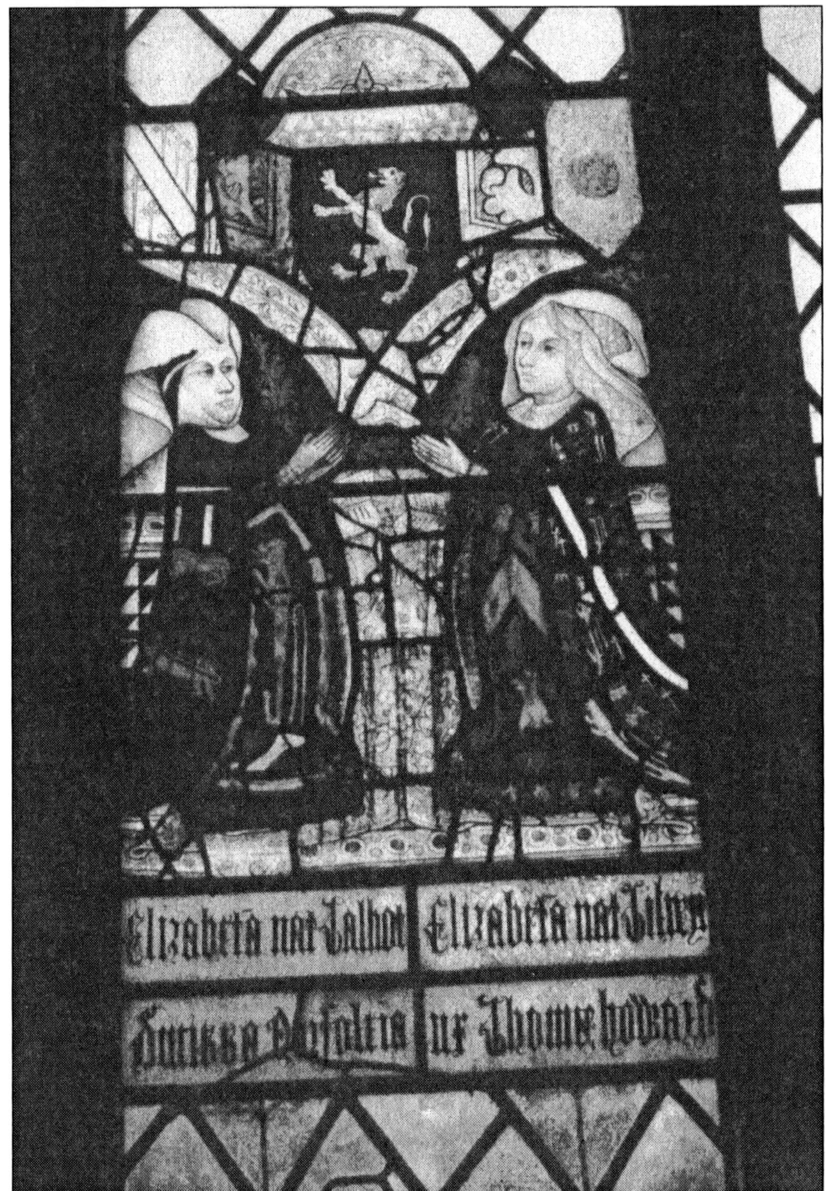

**Figure 3.2.** Elizabeth Talbot and Elizabeth Tilney, late fifteenth century, Holy Trinity Church, Long Melford. Photo Virginia Raguin.

When we return to Kempe, a closer look at some of her visions can point to the ways that she memorializes herself through her visions, how she uses her *Book* not only to record and memorialize a set of visions in which

Christ speaks directly to her and she plays a role in the life of the holy family but also to define a material legacy. In *Christ's Body*, Sarah Beckwith argues that Kempe's "identification with Christ's body may be seen as a subversive and dynamic private appropriation of an imagery that at least in eucharistic piety, was subject to intense and jealous clerical control."[23] While Kempe's uses of devotional imagery are no doubt appropriative on many levels, she positions herself in relation to an imagery that was also subject to an intense, and perhaps even jealous, *lay* control. As much as she identifies with Christ's body, she also situates herself dialogically and proximally to that body as a speaking image. Indeed, even though she claims to have transcended material desires when she describes her fashion requirements as a young woman, money continues to play a key role in her history; and needs for bodily glamour shift subtly to desires for money that she can use to endow churches and religious foundations. At several points in the *Book*, Kempe negotiates with the speaking Christ in material terms, pointing to her desire for the kind of money that would allow her to make public endowments.[24] Although Christ repeatedly praises Kempe for the gift of souls, at other points in the text he points to more material forms of patronage that she would have performed had she the means. For instance, after she has missed the ferry and hence failed to make an expected visit to the nuns at Denny, Christ consoles her, saying that he, who knows "every thowt of thyn hert" (ch. 84, 6869–70), also realizes she would have liberally endowed churches and abbeys if she had had the money: "And I knowe wel, dowtyr, that thu hast many tymys thowt, yyf thu haddist an had many chirchys ful of nobelys [money/nobles], thu woldist a yovyn hem in my name. And also thu hast thowt that thu woldist, yyf thu haddist had good anow, a made many abbeys for my lofe, for religiows men and women to dwellyn in, and a yovyn iche of hem hundryd powndys be yer for to ben my servawntys" (ch . 84, 6857–63). Christ's discourse, rich with consolation, is also rich with the language of payment and reward, even parsed in a specific figure, the generous hundred pounds a year with which she would endow the abbeys. The language of imagined charity throughout the chapter is contractual, Kempe's reward in heaven purchased either by the endowments to the abbeys and churches, purchased by endowments for priests (ch. 84, 6864), or purchased, as in Christ's discussion of lepers, by gifts of twenty pounds a year to each leper, so that each one could love and praise Christ (ch. 84, 6871).

The explicitly contractual nature of this exchange—perhaps not unlike the contract Kempe negotiates with her husband to secure her sexual autonomy—is echoed in Christ's discourse throughout the book and often expressed in fantasies of patronage that blur distinctions among contractual spirituality, the private contract with God, and public benefice. In an episode where Kempe describes her struggles with exclusion from St. Margaret's because of her excessive weeping, Christ consoles her with a picture of the power of immaterial goods, with a play on "price" (ch. 63, 5263) and poverty in reference to the beatitude: "Blessed are the poor": "Dowtyr, thu seyst oftyn to me in thi mende that riche men han gret cawse to lovyn me wel, and thu seyst ryth soth, for thu seyst I have yovyn hem meche good wherwyth thei may servyn me and lovyn me. But, good dowtyr, I prey the, love thu me wyth al thyn hert, and I schal yevyn the good anow to lovyn me wyth, for hevyn and erde schulde rathar faylyn than I shulde faylyn the" (ch. 63, 5270–75). In his role as fabulist, spiritual director/confessor, and alter-ego, Christ both acknowledges and soothes Kempe's preoccupation with her own poverty, her inability to endow and give, by promising her "good anow," goods enough that in this passage presumably are spiritual. Nevertheless, the language of the passage, "meche good" with which rich men serve and love God, is highly material, expressing a longing for the religious clout that one can buy with money.

The material inflections of longing in this passage may even specifically invoke the spectacle of "goods" possessed by the priory, to whose cloister she retreats when she fears her crying will get her ejected from the church (ch. 63, 5220). A preoccupation of this section of the text, in fact, which deals with her rejection from parish communities for her excessive weeping, concerns Kempe's ability or right to occupy space; when she is thrown out of the church, Christ speaks to her and promises her that the friar who has preached against her will be outside the church, and she will be in (ch. 63, 5250–51). A few chapters earlier in the text Kempe speaks, with particular intensity, of the moment of her houseling in the prior's chapel (ch. 56), painting a brief and suggestive picture of herself first ejected from a public space and then received, and even welcomed, even in a physical embrace, in a decidedly masculine and private clerical space:

> [B]ut than encresyd hir cryes and hir wepyngys in-so-meche that prestys durst not howselyn [give communion] hir openly in the chirche, but prevyly in the Priowrys Chapel at Lenne, fro the peplys audiens. And in that chapel sche had so hy contemplacyon and so meche dalyawns of owr Lord, in-as-meche as sche was putte owt of chirche for hys lofe, that sche cryed what tyme sche schulde ben howselyd as yyf hir sowle and hir body schulde a partyd asundyr, so that tweyn men heldyn hir in her armys tyl hir cryng was cesyd, for sche myth not beryn the habundawns [abundance]of lofe that sche felt in the precyows sacrament, whech sche stedfastly belevyed was very God and man in the forme of breed. (ch. 56, 4655–65)

Kempe's ecstatic record of this moment, focused on eucharistic ritual, recounts passage between spaces with markedly different material endowments. It also recounts a process by which she gains access, perhaps strategically, to clerical spaces that would have displayed a wealth of devotional objects and images. Rejected from the church as a liturgical pariah, Kempe is then fostered in a private ritual within a private chapel, which, according to Hope Emily Allen's note, may have contained the library as well as the "liturgical furniture."[25] Subsequently rejected from there as well (ch. 57), she is permitted, in a kind of negotiated settlement between her confessor and the prior, to take the sacrament at the high altar at St. Margaret's every Sunday. To what extent, we might ask, is Kempe's own sense of literal poverty, in this section of the text that recounts a history of exclusion from and privileged access to sanctified spaces, sharpened by her surroundings, and especially the priory, with its display of material wealth and ecclesiastical purchase-power?

While Kempe does not provide a literal answer for this question, nevertheless, her uses of devotional imagery throughout her narrative strongly suggest, I believe, that the power of meditative images in her text is inseparable from other contingencies that lend value to those images—and specifically contingencies of corporate and symbolic ownership in the culture of fifteenth-century East Anglia: class and gender that mediated not only ownership of but also physical access to images. While studies of patterns of ownership, inheritance, and donation indicate that women were increasingly owners of private devotional images, especially as these were represented in Books of Hours, access to images in forms of elite representation would be largely restricted to women of the upper classes who possessed, unlike Margery Kempe, both literacy and money.[26] The chief distinction that would allow men more frequent and more intimate visual access to expensive and beautiful images was clerical privilege. The high altar within the chancel space was traditionally the site of the most lavish endowments;[27] and the chancel, according to custom, was restricted to the clergy.[28] A curious exception that would seem to affirm this convention for Kempe's home church of St. Margaret's is even indicated in a by-law of the Corporation of Lynn, 1424–25, where the ordinance for the obit of John Burghard includes, according to Lynn historian Henry Hillen, "a strangely digressive clause which insists upon the attendance of the whole Corporation at feast days generally. Special permission was accorded the mayor and Jurats—24 only—to sit in the chancel."[29]

Within the nave, access to images was certainly determined in part by class, since well-to-do families often commanded private pews and chapels that were close to the chancel or had their own liturgical furnishings.[30] Pamela Graves, in her essay "Social Space in the English Medieval Parish Church," argues that late medieval English parishes, recipients of increasingly rich donations from both merchants and gentry, expressed corporate hierarchy and conflict in their very design.[31] While the architectural division between chancel and nave conventionally constituted and replicated a social division between clergy and laity who were variously responsible as well for the upkeep of the two spaces, a jostling for status in visible marks of patronage and in the strategic siting of ones' tomb or chapel within the parish altered these divisions, transforming all parts of the church into a site in which the status of its prominent lay patrons would have been inescapable. In a striking example, Graves cites a church at Ashton, in Devon, which was rebuilt in the fifteenth century to accommodate a private chapel for the local manorial family in the north aisle. Whereas images in the nave represent saints marked by signs and attributes, images within the chancel and chapel carry textual banners reflecting the Sarum rite and new fifteenth-century liturgical developments. As Graves interprets this program, it offers the manorial family marked access to the power of clerical ritual: "The family sat visually and physically separated from their tenants and viewed their religion as integrated with the textual form, whereas for the rest, it was dominated by image and action."[32]

## THE SPEAKING CHRIST AND THE MAN OF SORROWS

Certainly a key image structuring Kempe's *Book* and placing it—and her—at the center of liturgical ritual, metaphorically displayed on a highly visible platform, is the image of the speaking Christ, Kempe's vocal companion and superego throughout much of her narrated life. While Kempe's dialogue with Christ can be chiefly characterized by its verbal intimacy, Christ as a lover and companion who counsels her actions, the relationship is formalized in visual terms, and in terms, I would argue, that locate Kempe strategically in the position of a donor keeling below the image she has given. The narrative and iconographic detail with which Kempe endows Christ may even more precisely evoke a Man of Sorrows, one of the most popular new devotional images to appear in Kempe's time.[33] Typically portraying Christ, simultaneously both living and dead, as a half-length figure, hands crossed over his torso,[34] the Man of Sorrows became an important cult image in the fifteenth century, capturing the miracle of embodiment and transformation—the speaking Christ that is simultaneously flesh and eucharistic wafer, the body and the Mass.[35] The image also became an important indulgenced figure, especially in the popular form of the Gregorian Man of Sorrows, one of the most important eucharistic images of the fifteenth century. This legend, which appeared around 1400 and became an extremely popular subject for representation in glass, woodcuts, panel painting, and manuscript illustration in the fifteenth century, told the story that Christ, blood flowing from his wounds into the chalice at the altar, appeared to St. Gregory when he was saying Mass.[36] Many images representing the miracle include inscriptions explaining that an indulgence of thousands of years, said to have been granted by a Pope Clement, would be granted to those who prayed before it.[37]

Images of the Man of Sorrows in the Gregorian form as a half-length figure rising from the tomb and showing his wounds are extant in fifteenth-century English glazing at St. Peter Mancroft and elsewhere.[38] In East Anglian glazing the figure also takes the form of the pietà, the Man of Sorrows held in the Virgin's arms, as well as the Throne of Mercy with God the Father holding the body of his son in his arms, important new images in fifteenth-century English devotional art, although most extant images postdate Margery Kempe's *Book*.[39] Particularly suggestive, nevertheless, for its elision of the image with a figure of donation is a hybrid Man of Sorrows/pietà or Lady of Pity, from Long Melford, with a donor in blue below (figure 3.3). In this

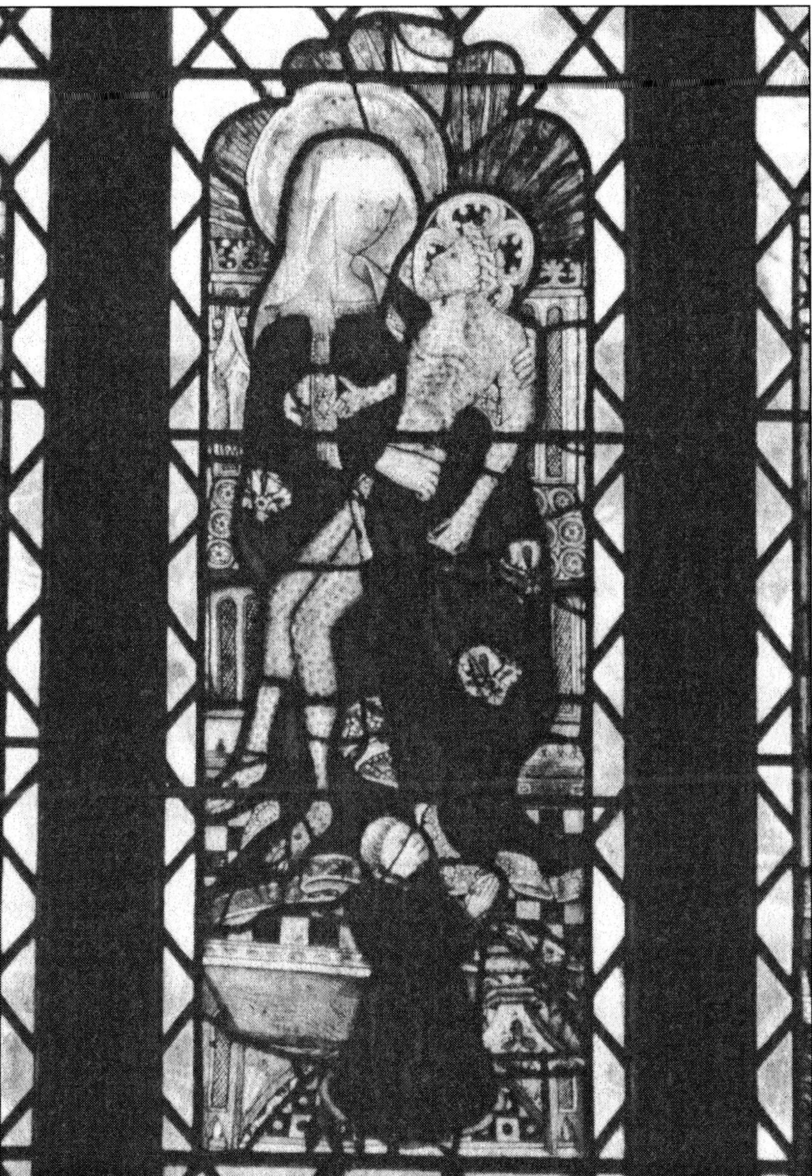

**Figure 3.3.** Lady of Pity, with donor, late fifteenth century, Holy Trinity Church, Long Melford. Photo Virginia Raguin.

image Christ, his body speckled with blood, looks up at his mother, who is holding him in her lap, and gestures with his right hand in emphasis. This image evokes an intimate drama, with the donor as evesdropper and eyewitness. Most arresting in this window is its powerful representation of emotional dialogue between the mother and son: both are equally prominent in the display, with her face reflecting pain and his body and gestures suggesting his attempt to explain his pain to her.[40] Miniaturized below this drama, the donor, a cleric—or, as Woodforde suggests, John Clopton, chief patron of the rebuilding of Long Melford Church in the late fifteenth century—maintains a prominent place in an ongoing devotional drama.[41] The donor's strategic placement below one of the central images in the glazing is above all a speech act for public continuity, a visual record to ease his soul through purgatory even as it entrenches family solidarity through its very presence.

Although it is difficult to say with any certainty where Kempe would have encountered an image of the Man of Sorrows in early fifteenth-century England, in her travels in Rome she well could have encountered like images, or even the famous wonder-working icon in Santa Croce in Gerusalemme, even though she does not list this particular church among her inventory of churches visited in Rome.[42] Nevertheless, the characteristics with which she endows Christ in their dialogue—bleeding wounds, ability to speak, powers of indulgence—suggest that she has constructed her narrative image after visual models that were beginning to be disseminated throughout England in her time. In the first episode in which Kempe describes Christ speaking to her, she recounts how she kneels below him, striking the pose of both a petitioner for indulgence and the donor: like the donor in blue in the Long Melford window, Kempe can be said to construct a textual image of herself that gives her a lasting place in a proximal posture to a speaking icon. Kempe also evokes the iconography of the Man of Sorrows by representing the speaking Christ as a hybrid figure of pity, suffering, and eucharistic power:

> Than on a Fryday beforn Crystmes Day, as this creatur, knelyng in a chapel of Seynt John wythinne a cherch of Seynt Margrete in N, wept wondir sore, askyng mercy and foryyfnes of hir synnes and hir trespas, owyr mercyful Lord Cryst Jhesu, blyssyd mot he be, ravysched hir spyryt and seyd onto hir:
>
> "Dowtyr, why wepyst thow so sor? I am comyn to the, Jhesu Cryst, that deyd on the crosse sufferyng byttyr peynes and passyons for the." (ch. 5, 491–98)

The Christ that Margery hears and seems to see as she kneels in the chapel of St. John in St. Margaret's would evoke the Man of Sorrows through his passional speaking, in which he expressly identifies himself as dead: "Jhesu Cryst, that deyd on the crosse sufferyng byttyr peynes and passyons for the."

As his dialogue continues, Christ also speaks to her as an indulgenced image who can grant contrition: "I am the same God that have browt thi synnes to thi mend and mad the to be schreve therof [who has brought your sins to your memory and made you to be shriven thereof]. And I graw[n]t the contrysyon into thi lyves ende (ch. 5, 501–03). Christ also expressly points to his eucharistic powers, reminding Margery that he is also available to her through ingestion and telling her it is his will that she take Communion every Sunday: "Also, my derworthy dowtyr, thu must forsake that thow lovyst best in this world, and that is etyng of flesch. And instede of that flesch, thow schalt etyn my flesch and my blod, that is the very body of Crist in the sacrament of the awter. Thys is my wyl, dowtyr, that thow receyve my body every Sonday" (ch. 5, 508–13). The movement to the Eucharist in Christ's account of himself and of his particular relationship to Kempe in this dialogue also encloses and memorializes her within a visual dyad, reenacting Kempe's presence as donor and penitent at the foot of the Man of Sorrows through her own participation in the eucharistic rite. Kempe constructs a complex relationship between herself and the speaking Christ that allows her to enter into an intensely affective relationship with him even as she in a sense takes on his powers, transforming herself into a missionary and eucharistic body through her emotive and gestural alignment with him.

Immediately after telling Kempe that it is his will that she take Communion every Sunday—an extraordinary injunction that prompts her to engage in a lengthy battle for clerical permission—Christ then tells her that she will become in effect a eucharistic wafer, though one that is also curiously debased. After telling her that she should receive his body every Sunday, he tells her that she will be eaten like the stockfish: "Thow schalt ben etyn and knawyn of the pepul of the world as any raton knawyth the stokfysch" (ch. 5, 515–16). On the one hand a eucharistic image, in that fish conventionally signify the last supper, Kempe's striking and domestic simile likening herself to a stockfish, gnawed by the rats of the community, may also recall a fifteenth-century riddle that hangs for its "humor," such as it is, on an antifeminist inversion in which women, who would normally be the ones to do the pounding that makes this dried fish palatable, become the ones that take the beating: "ther be 4 thyngs that take gret betyng . . . a stockfisch, a milston, a federbed, and a woman."[43] Even more directly, of course, the image of the stockfish evokes rats and common staples of the pantry and is perhaps a particularly local and familiar image for Kempe, living in Lynn with its important fisheries.[44] Ingesting Christ, Kempe in a sense becomes Christlike herself as an object of communal ingestion and also perhaps as a thing of community abuse, her litany throughout her book: Margery suffers as Christ suffers; Kempe in effect is Christ.

Kempe's first verbal instruction by the speaking Christ thus comes to wrap them in a close imagistic and affective embrace, even as the dialogue claims a figurative space within the church as an icon with donor portrait,

Kempe as donor/petitioner kneeling before an indulgenced Man of Sorrows. Locating her first vision within physical space—a chapel of St. John (no longer extant) in her family's parish church of St. Margaret's—Kempe establishes a physical, material locus for imaging, in effect staging a vision, as if the moment of Christ's address could appear as if lifted from the glass within the chapel. In imaging herself in an intimate speaking relationship with Christ, Kempe not only guarantees herself a certain purchase on the future but also places herself in a highly privileged place within the space of the church, picturing herself as petitioner before an important—and also new—kind of image. Through this semantic framing, Kempe memorializes herself in multiple ways: as dramatic agent, a figure of Christlike sacrifice; as a figure of intercession, one who prays to Christ and hence holds power for others over the afterlife; and as one whose every action serves to memorialize herself. Kempe locates her spirituality squarely in the community, even within its public buildings. However Christlike in her self-conception, taking on his burden as an outcast, pounded, perhaps, as a stockfish by the world, her uses of meditative images also allows her to claim an identity as a citizen of Lynn, a prominent social figure memorialized below the devotional image in the glazing.

## THE TRINITY AND THE BOOK OF LIFE

A second moment in which Kempe constructs a devotional meditation through a drama of patronage appears later in her text. Toward the end of the first book of her autobiography, Kempe describes a hallucinatory set of visions that are unlike any other in her *Book*. They each appear after she has fallen asleep and hence are cast into a particularly fictive framework, as if they appeared to her as small allegories, mini dream visions. They are also unusually pictorial and tactile: in the space of chapter 85, Kempe sees Christ in his manhood with his wounds bleeding; she sees Christ's body, ravishingly beautiful, lying supine but then assaulted by a man who slices him along the breast; in another sleeping vision she takes Christ's toes in her hand; and in yet another the Virgin speaks to her, "Dowtyr, wilt thu se my sone?" (ch. 85, 7050) and then swathes her son with a white kerchief.

Whereas the visions stand out in Kempe's *Book* for their drama, most of them a brief pictorial flash in which Kempe falls into a sleep and then sees herself as a direct participant in a closely focused devotional scene, the first of these scenes is striking for its explicit presentation as an illuminated manuscript. Unlike the following devotional images that Kempe imagines as animated with a vivid and even lurid life, the chapter opens with a presentation that is expressly representational. After falling to sleep, a fall she describes as into a trancelike state, Kempe sees a child-angel in white carrying a huge book that she recognizes as the Book of Life, inscribed with a gold Trinity. When she asks the child where her name is, he tells her that it is at the foot of the Trinity, and he disappears:

> On a tyme, as the sayd creatur was knelyng beforn an awter of the cros and seying on an oryson [prayer], hir eyne wer evyr togedirward [closed] as thow sche schulde a slept. And at the last sche myth not chesyn; sche fel in a lityl slomeryng, and anon aperyd verily to hir syght an awngel, al clothyd in white as mech [meek] as it had ben a lityl childe, beryng an howge boke beforn hym. Than seyd the creatur to the childe, or ellys to the awngel:
>
> "A," sche seyd, "this is the Boke of Lyfe."
>
> And sche saw in the boke the Trinite, and al in gold. Than seyd sche to the childe:
>
> "Wher is my name?"
>
> The childe answeryd and seyd: "Her is thi name, at the Trinyte foot wretyn," and therwyth he was a-go, sche wist not how." (ch. 85, 6958–70)

The Trinity that Kempe sees is a painted image, and the self that she demands to see in the image is a symbol of herself, her name, authorizing a relationship of herself to the Trinity. The image is overlaid with a complex set of social and iconic references: the angel bearing the Book of Life recalls the angel of Revelation, and his act suggests a ceremony of ritual presentation, a *liber vitae* presented to a wealthy patron. Imagining a Book of Life, Kempe may be aligning herself with St. Katherine, one of the saints most frequently named in her text. In an early fifteenth-century version of the life of Saint Katherine that includes the mystical marriage, when the virgins and martyrs present Katherine to the Virgin Mary, they say, "[A]t your commaundement we present hur, our der sistre, whose name ys specially wrytyn in the [boke] of euerlastyng life."[45] To have one's name written in a "Book of Life" is to have one's name recorded in a necrology. English monasteries kept registers known as *Liber Vitae*, which were lists of benefactors for whom masses would be recited.[46] In the *Liber Vitae* or New Minster Register, for example, is a list of the monks and benefactors who were to be commemorated during the services.[47] Kempe's insistence on seeing her own name etched below the image on the presentation page of a Book of Life thus transforms a conventional image denoting salvation into one of conspicuous patronage. She imagines the Book of Life as a literal book and locates her name visibly within it.

In beginning the set of visions of chapter 85 with this insistently personalized dedication page, Kempe sets the stage for "reading" the visions that follow as pictorial moments, images that also have been lifted from the pages of a manuscript. With this first image in particular Margery dramatizes an anxiously imbricated relationship between her vision and a devotional object, even establishing a pictorial hermeneutic that suggests that the subsequent visions in the sequence are also to be read through an encounter with text and visual gloss. But the image also presents us with a visual hermeneutic that overlays practices of reading those images with the multiple personae of Margery Kempe, both as a pious woman reliving crucial moments in the life of the holy family and as a powerful and socially visible patron of the devotional arts. With this image, indeed, as with her carefully constructed relationship to a speaking Christ, Kempe's meditations serve as a clearly material asset. She uses them not only to claim her privileged status and spiritual election; she also uses them to claim her place among the donors and patrons of Lynn.

But what, exactly, is the Trinity that Kempe pictures in the Book of Life? Although she explicitly names the image, she does not describe it in chapter 85, nor does she describe the images of the Trinity that she prays before elsewhere in her text. Her reference could suggest an image such as the circular and textual Trinity that surmounts the Man of Sorrows in Long Melford (figure 3.4) or the church's totemic rabbit-ear Trinity below, or even dually frontal, side-by-side composition as in the fourteenth-century East Anglian Ormesby psalter.[48] A more likely prototype for Kempe's reference, however, would be the closely framed grouping of God, crucifixion, and dove, a trinitarian form that survives widely in English alabasters, with eighty extant examples.[49] In the most common scheme, God is seated, the crucified Christ between his knees (Throne of Mercy), with the central grouping often surrounded by attendant figures, usually angels. The image is generally frontal and magisterial in spite of its dramatic postural paradoxes: the father dramatically larger than the son; the son's crucified body pendant, dead, in contrast to the seated muscularity of the father; the conflation of manly authority with a hint of maternal and even natal care, the small crucifix cradled between the father's knees, as is evident in the exquisite alabaster Trinity currently owned by the Boston Museum of Fine Arts (figure 3.5). As a common subject for altarpieces—so common, in fact, that by the fifteenth

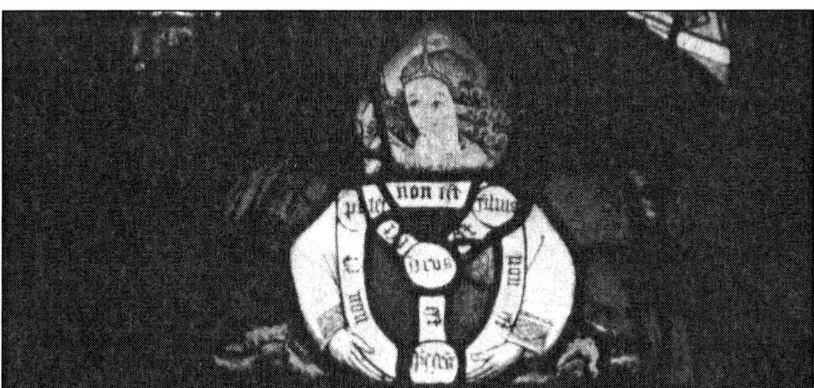

**Figure 3.4.** Trinity, late fifteenth century, Holy Trinity Church, Long Melford. Photo Virginia Raguin.

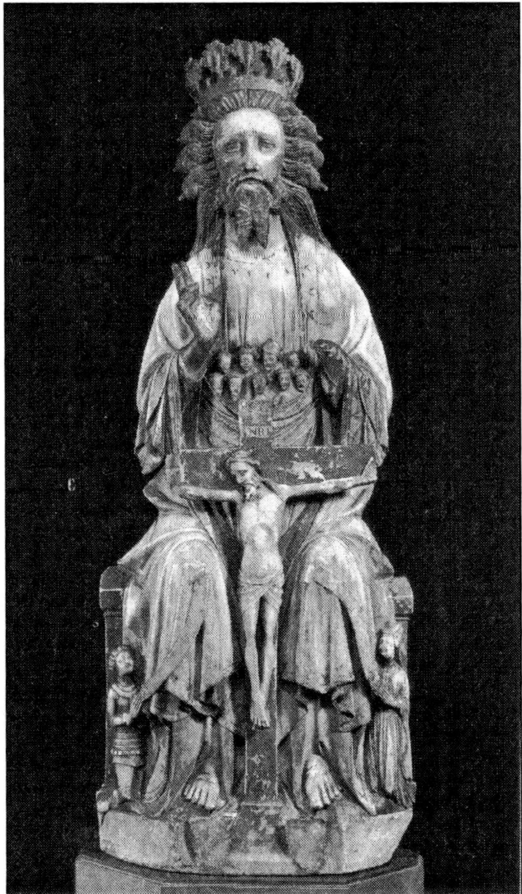

**Figure 3.5.** Alabaster Trinity, 1400–1450, Museum of Fine Arts, Boston. Courtesy Museum of Fine Arts. Photograph © 2003 Museum of Fine Arts, Boston.

century the small triptychs designed to stand on an altar were quite inexpensive[50]—the image was public and authoritative, frequently placed at the center of worship.

These records of surviving images and accounts of their placement and use in English parishes thus suggest that Kempe's vision is shaped around an image that is deeply conventional and squarely centered in liturgical ritual. Her vision of a Trinity at the center of a drama of donation would also seem to stake an important claim for her orthodoxy in the face of repeated accusations of Lollardy.[51] The Trinity, in its most conventional montage combining God, Crucifixion, and dove, was an image to which, Anne Hudson writes, "Wyclif and his followers took particular exception."[52] In its condemnation of offerings to "ymages of tre and of ston" the *Twelve Conclusions of the Lollards* singles out the "usual" image of the Trinity as particularly offensive and problematic: "And þow þis forbodin ymagerie be a bok of errour to þe lewid [ignorant] puple, yet þe ymage usuel of Trinite is most abhominable."[53]

However she pictures the image in this scene, what seems to matter most to her is the inscription of her name beneath the feet—which presumably would mean beneath the feet of the crucifix—in terms that clearly display her orthodoxy. The insistence on a gesture of donation, of finding her name inscribed in the frame, repeats one of the most characteristic features of Margery's *Book*, the drive to authorize herself, to name-drop (though here it is *her* name that is dropped), and connect herself with the most powerful clerical figures of her time. Yet although her insistence on self, her obsessive self-absorption and projection of a kind of in-your-face personality, are often perceived by her readers as remarkable or unique features of her orthography, they are in many ways typical of her social and cultural milieu. The dropping of one's name, leaving the visible trace of one's patronage on the church building, was as we have seen a gesture of wide currency in fifteenth-century England, even surviving in images of the Trinity that suggest parallels to her vision. At the Church of the Assumption of the Blessed Virgin Mary in Attleborough, East Anglia, a Trinity painted on the right central panel of the chancel parclose sits above the names of the donors below, inscribed with the conventional tag "*orate pro* . . ." An image of a donor kneeling below the Trinity in a clerestory window on the north side of the nave at Ringland,[54] and the donors flanking the Museum of Fine Arts' Trinity (figure 3.5),[55] all display a highly visible alliance between the image and its giver, as does a Carmelite missal, circa 1393, which depicts a lateral Trinity with Virgin and donors.[56] Even more suggestive for Kempe's vision in chapter 85, though it postdates her *Book*, is a late fifteenth-century window from Holy Trinity Goodramgate in which a Trinity hybrid with Man of Sorrows sags in the father's arms. The central image is flanked by the donor, John Walker, seen at the foot of the Trinity with a scroll, "*Te adoro et glorifico O Beata Trinitas* (figure 3.6)."[57]

To return to her vision of the Trinity, Kempe's account of the presentation of the Book of Life thus features herself prominently, situated as both the donor whose name is inscribed in the book and the recipient of the gift. Kempe's vision of the Trinity in chapter 85, introduced by her customary paratactic folk formula "on a tyme" that structures each chapter as a self-contained narrative unit, thus sits within and is in fact framed by a larger meditation on the spiritual rewards of material patronage. First Christ recognizes that she would endow the abbeys with one hundred pounds a year if she could; then an angel approaches with a magnificent book, as if to exhibit a specific devotional object that she has personally commissioned. The image, however brief, thus resonates with complex forms of desire—the desire for sanctity that Kempe exhibits throughout her book; the anxious insistence on orthodoxy in the face of accusations of Lollardy; the

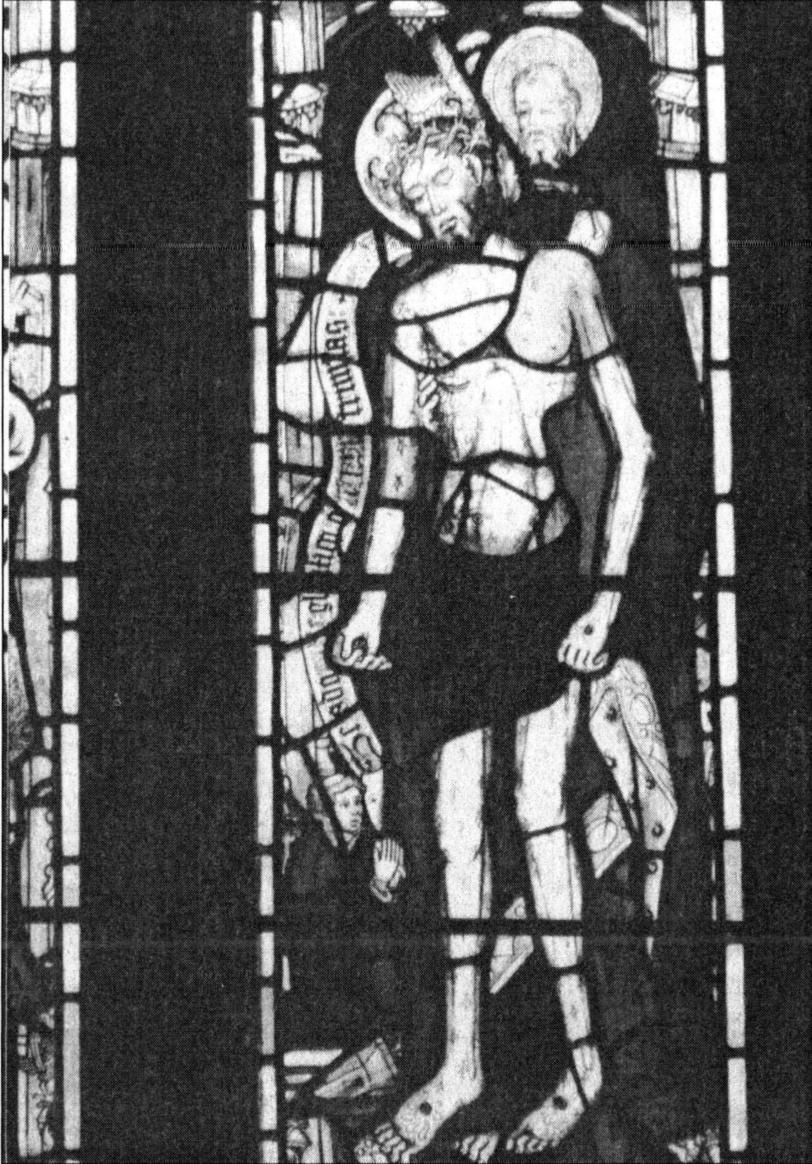

**Figure 3.6.** Trinity Man of Sorrows with donor John Walker, late fifteenth century, Holy Trinity Goodramgate, York. Photo Virginia Raguin.

desire for recognition by the socially elite—perhaps even with specific reference to the locally important Trinity guild to which her father belonged. Perhaps most tellingly, through her vision of her name in the Book of Life, with the surrounding discourse on the spiritual goods money can buy, Kempe achieves a place within a local building campaign and demands that her name be featured prominently on the list of patrons. Her question is poignant, even haunting, for it expresses a knowledge of exclusion from power and money: perhaps she asks the question because her name is there, but she is unable to read it.

The meditations that Kempe localizes at altars throughout the environs of Lynn thus color the panels, fill the niches, and glaze the main and tracery lights in a demonstration of a vividly imagined and enacted role as patron, donor, and with her figuration of herself praying before indulgenced images, as spiritual intercessor. Kempe's "devotional theater" not only takes its form from the images in glass, panel painting, and ecclesiastical ornament that would have surrounded her in fifteenth-century East Anglia but also takes its form from the dynamic rebuilding campaigns that were occurring throughout parishes and lay buildings in Norfolk and Suffolk,[58] including the St. Nicholas Chapel, St. Margaret's chapel of ease that figures so prominently in Kempe's text as the subject of a separatist plot, rebuilt circa 1429;[59] or the guildhall in Lynn, rebuilt in the 1420s, after the fire that Kempe describes. Kempe's "contemplacyon" and "meditacyon,"[60] private acts in which she imagines herself talking with Christ or participating with the holy family, are also highly public acts, we have seen, that make a startlingly assertive and keen-eyed use of images to imagine and construct an autobiographic self. The interactive and dramatic compositon of her "meditatacyons" repeatedly single out Kempe as phantasmatic donor, a visible patron gifted with the means and social power to endow and control the material life of the churches in which her meditations occur. Decorating the bare walls of the churches that she only describes by name, Kempe's visions splash her name and picture across the painted panels, in the spandrels of the glass, and in the very liturgical books that the priests intone. Kempe's question reverberates, as central to her *Book*, within the East Anglian redevelopment project of the fifteenth century. *Hic iacet. Orate pro nobis.* Here is my name.

## NOTES

1. See Gail McMurray Gibson, *The Theater of Devotion: East Anglian Drama and Society in the Late Middle Ages* (Chicago: University of Chicago Press, 1989), esp. chs. 2 and 4; Eamon Duffy, *The Stripping of the Altars: Traditional Religion in England c. 1400–1580* (New Haven: Yale University Press, 1992), 63–68, 155–60, 166–69; M. D. Anderson, *History and Imagery in British Churches* (London: Murray, 1971), 208–21; See also Joel T. Rosenthal, *The Purchase of Paradise: Gift Giving and the Aristocracy, 1307–1485* (London: Routledge and Kegan Paul); and C. Pamela Graves, "Social Space in the English Medieval Parish Church," *Economy and Society* 18 (1989): esp. 311–19.

2. Citations from *The Book of Margery Kempe* are from Barry Windeatt, ed. (Essex and New York: Longman, 2000).

3. Kempe's strategic self-construction through her body, voice, and persona is the subject of several recent full-length studies, including Lynn Staley, *Margery Kempe's Dissenting Fictions* (University Park: Penn State University Press, 1994) and Karma Lochrie, *Margery Kempe and Translations of the Flesh* (Philadelphia: University of Pennsylvania Press, 1991); see also David Aers, *Community, Gender, and Individual Identity: English Writing 1360–1430* (London and New York: Routledge, 1988), ch. 2; Sarah Beckwith, "A Very Material Mysticism: The Medieval Mysticism of Margery Kempe," in *Medieval Literature: Criticism, Ideology and History*, ed. David Aers (Sussex: Harvester, 1988), 34–57; Felicity Riddy, "Women Talking about the Things of God: A Late Medieval Subculture," in *Women and Literature in Britain, 1150–1500*, ed. Carol Meale (Cambridge: Cambridge University Press, 1993), 104–27; Sue Ellen Holbrook, " 'About Her': Margery Kempe's Book of Telling and Working," in *The Idea of Medieval Literature*, ed. James Dean and Christian Zacher (Newark: University of Delaware Press, 1992), 265–84; Rosalynn Voaden, "God's Almighty Hand: Women Co-Writing the Book," in *Women, the Book and the Godly*, ed. L. Smith and J. H. M. Taylor (Cambridge: Cambridge University Press, 1995), 55–65.

4. See for instance Gibson, *Theater of Devotion*, ch. 3, pp. 47–65; Sarah Beckwith, *Christ's Body: Identity, Culture and Society in Late Medieval Writings* (London and New York: Routledge, 1993), 78–111; Denise Despres, "Franciscan Spirituality: Margery Kempe and Visual Meditation," *Mystics Quarterly* 11, no. 1 (1984): 12–18; David Lawton, "Voice, Authority, and Blasphemy in the *Book of Margery Kempe*," in *Margery Kempe: A Book of Essays*, ed. Sandra J. McEntire (New York: Garland, 1992), 99; David Wallace, "Mystics and Followers in Siena and East Anglia: A Study in Taxonomy, Class and Cultural Mediation," *The Medieval Mystical Tradition in England*, ed. Marion Glasscoe (Cambridge: Brewer, 1984): 169–91; David Aers, *Community, Gender, and Individual Identity*, esp. 104–06.

5. Clarissa W. Atkinson, *Mystic and Pilgrim: The Book and the World of Margery Kempe* (Ithaca: Cornell University Press, 1983), 92–93.

6. According to Hope Emily Allen's note, "from an inventory of Lynn priory of 1454, the "capella" seems then to have contained the library as well as the liturgical furniture," in *The Book of Margery Kempe*, ed. Sanford Brown Meech and Hope Emily Allen, EETS (London: Oxford, 1940), 324/155.

7. According to the note in Meech and Allen, 316/131, this would have been the chapter house of the collegiate church of St. John the Evangelist, at Beverly (Beverly Minster). Although the chapter house is no longer extant, surviving chapter houses in England, such as at Salisbury, Lincoln, and Westminster, demonstrate typically elaborate sculptural programs; the entrance to the chapter house at Salisbury contains a sculptural program of the virtues and vices, and the spandrels of the arcading around the walls of the house itself show a set of carvings representing the Old Testament from the creation to the delivery of the ten commandments; Pamela Blum, "The Sculptures of the Salisbury Chapter-house," in *Medieval Art and Architecture at Salisbury Cathedral*, ed. Laurence Keene and Thomas Cocke (London: British Archaeological Association, 1996), 68–78.

8. On the exclusion of laity from the chancel during Mass see Duffy, *Stripping of the Altars*, 97; from the chancel in St. Margaret's, 111; and from touching liturgical vessels, 110; see also 157–61, for a discussion of the laity's experience of the high altar and especially the rood screen at a Sunday Mass. For the liturgical uses of the altar-

piece in fifteenth-century North European painting, see Barbara G. Lane, *The Altar and the Altarpiece: Sacramental Themes in Early Netherlandish Painting* (New York: Harper and Row, 1984), 8–10, 11; and Beth Williamson, "Altarpieces, Liturgy, and Devotion," *Speculum* 79 (2004): 341–406.

9. The chapel contained a representation of the nativity, which gave it its name (from Old French. *Gesine*, childbed), according to Henry J. Hillen, *History of the Borough of King's Lynn* (Norwich: East of England Newspaper Company, 1907), vol. 2:741–45, 814–15; see also note in Meech and Allen, *The Book of Margery Kempe*, 324; and discussion in Gibson, *Theater of Devotion*, 64.

10. The paucity of descriptions of devotional images may itself derive from a climate of anxiety about appropriate use, as expressed in the debate on graven images in *Dives and Pauper* where the repeated litany is to worship "aforn Þe ymage noght to Þe ymage"; in *Dives and Pauper*, ed. Priscilla Heath Barnum, EETS (London: Oxford, 1976), 85; for the debate, in Lollard texts and elsewhere, about appropriate use of images, see "Gold and Images" in *Faith and Fire: Popular and Unpopular Religion, 1350–1600*, ed. Margaret Aston (London: Hambledon, 1993), 219–29; and for the relationship between this debate and practices of ekphrasis in late medieval writing see Sarah Stanbury, "Visualizing," in *A Companion to Chaucer*, ed. Peter Brown (Oxford: Blackwell, 2001).

11. Sixten Ringbom, "Devotional Images and Imaginative Devotions: Notes on the Place of Art in Late Medieval Private Piety," *Gazette des Beaux-Arts* 73 (1969): 159–70. A particular example of this relationship can be seen in the story of a peasant whose sight-curing vision of St. Foy corresponded to an extant gilded statue and reliquary; see *Liber Miraculorum Sancte Fideis*, ed. A. Bouillet (Paris, 1897), 9–10, as noted in Margaret Aston, *Faith and Fire*, 221.

12. See especially Jeffrey Hamburger, "The Visual and the Visionary: The Image in Late Medieval Monastic Devotions," *Viator* 20 (1989): 161–204; Ringbom, "Devotional Images," 161–64, briefly discusses St. Catherine of Siena, St. Bridget, Julian of Norwich, St. Teresa of Avila, and St. Catherine of Genoa as evidence that "among fourteenth-century mystics the women seem to have been particularly responsive to images"; see also J. E. Ziegler, *Sculpture of Compassion: The Pietà and the Beguines in the Southern Low Countries, c. 1300–1600* (Brussels: Institut Historique Belge de Rome, 1992), 39–40, 117–39.

13. For a discussion of the role played by private ownership of images in the development of art connoisseurship at the end of the Middle Ages, see Belting, *Likeness and Presence: A History of the Image before the Era of Art*, trans. Edmund Jephcott (Chicago: University of Chicago Press, 1994), esp. 409–57.

14. I take the term *autoportrait* from Louis Marin, "Topic and Figures of Enunciation: It Is Myself That I Paint," in *Vision and Textuality*, ed. Stephen Melville and Bill Readings (Durham: Duke University Press, 1995), 195–214, who argues that Montaigne revolutionizes the concept of 'self' by creating, under a "dual drape," a self that is both visual and textual; Kempe, I believe, produces a similar double image.

15. See, for instance, Corine Schleif, "Hands That Appoint, Anoint and Ally: Late Medieval Donor Strategies for Appropriating Approbation through Painting," *Art History* 16, no. 1 (March 1993): 1–32; Richard Marks, *Stained Glass in England during the Middle Ages* (Toronto: University of Toronto Press, 1993), 1–27; and see especially Nigel Morgan, "Patrons and Devotional Images in English Art of the

International Gothic c. 1350–1450," in *Reading Texts and Images: Essays on Medieval and Renaissance Art and Patronage in Honor of Margaret Mannion*, ed. Bernard J. Muir (Exeter: University of Exeter Press, 2002), 93–121.

16. Sidney Cockerell, *Two East Anglian Psalters at the Bodleian Library, Oxford: The Ormesby Psalter, MS Douce 366 and the Brunholm Psalter, MS Ashmole 1523* (Oxford: Roxburghe Club, 1926), fig. 1, p. 19; see P. Lasko and Nigel. J. Morgan, *Medieval Art in East Anglia 1300–1520* (Norwich: Jarrold and Sons, 1973), 18 who point out that some of the numerous coats of arms throughout the manuscript represent Norfolk families.

17. Christopher Woodforde, *The Norwich School of Glass-Painting in the Fifteenth Century* (London: Oxford University Press, 1950), index, s.v. heraldic glass.

18. Large lettering on the north porch urges viewers to "Pray for ye sowlis of William Clopton, Margy and Margy his wifis, and for ye sowle of Alice Clopton and for John Clopto,' and for alle thooo sowlis' yt ye seyd John is bo'nde to prey for." Cited in Gibson, *Theater of Devotion*, 80.

19. Ibid., 101, 105; see also Graves on patronage in East Harling: "It may be suggested that the average inhabitant of East Harling witnessed at least one act of patronage during their lifetime . . . [and] the identity of the donor would be constantly in evidence through the repeated motifs of heraldry found throughout the fabric, to which the worshipper would be witness on every visit to church" (312).

20. Marks, *Stained Glass in England*, 12, notes that donors kneeling at the feet of saints and of Christ on the cross are common in English fourteenth-century glass. See also Schleif, "Hands That Appoint," 1.

21. Marks, *Stained Glass in England*, 4–5, 12, and fig. 1; the windows of the nave were glazed between 1291 and 1339 by clerical and lay donors, including members of the nobility and merchant class, which Marks notes as symptomatic of the transformation of English society to a complex structure embracing a "rich urban mercantile class," 4.

22. Ibid., 5–6; Gibson, *Theater of Devotion*, 79–96.

23. Beckwith, *Christ's Body*, 91; for Kempe's struggles with clerical control, see also Susan Dickman, "Margery Kempe and the Continental Tradition of the Pious Woman," in *The Medieval Mystical Tradition in England*, ed. Marion Glasscoe (Exeter: University of Exeter Press, 1980), 150–68.

24. On the mercantile rhetoric of Kempe's text see Sheila Delany, "Sexual Economics: Chaucer's Wife of Bath and *The Book of Margery Kempe*," *Minnesota Review* 5 (1975): 104–15; and Deborah Ellis: "Merchant's Wife's Tales: Language, Sex and Commerce in Margery Kempe and in Chaucer," *Exemplaria* 2 (1990): 595–626.

25. Meech and Allen, *The Book of Margery Kempe*, 324/155.

26. See Duffy's discussion of lay ownership of primers, 209–32. For an important study on fourteenth-century German nuns that argues that cloistered women may have comprised the largest audience for mystical and didactic literature and may have played a central role in the development of devotional imagery, see Jeffrey F. Hamburger, *The Rothschild Canticles: Art and Mysticism in Flanders and the Rhineland Circa 1300* (New Haven: Yale University Press, 1990), 3–5. Arguing for new possibilities for women to possess devotional images privately in the late Middle Ages, see also J. Ziegler, 129, who claims that women's new access to images in fourteenth-century beguinages marked a distinct change from earlier centuries where "sacred

objects had been the purview of male monastery, cloister, and cathedral, where they were used and enjoyed collectively"; see also 131. Ziegler notes, however, that precise documentation for possession and use is uncertain, 139, n. 80. For a study establishing a relationship between female readers and books of hours, see Sandra Penketh, "Women and Books of Hours," in *Women and the Book: Assessing the Visual Evidence*, ed. Jane H. M. Taylor and Lesley Smith (Toronto: British Library and University of Toronto Press, 1996), 266–80. Startling images suggesting dramatically different relationships to corporeal images appear in the prayer book of James IV, which shows James IV in a private chapel before a painted triptich, whereas the devotion of Queen Margaret in the same manuscript depicts her kneeling before a private altar but seeing the Virgin and child in a spiritual vision; illustration in Ringbom, "Devotional Images," 167; and in this volume, see figure 4.6.

27. On the privileging of the high altar as a locus for expensive gifts, in particular panel painting, in East Anglia, see Christopher Norton, David Park, and Paul Binski, *Dominican Painting in East Anglia: The Thornham Parva Retable and the Musée de Cluny Frontal* (Suffolk: Boydell, 1987), 83; Belting, *Likeness and Presence*, 398–404, 7; see also Freedberg, *The Power of Images: Studies in the History and Theory of Response* (Chicago: University of Chicago Press, 1989), 118ff. The special status of the high altar in a Suffolk church as a site for the most beautiful images is indicated in the valuable account by Roger Martin in the 1589s or 1590s: "The State of Melford Church and Our Ladie's Chappel at the East End, as I Did Know It." Martin gives a detailed account of the images at the Martin family chapel, the Jesus aisle that was to the south side of the chancel, but only after describing the clearly more elaborate Passion reredos behind the high altar and flanking gilt tabernacles housing carvings of the Trinity; see David Dymond and Clive Paine, *The Spoil of Melford Church: The Reformation in a Suffolk Parish* (Rope Walk, Ipswich: Salient, 1992), 1–2.

28. Duffy, *Stripping of the Altars*, 132: "In the course of the twelfth and thirteenth centuries a demarcation of responsibility had emerged between parson and people: he was to maintain the chancel, they the nave"; see also 97, 110–11; see 113–14 for a discussion of the control of nave altars by the laity; see also 157–61, for the laity's experience of the high altar and especially the rood screen at a Sunday Mass. Monasteries also replicated the gender distinction that privileged a male clergy with access to images, since in late medieval England monasteries outnumbered nunneries 6:1, according to Roberta Gilchrist, *Gender and Material Culture: The Archaeology of Religious Women* (London and New York: Routledge, 1994), 61; see also Norman. P. Tanner, *The Church in Late Medieval Norwich, 1370–1532* (Toronto: Pontifical Institute for Mediaeval Studies, 1984), 25, who indicates that this ratio was mirrored at the local level.

29. Henry Hillen, *History of the Borough of King's Lynn* (1907, reprint E.P., 1978), 168.

30. Duffy, *Stripping of the Altars*, 123–26, counters that documented concern by the gentry in the entire life of parish ritual leveled rather than privatized ritual experience. Nevertheless, the designation of certain spaces, and the images they contained, as special, entailed, or even exclusive would certainly have contributed to the mystification of structures of authority and hierarchy.

31. Graves, "Social Space," 301, 317.

32. M. Glasscoe, "Late Medieval Paintings in Ashton Church, Devon," *Journal of the British Archaeological Association* 140 (1987): 182–90; Graves, "Social Space," 319.

33. The image was also a popular image for private ownership in the late Middle Ages, as recorded by the Datini correspondence in which the merchant of Prato was counseled by Domenico di Cambio that an *imago pietatis* is the appropriate image for the bedchamber; see Hans Belting, *The Image and Its Public in the Middle Ages: Form and Function of Early Paintings of the Passion*, trans. Mark Bartusis and Raymond Meyer (New Rochelle, N.Y.: Caratzas, 1981), 232, n. 45.

34. One of the most famous of these images was the mosaic at Santa Croce in Gerusalemme in Rome, an image Bertelli argues was brought to the church in 1385 or 1386 and there became a pilgrimage shrine; see Carlo Bertelli, "The *Image of Pity* in Santa Croce in Gerusalemme," in *Essays in the History of Art Presented to Rudolf Wittkower* (London: Phaidon, 1967), 46. As Bertelli notes, 46, by the time the image appeared in Rome, the iconography of the Man of Sorrows was widespread in the West.

35. Gertrud Schiller, *Iconography of Christian Art*, trans. Janet Seligman (Greenwich, C.T.: New York Graphic Society, 1972), vol. 2, 197–201; Duffy, *Stripping of the Altars*, 107, 108–09; Belting, *Image and Its Public*, ch. 2; Patricia de Leeuw, "Unde et Memores, Domine: Memory and the Mass of St. Gregory," in *Memory and the Middle Ages*, ed. Nancy Netzer and Virginia Reinburg (exh. cat. Boston College Museum of Art, 1995), 33–41; Lane, *Altar and Altarpiece*, 128–31.

36. See de Leeuw, 33–41; Schiller, 200; Belting, *Image and Its Public*, 36–38. A version of the legend of Gregory also appears in the *Mirrour of the Blessed Lyf of Jesu*, ed. L. G. Powell (1908), 308–09, as discussed in Duffy, *Stripping of the Altars*, 103; and an *imago pietatis* forms the central drama of the *Croxton Play of the Sacrament*, ed. Norman Davis, *Non-Cycle Plays and Fragments*, EETS (London and New York: Oxford, 1970); see Duffy, 107–08.

37. J. A. Endres, "Die Darstellung der Gregoriusmesse im Mittelalter," in *Zeitschrift für christliche Kunst* 30 (1917): 148, dates the earliest reference to the image's powers of indulgence to an inscription on a relief in Regensburg from the beginning of the fifteenth century; cited in Bertelli, 46. See also De Leeuw, "Unde et Memores," 35; Woodforde, *Norwich School of Glass Painting*," 23; Ringbom, "Devotional Images," 165. On the history of indulgenced images in general, see Belting, *Image and Its Public*, 14–15, 64, 132–33.

38. Woodforde, *Norwich School*, 23.

39. For a discussion of English representations of the Man of Sorrows, see Campbell Dodgson, "English Devotional Woodcuts of the Late Fifteenth Century, with Special Reference to Those in the Bodleian Library," *Walpole Society* 17: 94ff.

40. Also suggesting an alliance between the image of the Man of Sorrows and the donor figure who is both giver of the image and receiver of an indulgence through his or her placement below the figure, a Man of Sorrows appears in the glazing at Long Melford in close conjunction with a figure of Lady Annes Fray, with the inscription below her, "pray for dame Annes Fray"; see Woodforde, *Norwich School of Glass Painting*, 121. It is by no means certain, however, that these images were proximal in the original program of the glazing.

41. Woodforde, *Norwich School*, 117–88.

42. Bertelli, "The *Image of Pity*," 45, n. 37, also notes that the Man of Sorrows was frequently represented on church portals and on chapels represented in Italian Trecento paintings.

43. *Middle English Dictionary*, 770. This usage is reported from c. 1475.

44. A bench end, now in the Victoria and Albert Museum, from St. Nicholas' church, the chapel of ease that was the Brunham family chapel, shows a carving of three dried fish, or stockfish; see Anderson, *History and Imagery in British Churches*, 217.

45. *St. Katherine of Alexandria: The Late Middle English Prose Legend in Southwell Minster MS 7*, ed. Saara Nevanlinna and Irma Taavitsainen (Cambridge: Brewer, 1993), lines 446–48, p. 80. A similar reference appears in Capgrave's version of the St. Katherine legend, c. 1440, when Katherine prophesizes that the name of Porphyry and of Maxentius' queen "shul be wreten in the book of lyf," John Capgrave, *The Life of St. Katharine of Alexandria*, ed. Carl Horstmann, EETS (London: Paul, Trench, and Trübner, 1893), line 860, p. 366.

46. G. H. Cook, *Medieval Chantries and Chantry Chapels* (London: Phoenix House 1947, rev. edition, 1963), 3–5.

47. C. M. Kauffmann, *Romanesque Manuscripts, 1016–1190*, in *A Survey of MSS Illuminated in the British Isles*, vol. 3 (London: Miller, 1975), item no. 78, describes the New Minster Register (Liber Vitae), London, British Library MS Stowe 922. I am grateful to Madeline Caviness for this reference.

48. Rickert, figure 125.

49. Anderson, *History and Imagery in British Churches*, 95; see also Francis W. Cheetham, *English Medieval Alabasters: With a Catalogue of the Collection in the Victoria and Albert Museum* (Oxford: Phaidon-Christie's, 1984), 296; it has been suggested that Norwich may have been a center for alabaster carving, particularly for stone fonts, though Cheetham, 15, considers it unlikely.

50. Cheetham, 31.

51. For discussions of Kempe's orthodoxy, see esp. Lynn Staley, *Margery Kempe's Dissenting Fictions*, who argues that Margery is a fictive persona created by Kempe who strategically negotiates charges of Lollardy even as she lodges a critique against orthodoxy 5–11; Sarah Beckwith, "A Very Material Mysticism, 45–46; for a discussion of Kempe's anticlericalism, see Beckwith, *Christ's Body*, "The Uses of Corpus Christi and Margery Kempe," 78–111.

52. Anne Hudson, ed., *Selections from English Wycliffite Writings* (Cambridge: Cambridge University Press, 1978), 153/97.

53. Ibid., 27.

54. Woodforde, *Norwich School of Glass Painting*, 70–71.

55. For alabaster Trinities with donors, see Francis Cheetham, *Alabaster Images of Medieval England* (Woodbridge: Cultural Exchange and Boydell, 2003), 147–53.

56. British Library MS Add. 29705, fol. 193v, illus. in Marks, *Stained Glass in England*, fig. 138, p. 172.

57. Marks, 34, 252 n. 41.

58. For a discussion of the extensive rebuilding of churches in fifteenth-century East Anglia, see Norman Tanner, *The Church in Late Medieval Norwich*, 1370–1532, Pontifical Institute Studies and Texts, no. 66 (Toronto: Pontifical Institute of Mediaeval Studies, 1984), 4; see also Gibson, *Theater of Devotion*, 26; Graves, "Social Space," 312–13; and Duffy, *Stripping of the Altars*, 132, who notes that "maybe as

many as two-thirds of all English parish churches saw substantial rebuilding or alteration in the 150 years before the Reformation."

59. Hillen, *Borough of King's Lynn*, 879, describes the chapel as "Newly built and constructed from the alms of the benevolent" in 1429. That the rebuilding of the chancel was the result of a long capital campaign is indicated from a 1371 record that Pope Gregory XI granted a bull for rebuilding St. Nicholas and from a 1399 record of a gift of thirty pounds towards rebuilding and a further twenty pounds from the residue of his estate; see Hillen, 877.

60. For a discussion of these terms in the *Book*, see Despres, "Franciscan Spirituality."

## FURTHER READING


Aston, Margaret. *Faith and Fire: Popular and Unpopular Religion, 1350–1600*. London: Hambledon, 1993.

Beckwith, Sarah. "A Very Material Mysticism: The Medieval Mysticism of Margery Kempe." In *Medieval Literature: Criticism, Ideology, and History*. Ed. David Aers. Sussex: Harvester, 1986.

Belting, Hans. *The Image and Its Public in the Middle Ages: Form and Function of Early Paintings of the Passion*. Trans. Mark Bartusis and Raymond Meyer. New Rochelle, NY: Caratzas, 1981.

Delany, Sheila. "Sexual Economics: Chaucer's Wife of Bath and *The Book of Margery Kempe*." *Minnesota Review* 5 (1975): 104–15.

Despres, Denise. "Franciscan Spirituality: Margery Kempe and Visual Meditation." *Mystics Quarterly* 11, no. 1 (1984): 12–18.

Duffy, Eamon. *The Stripping of the Altars: Traditional Religion in England c. 1400–1580*. New Haven: Yale University Press, 1992.

Gibson, Gail McMurray. *The Theater of Devotion: East Anglian Drama and Society in the Late Middle Ages*. Chicago: University of Chicago Press, 1989.

Graves, Pamela. "Social Space in the English Medieval Parish Church." *Economy and Society* 18 (1989): 297–322.

*Mapping Margery Kempe* (website). Ed. Sarah Stanbury and Virginia Raguin. www.holycross.edu/kempe.

Marks, Richard. *Stained Glass in England During the Middle Ages*. Toronto: University of Toronto Press, 1993.

Rosenthal, Joel. T. *The Purchase of Paradise: Gift Giving and the Aristocracy*, 1307–1485. London: Routledge.

Staley, Lynn. *Margery Kempe's Dissenting Fictions*. University Park, PA: Pennsylvania State University Press, 1994.

FOUR

# REAL AND IMAGED BODIES IN ARCHITECTURAL SPACE: THE SETTING FOR MARGERY KEMPE'S *BOOK*

Virginia Chieffo Raguin

MUCH OF THE RECENT LITERATURE concerning Margery Kempe has centered on her ability to transcend time and place by the force of her visionary experiences. Despite her extraordinary accomplishments in constructing a place beyond the norm, Kempe still defined her persona through her status as a mayor's daughter and resident of Lynn. Deborah Ellis notes that Kempe "often expresses her struggle, as a sort of metatownswoman, through house imagery."[1] For medieval women, the home was a pervasive symbol, determining both the sense of personal integrity and the larger concept of "community." The *Book of Margery Kempe* is rife with specific notation of place. Not only does Kempe cite a large number of events happening in her town, but she refers throughout her text to "homey" issues of clothes, meals, lodging, and domestic duties. Most crucial of her references to buildings, however, are those to churches, places where the power of the town intersected with that of the heavenly realm. Through her references to buildings she transfers the images of the actual cities to her inner world, the "city of the soul" (ch. 28, 1574–75). It is from this association of the personal self with the heavenly one that she builds her authority.

## LITURGICAL SPACE AND SOUND

In over thirty-five named church sites, she links her experience to church practice.[2] She is present for sermons (ch. 69), participates in processions (ch. 72, 5802–07), and she hears Mass, even being granted a miraculous vision of the host fluttering as a dove (ch. 20, 1512–15). She attends seasonal liturgies such as Palm Sunday rituals of the priest lifting up of the veil before a crucifix (ch. 78, 6274–77), private devotions such as the dressing of a statue of the infant Jesus (ch. 30, 2524–53), private prayer at the chapel of the Virgin called the "Gesine" (childbed) at St. Margaret's,[3] or individual conference with a confessor in a designated chapel (ch. 69, 5681–84). Most frequent, understandably, are her references to her parish church, St. Margaret's of Lynn (figures 4.1–4.3). Although the church has had many sections rebuilt and the nave constructed in 1745 after the collapse of the south tower during a storm, it has substantially the same dimensions as in Kempe's time. The extremely deep choir (figure 4.2), reserved for the clergy, was constructed in the early thirteenth century.[4] The choir screens date from before Kempe's time, so we can imagine what it was like when sections of the church were relegated for use according to status and class. Kempe negotiated her presence and her privilege of access to see both ritual and object, such as the tabernacle that held the reserved host, the Easter Sepulcher, and relics, by her construction of herself as a mystic.[5]

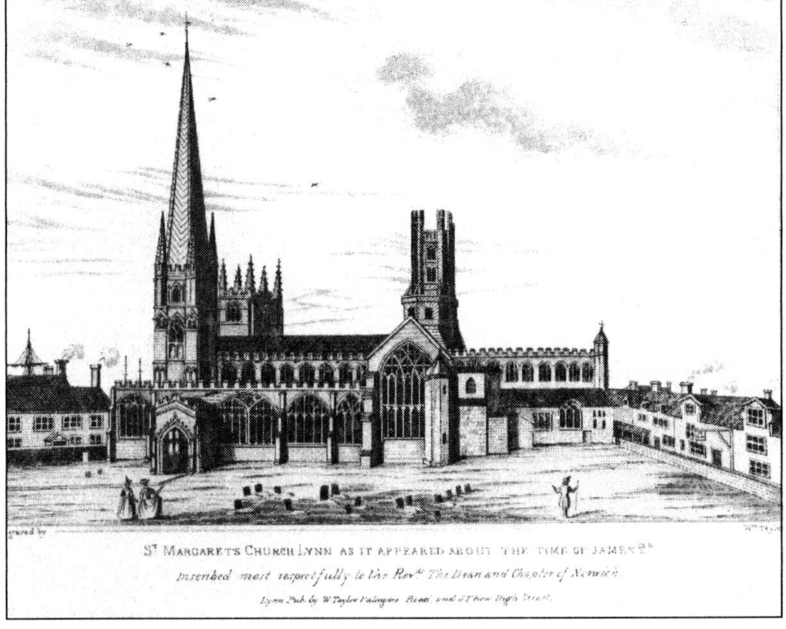


**Figure 4.1.** King's Lynn, St. Margaret's, exterior, south side. After William Taylor, *The Antiquities of King's Lynn* (London, 1844).

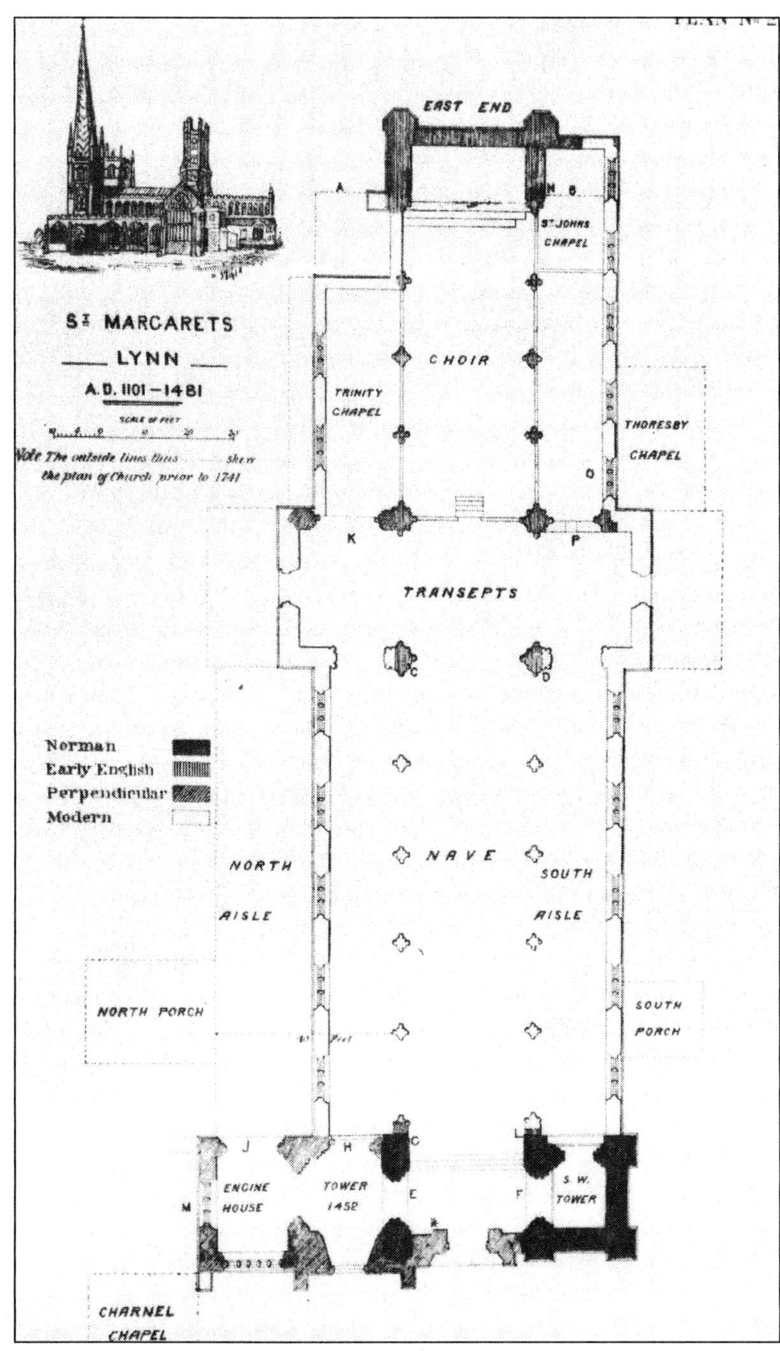


**Figure 4.2.** King's Lynn, St. Margaret's, plan 1102–1481, length 236 feet. After E. M. Beloe, F.S.A., *Our Borough: Our Churches: King's Lynn, Norfolk* (Cambridge, 1899).

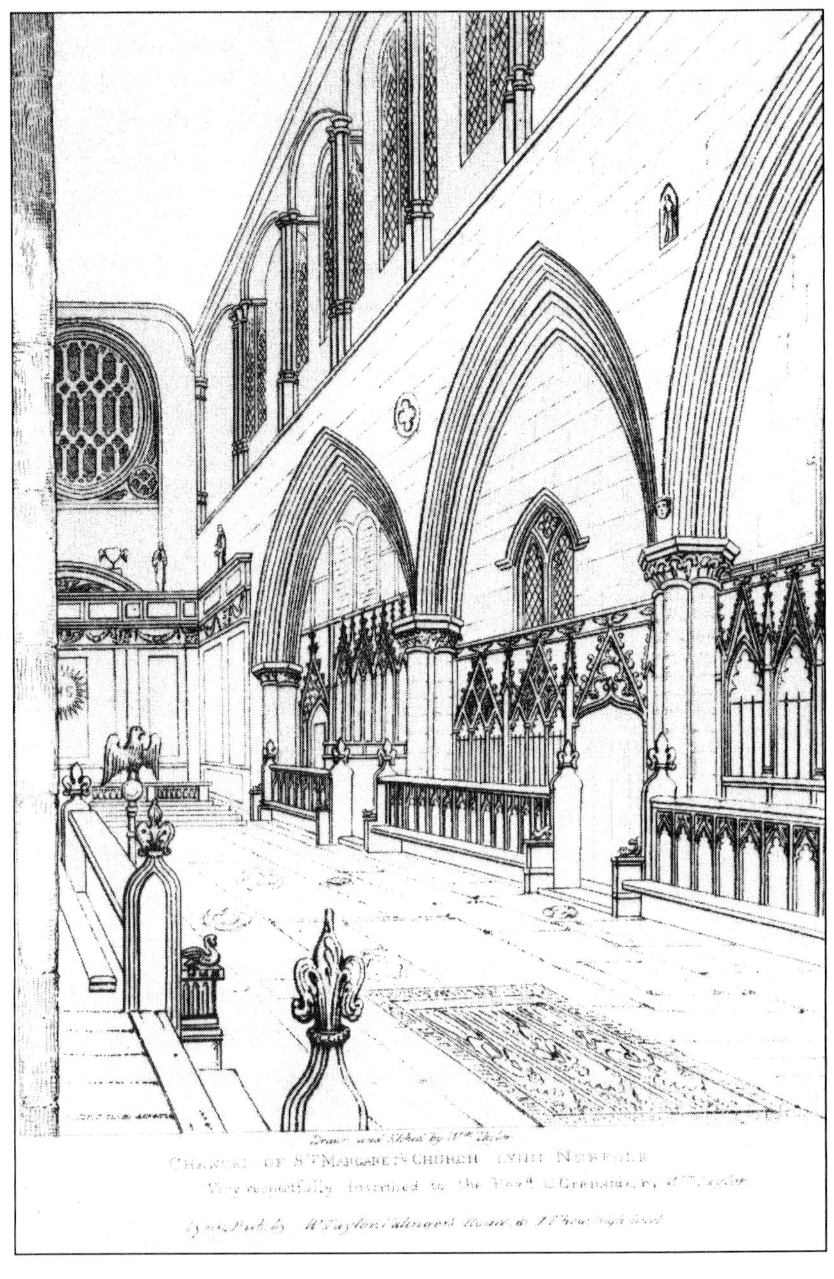


**Figure 4.3.** King's Lynn, St. Margaret's, interior of choir, south side. After William Taylor, *The Antiquities of King's Lynn* (London, 1844).

To the modern reader, Kempe's citations of the places can appear peripheral.[6] In comparison with medieval descriptive texts, however, they are quite rich. Bridget's *Revelations*, produced by a woman even more public and well traveled than Margery Kempe, contain far less localizing physical context.[7] Even guides to sites, such as *The Pilgrim's Guide to Santiago de Compostela*,[8] are also highly selective, the primary obligation being an enumeration of the purpose of the monument and the veneration of the specific saint. The stories of the saints and their virtues, much like Kempe's stories of virtuous or nonvirtuous actions, are foremost. For the *Guide*'s description of the monastery of St. Foi at Conques, as an example, the reader is treated to a paragraph on the courage of the early Christian martyr, then simply told that "the most precious body of the blessed Faith, virgin and martyr, was buried with honour by the Christians in a valley commonly called Conques, above which a beautiful basilica was built."[9] Even in the ninth chapter of the *Guide*, dedicated completely to a description of the basilica of St. James at Compostela, the writer's most frequent concern is the listing of the saints contained in the altar dedications within the basilica. The most elaborate description is reserved for the metalwork of the altars where the images and stories of the saints are depicted.

To picture Margery Kempe's strategic placement of herself within church space, in particular, it is useful to look at some donor portraits in Books of Hours. Seen within the parallels of contemporary clerical structure, Kempe's behavior is logical and even conventional. When contrasted to liturgical practice, her vocal outbursts appear appropriate, and compared with lay representation in manuscripts, stained glass, and sculpture, her self-imagery takes on new meaning. Kempe's descriptions of herself at prayer find their most vivid evocation from manuscripts produced some twenty to fifty years after she dictated her book to her priest-scribe. These lavish manuscripts, as Sarah Stanbury develops in this volume, are the kinds of books that Kempe could never hope to use, much less commission. Her illiteracy as well as her relative poverty precluded the act. Yet these books reflect the climate within which Kempe developed her strategies of placement. Most telling is the setting of donor portraits, depicted within an architectural setting, in the act of devotion.

Almost as if relying on Kempe's text, the Master of Mary of Burgundy produced illuminations for princely patrons of the later fifteenth century, among them Mary of Burgundy.[10] In this exquisite and well-known manuscript, Mary reads her hours within a well-appointed oratory (figure 4.4), complete with shutters equipped with bulls-eyes glass lattice, a glass vase with tall stalks of iris, and a pet dog. The spacious setting of the choir of a church is seen through the open shutters, a large building in Gothic style of glazed aisles and clerestory with four light windows and blind triforium. The setting is specifically within the choir, in front of the high altar, a space into which Mary either projects or remembers herself, accompanied by her female

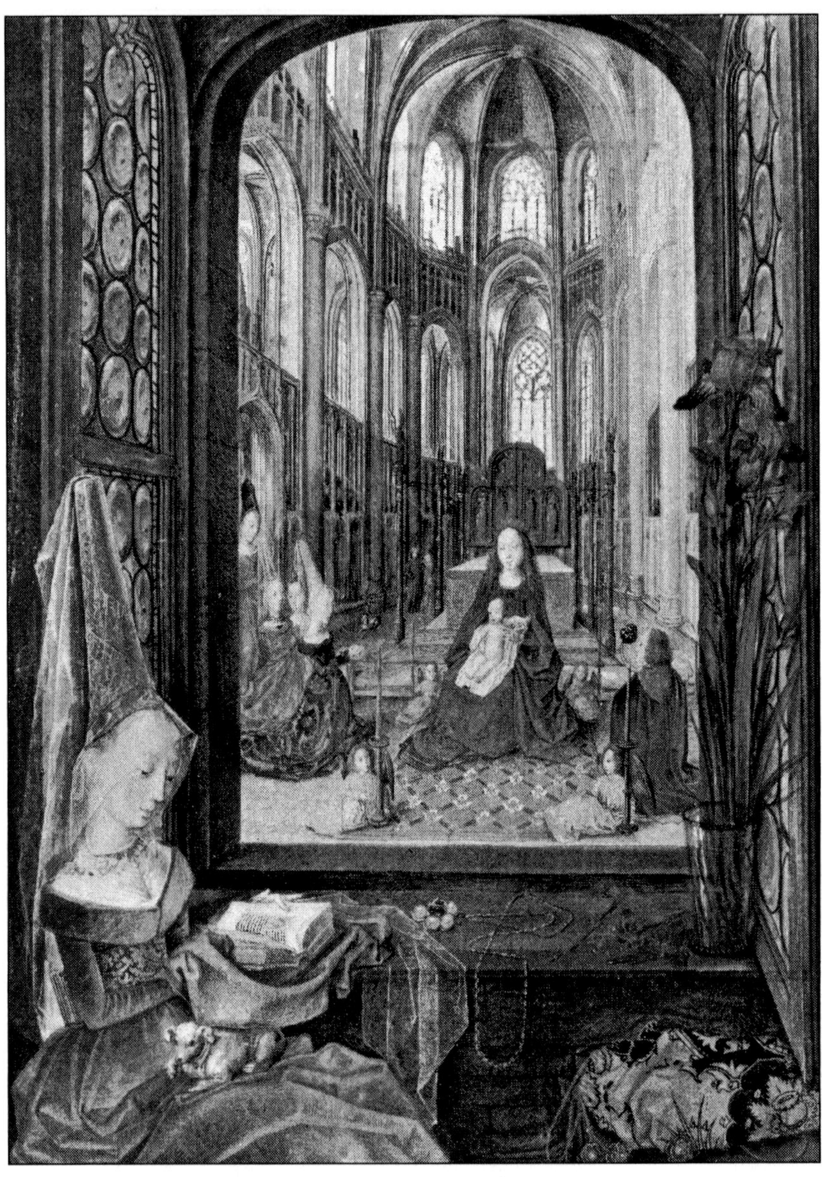

**Figure 4.4.** Mary of Burgundy at Prayer, *Hours of Mary of Burgundy*, ca. 1477, Vienna Österreichische Nationalbibliothek, Cod. Vind. 1857, fol. 14v. Courtesy Österreichische Nationalbibliothek, Bildarchiv d. ÖNB, Wien.

companions, with a male devotee, possibly her husband Maximilian of Hapsburg, who prays before the Virgin, honoring her with a censor. Four child-angels guard the candles set at the edges of the cloth of honor on which the Virgin and Child are isolated, the child looking toward Mary. The choir's solid screen and the archway through which Mary arrives are visible. Both the interior and the framing, Mary holding her book, in all probability reading the *Obsecro te*, a prayer specifically addressing the Virgin as intercessor, locate action and place to foreground the patron's access to ritually central clerical space.[11]

The desire to see and be seen and to construct representation fixed within the actual place of devotion extends to male as well as female commissioners.[12] In another Burgundian manuscript, dated about 1460 (figure 4.5), Philip the Good is seen attending Mass.[13] The choir of the chapel is

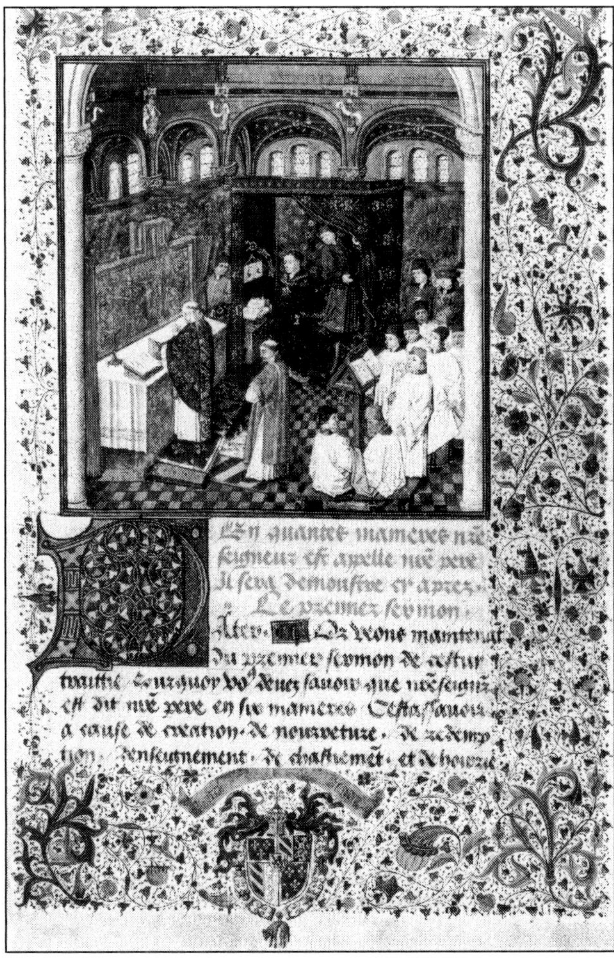

**Figure 4.5.** Philip the Good Attending Mass, *Traité sur l'oraison dominicale*, trans. Jean Miélot, Lille(?), ca. 1460, Brussels, Royal Library, MS 9092, fol. 9. Courtesy Brussels, Royal Library.

isolated by long red curtains strung between the capitals of the hemicycle. Within, Philip kneels under the royal blue baldaquin of his private oratory, a servant drawing back the curtain to allow him to see the Mass. The Duke's prayer book rests on a small prie-dieu; above it, a diptych shows the Virgin and Child to the left, and to the right a portrait of the kneeling duke in black. A retable before the priest and deacon contains three scenes of the Passion and a five-flame candlestick to symbolize the Five Wounds. Lest there be any doubt as to the identity of the worshipper and donor, the Duke's shields are woven in the rug before the altar and the Burgundian insignia on the blue drapery of the baldachin.

A similar enclosed space, one even closer to those described by Kempe, is represented in the *Book of Hours of James IV*.[14] Presumably made for his marriage in 1503 to Margaret Tudor, daughter of Henry VII, the manuscript shows Margaret at her devotions (figure 4.6) and in marked contrast to the

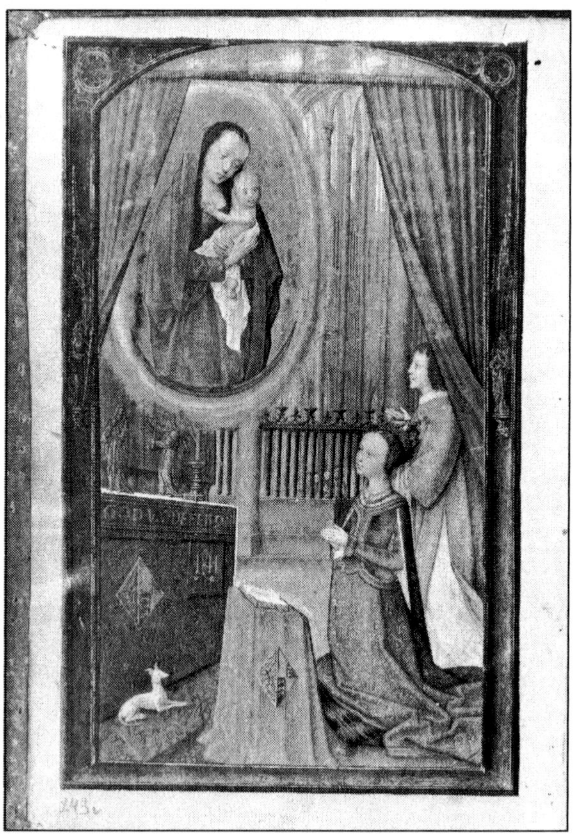

**Figure 4.6.** Margaret Tudor at Prayer, *Book of Hours of James IV*, ca. 1503, Vienna Österreichische Nationalbibliothek, Cod. 1897, fol. 243v. Courtesy Österreichische Nationalbibliothek, Bildarchiv d. ÖNB, Wien.

devotions of her husband, as Sarah Stanbury points out in chapter 3 of this book (note 26). Like that of the *Hours of Mary of Burgundy*, the setting is a tall Gothic church. Margaret kneels in a private oratory, her own Book of Hours before her on a prie-dieu set in front of an altar holding a statue group of the Annunciation. Green drapes frame the image, evoking the real drapes often embellishing the architectural enclosure but acting here as a foil for Margaret's vision of the Virgin and Child above the crescent moon that hovers in a type of elongated globe over the altar. A cleric, in deacon's dalmatic, stands to her side. Behind her is the grill of the chapel's enclosure, and crowding behind it are the onlookers who are excluded from Margaret's privileged space.

The importance of architectural settings in the definition of self is also evidenced in the medieval practice of the arts of memory and suggests that Kempe's insistent references to place may serve as memorial aids or even structural principles in her *Book*. Memory aids in the Middle Ages were primarily structured around architectural models. For both literate and illiterate, passages to be learned, lists of rules, or categories of order would be subject to stratagems of memory based on images of buildings and their contents. This journey through memory, as if one is moving through rooms in a building, was grounded in classical treatises such as the *Ad Herennium*, a text book compiled by an anonymous teacher of rhetoric in Rome in the first century BCE. Frances Yates summarizes what were then the standard methods of architectural imagination:

> In order to form a series of places in memory . . . a building is to be remembered, as spacious and varied a one as possible, the forecourt, the living room, bedrooms, and parlours, not omitting statues and other ornaments with which the rooms are decorated. The images by which the speech is remembered . . . are then placed in imagination on the places which have been memorized in the building. This done, as soon as the memory of the facts requires to be revived, all these places are visited in turn and the various deposits demanded of their custodian. We have to think of the ancient orator as moving in imagination through his memory building *whilst* he is making a speech, drawing from the memorized places the image he has placed in them.[15]

Memory systems, using the real experience of a known city or camp or constructing artificial building structures in the mind, were continued in the Middle Ages through such influential teachers as Albertus Magnus at the University of Paris in the thirteenth century.[16] Thomas Aquinas continued his work, encouraging the student to select memory spaces for which he felt affection or that were striking and vivid, rare and unusual, so the memory would remain more fixed. A number of commentaries, such as the Italian book *Rosaio della vita* 1373, speak of memorization of lists of virtues and vices, describing natural palaces such as trees in a field and artificial places such as those within buildings—a study, a window, or a coffer.[17]

Although Kempe would not have made a formal study of rhetorical devices, she was by no means naive. Mercantile practices such as the accounting required to maintain the brewery or mill (ch. 2) that she owned must have entailed some form of memory aids. Even household management invariably demanded as much structure.[18] Significantly, St. Bridget of Sweden (1307–73) uses a memory system based on imagining three houses of spiritual goods in her *Revelations*, a text with which Kempe was familiar.[19] Constructing a sort of allegorical housekeeping, the important mystic exploits the model of three houses in order that the spouse of Christ place in memory the kinds of virtues needed and their hierarchical order. The first is filled with food, "bread of goodwill, drink of goodly premeditation, and foods of goodly wisdom"; the second house contains clothing, linen of peace and patience, woolen of mercy, and silk of purity; and finally the third house contains the virtuous actions of the Christian thus nourished and clothed.

Margery Kempe's experience of architecture as both structuring memory and defining a space of honor extends throughout her text. Her memory of events is invariably linked to the physical experience of the site.[20] The setting of every defining moment is recorded. Her husband's acquiescence to her wish for chastity is granted on a trip from Lynn to Bridlington, as "hyr husbond sett hym down undyr the cros" (ch. 11, 743–44)[21] at the wayside. With the exception of her first revelation, Christ appearing to her while she is suffering from severe depression after childbirth and "syttyng upon hir beddys syde" (ch. 1, 229–30),[22] all her visions seem to have been experienced in specific church buildings. Most memorable may be her vision in the Tomb of the Holy Sepulcher in Jerusalem (ch. 28, 2197–225). It is in this holiest of pilgrimage sites, the one most calculated to evoke remembrance of Christ's death and resurrection, that she receives the gift of tears: "and cryed wyth a lowde voys as thow hir hert schulde a brostyn asundyr" (ch. 28, 2209–10).[23] Kempe consciously or unconsciously parallels the powerful visions received by St. Bridget at the Holy Sepulcher, in which the saint is also given the sight of Christ's Passion and is reassured that the Virgin had protected Bridget's son from the snares of the devil at the moment of his death.

## VOCALIZATION

Unlike Bridget's account, however, Kempe gives far more precise attention to her remembered experience, telling us that it took place between one evening and the next. Her first vocal manifestation of a mystical experience is intimately linked to her hearing the clergy demonstrate its intimacy with Christ through sound. The time in the Holy Sepulcher lasts from "the to day at evynsong-tyme . . . til the next day at evynsong-tyme (ch. 28, 2197–98).[24] She hears the sound of the clergy chanting the Divine Office opening and closing her experience, to which she adds her own great sound of weeping when "in the cite of hir sowle sche saw veryly and freschly how owyr Lord was crucifyed" (ch. 28, 2210–11).[25] In this signal event, Kempe is precise about informing the reader that "this was the fyrst cry that evyr sche cryed in any contemplacyon" (ch. 28, 2217–18). Kempe's evocation of the architectural metaphor of the "city of her soul" responds to biblical tradition as well as to her awareness of her pilgrimage to this specific place. She conflates an image of the historic Jerusalem in which she finds herself with the Jerusalem to come, the heavenly city with its additional metaphor of the female body, "coming down out of heaven . . . prepared as a bride adorned for her husband" (Rev. 21:2).

The experience in Jerusalem and her manifestation of her first gift of tears are logical responses to extraordinary events. Kempe's avoidance of chronology in her associative-driven exposition blurs much of this normalcy, however, as she presents first highly emotional, apparently unstable moments, her depression before and after childbirth, her struggles to avoid sexual relations in marriage, and visions. Her behavior most often cited as aberrant, her vocal outbursts, "boistows sobbyngys, wepyngys, and lowde cryes" (ch. 60, 4937–38)[26] and her falling to the floor prostrate were not professed until after a crowning moment in a devotee's life—a night of prayer and meditation cloistered by the tomb that sheltered Christ. As a lay person, and as one removed from literate expression or organizational ties, such as confraternities, Kempe was left with physical manifestation as a proof of the quality of her calling.

Not only buildings but also liturgical procedures manipulated sound and sight in structures of deprivation and reward, inclusion and exclusion. In her powerful responses to clerical space, Kempe also reveals herself to be strategically attentive to the sounds and textures of liturgical ritual within those spaces and even to the politics of spatial inclusion and exclusion. Much of the imagery we take for granted in churches today was often closed off from customary view by screens and covers and only revealed to worshippers at specific times and during designated ceremonial display. Those close to the choir screens might be allowed squints for seeing the elevation, as described in the introduction to this volume; at other times, sound would have to be substituted for sight, as during Lent when a veil was hung in St. Margaret's, as Duffy explains, "within a foot of the ground, completely blocking the laity's view of the celebrant and the sacring."[27] The Mass became a heard experience, the importance of which can be seen from thirteenth-century disputes. For example, in response to a complaint by the prior of St. Margaret's, the chaplain of the Hospital of St. John in Lynn was limited to a single Mass per day, said only in a low voice (*submissa voce*).[28] Neither could the hospital ring bells.

When we view buildings from Kempe's time and mentally reconstruct their original settings, with statues, wall hangings, lighted candles, shrines, stained glass, and numerous chapels, we can understand this interest in placement; and if we could view rituals of procession, such as the exposition of the sacrament, singing of devotions, wafting of incense, and sounds of the bells of the church and of the Mass, we might understand more easily her choices of communication, her famous weeping and shouting. Kempe's vocal outbursts, in fact, seem quite reasonable in the context of such clerical control of sound. Her authority (from God) was declared in loud weeping just as the priestly authority was known from the bells and sung offices, both manifesting mysteries unseen but experienced for others through sound. The medieval church was a busy, colorful, image-redolent, and above all, noisy place. Not only was ritual prayer by the clergy a heard event; even private prayer was characterized by the saying aloud of beads, ejaculations, voiced phrases. Even reading was still an oral practice, and sound figures prominently in Kempe's text. Music, the wind, and even natural sounds were interpreted as signs of God's favor.[29] A defining moment is Kempe's description of lying in bed with her husband and hearing "a sownd of melodye so swet and delectable, hir thowt, as sche had ben in paradyse." She exclaims, "Alas, that evyr I dede synne, it is ful mery in hevyn" (ch. 3, 325–28).[30] The intimacy that she enjoys with her husband and her abiding affection for him, as well as his for her, is clear throughout the text; yet here we are told that although sex may be good, heaven is better. And it is music that makes this clear. Kempe's experience is patterned after the music that she has heard in liturgical settings that communicate the sense of the otherworldly. She tells us that in St. Stephen's in Norwich her meditation on the Passion of Christ is rewarded with "so hedows a melodye that sche mygth not ber it" (ch. 17, 1242).[31] She falls to the floor and lies still for a great while. "Sowndys and melodiis had sche herd nyhand every day the terme of xxv yere . . . and specialy whan sche was in devowt prayer" (ch. 35, 2870–72)[32] include a "maner of sownde, as it had ben a peyr of belwys blowyng in hir ere . . . the voys of a dowe, and . . . of a lityl bryd whech is callyd a reedbrest" (ch. 36, 2966–70).[33] Sweet smells, like the incense that accompanied high masses and religious processions, heralding the presence of the sacrament, are likewise prototypes for her experience of mystical revelations, when she sensed "swet smellys, . . . swettar, hir thowt, than evyr was ony swet erdly thyng that sche smellyd beforn" (ch. 35, 2864–66).[34]

Kempe's construction of her public persona thus relies heavily on the model given by the clergy, especially their sounds. Such an interpretive approach does not contradict the many studies that have addressed Kempe's reliance on family and marriage as the experiential basis for her relationship with Christ; he is at once her child, lover, father, husband, and redeemer, assuring her, "I schal ordeyn for the, dowtyr, as for myn owyn modyr and as for myn owyn wyfe" (ch. 63, 5280–81).[35] These are, naturally, affective structures of the lay world. Kempe, however, constructs her *Book* and her behavior to transcend the limitations of the laity. As the clergy are her primary inspiration, we see Kempe eagerly embracing their ritual.[36] All manner of devotional practices, such as the recitation of the rosary, are dear to her, and she confesses that when she was involved in writing her books she "seyd fewer bedys for sped of wrytyng than sche had don yerys beforn" (ch. 88, 7274–75).[37] She does not contravene the authoritarian structure of the church, but simply claims Christ as her confidant and her ultimate confessor. The Father of Heaven "dalyd to hir sowle as pleynly and as veryly as o frend spekyth to another be bodyly spech" (ch. 17, 1251–52).[38] Thus even as she shifts the power of authority from clerical control to her own revelation, she does it through reiterating the structure of church practice, the speech of a confessor to his charge. Her stratagem shifts the authority to guide her from priest to Christ and the Trinity itself.

## ENCLOSURE

Although Kempe is far from cloistered, her desire to linger with communities of religious and to occupy the "cloistered" spaces of the choir and private chapel operates within a metaphor of architectural structure. She often refers to her visits to convents in Rome (ch. 39), Venice (ch. 27), and around England, such as the Franciscan convent of Denny in Cambridgshire (ch. 84). This metaphor of architecture, as Kempe says, the city of her soul (ch. 28, 1574–75), was elaborated in cloister imagery of the time. Although most of these foundations, or at least their imagery, have been lost in England, extant Continental structures reveal what they were like. A close look at actual architectural space as depicted for (or by) cloistered women can help explain the climate within which Margery Kempe acquired her visual language.[39]

A house for noble women in northern Saxony shows imagery and architecture articulating female devotional ideals.[40] Ebsdorf, founded as a Benedictine nunnery in the twelfth century, was supported by the patronage of the Braunschweig-Lüneburg ducal house. The cloister was finished by 1386 and glazed about 1400/1410 with a program based on the *Speculum humanae salvationis*, one of the popular spiritual guides that encouraged an understanding of Christ's message through juxtaposition with precedents from Jewish tradition. The three-part windows accommodated such a typological structure; the New Testament scene appeared in the center, Old Testament prototypes at the side, and prophets in tracery lights. Ulf Korn's reconstruction shows fifteen windows reproducing eighteen pages of the manual, using as his model the manuscript of the *Speculum* from about 1360, now in Darmstadt's municipal library.[41]

The designers of the glazing program's most marked change from the manuscript to the window is the insistent representation of buildings. Mimicking the space that contains them, the pictures on the nunnery's windows echo the real architectural cloister that contains them, reinforcing the metaphor of spatial enclosure. In the window depicting the cloister, an image of

Christ the Good Shepherd (figure 4.7) is not one of bucolic isolation, but of a savior explicitly directing the faithful to gather within a Gothic church. Although the image is dependent on a male-dominated clerical system, it is yet egalitarian in assurance of the value of each individual soul and Christ's closeness to the faithful, depicted in very human terms of cradling a small lamb before a church replete with rose window, gable facade, and stained glass. In the image of the Resurrection, Christ appears to step out of his tomb and into the space of the cloister. His arcaded sarcophagus engenders images of a temple seen from above, as if a giant figure were astride it. This architectural resonance is supported by the similar reconfiguration for the flanking Old Testament panels, the *Stone that the Builders Rejected* and *Samson with the Gates of Gaza*. The theme of the stone rejected is shown as the construction of a tower, with workers laboring within and without the building. Samson is not simply silhouetted with the doors on his shoulder, the more common

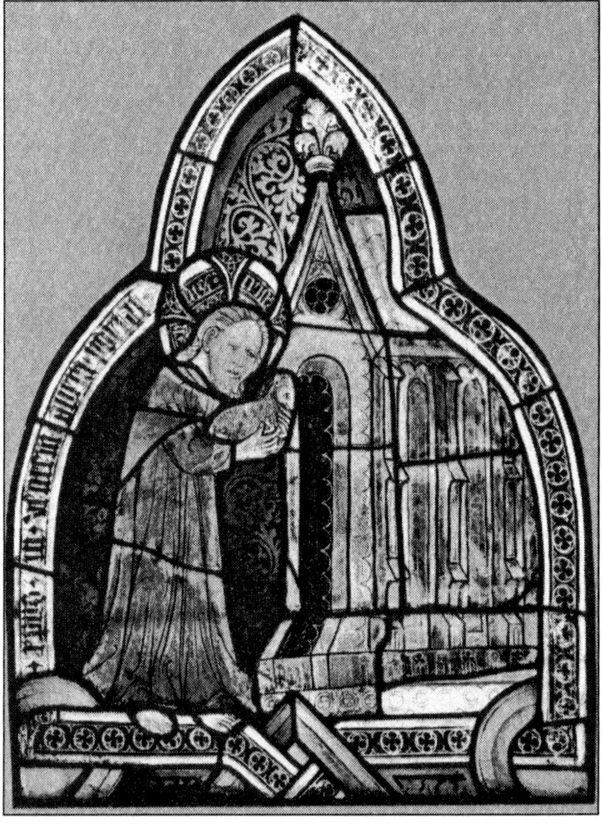

**Figure 4.7.** Christ the Good Shepherd, Ebsdorf, Benedictine nunnery, Cloister window, 1400–1410. Courtesy Corpus Vitrearum Deutschland, Freiburg i. Br. (R. Becksmann) Akademie der Wissenshaften un der Literatur Mainz.

representation, but is surrounded by the walls and tower of a complex city. The Arc of the Covenant, more commonly represented as a litter, is shown as a church complete with tower. It is presented twice, first flanking the Presentation in the Temple and then carried through the Red Sea as part of the window of Christ's Baptism. Although the Arc does not copy any known building, the image clearly includes tall windows, specifically of Romanesque rounded arches, and levels of roofs associated with Western medieval architecture. The specificity of the early medieval forms for an Old Testament image is undoubtedly a self-conscious contrast to the Gothic form of the New Testament image of the Good Shepherd.

The Parable of the Vine-dressers (Matt. 21:33–39), as portrayed in the glazing at Ebsdorf, addresses enclosure as a value for the female religious and may also provide a useful analog for understanding the representation of cloistered interiors in Margery Kempe's text. The owner of the vineyard "made a hedge around it, and dug in it a press, and built a tower," then let the vineyard to husbandmen while he was absent. It is, indeed, the *hortus conclusus*, the enclosed garden of the Song of Songs. The Darmstadt manuscript of the *Speculum humanae salvationis* shows an animated scene of two men brutally ambushing the owner's son (figure 4.8), which is set in front of a vineyard with a Gothic gate and watchtower, but whose walls are interwoven branches, the hedge of the biblical text. The cloister program (figure 4.9), however, creates a city wall, contrasting the complementary colors of red and green as visual signifiers of polarity. The inviting growth of the green vineyard is thus set against the hard, impenetrable red stone of the wall. The scene depicted is the slaying of the owner's son who is sent back to claim the fruits of the vineyard. All three men, victim and perpetrators alike, are of the same elite, golden-haired class, and all wear the same elegant short tunic exposing the stockinged leg. The conflict is bloodless, rather like a ritual stage play or knightly entertainment. The vivid naturalism of the manuscript has been transformed into a symmetrical statement of the wall as enclosure, with the male action placed outside. It seems likely, as Caviness has suggested in her study of the early fourteenth-century *Hours of Jeanne d'Evreux*, that the image depicts individuals of the male sex that the enclosed noblewomen are to avoid.[42] Violent lives of fathers and brothers, as well as of rejected suitors, are set outside the wall that marks the peace of the enclosed garden of the women.

Buildings imply safety and status. As Christ comforts Kempe, he likens his ability to protect her on her travels to the safety of the "strengest chirche in alle this worlde" (ch. 42, 3341–42). Representations of buildings that evoke the women's cloister help define the meaning of the convent's physical space, validating the very nature of enclosure within the real building. To women living out their lives within the enclosure of the convent, the house itself can function as metaphor for protection and power. The extant glass of the nuns' choir in Ebsdorf shows complex and varied building motifs in

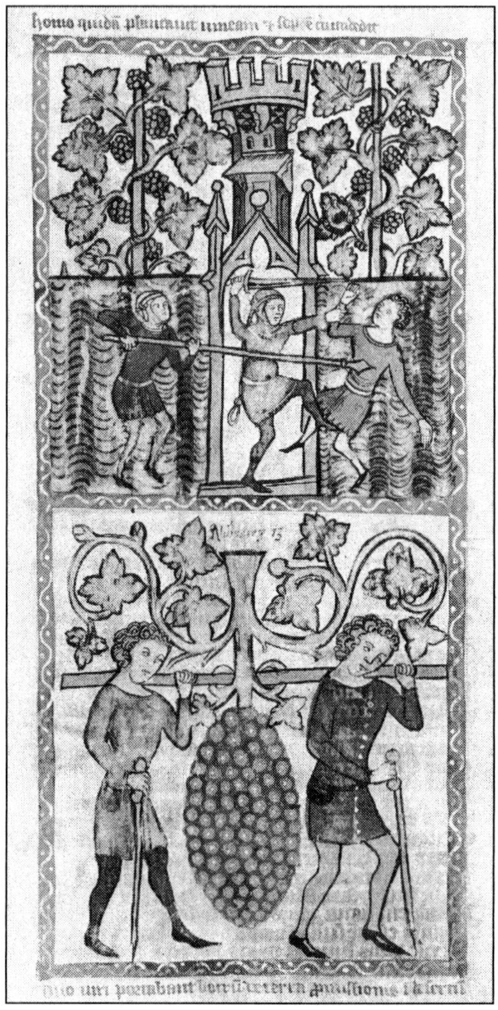

**Figure 4.8.** Parable of Vine-dressers, *Speculum humanae salvationis*, ca. 1360, Darmstadt, Hessische Landes und Hochschulbibliothek Hs 2505, fol. 41r.

architectural canopies under grisaille ornament.[43] Despite the loss of the lower figural panels, the large expanse of glazing done in grisaille patterns with gold, green, and red strapwork or in white architecture against blue backgrounds suggests purposeful design. The striking color combinations and great beauty articulate the importance of seeing the window, or any work of art, in situ, its meaning conditioned by its place within a large complex. The richness of the illusionist architecture as drawn in the glass can become a foil for the real, perhaps even questioning the banality of the "sensually real" in comparison to the spiritually depicted.

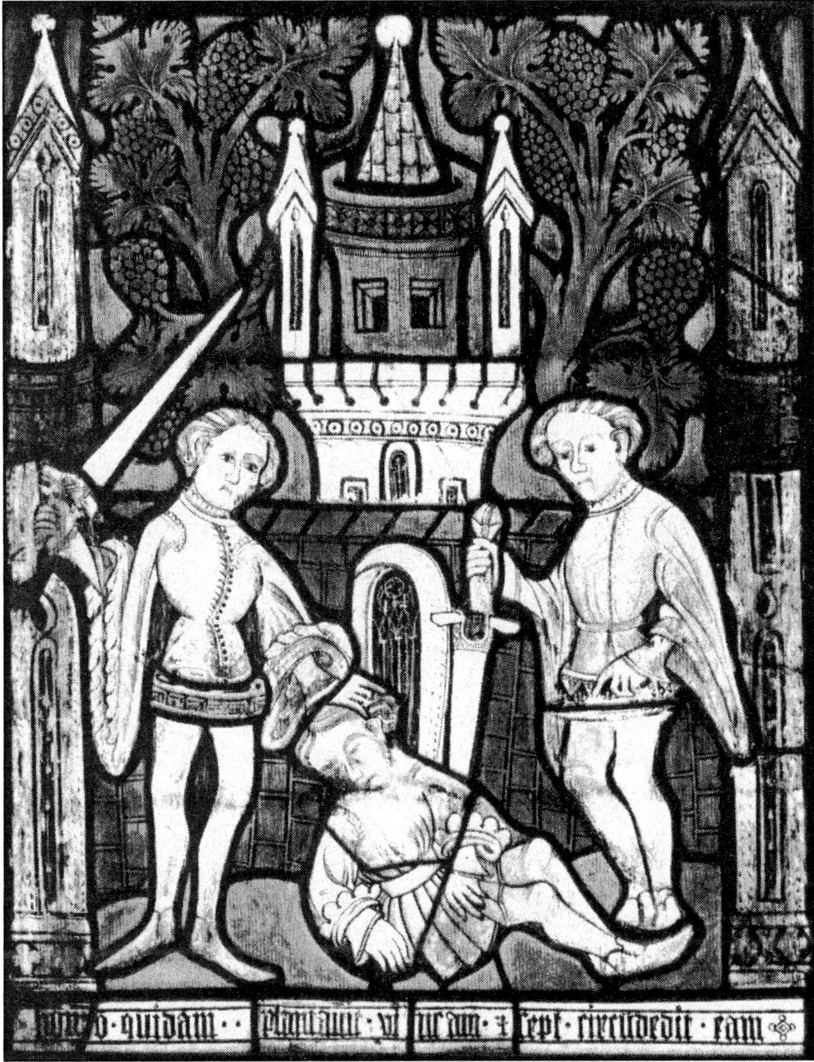

**Figure 4.9.** Parable of Vine-dressers, Ebsdorf, Benedictine nunnery, Cloister window, 1400–1410. Corpus Vitrearum Deutschland, Freiburg i. Br. (R. Becksmann) Akademie der Wissenshaften un der Literatur Mainz.

These images of architecture bring us back to the function of architecture in medieval patterns of memory. Mary Carruthers's *The Book of Memory* discusses the medieval use of "mental buildings" as memory devices.[44] Such ideas correspond to the injunction that the pious soul must store up treasure in heaven, not on earth. The framing of each of the Ebsdorf cloister images as if placed in little boxes echoes the tradition of the mind likened to a treasure box, a thesaurus. Synonyms for thesaurus include *cella* or monastic cell, and *arca*, or ark. The vivid nature of the image, especially with its brilliant "unnatural" color and its internal proportions, must relate to the medieval discussion of the power of *phantasia*, retentive imagination. Antique memory devices included intercolumnation, the spaces between columns as backgrounds for things to be remembered. What better place than a cloister with images set between designated columns?

## SPACE AS STATUS

Kempe's right to enter privileged spaces formerly reserved for the clergy and her concomitant uses of "voice" are demonstrated by a struggle with the prior of St. Margaret's. The relationship shows the apportioning of power between clergy and town, with the bulk of the power being maintained by the clergy through administration of the sacraments and their ability to withhold access. The entire structure of the medieval church reflected the social divisions, arguably more operative in early medieval times, among those who worked (peasants), those who fought (nobility), and those who prayed (clergy). Churches were early designed with choir areas so that the clergy, monastic or secular, could regularly have unfettered access to reserved space for the communal recitation of the canonical hours, one of their major obligations. Churches were also established within a line of hierarchical authority. St. Margaret's was founded in 1101 by Bishop Herbert of Norwich and dependent for its staffing and ordinances on the Benedictine priory at Norwich. It was jealous of its privileges and, like most ecclesiastic institutions, had a long history of defending its rites to property and to jurisdiction of ritual, as noted above. The bishops of Norwich were also in conflict with the Town Council of Lynn,[45] and the parishioners of the Church of St. Nicholas, which Kempe mentions in chapter 25, were at odds with the jurisdiction of the mother parish of St. Margaret's.

Kempe must have already enjoyed access to the normally reserved choir when her privileges were threatened by incoming clergy who must have been shocked to see a woman, and a laywoman without social rank, disturbing canonical, reserved space. She records that a new monk came to Lynn "whech lovyd not the sayd creatur ne wolde suffryn hir to comyn in her chapel, as sche had do before that he cam thedir" (ch. 57, 4671–73).[46] The prior, presumably embarrassed by his previous acquiescence, took the side of the newcomer and forbade Kempe's confessor from administering her Communion in the clergy's space. The prior's authority could only be countermanded by an authority higher than him. Robert Spryngolde, her confessor, produced a letter of dispensation that Kempe had received from the Archbishop of Canterbury, which gave him power to hear Kempe's confession and administer the sacrament "as oftyn as we ben reqwiryd" (ch. 57, 4684), explicitly in clerical, reserved space. The next line of Kempe's text tells us that the monks were forced to allow her to receive communion "at the hy awter in Seynt Margaretys Chirche." Not only does Kempe's text elaborate the process of negotiating levels of authority, but she then appropriates the ultimate authority by describing how God himself gave approval by so filling her with his love that she cried with great force: "owr Lord visited hir wyth so gret grace . . . that sche cryed so lowde that it myth ben herd al abowte the chirche and owte of the chirche (ch. 57, 4686–88).[47] Her sounds confirmed her rights.

The privilege of entering the choir was a major dispensation, and Kempe's text is meticulous in mentioning moments that include her location. Susan Morrison notes that Kempe's performance of self includes her "writing herself in spatially privileged space" and thus into acceptance by religious authority.[48] Kempe describes funeral ceremonies when she was in the "cherch of Seynt Margarete in the qwer [choir] wher a cors was present" (ch. 23, 1705–06). She recalls dream/visons in the choir (ch. 85, 6992–7010). When told of the illness of Master Aleyn, "sche ran into the qwer at Seynt Margaretys Chirche, knelyng down beforn the sacrament" (ch. 70, 5695–96) and thus was clearly privileged to be in the choir. When seen by others Kempe's body would appear in physical proximity to the devotional image. Indeed, next to the high altar, she would appear among its images of statues and painted panels and even on line with the door of the Easter Sepulcher. The ceremony of the Easter Sepulcher was conducted in the choir and the host taken from the altar and buried symbolically by placing it in a recess behind a door to the left (or the to the honorary right side) of the altar (ch. 57, 4697–701).

In the manuscripts mentioned at the beginning of this chapter, donors/owners appeared sometimes with the narrative image behind them and at other times directly addressing the sacred image. In a manuscript from Kempe's time, the "Belles Heures" in the Cloisters Museum, the Duchess of Berry is at prayer, and her eyes are directed to another miniature containing an image of the Trinity.[49] Whether across marginal space or across conflation of space and time, the constant was the real, named individual juxtaposed with the sacred image on view for the spectator. Kempe made herself into a such a figure through her strategy of placement on eye line with the inhabitants of Lynn. As they looked toward the altar, they would see Kempe interjected between their line of sight and its object. Such positioning of self in sacred space would be amplified in the later fifteenth century. Prominent lay persons would construct private chapels that engulfed clerical space, as in the disposition of chapels surrounding the altar in Long Melford. There a John Clopton or John Baret, as in St. Mary's in Bury St Edmunds, could be seen, in prayer or in the repose of death, in proximity to the sacred image.[50] Similar lay ascendancy occurred at St. Margaret's. The Trinity Guild gained the right to consecrate the north choir aisle as a chapel in 1472, in which Walter Coney, four times mayor of Lynn, set his large memorial brass.[51]

Kempe appears keenly aware of this intersection of social and religious privilege, as evidenced by her vehement opposition to the granting of independence to the church of St. Nicholas in Lynn, founded as a chapel of St. Margaret's.[52] In 1374 and again in 1432, coinciding, it seems, with new building campaigns, the parishioners of St. Nicholas sued to have a christening font, to conduct marriages, and to perform the rite of purification after childbirth. Kempe introduces this issue by an oblique statement, characteristic in her work, that this dispute arose "in a worshepful town." In reality, her father, while mayor, had also been opposed to this innovation,[53] and Kempe appears equally aware of the issue as one of access to power. Christenings and Purifications were clearly two very popular social activities. Authority to perform these rites would have made "the chapel eqwal to the parysch cherch" (ch. 25, 1916). Kempe has a revelation, an understanding in her soul, that though the parishioners behind this scheme would give a bushel of money, "thei schuld not have it," and because of her foreknowledge, "sche was the mor bold to preyn owyr Lord to wythstonde her intent and to slakyn her bost" (ch. 25, 1930–31).[54] Her attitude testifies to her completely ingrained understanding of ritual and the site of ritual as powerful aspects of social discourse.

Studies of Kempe have often concentrated on her deprivations and her refusal to follow societal norms, such as her desire to break off sexual relationships with her husband with whom she had fourteen children. These actions, however, should be seen not so much as denials but as steps toward a more valued status. Kempe could envision a more distinguished social class, a greater acquisition of power (impinging on clerical power), and a greater sense of self as an active part of Christ's plan of salvation. In the late Middle Ages almost all of one's life was structured by community rituals. Her visions enabled her to move into a new community, one of greater status than the earthly one she enjoyed. At every turn she describes her place in heaven as within a company, even within a great crowd as if in a church. Christ tells her that at her end she will be with "my blyssed modyr and myn holy awngelys and twelve apostelys, Seynt Kateryne, Seynt Margarete, Seynt Mary Mawdelyn, and many other seyntys that ben in hevyn" (ch. 22, 1630–55).[55] She will "dawnsyn in hevyn wyth other holy maydens and virgynes" (ch. 22, 1684–85). The description of her mystical marriage to Christ is particularly redolent with the earthly memories of elaborate ceremonies. She describes, as do other mystics, a great audience witnessing the event,[56] bringing to mind the medieval witness validation of legal contracts. In addition, she documents the moment as set within the Church of the Holy Apostles in Rome. Signal events were staged before designated authorities, or as public ceremony, and testimonies in trials would demand that witnesses swear to what they had seen. Thus Kempe presents the event as if it were a well-attended church ceremony in a highly prestigious place, even to the function of God the Father taking her by the hand to give her away to his son, "befor the

Sone and the Holy Gost, and the Modyr of Jhesu and alle the twelve apostelys and Seynt Kateryn and Seynt Margarete and many other seyntys and holy virgynes, wyth gret multitude of awngelys" (ch. 35, 2849–51).[57] They all see the hands clasped and hear Christ's words, "I take the, Margery, for my weddyd wyfe" (ch. 35, 2853).

Kempe's community and her privileges of inclusion also extend backward in time. This is demonstrated primarily through her efforts to get physically close to sacred relics housed at religious sites. Her many quests and pilgrimages are a manifestation of the belief in the extended Christian community, the *praesentia*, as developed by Peter Brown.[58] In Santa Maria Maggiore, for example, she is at the tomb of St. Jerome. As a matter of faith, the Christian is taught to see the mystical body of Christ as encompassing all souls. Kempe gives a vivid actuality to that tenet of faith by not only meditating on the virtues of the saint and praying for his intercession, but by actually receiving an answer from the Church Father. Jerome appears to her, reassuring her of the righteousness of the most troubling public aspect of her behavior. He tells her that her tears are divinely approved, a "specyal gyft that God hath yovyn the," with Kempe telling us that "wyth swech maner of dalyawns he hily comfortyd hir spiritys" (ch. 41, 3270).[59]

In the medieval Christian community, the physical site itself was the means by which members of the community engaged in rituals that defined the notion of responsibility, privilege, protection, and hierarchy. The medieval church was invariably the largest and most elaborate structure of personal experience. It functioned as a metaphor for the ultimate goal of the Christian's life, a communal "home," a stronger, more power site than her domestic home. The urban setting was a place of safety, set against the unknown open country, a major thematic device in art, from Giotto's 1300 cycle of the *Infancy of Mary and Life of Christ* in the Arena chapel, Padua, to Piero di Cosimo's 1490 *Discovery of Honey*.[60] Kempe's own city of Lynn was encircled by walls whose gates screened access.[61] The gates ensured that both the privilege to tax and freedom from intrusion were preserved. In a juxtaposition of the city as safe (very different for the late-twentieth-century reader) and country as unsafe, the sense of bonding with an institution is clear. In Rome, Kempe receives assurance that she will be safe as she journeys to pilgrimage sites and to her home, as if she were protected within a church. Christ tells her, "I am as mythy to kepyn the her in the felde as in the strengest chirche in alle this worlde" (ch. 42, 3341–42).[62]

## INCLUSION AND COMMUNAL SPACE

Inclusion—or as Stanbury phrases it, "being there"—did indeed dominate Kempe's constructions. She reveals a keen awareness of these rituals of presence when she is either included or excluded through the intimacy of sharing a meal. The secular meal parallels liturgical meals, the church ritual of receiving the sacrament, for which Kempe had been given special dispensation. Twenty-four references to shared meals and seating arrangements, mirroring social placement within the church, as Katherine L. French explains in her chapter, enrich her text. Indeed, her cherished goal of chastity within marriage is allowed to her by her husband when he is assured, in recompense, that she will pay his debts before going to Jerusalem and will sit with him and eat, sharing his meals, on Fridays (ch. 11, 740–80). She notes when she is invited to a meal in Lincoln and the "Bysshop hymself sent hir ful gentylly of hys owyn mees" (ch. 15, 1101–02),[63] when the Grey Friars in Bethlehem "receyved hir into hem and sett hir wyth hem at the mete that sche schuld not etyn alone" (ch. 29, 2389–90),[64] or when a worthy lady "set hir at hir owen tabil abovyn hirself, and leyd hir mete wyth hir owyn handys" (ch. 38, 3063–64).[65] Kempe is equally explicit about the indignities she suffers by individuals who place her in lowly positions. In Constance her companions are annoyed with her and "madyn hir to syttn at the tabelys ende benethyn alle other, that sche durst ful evyl spekyn a word" (ch. 26, 2009–10).[66] To contradict the effect of such treatment, she is quick to explain that despite such malice, wherever they go, she is held in more esteem by others than are her companions.

Kempe's bodily presence in the churches she visits, as discussed by Stanbury in this volume, develops within a world that routinely placed female bodies in heraldic display in windows and on the written page, the woman's body bearing the impaled arms of family and of marriage.[67] Kempe's own concerns about dress and about her placement within churches may be connected to this tradition of donor presence where female costume, and specifically heraldic dress, was crucial to the meaning of the image. Despite what we may think about Kempe's independence, her identity still rests on her association with family, the triangulation of father, husband, and self. She answers to a question of identity with definition of place, paternity, and marriage: "I am of Lynn in Norfolke, a good mannys dowtyr of the same Lynne, whech hath ben meyr fyve tymes of that worshepful burwgh, and aldyrman also many yerys, and I have a good man, also a burgeys of the seyd town, Lynne, to myn husbond" (ch. 46, 3684–88).[68] However, the ability to depict herself as a donor, as consistently seen in wall painting, stained glass (figures 3.3, 3.6), and tomb sculptures, is denied Margery Kempe. [69] Nevertheless, she finds ways to embody the self, even physically, in these very same places, as Stanbury argues. She is a fixture, praying in the choir of St. Margaret, just as if she were a painted image of a donor before the cross.

Her most dramatic moments, however, are not simply before the cross, but prone, sprawling on the pavement of the building, rapt in her ecstasy of feeling. She describes entering churches at night to prostrate herself on the floor. At St. Stephen's in Norwich, she goes to the high altar and falls down on the tomb of the vicar who has been her confessor many times (ch. 60, 4933–36). This position was common in private prayer, and she describes herself "as she lay stille" (ch. 85, 7004) in the choir, and as she "lay in the qwer in her prayers" (ch. 23, 1714). If she emphasizes this attitude and placement, she is following a tradition of claiming the church floor as a space of privilege, as seen, for example, by the tombs placed on the floor of the Cavalcanti/Acciaiuoli chapel in Santa Maria Novella, discussed by Ena Giurescu Heller in this volume. Kempe's prone body echoes those of others. In St. Margaret's, she is juxtaposing her real, living presence with the imaged presence in monumental brasses of the most successful persons of her class, merchants and former mayors of Lynn.

The custom of burial within the church for prominent ecclesiastics was common, inspired by the internment of relics of saints as rituals of foundation. The more closely one could align one's body, either as worshipper or as defunct, to the sainted dead, the greater the honor. The nobility negotiated similar privileges, and as power was acquired by the merchant classes they also claimed inclusion.[70] Lynn was early a site of lay ascendancy, as can be seen through its brasses. St. Margaret's, in fact, had of some of the most important fifteenth-century sepulchral brasses in England.[71] In the early eighteenth century, eleven large-scale figural brasses were still extant in St. Margaret's.

> I. Adam de Walsokene and w. Margt. 1349. In choro. [figure 4.10]
> II. Robert Braunche and ws. Leticia and Margt. 1364. In choro. [figure 4.11]

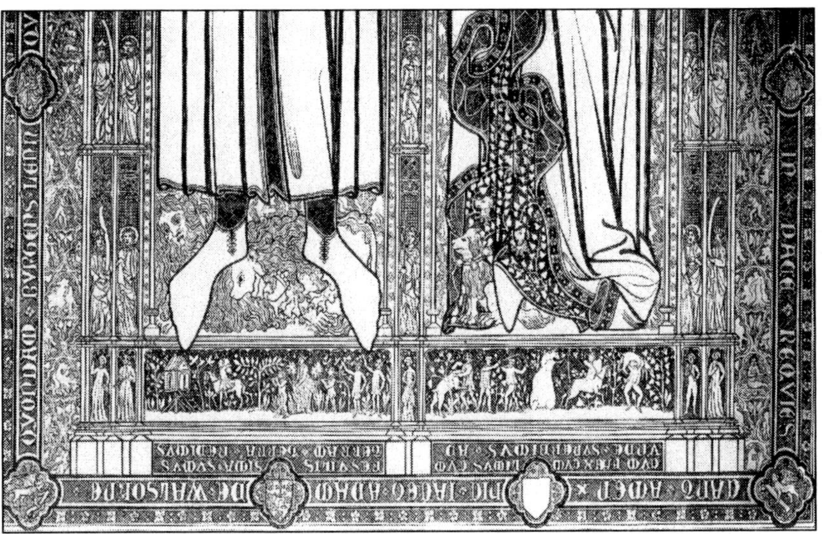

**Figure 4.10.** Brass of Adam de Walsoken and wife Margaret, 1349, St. Margaret's, King's Lynn, Detail of bottom, men carry grist to mill and carry Walsoken in litter over stream. After John Sell Cotman, *Engravings of Sepulchral Brasses in Norfolk* (London: Bohn, 1838).

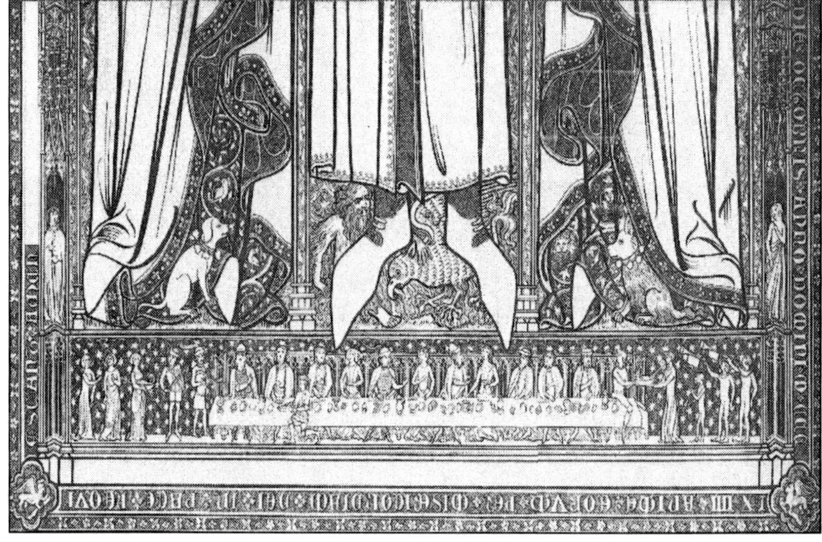

**Figure 4.11.** Brass of Robert Braunche with Leticia, first, and Margaret, second wife, 1364, St. Margaret's, King's Lynn, Detail of bottom, Peacock Feast. After John Sell Cotman, *Engravings of Sepulchral Brasses in Norfolk* (London: Bohn, 1838).

III. Robert Attelath and w. Johanna. 1376. In medio capellae S. Trinitatis.
IV. Simon Scotland and w. Johanna with mchts mark. c. 1450. In navi ecclesiae.
V. Walter Kintan and w. Johanna. 2 shields. 1468. In ala boreali orientem versus.
VI. Walter Coney. "Mercator huius villae." 1479. In ala boreali orientem versus.
VII. John Bulney, and ws Johanna and Agnes. 1487. "Burgensis et Glover Burgi de Lenn." 4 shields, 2 charged with shears, 2 with gloves. In ala boreali orientem versus.
VIII. John Trounche and 4 wives Margt., Marget., Isabella & Johanna. 1496. 4 mchts mks.
IX. Adam Bensting "Pryst" 1506. Juxta baptistorium.
X. William Tresby, 1511. In ala obliqua ecclesiae inter choru & navim.
XI. Thos. Trounche and w. Margt. and dau. Johanna in shroud. Eff. of w. then lost. 1535. In ala obliqua Ecclesiae.[72]

The three earliest brasses, those present in Kempe's time, came from a common workshop, probably Lübeck in East Prussia, and these merchants were part of the powerful Hanseatic trading league. The importance of the brasses can be seen in the overview of this material by John Sell Cotman, in 1838 when far more examples were extant.[73] The monument to Mayor Adam de Walsoken and wife Margaret (figure 4.10) is still extant. At the bottom of the brass we see Walsoken's men carrying grist to his mill and carrying Walsoken in a litter over a stream—a curious connection to Kempe, who records her own experience with running a mill (ch. 2, 275–78) as a demonstration of her pride, attributing to divine intervention the remarkable reluctance of the horses to pull. The brass of the merchant Robert Attelath and wife, Johanna, is now lost, but the male figure is known from a rubbing.[74] For Robert Braunche, mayor, the brass shows both Leticia, his first, and Margaret, his second wife. At the bottom of the image Braunche had commissioned a representation of the Peacock Feast he instituted (figure 4.11).

Kempe would also have seen similar brasses, as magnificent as the Braunche brass, in St. Nicholas. The St. Nicholas brasses date to 1380 and 1400, when it appears that large brasses were not being made for St. Margaret's. This evidence corroborates the historic records and Kempe's references to the position of the chapel as a site of conspicuous wealth towards 1400 and an actual threat to St. Margaret's supremacy. Kempe characterizes the parishioners as "ryche men, worshepful marchawntys, [who] haddyn gold anow, whech may spede in every nede" (ch. 25, 1901–02). The description of the now lost brass of William Bittering and wife Juliana from the 1380s bears this out:

> 'Tis 10 feet—inches long and 6 feet—inches broad, all cover'd with brass plates finely engraven with ye effigies of the person and his consort there interred in the middel at full length, embellished with figures of ye 12 apostles and many other saints, etc. . . . Adorned likewise with artfull decorations round ye verge where see also ye sdame—the like is in a south window just near it, and under their feet is a hexastick of monkish Rhythiming verses for ye epitaph, intimating their qualifications and distinctions, etc.[75]

The brass for Thomas Waterdeyn and wife, Alice, of about 1400 showed two hearts joined together suspended from a tree flanked on either side by Waterdeyn's merchant mark. The inscription reads: Where your true joy is fixed, so will be your hearts.[76]

Even a superficial study of Norfolk churches, as provided by Cotman, mentioned above, confirms that the tradition of figural images in brass was common, but Lynn was distinguished for number and quality, even surpassing Norwich and its cathedral. The brasses not only were structured of a highly valuable material (the cause of their confiscation in later centuries) but also were modeled in technique that permitted extreme delicacy of depiction. They presented complex inscriptions, details of dress, and natural as well as symbolic forms. The little dogs that represent fidelity at the feet of the women, in particular Leticia, and Margaret, wives of Robert Braunche (figure

4.10) show differentiation that identifies the animals popular as pets for the wealthier classes, a terrier and spaniel.

The careful attention to dress as shown in the brasses is evocative of Kempe's own interest in clothes. She confessed that even after her revelation from Christ during her illness, she maintained her showy manner of dressing, her "pompows aray" (ch. 2, 256), detailing her use of gold trim, brilliant colors, and contrasting hues revealed by the slashes in her sleeves. Kempe's constant awareness of how she is seen by others is revealed by her confession that she scrutinized others' apparel and had known "ful greet envye at hir neybowrs, that thei schuld ben arayd so wel as sche" (ch. 2, 270–71).[77] Even in her most pious gestures, such as her quest for operative virginity, her desire is manifested by clothes. For Kempe, the ability to wear white (ch. 44, 3417–48, ch. 37, 3000–02), for which she needs clerical approval, is the confirmation of her achievement of virginity and eligibility for Christ's espousal.[78] I believe that for herself, just as much as for her viewers, external appearance is the construct and the guarantee of her interior state.

Margery Kempe, both fascinating and liminal, was still a woman of her time and conventional in many ways. She emulated the proven strategy of clerical performance, staged within church buildings, but subverted it to allow her to claim her own inclusion. We see Kempe's position as in between: as wife and mother and also "public" virgin; as a humble follower of Christ who still notes where she is seated in the hierarchy of meals; or as a woman consistently challenging clerical hegemony but using as her weapons the very rituals and structures of the corporate church. A definitive proof of her voice may be its power in her finances. The clergy preach, sing, read, and study, dispensing words and actions. Kempe cries, roars, weeps, and talks and for this is rewarded by sweet voices from her Lord in Heaven. But she, like the clergy, is also rewarded on earth. Some pilgrims "yovyn hir iii halfpenys, in-as-meche as sche had in comownying telde hem good talys. And than was sche rygth glad and mery" (ch. 44, 3372–74).[79]

Our current interest in *The Book of Margery Kempe* says much about our own society's concerns with gender, class, and religion as constructs of status. Direct testimony from medieval texts of these intersections is extremely rare, and it bears repeating that these highly unusual instances of medieval self-revelation were invariably a product of resistance. Abbot Suger's description of his reconstruction and embellishment of the abbey church of Saint-Denis is contextualized by the powerful influence of St. Bernard on twelfth-century attitudes about the inappropriateness of imagery and lavish display in monastic confines.[80] Kempe's text is dictated by the female child of a once-wealthy family, in decline, at a moment of transition from clerical dominance to lay power. Strangely, it seemed as I compared Kempe's behavior to actual building practice, she parallels practices of patronage that appear a full half-century later. Her intensity of place, I would suggest, comes from her position as a member of the *illiterati*.[81] Her absorption of tenets of faith came not with the written page but with corporeal experience, a voice heard within a specific setting, or an image seen as painted retable or sculpture set in architectural space. Thus her structure of recall is always associative, and always site-specific. We benefit from this highly unusual moment when an unlettered person leaves us a written memoir. We "read" her constructing a self-image based on experience within spaces, seeing herself as an image in sepulchral brasses, transfixed by a night within the basilica of the Holy Sepulcher, journeying to pilgrimage site, and grounded in the routine of daily experience of her parish church.

## NOTES

I first read *The Book of Margery Kempe* in a team-taught course on art and literature with Thomas M. C. Lawler and later in the seminar Visionary Art and Literature with Sarah Stanbury. I am grateful for both these opportunities. I wish to thank the Research and Publications Fund of the College of the Holy Cross for support of research that Sarah Stanbury and I jointely pursued in East Anglia, summer 1995. Portions of this chapter were presented at the International Congress on Medieval Studies, Kalamazoo, Michigan, May 1996; the International Congress on Medieval Studies, Leeds, July 1996; the Holy Cross Women's Studies Conference, 1996; and for a medieval literature course taught by Kathleen Ashley, University of Southern Maine, in 1966. For many images of medieval Rome, Venice, England, and other sites mentioned by Kempe and discussed in this chapter, see the Website Mapping Margery Kempe www.holycross.edu/kempe. Citations in this chapter are from *The Book of Margery Kempe*, ed. Barry Windeatt (Essex and New York: Longman, 2000). Modern English translations in the notes with page numbers are from *The Book of Margery Kempe*, trans. Barry Windeatt (London: Penguin Books, 1985).

1. Deborah S. Ellis, "Margery Kempe and King's Lynn," in *Margery Kempe: A Book of Essays*, ed. Sandra J. McEntire (New York: Garland, 1992), 140.

2. Although not explicitly detailed in her text, Kempe was certainly exposed to architectural meanings. Relationships of scale—for example, the contrast between the size of the cathedrals of Norwich and Lincoln and Lynn's parish churches—create a language of power and authority, one that is enhanced by contrasts in materials, and arguably, skill of workmanship. The dominance of Lincoln's profile, or the Norman strength of Norwich's hemicycle, depend on materials as well as massing. Cut stone, Purbeck marble, and the highly refined techniques of Lincoln's Angel Choir, whose cathedral Kempe must have visited during her three-week wait for the Bishop (1055–57), demonstrate legitimacy of control. The parish churches were drawn into this dialogue of materials and power. The local use of flint in polychrome exteriors mimics the dark and light contrast of the limestone and Purbeck marble shafts of Lincoln's arcades. The timbered angel roofs, as at St. Nicholas, seem a reply to the elaborate stone vaulting and angel iconography. Peter Brieger, *English Art 1216–1307* (Oxford: Oxford University Press, 1957), esp. 189, figs. 3, 4, 6a, 16a, 71.

3. The location of the chapel is not clearly located in the documents. See H. Harrod, Esq., *Report on the Deeds and Records of the Borough of King's Lynn* (King's Lynn: Thew and Son, 1874), 14–15; *The Book of Margery Kempe*, ed. Sanford Brown

Meech and Hope Emily Allen, EETS, o.s. 212 (London: Oxford University Press, 1940), 324/155, 329/169. The chapel of the Gesine is mentioned in a deed of 1366 locating property as bounded on one side by "the stile by which the church of St. Margaret was entered at a certain chapel of the Blessed Mary called 'Gyssyne' to the east" and on the other by "another conduit that leads to the same church west." Since it is highly unlikely that the chapel, which was used commonly by the townsfolk, would be in the choir at this time, it was probably, like the chapel of St. Anne at Chartres, in the north transept.

4. The distinction between the choir (or chancel) and the nave is clear in fifteenth-century documents concerning the rebuilding of the roof and clerestory. The minutes of the town council, 21 March 1481, record (in English): "the commons shall close and defend the church of St. Margaret's and take down the old roof and . . . the executors of Walter Cony grant to make the clerestories on both sides of the same church." Henry Hillen, *History of the Borough of King's Lynn* (Norwich: East of England Newspaper Company, 1907), 128–31; and Edgar Milligen Beloe, *Our Borough: Our Churches: King's Lynn, Norfolk* (Cambridge: Macmillan and Bowes, 1899), 92. Beloe gives the full wording of the resolution, which makes it clear that all that is referred to as "church" is truly the nave. He comments that "the chancel was still in the hands of the prior of Lynn, representing the Monastery of Norwich, and we therefore have no record among the Lynn Muniments of the rebuilding of its clerestory" (Beloe, 94). The style of the chancel, however, argues for a date very close to that of the nave. For reconstruction of the earlier state of St. Margaret's see Benjamin Mackerell, *The History and Antiquities of the Flourishing Corporation of King's-Lynn* (London: Cave, 1738), 3–10.

5. For the Easter Sepulchre see Meech and Allen, *Book of Margery Kempe*, 319/139; Pamela Sheingorn, *The Easter Sepulchre in England* (Kalamazoo, Mich.: Medieval Institute Publ. WMU, 1987). After the Renaissance and nineteenth-century renovations to the chancel of St. Margaret's, we have lost the original disposition of the Easter Sepulchre of Kempe's time.

6. Donald R. Howard, *Writers and Pilgrims: Medieval Pilgrim Narratives and Their Posterity* (Berkeley and Los Angeles: University of California Press, 1980), 35, complains that "there is not in her book a scintilla of traveller's curiosity." Clarissa W. Atkinson, *Mystic and Pilgrim: The Book and the World of Margery Kempe* (Ithaca: Cornell University Press, 1983), 92–93, comments that Kempe did not write about what she saw, although it is reflected in her meditations.

7. See Julian Bolton Holloway, "Bride, Margery, Julian and Alice: Brigit of Sweden's Textual Community in Medieval England," in *Margery Kempe: A Book of Essays*, ed. Sandra J. McEntire (New York: Garland, 1992), 203–21.

8. Paula Gerson, Annie Shaver-Crandall and Alison Stones, *The Pilgrim's Guide to Santiago de Compostela* (London: Miller, 1995–98), vol. 2.

9. Ibid., vol. 2, 43.

10. *Hours of Mary of Burgundy*, Bruges, ca. 1477, Vienna Österreichische Nationalbibliothek, Cod. 1857, fol. 14v.; Otto Pächt, *The Master of Mary of Burgundy* (London: Faber and Faber, 1948); Pächt, *Book Illumination in the Middle Ages: An Introduction* (London: Miller, 1986); *The Hours of Mary of Burgundy*, commentary by Erik Inglis (London: Miller, 1995).

11. Sandra Penketh "Women and Books of Hours," in *Women and the Book*, ed. Jane Taylor and Lesley Smith (Toronto: University of Toronto Press, 1996), 266. For discussion of the cultural context of Books of Hours and prayers such as the

Obsecro te, see Roger Wieck, *Time Sanctified: The Book of Hours in Medieval Art and Life* (Baltimore: Walters Art Gallery, 1988); John Harthan, *The Book of Hours* (New York: Crowell, 1977).

12. See, for an extended treatment of visualizing women in fifteenth-century Italian contexts, Adrian Randolph, "Regarding Women in Sacred Space," in *Picturing Women in Renaissance and Baroque Italy*, ed. Geraldine A. Johnson and Sara F. Matthews Grieco (Cambridge and New York: Cambridge University Press, 1977), 17–41.

13. *Traité sur l'oraison dominicale*, trans. Jean Miélot, Lille?, ca. 1460, Brussels, Bibl. royale, MS 9092, fol. 9. L. M. J. Delaissé, *Medieval Miniatures from the Department of Manuscripts, The Royal Library of Belgium* (London: Thames and Hudson, 1965), 172–73, no. 40.

14. *Book of Hours of James IV*, Gerard Horenbout (?), Ghent or Bruges, ca. 1503, Vienna Österreichische Nationalbibliothek, Cod. 1897, fol. 243v. Christopher de Hamel, *A History of Illuminated Manuscripts* (1986, London: Phaidon, rev. ed. 1994), pl. 148.

15. Frances A. Yates, *The Art of Memory* (Chicago: University of Chicago Press, 1966), 3.

16. Albertus Magnus, *De bono*, in *Opera omnia*, ed. Bernhard Geyer (Aschendorff: Monastery of Westfalia, 1951), XXVII, 82ff.; Yates, *Art of Memory*, 61–69.

17. Yates, *Art of Memory*, 90; see Paolo Rossi, *Clavis universalis: Arts de la mémoire* (Grenoble: Millon, 1993, translated from the Italian, 1960), 272.

18. Ellis, "Margery Kempe and King's Lynn," 140.

19. *Saint Bride and Her Book: Birgitta of Sweden's Revelations*, translation and essays by Julia Bolton Holloway (Newburyport, Mass.: Focus Texts, 1992), II, 24–27, 38–40. Kempe mentions Bridget frequently in her *Book*. Atkinson, *Mystic and Pilgrim*, esp. 34–35; Louise Collis, *Memoirs of a Medieval Woman: The Life and Times of Margery Kempe* (New York: Harper and Row, 1964), 139–43.

20. See, esp. Gail McMurray Gibson, *The Theater of Devotion: East Anglian Drama and Society in the Later Middle Ages* (Chicago: University of Chicago Press, 1989), for a broad sense of the physicality of experience. The concept of 'habitus' may help to clarify the pervasive importance of these architectural settings. Only a small part of our ability to position ourselves in three-dimensional space (depth perception) is purely physiological, a product of binocular vision. Most of our ability to place ourselves in a working relationship to the world, such as the ability to recognize the fourth leg of a rectangular table when seen at an angle, is learned. We invariably believe such knowledge to be natural. Kempe's culture, traditional and marginally literate, communicated most of its values through physical experience.

21. "her husband sat down under the cross" (59).

22. "sitting upon her bedside" (42).

23. "and cried with a loud voice as thought her heart would have burst apart" (104).

24. "from evensong time . . . until evensong on the next day" (104).

25. "in the city of her soul she saw truly and freshly how our Lord was crucified" (104).

26. "violent sobbings, weepings, and loud cries" (186).

27. Eamon Duffy, *The Stripping of the Altars: Traditional Religion in England c. 1400–1580* (New Haven: Yale University Press, 1992), 111, on squints see 97–98,

figs. 44–46, 52–53. See also Corine Schleif, *Donatio et Memoriae, Stiftungen und Motivationen an Beispielen aus der Lorenzkirche in Nurnberg* (Munich: Deutscher Kunstverlag, 1990) for the intrusion into clerical space by the burghers of fifteenth-century Nuremberg.

28. The chaplain of the Hospital of St. John, built on Dam Gate in the northern section of Lynn, had been saying Mass and administered the sacraments; the prior of St. Margaret's moved to suppress the legitimacy of such privileges. The dispute over jurisdiction was referred to the priors of Bury-St.-Edmunds and Thetford, whose judgment is preserved in a document of 11 February 1234, giving almost all advantage to St. Margaret's. The private chaplain (*proprius capellanus*) may say no more than one Mass a day and only in a low voice (*submissa voce*), and whatever offerings are made at the altar must be given without diminution or deceit to the church of St. Margaret's. The order further instructs that the brothers and sisters dying in the hospital are to be buried through St. Margaret's and that the chaplain is not to hear confessions or give pardon. The hospital's bell can only be rung to convoke the brethren (as opposed to signaling church ceremonies (such as Mass or prayers), and the prior of Lynn is to visit the hospital each year. Not only would such a visit be one that allowed inspection of the premises to insure compliance, but a typical state visitation by a superior would necessitate an outlay of requisite hospitality. Beloe, *Our Borough*, 75, document in archives of the dean and chapter, Norwich. For some indication of the finances of St. Margaret's and its collection of rents and fees, see sources of revenue and expenses for the years 1437 through 1438 in William Taylor, *The Antiquities of King's Lynn* (London: Thew, 1844), 14–15.

29. *The Life of the Holy Hildegard*, monks Gottfried and Theoderic, trans. James McGrath (Collegeville, Minn.: Liturgical, 1995). Music is a major aspect of Hildegard's spirituality.

30. "a melodious sound so sweet and delectable that she thought she had been in paradise. Alas that I have sinned. It is full merry in heaven" (46).

31. "so terrible a melody, that she might no bear it" (74).

32. "Sounds and melodies she had heard everyday for twenty-five years . . . and especially when she was in devout prayer" (124).

33. "kind of sound as if it were a pair of bellows blowing in her ear . . . the voice of a dove, and . . . the little bird that is called the 'redbreast' " (127).

34. "sweet smells . . . sweeter she thought than any earthly thing ever was that she smelled before" (124).

35. "And I shall provide for you, daughter, as for my own mother and as for my own wife" (196).

36. Her carefully constructed memories of successful defenses of the charges of Lollardy can be read as acts of self-preservation but also genuine evidence of her attraction to the ritual structure of the church and orthodox beliefs. The Lollard position challenged rituals and clerical offices, including belief in "transubstantiation, clerical celibacy, Friday fasts, images, pilgrimages, special prayers for the dead, and the belief that confession to a priest was necessary for salvation." See Atkinson, *Mystic and Pilgrim*, 104–08, 110–12. Lynn Staley, *Margery Kempe's Dissenting Fictions* (University Park: The Pennsylvania State University Press, 1994), argues that Margery Kempe is constructing a fictional persona who fulfills contemporary expectations of pious behavior, but to her own purposes. For Lollardy, see Margaret Aston, *Lollards and Reformers: Images and Literacy in Late Medieval Religion* (London: Hambledon, 1984). For addi-

tional development of Kempe's clerical relations, see Sarah Beckwith, *Christ's Body: Identity, Culture, and Society in Late Medieval Writings* (London and New York: Routledge, 1993), 94–111. See on general female prophecy, Diane Watt, *Secretaries of God: Women Prophets in Late Medieval and Early Modern England* (Woodbridge, Suffolk, and Rochester, N.Y.: Boydell and Brewer, 1997).

37. "said fewer beads than she had done for years before, in order to speed the writing" (257).

38. "conversed with her soul as plainly and as certainly as one friend speaks to another through bodily speech" (75).

39. Madeline Caviness, "Anchoress, Abbess, and Queen: Donors and Patrons or Intercessors and Matrons?" in *The Cultural Patronage of Medieval Women*, ed. June Hall McCash (Athens: University of Georgia Press, 1996), 105–54. Caviness argues the ambivalence of these situations where evidence may suggest either control of imagery by women or images produced as a means of control of women.

40. Rüdiger Becksmann and Ulf-Dietrich Korn, *Die mittelalterlichen Glasmalereien in Lüneburg und den Heidenklöstern*, Corpus Vitrearum Medii Aevi, Deutschland, 7/2 (Berlin: Deutscher Verlag für Kunstwissenschaft, 1993), 29–74.

41. Darmstadt, Hessische Landesmuseum und Hochschulbibliothek Hs 2505, ca. 1360. Becksmann and Korn, *Glasmalereien in Lüneburg und den Heidenklöstern*, 34–36, pls. 6, 9. See also the printed edition of ca. 1475, *"The Mirour of Mans Saluacioun": A Middle English Translation of the Speculum Humanae Salvationis*, ed. Avril Henry (Philadelphia: Pennsylvania University Press, 1987). esp. illustrations on 128, 166, 167, 182.

42. Madeline Caviness, "Patron or Matron? A Capetian Bride and a 'Vade Mecum' for Her Marriage Bed," *Speculum* (special issue, Studying Medieval Women: Sex, Gender, Feminism, ed. Nancy F. Partner) 68, no. 2 (1993): 333–62.

43. Becksmann and Korn, *Glasmalereien in Lüneburg und den Heidenklöstern*, 3–20, pls. 3, 5.

44. Mary Carruthers, *The Book of Memory* (Cambridge and New York: Cambridge University Press, 1990).

45. Harrod, *Deeds and Records*, 64; Atkinson, *Mystic and Pilgrim*, 76; riots accompanied a dispute over the major's and bishop's authority, even for ceremonial precedence, one of them in 1377 when John Brunham, Margery Kempe's father, held the office of mayor.

46. "who had no love for the said creature, nor would allow her to come into their chapel, as she had done before he came there" (178). Meech and Allen, *Book of Margery Kempe*, 338/209, note that Kempe's devotions usually take place in the choir, which "was of course extra-parochial."

47. "after this time she received Communion at the high altar of St. Margaret's church and our Lord visited her with such great grace . . . that she cried so loudly that it could be heard all round the church, and outside as well" (178). Hope Emily Allen notes 2/20, 6/4, 84/10, 140/25, and 09/29 present a serious discussion of the medieval virtue of tears. She is the single commentator, I have found, who describes Kempe as "making her tears . . . a supplemental liturgy," p. 256. See also Gibson, *Theater of Devotion*, 15, 47–49, who counters contemporary readers' characterization of Kempe's outbursts as pathological; Beckwith, *Christ's Body*, 88–91.

48. Susan Signe Morrison, *Women Pilgrims in Late Medieval England: Private Piety and Public Performance* (London and New York: Routledge, 2000), 131.

49. *Jeanne de Boulogne Praying to the Trinity*, 1405, Metropolitan Museum of Art, The Cloisters, *Belles Heures*, fol. 91v, Millard Meiss, *French Painting in the Time of Jean de Berry: The Limbourgs and Their Contemporaries* (New York: Braziller, 1974), fig. 385.

50. Gibson, *Theater of Devotion*, 72–96; Duffy, *Stripping of the Altars*, 38–40, 97–98, 307. Samuel Tymms, *An Architectural and Historical Account of the Church of St. Mary, Bury St. Edmunds* (Bury St. Edmunds: Barker and Son, 1854), 18, 35. In 1467 the will of John Baret was able to convert the Lady Chapel, to the south of the high altar of St. Mary, into his private chantry. In 1480 John Smyth's will effected conversion of the altar of St. John, on the north, into the Smyth chantry. See Bury St. Edmunds, Long Melford, and other sites on the Website www.holycross.edu/kempe.

51. Dated 1476, Motto Laus Trinitati (Praise to the Trinity) on scrolls and Coney's merchant's mark on shield (the commoner's substitute for heraldic charge). Coney was a prominent member of the Trinity Guild, to which Kempe had been admitted in 1438. Hillen, *Borough of King's Lynn*, 220–22, 741–45, 813–14. Brass, largely destroyed, known from rubbing. Taylor, *Antiquities of King's Lynn*, 49–51, ill.; Mackerell, *History and Antiquities*, 29.

52. A chapel since the midtwelfth century, it was rebuilt shortly after 1200, and modifications were made ca. 1370. Most of the church's construction dates from 1421 to 1423 for the chancel/choir, and through the late fifteenth century, the south porch. For development of Kempe's relationship with her city, see Ellis, "Margery Kempe and King's Lynn."

53. Harrod, *Deeds and Records*, 61–63; Meech and Allen, *Book of Margery Kempe*, 372–73; Taylor, *Antiquities of King's Lynn*, 121–22, text of 1432 letter; Beloe, *Our Borough*, 139–48, with photographic illustration of the letters and minutes of corporation; Hillen, *Borough of King's Lynn*, 148–50, The mayor "John de Brunham" appears in the three lists of burgesses attesting in 1478 to reasons to refuse privileges of the sacraments of marriage, baptism, and purification. Brunham had been mayor in 1370, then for two consecutive terms, 1377 through 1378, and in 1385 and 1391. Harrod, *Deeds and Records*, 168; Atkinson, *Mystic and Pilgrim*, 76.

54. "She was the more bold to pray our Lord to withstand their intention and to deflate their boasting" (95).

55. "my blessed mother, and my holy angels and twelve apostles, St. Katherine, St. Margaret, and St. Mary Magdalene, and many other saints that are in heaven" (86).

56. On ceremonial imagery see Meech and Allen, *Book of Margery Kempe*, 301/87.

57. "before the Son and the Holy Ghost and the Mother of Jesus, and all the twelve apostles and St. Katherine and St. Margaret and many other saints and holy virgins" (123). Very little remains visible of the fifteenth-century appearance of the Church of the Holy Apostles. I wish to thank Alison Fleming for her extensive help in researching the buildings of Rome for the *Mapping Margery Kempe* Website and for her advice on all these issues of Roman architecture.

58. Peter Brown, *The Cult of the Saints in the Early Church* (Chicago: University of Chicago Press, 1985), esp. 88–105.

59. "special gift from God . . . and with such manner of conversing he highly comforted her spirits" (136).

60. James H. Stubblebine, *Giotto: The Arena Chapel Frescoes* (New York: Norton, 1969); Sarel Eimerl, *The World of Giotto* (New York: Time, 1967). It is interesting that the city gate of Jerusalem, illustrating Joachim's return to honor, was selected (but without explanation) as the cover illustration of Osbern Bokenham's *A Legend of Holy Women*, trans. Shiela Delany (Notre Dame: University of Notre Dame Press, 1992). *Discovery of Honey*, Worcester Art Museum, 1937.76 in Sharon Fermor, *Piero di Cosimo: Fiction, Invention and "Fantasia"* (London: Reaktion Books, 1993), 62–92.

61. See the description of Gatekeeper's duties, 25 August 1436 (the year Kempe dictated her book): "The same day it was agreed that the keeper of East Gate shall carry about him a club, and duly perform his office of Porter, and shall permit men at due seasons to enter in and go out coming to the said gate, and shall keep fresh water at the house appointed for the said water," after which follows further duties, especially the regulation of goods for sale at the Tuesday and Saturday markets, so goods would not be brought out of town for transaction "to the hurt of the corporation." Taylor, *Antiquities of King's Lynn*, 157.

62. "I am as mighty to keep you safe here in the fields as in the strongest church in all this world" (138).

63. "the Bishop himself very kindly sent things to her from his own table" (70).

64. "took her in with them and seated her with them at meals, so that she would not eat alone" (109). For discussion of this passage see Meech and Allen, *Book of Margery Kempe*, 295/73. See also Arnould Greban, *Le Mystère de la Passion*, ed. Gaston Paris and Gaston Raynaud (1878, Geneva: Slatkine Reprints, 1970), 426–67. The text was written before 1452. When the apostles and holy women sit down to a meal just before the appearance of the resurrected Christ (verses 32486–563), there is a long discussion of the seating arrangements. The Virgin at first tries to defer to St. Peter, then accepts the first place, thanking Peter for his "courtoisie."

65. "seated her at her own table above herself, and served her food with her own hands" (130).

66. "made her sit at the end of the table below all the others, so that she scarcely dared speak a word" (98).

67. Christopher Woodforde, *The Norwich School of Glass-Painting in the Fifteenth Century* (London: Oxford University Press, 1950), 74–127, pls. 23–26; H. Munro Cautley, *Suffolk Churches* (Cambridge: Suffolk Historic Churches Trust, 1937; 5th ed., 1982), 196–214, col. pl. 5; also Richard Marks, *Stained Glass in England During the Middle Ages* (Toronto: Toronto University Press, 1993), esp. 3–25; Joan Evans, *English Art 1307–1461* (Oxford: Clarendon, 1949, reprint 1981); Peter Lasko and Nigel Morgan, *Medieval Art in East Anglia 1300–1520* (Norwich: Jarrold and Sons, 1973). For description of the decorative programs in St. Margaret's see Mackerell, *History and Antiquities*, 8–10; William Richards, *The History of Lynn* (Lynn: Wittingham, 1812), 1089–91.

68. "I am from Lynn in Norfolk, the daughter of a good man of the same Lynn, who has been five times mayor of that worshipful borough, and also an alderman for many years, and I have a good man, also a burgess of the said town of Lynn, for my husband" (149). For documents relating to the high status of both men see Meech and Allen, *Book of Margery Kempe*, 358–68, and Hillen, *Borough of King's Lynn*, 133–34.

69. Atkinson, *Mystic and Pilgrim*, 212–13, discusses the conflict between the domestic role assigned to Margery Kempe and the public lives permitted her brother.

70. See elaboration of negotiated spaces to achieve proximity to formerly exclusive clerical areas of Nuremberg's churches in Schleif, *Donatio et Memoriae*.

71. A system operative since the thirteenth century divided the citizens into Potentiores, Mediocres, and Inferiores. Hillen, *Borough of King's Lynn*, 87–89. The Brunham family were of the highest class of Potentiores.

72. Edgar Milligen Beloe, "A List of Brasses Existing in the Churches of St. Margaret and St. Nicholas, King's Lynn, in the year 1724," *Transaction of the Cambridge University Association of Brass Collectors* 2/1 no. 11 (1892): 57–59, many minor inscriptions without figures are also noted. Taylor, *Antiquities of King's Lynn*, 52–53, records the brasses of X. Tresbe, VIII and XI Trounche, IV Scotland. Mackerell, *History and Antiquities*, made a complete record of the numerous brasses extant in 1738 when tomb inscriptions littered the interior of all the churches in Lynn.

73. John Sell Cotman, *Engravings of Sepulchral Brasses in Norfolk* (London: Bohn, 1838), xxii–iii, 3–5, 7–8, pls. 2, 3, 7 (for Lynn); On the Hansa, see Hillen, *Borough of King's Lynn*, 172–78. For the brasses: Mackerell, *History and Antiquities*, 19–20; Herbert W. Macklin, *The Brasses of England* (London: Methuen, 1907), 308–09; Henry H. Trivick, *The Craft and Design of Monumental Brasses* (London: John Baker, 1969), 28–30; H. K. Cameron, "The Fourteenth-century Flemish Brasses at King's Lynn," *Archaeological Journal* 136 (1979): 151–72; Nigel Wilken, "The Birds, the Bishop and the Music of Brass," *Transactions of the Monumental Brass Society* 14, no. 3, (1988): 205–16, discusses the peacock feast frieze at the foot of the brass of Robert Braunche based on the Alexander romance *Les voeux du paon*, composed ca. 1310 by Jacques de Longuyon. Walsoken's measures 118 x 68 inches, Braunche's 106 x 61 inches.

74. In the collection of brasses made by Sir John Cullum and Craven Ord and bequeathed by Frances Douce to the British Museum, impression taken in 1780. It measures 5 feet 10 inches. Cotman, *Engravings of Sepulchral Brasses*, 8, pl. 7; Beloe, "A List of Brasses," 58; Taylor, *Antiquities of King's Lynn*, 51.

75. Bittering was mayor in 1351, 1352, 1358, and 1365. Mackerell, *History and Antiquities*, 133–34; Beloe, "A List of Brasses," 59: "This is the most ancient and most remarkable tombstone we meet with in this chapel, which denotes its antiquity," also assumed it to be one of the foreign brasses; the verses read:

Moribus ornatus Wilielmus civis amatus
De Bitering natus jacet hic sub marmore stratus
Lege dei plana cvjvs conjvx Jvliana
Hesit ei vita nunc linquit morte sopita
Que seperat fvnus. . . . ille tribunus
Hijs se det munus unit quos tumulus unus

76. Ubi vera sunt gaudia nostra ibi fixa sunt corda, followed by: Orate pro Animabus Thome Watyrdeyn et Alice consortis Sue quorum Animabus propiciet Deus. Waterdeyn was mayor in 1397 and 1404. Mackerell, *History and Antiquities*, 102; Taylor, *Antiquities of King's Lynn*, 75; Beloe, "A List of Brasses," 59.

77. "was enormously envious of her neighbors if they were dressed as well as she was" (44).

78. The issue of wearing white and the importance of dress in the Middle Ages is a vast topic, deserving serious attention. Kempe, however, serves to focus attention

on this subject for many readers who would not necessarily realize the power of such social norms. Kempe's desire for virginity reflects English models of sanctity she would have known. Heffernan's study of English lives of saints made him conclude that by the thirteenth century, virginity had become the queen of all virtues. Thomas J. Heffernan, *Sacred Biography: Saints and Their Biographers in the Middle Ages* (Oxford: Oxford University Press, 1988), 267, and entire chapter "Virgin Mothers." See also, for continental sources, André Vauchez, *The Laity in the Middle Ages: Religious Beliefs and Devotional Practices*, trans. Margery J. Schneider (South Bend: University of Notre Dame Press, 1993), 185–203.

79. "gave her three halfpence because she, in conversation, told them some holy tales. And then she was very glad and cheerful" (139). For explanation of her absorption of texts, which for her and other illiterate women "become physically reformed in their bodies and can be immediately accessed for the instruction of others," see Ralph Hanna III, "Some Norfolk Women and Their Books," in *Cultural Patronage of Medieval Women*, 288–305, at 297.

80. *Abbot Suger on the Abbey Church of St.-Denis and Its Art Treasures*, ed. and trans. Erwin Panofsky; second ed., Gerda Panofsky-Soergel (1946, Princeton: Princeton University Press, 1979). *The Works of Bernard of Clairvaux* (Spencer: Cistercian Publications, 1970), and Jean Leclercq, *Bernard of Clairvaux and the Cistercian Spirit* (Kalamazoo, Mich.: Medieval Institute, 1976), esp. 12–36, "Saint Bernard and His Work;" Conrad Rudolf, *The "Things of Greater Importance": Bernard of Clairvaux's Apologia and the Medieval Attitude toward Art* (Philadelphia: University of Philadelphia Press, 1990).

81. Even if she could read to some extent, as some maintain, there is little indication that her reading was a private, self-empowering action, when the personal absorption in the text creates the reader's own imagined community. Kempe insists on her illiteracy; see Staley, *Margery Kempe's Dissenting Fictions*, 32, and Beckwith, *Christ's Body*, 95. See comprehensive review of literacy and image by Lawrence G. Duggan, "Was Art Really the 'Book of the Illiterate'?" *Word and Image* 5/3 (1989): 227–51.

## FURTHER READING


*The Book of Margery Kempe*. Ed. Sanford Brown Meech and Hope Emily Allen. Early English Text Society. o.s 212 London: Oxford University Press, 1940.

*The Book of Margery Kempe*, Ed. Barry Windeatt. Essex and New York: Longman, 2000.

*Age of Chivalry: Art in Plantagenet England 1200–1400*. Ed. Jonathan Alexander and Paul Binski. Exh. cat. Royal Academy of Arts, London, 1987.

Beloe, Edgar Milligen. *Our Borough: Our Churches: King's Lynn, Norfolk*. Cambridge: Macmillan and Bowes, 1899.

Cautley, H. Munro. *Suffolk Churches*. Cambridge: Suffolk Historic Churches Trust, 1937; 5th ed., 1982.

Cotman, John Sell. *Engravings of Sepulchral Brasses in Norfolk*. London: Bohn, 1838.

Fanous, Samuel. "Measuring the Pilgrim's Progress: Internal Emphasis in *The Book of Margery Kempe*." Ed. Denis Renevey and Christiania Whitehead. Toronto: University of Toronto Press, 2000: 157–76.

Hillen, Henry. *History of the Borough of King's Lynn*. Norwich: East of England Newspaper Company, 1907.

Lasko, Peter, and Nigel Morgan. *Medieval Art in East Anglia 1300–1520*. Norwich: Jarrold and Sons, 1973.

Mackerell, Benjamin. *The History and Antiquities of the Flourishing Corporation of King's-Lynn*. London: Cave, 1738

Marks, Richard. *Stained Glass in England during the Middle Ages*. Toronto: Toronto University Press, 1993.

Taylor, William. *The Antiquities of King's Lynn*. London: Thew, 1844.

Yates, Frances A. *The Art of Memory*. Chicago and London: Chicago University Press, 1966.

FIVE

# THE SEAT UNDER OUR LADY: GENDER AND SEATING IN LATE MEDIEVAL ENGLISH PARISH CHURCHES

Katherine L. French

DURING MASS, THE SPACE WITHIN an English parish church was divided between the clergy, who were in the chancel and the laity, who were in the nave.[1] A rood screen, an elaborately carved fence, separated these two areas. When the laity installed permanent pews in the nave, seating arrangements further divided the nave into male and female spheres. Parishes followed a variety of arrangements. Most seem to place men on the south side of the nave and women on the north, although some parishes switched this order or placed men in the front and women in the back.[2] Whatever the placement, seating arrangements created a context for religious and social interactions among parish men and women. Seating delineated spaces within the nave where an individual fashioned his or her personal identity and where groups, or even cliques, acted out their differences and boundaries.[3]

Reliance on these generalizations alone does not help us to understand the different ways in which the laity used the space within the church and what that space meant to them.[4] Generalizations about separating men and women hide a myriad of local gender concerns that the laity played out in their seating arrangements. As each church and its internal organization was unique, seating arrangements became places to create and maintain local culture and act out local gender concerns. The internal organization of each nave affected social interaction by helping to determine how and when men and women encountered one another, investing each individual with a set of locally understood set of social norms and revealing what sort of value the parish placed on intragender interactions.

Pews were not commonly found in churches until the fifteenth century.[5] Their introduction began gradually and in an unorganized fashion. Prior to that, parishioners either stood or brought their own stools.[6] Once the laity began to install permanent seats in the nave, seats began to play a role in the social dynamics of the parish as they came to be visibly associated with the status of the parishioners occupying them. Some parish administrations sold seats as part of an overall plan to finance the care and upkeep of their section of the church. Purchasing a seat, therefore, involved the purchaser, often a woman, in parish administration and parish support of the nave.

Not all parishes sold seats, however. Some parishes installed them but left the negotiation over who sat where to oral culture and local custom. In rural areas, the right to hold a seat was often based on land holding. In an early sixteenth-century pew dispute from the Somerset parish of Minehead, the defendant Giles Dobell told the Star Court that he "hath been seasid in his demesne as of fee of and yn on[e] mesuage or tenement with th'appurtenaunces in Mynhed in your countie of Somercett and by reson therof hath usid to have a sette or a pue for hym and his wyff in the sid churche of Mynhed."[7]

Not all seats within the men's or women's sections were equal. In those parishes where there are records from the sale of seats, we can see something of the different value systems at work in determining the location of a seat. Despite their higher cost, some parishioners considered a seat's proximity to the chancel, side altars, or favorite cult image when buying it. In 1547, William Dorman, a parishioner in Ilminster, Somerset, bought the seat under the image of St. Christopher.[8] It was popularly believed that seeing an image of St. Christopher would protect one from mishap the rest of the day. Buying a seat demonstrated more than piety; the purchase of a good seat, usually one closest to the chancel, also displayed wealth and status. Only those with enough disposable income could afford to buy seats. Gender and wealth worked together to create seating plans.

The practice of separating men and women during worship predates Christianity. Jewish men and women did not worship together. At least as far back as the third century, Christians also separated men and women.[9] The early church seems to have placed women in the back of the church, at the west end, keeping them as far as possible from the chancel. This arrangement apparently grew out of concern over the threat of female pollution. Many clerics in the later Middle Ages continued to believe that seating women apart from men helped to confine the danger and impurity that women posed to men. Robert Mannyng, in his early fourteenth-century instructional text *Handlyng Synne*, said it was not proper for either lay men or women to be in the chancel, but when women stood among the clergy in the chancel, they did greater harm with their presence. They distracted the clergy and led the weak ones to temptation and sin:

> But ȝyt do wymmen gretter folye
> Þat use to stonde among þe clergye,
> Oþer at matyns or at messe,
> But ȝyt hyt were yn cas of stresse.
> Fir þer of may come temptacyun.
> And dystourblyng of deuocyun.[10]

By the late Middle Ages, however, the more usual arrangement relegated women to the north side. The traditional explanation for this practice lies in the association of both the north and women with things dark, damp, and demonic, as Corine Schleif explains in her chapter in this volume.[11] An alternative view, put forth by Margaret Aston and Roberta Gilchrist, is that women sat on the same side as Mary relative to her position to Christ on the cross on the church crucifix located on top of the rood screen.[12] The association of Mary with the north side also carried to other spatial arrangements. The Marian chapel was usually on the north side of the church, usually behind or next to the chancel.[13]

Faced with seating irregularities, the late medieval clergy did not typically resort to arguments about the dangers of female pollution. They continued, however, to see women "out of place" as a problem, as apparently did many members of the lay community. Although the laity almost certainly absorbed the association of women sitting in the north side with attendant concerns for their purity, the laity overtly cast proper maintenance of the nave's organization as acts of community membership and respectability.[14] Their concerns were related to broader societal concerns about women who were difficult to control or classify, whether physically, socially, or even geographically. When women moved out of their expected places or categories, many questioned their morality or propriety, assuming the worst motivations.[15] Seating arrangements recreated these dynamics on a smaller scale. For example, in the Lincoln parish of Grayingham, several women were cited for sitting among the men and sharing the kiss of peace with them.[16] Both the wardens who reported their behavior and the clerics who reprimanded them worried that the kiss of peace, a sign of Christian community and charity, would be sullied by the mixing of the sexes. The women were not performing a message of Christian charity but rather were behaving in a wanton manner. In another legal confrontation over seating, the churchwardens of the London parish of St. Martin Vintry brought suit against Maria, alias Mariot Harington, a common bawd, for sitting in a seat during Mass.[17] Maria's status as a known prostitute made it inappropriate, the wardens felt, for her to sit among the respectable members of the parish. There was also the fear that she might try to recruit other women to her line of work. Respectable women, those who could afford a seat in the nave, were not expected to mix with such company, at least in such a public manner.[18] The wardens saw her presence as both an intrusion and a threat to the moral order of "respectable society." Although the churchwardens made appeals to respectability, in both cases respectability could mask more deep-seated concerns about purity.

Separating women from men might mark them as inferior in the eyes of the church, but the women's section of the nave was also a place for the creation and practice of women's culture. The space within the nave did not mean the same thing to men and women. Each sex used seat location to act out their own hierarchies and social organization. To be sure, women's status was often predicted on their husbands' or fathers' status, but that does not lessen the importance of status, however acquired, to women's subculture. The existence of a women's subculture is something that most men seem to have taken for granted, even if they did find it threatening.[19] That the potential subversiveness of female subculture could be acted out in the nave of the church, one of the few places where women could gather in all-women groups and socialize with each other, was, however, of concern to many. The Middle English poem "What the Goodwife Taught Her Daughter" speaks directly to this anxiety:

> Whanne þou sittest in þe chirche, þi beedis þou
> schalt bidde;
> Make þou no iangelynge to freende nor to
> sibbe;
> Lau3e þou to scorne neiþer oolde bodi ne
> 3ounge,
> But be of fair beerynge & of good tunge.[20]

Even if women followed the Goodwife's advice, women's culture was not limited to conversation only. Their part of the nave was also a place to display women's material culture, such as prayer books, rosaries, clothing, and jewelry.

When we compare the seating arrangements of two parishes, St. Margaret's in Westminster and St. Mary's in Bridgwater, Somerset, we can see the different roles seating arrangements could play in local parish life. Although a comparison of only two parishes cannot offer broad conclusions, it does show the relationship between specific local issues and seating arrangements and suggests something of the connection between seating and the role of women in specific parishes. There seems to be a correlation between the creation or elimination of particularly female spaces within the nave and a lay parochial administration's willingness to integrate women's subculture into the rest of parish life. R. A. Houlbrooke argues that women in preindustrial societies begin to act collectively when there is an infrastructure of specifically female social and economic contacts.[21] Through its seating arrangements, the organization of space within a parish church could create or eliminate just such an opportunity. The very different seating plans and very different roles that women played in these two parishes would seem to support this hypothesis. The churchwardens' accounts show that the arrangement of the naves in these two churches changed several times over the two hundred years prior to the Reformation.[22] In both communities the parishioners expanded the nave's size, built new chapels, and added new aisles. Each new arrangement of the nave altered the value placed on space within the nave and changed what it meant to attend Mass. Included in the changes was the building of permanent seats. Seating arrangements reflect not only shared Christian concerns about the proximity of men and women to each other, but when considered within the broader context of lay involvement in parish life, they reveal how localized gender relations could be.

## ST. MARGARET'S, WESTMINSTER

The female parishioners of St. Margaret's in Westminster played a dominant role in this parish's seating arrangements. Through their decisions about where to sit and when to move, women demonstrated a variety of individual and familial concerns that comprised part of a women's subculture. These concerns were further integrated into parish life through other parochial activities.

St. Margaret's was an urban parish with between two and three thousand parishioners, whose livelihoods came predominantly from trading, manufacturing, and victualing.[23] The parish was next to Westminster Abbey; pilgrims to the shrine of Edward the Confessor, as well as the monks living in the abbey, helped to benefit the local economy. Despite the abbey's presence, this was not a particularly wealthy community.[24] Yet even with its modest means, between 1487 and 1523 the laity financed the demolition of its old church and the building of a new one. The enthusiasm and speed with which the parishioners raised both the money and the walls is a clear example of how important the parish was to the local community.

Part of the extensive rebuilding included the gradual construction of pews in the new nave. Each year, the wardens sold the available seats to the parishioners. Seats were made available when new seats were built or when the previous occupant died or moved to another seat. The sale of pews allowed the parish to raise additional money. Construction of pews was haphazard and occasional. In 1478, John Russell received thirty-three pence for making eleven new pews in the south aisle, also called the "Trinity aisle."[25] After 1501, when the new north aisle was finished, a large crew of carpenters and joiners outfitted it with new pews.[26] In the same year, the parish also had thirteen more seats added to other parts of the nave; seven were placed in the south aisle, and six double pews were added to the central part of the nave.[27] In the following year more seats were built for the Trinity aisle, and in 1512, the wardens contracted with James Mylner for an additional seven pews.[28]

Each year, the churchwardens' accounts record the names of those buying or changing seats. Periodically the records also provide information about the location of these seats. In 1523, Elizabeth Pomfriet, wife of John, a prosperous brewer, bought a seat for herself and her daughter "under our lady."[29] The notation goes on to suggest, however, that Mistress Clasy already sat there and was not to be displaced. Detailed though much of this information is, there is no exact information on where women sat, although we might assume that they sat in the north aisle, also known as St. George's aisle. Information is a bit more certain for male seating. Records of purchasers of seats in the south aisle name only men. These seats typically cost three shillings, four pence, although Master Foster paid twice that in 1505.[30] Additionally, only men bought seats near the St. Erasmus altar and St. Cornelius altar, which also suggests that they too were located somewhere along the south aisle.[31]

Although the records do not usually explain where the seats were, tracing who bought seats and who moved their seats reveals that men and women made different decisions with regard to their seating. From these choices we can extrapolate differences in priorities. Because the selling of seats was part of a lay initiative to raise money, seating arrangements were of institutional and financial interest to the community as a whole; and because of the formal financial relationship, seating was more fully institutionalized at Westminster than it was in communities where the wardens did not sell seats. The seating arrangements and the subcultures created by them and reinforced by them thus received official recognition by the parish. As seating arrangements evolved, the spaces within the nave took on differing significance to different segments of the parish population. For some seat placement was an opportunity to display piety or status; for others it was a chance to socialize, and for still others it was a health requirement.

In St. Margaret's, church seating appears to be primarily a women's issue, as women bought the vast majority of seats. Between 1460 and 1530, 737 women bought seats, whereas only 275 men did.[32] Women also changed their seats more often then men.[33] Only 13 percent of men compared to 22 percent of women changed their seats.[34] When we look in greater detail at the decisions surrounding church seating, we see further differences in men and women's behavior and choices (see table A).

**Table A Westminster Seating, 1460–1530**

| Sex | Buy Seats | Move Seats |
|---|---|---|
| women | 737 (73%) | 166 (22%) |
| men | 275 (27%) | 35 (13%) |
| total | 1012 | 201 |

Whether or not one's spouse had a seat was an important factor in determining whether one purchased a seat and when one moved to a different seat. The men who bought seats fall in two groups: those whose wives also bought seats and those who either did not have wives or had wives who did not buy seats.[35] These two groups of men display very different behavior with respect to seating (see table B).

**Table B** **Men's Seating: Westminster Seating, 1460–1530**

| Status | Buy Seats | Move Seats |
|---|---|---|
| with wives | 138 (50%) | 30 (22%) |
| without wives | 137 (50%) | 5 (4%) |
| total | 275 | 35 |

It would seem that having a wife with a seat propelled men into changing their position in the nave more frequently. Of the 138 men whose wives purchased seats, 30 (or 22 percent) moved their seats, whereas of those 137 men whose wives bought no seats, or had no wives, only 5 (4 percent) moved their seats. We can further analyze this first group of men, in terms of when they and their wives bought their seats in relation to each other.

**Table C** **Seat Purchasing in Relation to Spouse: Westminster Seating, 1460–1530**

| Status | Buy Seats | Move Seats |
|---|---|---|
| before husband | 88 (64%) | 50 (57%) |
| with husband | 27 (20%) | 5 (20%) |
| after husband | 20 (15%) | 9 (45%) |
| uncertain | 3 (2%) | 3 |
| total | 138 | 67 (49%) |

Whereas 15 percent bought seats before their wives, and 20 percent bought seats the same year as their wives, most men (64 percent) bought seats after their wives. Those who bought seats together moved the least often. With the exception of Lewis Turfote and John Wryggor, the men who purchased seats jointly with their wives held no offices within the parish or the city.[36] These couples may have bought their seats in old age or ill health when their primary concern was comfort and physical assistance during worship, rather than social advancement, or they bought their seats as a sign of having achieved as a family a level of economic prosperity and respectability. On the whole, most men seem to have had little inclination to move about the nave as better seats became available. For the men, a pew seems to have been a sign of success, a way of maintaining visibility after they had finished their time in office. It confirmed their position within the community, but it did not help create it.

Women made rather different use of seating. The wives of the men who purchased seats can be distinguished from the rest of the women who bought and changed seats. Although women as a group moved more often then men, women with husbands sitting in the nave moved much more often than those without husbands sitting in pews (49 percent compared to 16 percent) (see Table D).

**Table D Women's Seating: Westminster Seating, 1460–1530**

| Status | Buy Seats | Move Seats |
|---|---|---|
| with husband | 138 (19%) | 67 (49%) |
| without husband | 427 (58%) | 68 (16%) |
| on own | 172 (23%) | 31 (18%) |
| total | 737 | 166 (22%) |

Those wives who bought seats before their husbands moved the most frequently (57 percent). Half of this group of women had husbands who served as parish or city officers. A typical example is the wife of Thomas Middleton. Thomas was churchwarden from 1506 through 1508.[37] His wife bought her first seat in 1475 for 2 shillings. She moved in 1479, the same year Thomas bought his seat. She moved again twice more, in 1502, and in 1505, the year before Thomas became churchwarden.[38] Most men seem to have bought seats after their public service, but their wives bought them before. This behavior suggests that men and women had different motivations for purchasing seats and that seating meant different things to this group of men and women. For the group of women whose husbands had local political careers, seating choices would seem to be strategically motivated to further their husband's political or communal aspirations. In a world where women only held public office in exceptional circumstances, a husband's political successes might also be his wife's. Moving to ever more visible or desirable seats might have been a way for a woman to promote her family's or her husband's reputation. Good seats were close to the front, where the occupant could be closer to the host and the preacher. Those who sat in them could be presumed to have a certain level of piety and affluence, both of which were desirable attributes for local leaders.[39] A good seat also allowed a woman to mix with other like-minded women, whose husbands might be able to further her husband's career. Seating was a socially sanctioned way for women to promote the interests of their husbands or families. Men in this parish had other ways of furthering their own careers and creating visibility.

This mobile and visible group of wives was, however, only a small part of the total number of women who bought seats. Most women who had seats did not have husbands with seats in the nave. The churchwardens' accounts list this much larger group of women in one of two ways. A woman is identified either as the wife of a particular man, or she is listed by her own name. Being listed by one's full name does not automatically mean the woman was single, although many were.[40] When we look at those women clearly identified as wives, but whose husbands bought no seats, the rate of movement declines to 16 percent. This group did not aggressively seek out ever better seats, even if a seat gave them a certain level of respectable visibility and comfort. In marriages where only the wife was a seat owner, seating was not an obvious part of a larger family strategy for advancement.

The final group of women, those identified by their own names, are the most diverse group. Some, like Mother Hubberd who bought a seat in 1504, were undoubtedly widows.[41] Others, such as Joan Ferris, were probably single.[42] Still another group, of whom Agnes Baynbrygge and Mistress Atwell were a part, comprised the wives of prominent, if not wealthy, men of the city and parish.[43] Their husbands had both served in the parish's administration.[44] What these women have in common, besides the financial wherewithal to buy a seat, is the manner in which the churchwardens' accounts describe them. The accounts identify them independently of their husbands, if they had them.

Because these women are identified by their own name and not by their relationship to their husbands, they appear to be acting on their own, buying their seats in person from the churchwarden. What is more, as a group, these women changed seats at a slightly higher rate (18 percent) than those women whose husbands did not have seats. This group of women had different priorities and made different decisions about their seating than the other two groups of women. Although status and visibility were probably still concerns, their decisions about when to move and where to sit were not so obviously determined by their husband's status, if indeed they had one. Rather, their negotiations for seats within the women's half of the nave seem based on values that had more to do with their own interactions with other women. For example, Alice Lucas, who bought a seat under her own name, specifically requested a seat with Margaret Eldersham.[45] In 1515, Agnes Tebbe, wife of a parish carpenter, died, and Mistress Stevenson requested her vacant seat.[46] Agnes had occupied that seat since 1504.[47] With their husbands seemingly a nonissue with respect to seating, occupation of the women's space within the nave became a place to create a different kind of women's culture—operating alongside those women who were also trying to promote their families. Although this culture was by no means independent of or cut off from men, it points to a social and cultural community somewhat less defined by male authority.

The various decisions made by individual women in all three groups hint at some of the dynamics and priorities that informed their decisions. Although friendship or shared religious interests might have motivated Alice

Lucas and Margaret Eldersham, the behavior of Mistress Stevenson hints at a sort of competition behind some seating decisions. Similarly, Elizabeth Pomfriet, who bought the seat "under our lady," may have been displaying piety and devotion to St. Mary or a desire for visibility and self-promotion. Better or worse locations offered women opportunities to improve their position at the expense of another. The better seats were a sign of status and a means of visibility in and of themselves. Other women were clearly balancing a desire for communal acceptance and standing with their family's personal needs. Robert Watts' wife, who had moved twice by 1515, moved to a third seat in 1516 to sit with her mother, who might have been quite elderly.[48] For John Clerk's wife, the reasons for her move also seem to have had less to do with status and more to do with health. In 1500, she had her own pew, but in 1526, her husband, John the elder, took the unusual step of buying them a pew together.[49] The low price of his pew, twelve pence, and the low price for her move, four pence. as opposed to the more usual eight pence or twelve pence, suggests that this was not a particularly favorable spot in the nave. That they were to sit together suggests that one or the other needed constant help or supervision during the services. These examples suggest that concern for the spiritual and physical well-being of a family member could also be important reasons for buying a seat. Without a seat, an infirm member of the family might not be able to attend church. Thus seating decisions illuminate some of women's roles as caregivers.

Finally, small hints in the accounts suggest that life-cycle changes altered one's relationship to the space in the nave. Those in similar circumstances sat together. Changes in circumstance from single to married to widowed prompted some to change seats. In 1499, the parish built a pew for women to sit in during their churching, and in 1512, Henry Nowyk repaired it.[50] While women were in this state of being reintegrated back into the community after their confinement, they sat in a different seat that marked their status. In 1518, Mistress Pen bought the seat that Mistress Morley's daughter sat in before she was married, implying that Morley's daughter changed seats after her marriage.[51] Some parishes even had the maidens sit separate.[52] Simon Smith's wife only bought her pew in 1504, while her husband, the parish locksmith, had held his pew since 1486.[53] Simon died in 1504; his wife's pew might have been in recognition of her new status as widow.[54]

Although we do not know the exact arrangements of the nave, the detailed information about those who bought seats shows that marital status as well as social status shaped some of the laity's decisions about how to use the nave. For other parishioners, the motivations had more to do with personal circumstances, friendship, and piety. Whatever the reasons, the uses of space within the men's and women's sections were shaped by local social and economic pressures and bespeak a more complex set of desires than simply a need to protect men from the perceived dangers of women. Seating became a way for women to participate in parish life and to display their own priorities and concerns.

The concerns over status and marriage that women expressed in their seating appeared in other areas of this parish's culture. Women in this parish were particularly involved in fund-raising. Building a new church took a great deal of money, and St. Margaret's was very resourceful in creating activities to help finance its expanding church and its expanding liturgy. Some of these activities appear to have drawn upon the associations and connections women had already made while sitting within their half of the nave. In addition to benefiting the parish, women's fund-raising activities expressed concerns similar to those motivating seating decisions. Women's ability to articulate concerns over marriage and status in both seating and fund-raising shows the level to which their interests had been absorbed and legitimized by the rest of the parish.

At the end of the fifteenth century, under the guidance of the churchwardens and their wives, the married couples in the parish started celebrating the holiday of Hocktide, which fell on the second Monday and Tuesday after Easter.[55] On Hock Monday, the wives captured the husbands and held them for ransom, and on Tuesday they reversed the roles.[56] The money raised by the ransoms went to help build and furnish the new parish church. The women specifically used the proceeds from their 1509 celebrations to buy a new banner for St. Margaret's shrine.[57] By the early sixteenth century, there was also a guild for the unmarried women of the parish.[58] The "virgins," as they were called, raised money with a door-to-door collection to help finance the ever-expanding festival at St. Margaret.[59]

We can read both sets of women's activities as ways for the whole parish to address concerns revolving around gender. Through rituals of inversion, Hocktide helped the parish deal with the tension around the involvement of women in parish affairs. The celebration allowed married women to organize and raise funds for the parish, but while their work benefitted the parish, their domination over men was not permanent. When the holiday was over, they returned to their subordinate position, yet the parish remained permanently better off because of their activities. Similarly, the virgins' guild provided unmarried women with a chance to work with each other, demonstrate their piety and commitment to the church, and possibly attract a mate. As with Hocktide, the parish provided a safe context for women to act in ways not usually deemed appropriate. If single women had solicited money door-to-door outside the confines of their guild, the community would have viewed it and them in a very different way. In both instances, women, under the supervision of the parish administration, addressed concerns for women's status—the very concerns that their seating arrangements and use of space also addressed. Although the rise of Hocktide and the development of a women's guild were not predicated upon the prominence of women in church seating, we can see how one fueled the other. With the visibility that seating gave women, it was not a big step for them to involve themselves in other areas of the parish, especially with the financial needs that building a new church created. Having created such opportunities, seating arrangements continued to reinforce women's visibility and parish participation.

## BRIDGEWATER, SOMERSET

The Parish of St. Mary's in Bridgwater in central Somerset organized seating arrangements within their nave in a strikingly different way and to a much different purpose.[60] The addition of more pews in this nave served not to integrate women into the parish but rather to exclude them. The churchwardens' accounts for Bridgwater are earlier and more irregular than those from Westminster. Nonetheless, they still provide enough information to reconstruct some of the parish's seating priorities during one period in its history. Changes to Bridgwater's seating plans suggest the elimination of an institutionally sanctioned women's section in the nave. The nave became a place to demonstrate men's status gained from public office in the town. Comparing Bridgwater to Westminster highlights the local nature of parish culture and the ways in which seating arrangements manifested other concerns.

This parish included the prosperous port town of the same name on the Parrett River and seven surrounding hamlets.[61] In addition to trade in wine, dyestuffs, and food, Bridgwater was an important cloth-finishing center. By 1400, the population was about sixteen hundred.[62] By the midsixteenth century, however, the town had decayed and the parish served only six hundred communicants, probably half of what it had in the fifteenth century when the town had been more prosperous.[63] During the second half of the fourteenth and most of the fifteenth centuries, the period for which we have records, the parishioners continually expanded the parish church of St. Mary's. Starting in 1364, the parish rebuilt the tower. By 1471, the date of the last surviving pre-Reformation churchwardens' account, the parishioners had added eight identifiable chapels. While Westminster was built all at once and is of a uniform architectural style, Bridgewater is a combination of styles reflecting the piecemeal expansion of the church. The continual addition of chapels was a manifestation of the growing interest in new devotions. The parish paid for all this expansion with a parishwide assessment based on wealth, though later the parish switched to rental property as a source of income.[64] Selling seats earned the parish only a small amount of money; it was a convenience to those who needed it, not a major fundraiser. Unlike Westminster, however, seat arrangements in Bridgwater did not offer parish women the opportunity to expand on their own local subculture and gain a visible place in parish involvement. Instead, they restricted their involvement and visibility.

Between 1366 and 1471, there are twenty-six surviving churchwarden's accounts.[65] They record the names of fifty-nine people who bought seats from the wardens from between 1418, when the wardens first record selling seats, and 1471, the last surviving pre-Reformation churchwardens' account. There is even a rudimentary church seating plan from 1454 after the parish had outfitted part of the nave with new seats the previous year.[66] Those individuals listed in both the churchwarden's accounts and the seating plan can be cross-referenced in the borough records to assess their occupation or relative status.[67] The result is that we can see how seating changed in significance over time. The most abrupt change came with the installation of new pews in 1454.

When Bridgwater's wardens started to sell seats in 1418, there were only a few, they did not cost very much, and those who bought them seemed to have been the elderly or infirm. In this early phase, seating was a service to those in need. Before 1454, half of the people who had purchased pews were men, and half were women. Both groups appeared infrequently in the municipal records; the women were not part of prominent families, nor were their husbands holders of civic or parish offices or major land holders. The same is true for the men buying seats. Prior to the installation of new seats, only two bailiffs and a churchwarden purchased seats. This could be related as much to infirmity and poor health as to social status.

After the parish built new pews, however, the profile of those purchasing seats changed substantially. Seat purchasers were now men of substance active in town rather than in parish affairs. One was even a member of Parliament. A correlation of those who bought seats, both before and after 1454, with the amount they were assessed for the annual parish rate, shows similar and predictable changes. Those buying seats after 1454 were better off financially and lived in the wealthier neighborhoods than those who bought seats before 1454.

While the records list many important public officials as purchasers of parish seats, they do not show a similar correlation for holders of parish offices. The lack of men who *both* bought seats and held the parish offices of either churchwarden or guild warden suggests that running the parish did not impart the same level of social prominence as the town offices did. Status and prestige appear to have come from outside the parish and could be demonstrated by how much one gave to the church and where one sat in the nave. It is of course possible that churchwardens automatically received a seat upon assuming their office. Yet even if this is true, it does not significantly change the profile of the group. Although the new seating arrangement attracted wealthier and more prominent parishioners, the previous arrangement had reserved seats for those in physical need.

Adding new seats to the nave also altered the ratio of the men and women who held seats, and this change reflects other changes in the role of women in this community. Before the installation of the new pews, women, both on their own and through their husbands, had purchased 50 percent of the seats. With the introduction of more pews, the percentage of women purchasing seats declined to 37 percent. Although there is no indication of how complete the plan is, it only lists men. The plan itself also shows how men had begun to dominate the nave, even in those areas traditionally used by women. According to the plan, seating was in four parts of the nave: the church (probably the central part), the northern part, the southern part, and by the chapel of St. George. Men sat in all parts, even in the north side. Male domination of both sides of the nave further suggests that the women might have been relegated to the back (the west end) of the church, as far away from the chancel as possible. Women were cut off from typical ways one demonstrated piety, since from the back of the church it was more difficult to see the elevation of the host at the high altar. However incomplete the plan, its existence and the lack of women in it further indicate how the significance of seating had changed.

The installation of new seats appears to have been part of a fundamental rethinking of the parish's position in the town and of the role of the parishioners in the parish, although what exactly motivated this change remains unclear. Repewing the church came at the same time that the parish dropped its annual rate as a form of fund-raising. Previously, all heads of households, which sometimes meant women, had supported the parish through the annual collection.[68] Now the household was no longer a unit of parish support. According to the churchwardens' accounts, the parish began to finance itself exclusively through the collection of rents from houses it owned and from pious gifts. Clive Burgess recently argued that churchwardens are only one layer of church administration and record keeping. If this is true in the case of Bridgwater, there might be other sources of income that were not a part of the churchwardens' duties and hence did not make it into their accounts.[69] Nevertheless, unless women rented property or left a testamentary bequest, they could not directly support the parish. These changes also affected the men of the parish. However, unlike women, men could serve in parish offices and work as individuals to maintain the parish. As individuals they might be excluded from parish offices, but not as a sex.

The parish of Bridgwater thus eliminated several aspects of its parish culture that had included women and began displaying status that was largely created in the male public domain, outside the parish's lay organization. Before the midfifteenth century, single women as heads of households and women who bought seats had achieved a level of visibility and participation in this parish. These avenues of involvement were now curtailed. To be sure, women were still encouraged to demonstrate their piety, but now only through their subordination to family identity. Unlike Westminster, widows or unmarried women remained largely invisible in the parish records, because they had little or no official involvement in parish affairs and because they were excluded from civic offices.

Also unlike Westminster, Bridgwater held no such festivals as Hocktide and had no guild for married or unmarried women.[70] The churchwardens' accounts list few gifts from women. Parish leaders gave no officially recognized space to women in parish culture, both literally and figuratively. The space of the nave became a venue in which to display male status—a space in which women were notably absent. Although women might still have brought their own stools, the new use of seats in Bridgwater's parish church transformed the way the parishioners used and valued the space within the nave and reflected the town's domination of the parish. Despite this situation, we can hypothesize that the women in Bridgwater shared some of the same concerns expressed by women in Westminster. Because the Bridgwater women were operating outside of the concerns of the parish's administration they were not visible or legitimized. In essence, the lay space of Bridgwater's parish came to mirror the male space of public affairs.

The parish was a religious community of both men and women, even if the female half appears less often in the surviving records. Women's lack of political power and financial and legal influences usually meant that their contributions to the parish are obscured by their family role. A pious bequest listed as coming from an individual man might in fact have been a family decision, even if the churchwardens' accounts do not record it as such. Considering then how parishioners arranged themselves when they attended Mass provides a way of seeing women in parish life when they are otherwise hidden in the documents. How the community allocated and valued that space supplies further insight into the place of gender in local religion. Yet when we finally move to how women themselves used seating arrangements, we see something of their own priorities and concerns of family and caregiving but also status and competition as they were played out in these social conditions.

Comparing the arrangements of particular naves demonstrates the exceedingly local character of spatial organization and gender relations. Parishioners would probably have been familiar with the symbolism and associations of the north side and the right hand of God, as Corine Schleif describes in her chapter, but they did not confine their organization of space within the church to only these concerns. Although gender was an organizing principle for seating arrangements, it was more complicated than the mere separation of the sexes. Giving women a space within the nave was recognition that they were a part of the parish community, but a part that needed definition and perhaps confinement. At the same time, the nave could become a place to develop and articulate both social and religious concerns that were specific to them. Official recognition by the parish administration served to publicize and legitimize their concerns. Once legitimized, women were able to claim a larger role in their parish's communal activities. Conversely, limiting women's space within the nave was a way of limiting their involvement in the publicly recognized ways of practicing religion and thus limiting their involvement in the parish.

In some ways, the women's activities in Westminster are unusual, although by no means unique.[71] My point is not that having a women's half of the nave automatically led to the formation of women's guilds or women's festivals. Rather, I am arguing that space within the nave could serve as a site for articulation of an individual or collective identity, in a number of differing ways. Women sat together because they were women, but smaller groups of women as defined by social or marital status or pious interests also sat together. These shared conditions and identities brought them together in the nave in particular configurations. These arrangements legitimized them, and this legitimacy served as a catalyst for further social and economic contact and involvement.

## NOTES

The research in this chapter is part of a longer study, *The Good Women of the Parish*, forthcoming from the University of Pennsylvania Press.

1. Medieval English canon law further emphasized this division by dividing responsibility for the care of parish churches between the rector and the laity. The chancel was the rector's concern, and the nave, the laity's. Charles Drew, *Early Parochial Organisation in England: The Origin of the Office of Churchwarden*, St. Anthony Hall Publications, no. 7 (York: Borthwick Institute of Historical Research, 1954).

2. Margaret Aston, "Segregation in Church," in *Women in the Church*, ed. W. J. Sheils and Diana Wood, Studies in Church History, vol. 27 (Oxford: Blackwell, 1990), 237–81.

3. Roberta Gilchrist, *Gender and Material Culture: The Archaeology of Religious Women* (London: Routledge, 1994), 150.

4. H. L. Moore, *Space, Text, and Gender: An Anthropological Study of the Marakwet of Kenya* (Cambridge: Cambridge University Press, 1986), 78.

5. In some parishes, the earliest seats were probably reserved for the aged, infirm, and women. See J. Charles Cox, *Bench-ends in English Churches* (Oxford: Oxford University Press, 1916), 10. Yet some clergy felt that it was inappropriate and against the rules for women to have seats. In the visitation of the Hereford conducted in 1397, the visitor claimed that "it is ordained from antiquity that women should not sit in the church." Because the parishioners of Brunley did not observe this rule they were fined six shillings, eight pence. A. T. Bannister, ed., "Visitation Returns of the Diocese of Hereford in 1397," *English Historical Review* 45 (1930): 449.

6. As pews became more prevalent in the late fifteenth century, they sported a new genre of decorative carving. Cox, *Bench-ends*; J. D. C. Smith, *Church Woodcarvings: A West Country Study* (New York: Kelly, 1969); Peter Poyntz Wright, *Rural Benchends of Somerset* (Amersham, England: Avebury, 1983).

7. Public Record Office, STAC 2/12/224–226: " "held as his demesne as of fee 1 messuage or tenement with appurtenances in Minehead in your county of Somerset and by reason thereof used to have a seat or pew for him and his wife in the said church of Minehead."

8. Somerset Record Office (S.R.O.), D/P/ilm 4/1/1 fol. 5.

9. Aston, "Segregation in Church," 238–42.

10. Robert Mannyng, *Handlyng Synne*, ed. Idelle Sullens (Binghamton: Medieval and Renaissance Texts and Studies, 1983), 221: "Women do great folly/When they stand among the clergy/Whether at matins or at mass/Unless it is from need,/ For of it may come temptation/And disturbing of devotion."

11. See also Aston, "Segregation in Church," 238–42; Gilchrist, *Gender and Material Culture*, 133.

12. Aston, "Segregation in Church," 269–81; Gilchrist, *Gender and Material Culture*, 133–35.

13. Gilchrist, *Gender and Material Culture*, 133–35.

14. I am drawing here on Henretta Moore's distinction between the movement through space and its implications for cultural analysis and an analysis of spatial organization. See H. L. Moore, *Space, Text, and Gender*, 79–90.

15. Barbara Hanawalt, "At the Margins of Women's Space in Medieval Europe," in *"Of Good and Ill Repute:" Gender and Social Control in Medieval England* (New York: Oxford University Press, 1998), 70–87.

16. Lincoln Record Office, *Calendar of Memoranda Book of Bishop John Dalderby of Lincoln*, vol. 3, 474. I am grateful to Sandy Bardsley for this reference.

17. London Guildhall Library, MS 9064/2 (Commissary Court Act Book), fol. 163v. I am grateful to Shannon McSheffrey for this citation.

18. Ruth Mazo Karras, *Common Women: Prostitution and Sexuality in Medieval England* (New York: Oxford University Press, 1996), 95–101. On a day-to-day basis, so-called respectable women might in fact meet up with and interact with prostitutes. Some prostitutes provided women with sex education and information about prospective husbands. See Karras, 95–97.

19. Steve Hindle, "The Shaming of Margaret Knowsley: Gossip, Gender and the Experience of Authority in Early Modern England," *Continuity and Change* 9:3 (1994): 391–419.

20. "How the Good Wife Taught Her Daughter," in *The Babees' Book*, ed. F. J. Furnivall, EETS OS 32 (London: N. Trübner, 1868), 37: "When you sit in the church, you should pray/ your beads;/ Make no chattering to friends or/relations;/ Do not scorn either the old or the/ young,/ But be of fair bearing and of good tongue." See also Felicity Riddy, "Mother Knows Best: Reading Social Change in a Courtesy Text," *Speculum* 71 (1996): 66–86.

21. R. A. Houlbrooke, "Women's Social Lives and Common Action in England from the Fifteenth Century to the Eve of the Civil War," *Continuity and Change* 1:2 (1986): 171–89.

22. The postplague period was a time of great growth and expansion in parish churches throughout England. Edwin Smith, Graham Hutton, and Olive Cook, *English Parish Churches* (New York: Thames and Hudson, 1979), 117–24. See also Beat Kümin, *The Shaping of a Community: The Rise and Reformation of the English Parish, 1400–1560* (Aldershot, Hants: Scolar, 1996), 125–47.

23. Gervase Rosser, *Medieval Westminster: 1200–1540* (Oxford: Oxford University Press, 1989), 168–76. The chantry certificate lists twenty-five hundred communicants for St. Margaret. C. J. Kitching, ed., *London and Middlesex Chantry Certificates: 1548*, London Record Society, vol. 16 (1980), no. 139. For occupations of Westminster, see Rosser, *Medieval Westminster*, 119–65.

24. Rosser, *Medieval Westminster*, 221–24, 26769.

25. Westminster City Archives (W.C.A.), E1, fols. 161–62.

26. W.C.A., E1, fols. 431, 453–54.

27. W.C.A., E1, fol. 487.

28. W.C.A., E1, fol. 514, E2 (1512).

29. W.C.A., E2 (1523).

30. W.C.A., E1, fols. 111, 369–70, 417, 447, 514.

31. W.C.A., E1, fol. 336, E2 (1516).

32. In a parish of 2000, this meant that only a portion—the more financially well-off portion—of the parish was involved in seating concerns in any given year. Most still brought their own stools or stood in the back. Wealth would seem to increase the level to which an individual would identify with a particular space.

33. Cox also notes, with great unease, that women buy more seats. He suggests that women buy more seats because more women attended Mass, an observation others have made as well. Cox, *Bench-ends*, 20–25.

34. There is always a question of how accurate these records are. It is clear that there were individuals sitting in seats that are never recorded as purchasing a seat. There are also individuals who move seats for whom there is no record of the original purchase. My statistics include both those listed as moved and those who the records claim have moved.

35. Married men are generally identified in the churchwardens' accounts through their wives who are listed as the wife of so-and-so. Further prosopographical research may identify more married couples.

36. Rosser, *Medieval Westminster*, appendix 8, 403, 405.

37. W.C.A., E1, fols. 101–02; 156–57, 447, 534.

38. W.C.A., E1 fol. 545.

39. David Gary Shaw, *The Creation of a Community: The City of Wells in the Middle Ages* (Oxford: Oxford University Press, 1993), 177–215.

40. For more on the number of life-long single women in the English population, see Maryanne Kowaleski, "Single Women in Medieval and Early Modern Europe: The Demographic Perspective," in *Single Women in the European Past, 1250–1800*, ed. Judith Bennett and Amy Froide (Philadelphia: University of Pennsylvania Press), 38–81.

41. W.C.A., E1, fols. 471–73.

42. W.C.A., E1, fols. 369–70. She bought her seat in 1500 for two shillings. She supervised the virgins' guild in 1503 (fol. 446) and gave to the parish's benevolent fund under her own name in 1504 (fol. 479). She died in 1505 (fol. 526). The accounts never mention her in conjunction with a man, nor have I found mention of a man with the same last name.

43. W.C.A., E1, fols. 212, 447.

44. Baynbrygge was churchwarden from 1476 through 1478, and Atwell, warden of the parish's assumption guild from 1505 through 1508. Rosser, 368, 371.

45. W.C.A., E2 (1518).

46. W.C.A., E2 (1515).

47. W.C.A., E1. Agnes bought her first seat in 1503, when the north aisle received its new pews. Her husband gave a special gift for the building of new pews and bought a seat for himself that same year (fols. 471–75). Agnes then paid twelve pence the next year to move her pew. It was this seat she occupied for the rest of her life (fol. 508).

48. W.C.A., E1, fol., 554, E2 (1511) (1516).

49. W.C.A., E2 (1526).

50. W.C.A., E1, fol. 380, E2 (1512).

51. W.C.A., E2 (1518).

52. Cox, *Bench-ends*, 21; Aston, "Segregation in Church," 287.

53. W.C.A., E1, fols. 471–73, 233–34 (for his activities as locksmith see fols. 191, 288, 290, 339).

54. W.C.A., E1, fol. 469.

55. W.C.A., E1 fol. 335 (first appearance).

56. Katherine L. French, " 'To Free Them from Binding': Women in the Late Medieval English Parish," *Journal of Interdisciplinary History* 27:3 (1997): 387–412; Sally-Beth MacLean, "Hocktide: A Reassessment of a Popular Pre-Reformation Festival," in *Festive Drama*, ed. Meg Twycross (Cambridge: Brewer, 1996), 233–41.

57. W.C.A., E1, fol. 574.

58. W.C.A., E2 (1512) (1513) et passim.

59. For more on the festival see Rosser, *Medieval Westminster*, 272–74; for the virgins see Katherine L. French, "Maidens' Lights and Wives' Stores: Women's Parish Guilds in Late Medieval England," *Sixteenth Century Journal* 29: 2 (1998): 399–425.

60. For more on Bridgwater see Katherine L. French, *The People of the Parish: Community Life in a Medieval English Diocese* (Philadelphia: University of Pennsylvania Press, 2001).

61. Thomas B. Dilks, ed., *Bridgwater Borough Archives: 1200–1377*, vol. 1, Somerset Record Society, vol. 48 (London: Somerset Record Society, 1933), xxxvi.

62. R. W. Dunning, ed., *VCH-Somerset*, vol. 6 (Oxford: Oxford University Press, for Institute of Historical Research, 1992), 197.

63. *VCH-Somerset*, vol. 6, 197–200.

64. Katherine L. French, *People of the Parish*, 99–141.

65. SRO, D/P/bw. See also Thomas Bruce Dilks, ed., *Bridgwater Borough Archives: 1200–1468*, vols. 1–4. ed., Somerset Record Society, vols. 48, 53, 58, 60 (Somerset: Somerset Record Society, 1933, 1938, 1945, 1948).

66. SRO, D/P bw no. 99.

67. *Bridgwater Borough Archives: 1200–1468*, vols. 1–4.

68. There are collections surviving for three years: 1445, 1446, and an undated one from about the same time. In the first two lists, women comprise 5 percent of the listed individuals and gave 5 percent of the total income. In the undated list, the percentage of income is higher (11 percent) as is the percentage of women (22 percent). This last list also included servants, which helps account for the increase in women. SRO, D/P/bw no. 806, 807, 1649. See also *Bridgwater Borough Archives*, vol. 4, 7–34.

69. Clive Burgess, "Pre-Reformation Churchwardens' Accounts and Parish Government: Lessons from London and Bristol," *English Historical Review* 17:1471 (April 2002): 306–32.

70. There is a gap in the churchwardens' accounts from 1472 to 1548. The 1549 account does not show the development of women's activities in the intervening years. Although this is not conclusive, it is suggestive. The 1549 account does sell six seats; only two are to women, and they are of a much lower price than the four men's seats. SRO D/B/bw 1447.

71. The women in the Salisbury parish of St. Edumund's had similar experiences. Like the women in Westminster, the women in St. Edmund's bought most of

the seats, and also like Westminster, there was a Hocktide celebration and a women's guild. Henry James Fowle Swayne, ed., *Churchwardens' Accounts of S. Edmund and S. Thomas Sarum, 1443–1702*, Wiltshire Record Society, vol. 1 (1896).

## FURTHER READING

Margaret Aston, "Segregation in Church." In *Women in the Church*, ed. W. J. Sheils and Diana Wood, Studies in Church History, vol. 27. Oxford: Basil Blackwell, 1990.

Cox, J. Charles. *Bench–ends in English Churches*. Oxford: Oxford University Press, 1916.

Eamon Duffy, *Stripping of the Altars: Traditional Religion in England, 1400–1580*. New Haven, Connecticut: Yale University Press, 1992.

Katherine L. French, " 'To Free Them from Binding': Women in the Late Medieval English Parish." *Journal of Interdisciplinary History* 27:3 (1997): 387–412.

———. "Maidens' Lights and Wives' Stores: Women's Parish Guilds in Late Medieval England." *Sixteenth Century Journal* 29:2 (1998): 399–425.

Pamela Graves, "Social Space in the English Medieval Parish Church." *Economy and Society* 18:3 (1989): 297–322.

SIX

# ACCESS TO SALVATION: THE PLACE (AND SPACE) OF WOMEN PATRONS IN FOURTEENTH-CENTURY FLORENCE

Ena Giurescu Heller

PRIVATE INITIATIVES IN COMMISSIONING ART and architecture abound in fourteenth-century Florence. In the newly built (or rebuilt) churches of the mendicant orders, wealthy Florentines endowed funerary and commemorative chapels and altars, embellishing them with frescoes, altarpieces, and liturgical objects.[1] These individuals were often well-known figures of the urban elite, who contributed to the commune's political and economic strength; they were merchants, bankers, soldiers, politicians, and ecclesiastics. Their names were Donato Peruzzi, Mico di Lapo Guidalotti, Tommaso di Rossello degli Strozzi, today remembered, respectively, through Giotto's frescoes in the Peruzzi Chapel in Santa Croce; the chapter house in the cloisters of Santa Maria Novella and its frescoes by Andrea da Firenze; the altarpiece by Andrea Orcagna in the Strozzi Chapel in Santa Maria Novella (figure 6.1). They were all men. For the same place and period, how many women's names does one associate with chapels, frescoes, or altarpieces? I suspect that only those of us who have studied Florentine fourteenth-century chapel patronage in depth would think of Guardina Tornaquinci, Andrea Acciaiuoli, and Gemma Velutti. Most studies of patronage do not even pause to ponder why so few women are ever mentioned, and those dedicated

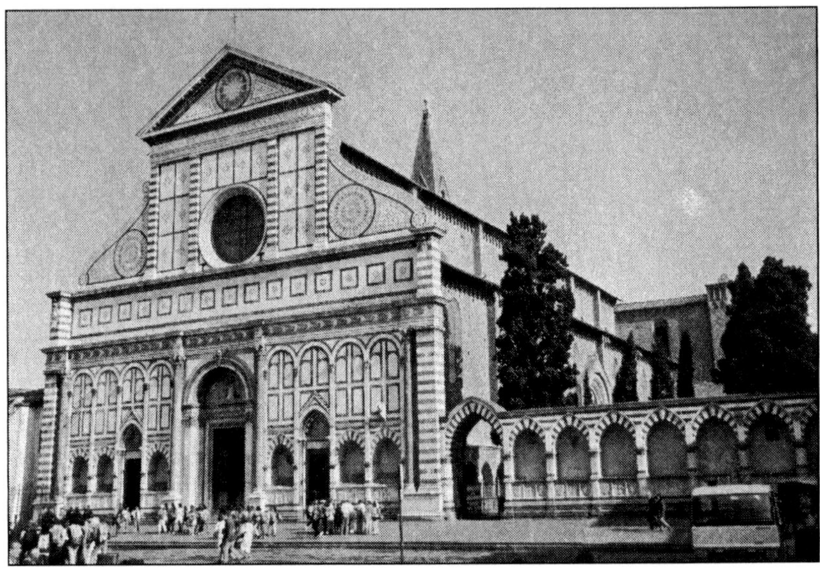

**Figure 6.1.** Santa Maria Novella, Florence, facade of the church. Ena Giurescu Heller.

specifically to women patrons invariably remark on the rather small percentage of female initiatives among the commissioning of art and architecture.[2] One cannot help but ask, why were there so few women patrons in a society so rich in liquid wealth and so inclined to spending on art? More important, why do we know so little even about the few documented cases?

This study, which focuses on the sacristy/chapel of Santa Maria Novella, was in part prompted by these questions. The sacristy's history is a revealing source of information on fourteenth-century women patrons, and its historiography sheds light on their subsequent oblivion. Presented against the background of known data about fourteenth-century Florentine society and other documented cases of female patronage, the sacristy/chapel of Santa Maria Novella is a case study that provides a starting point in a more comprehensive and much needed study of the place and space of women patrons in *trecento* Florence.

Mainardo Cavalcanti's will of 25 January 1380 (1379 Florentine style) provided for the building of a chapel in the southwest corner of Santa Maria Novella's transept (figure 6.2).[3] Dedicated to the Virgin Annunciate, the structure was intended dually as sacristy for the Dominicans and funerary chapel for the Cavalcanti family. Its architecture replicates, albeit on a larger scale, the plan and elevation of earlier chapels in the church: it is a single rectangular bay covered with a quadripartite rib vault and has a large triple lancet window centered on the wall opposite the entrance.[4] The altar, adorned

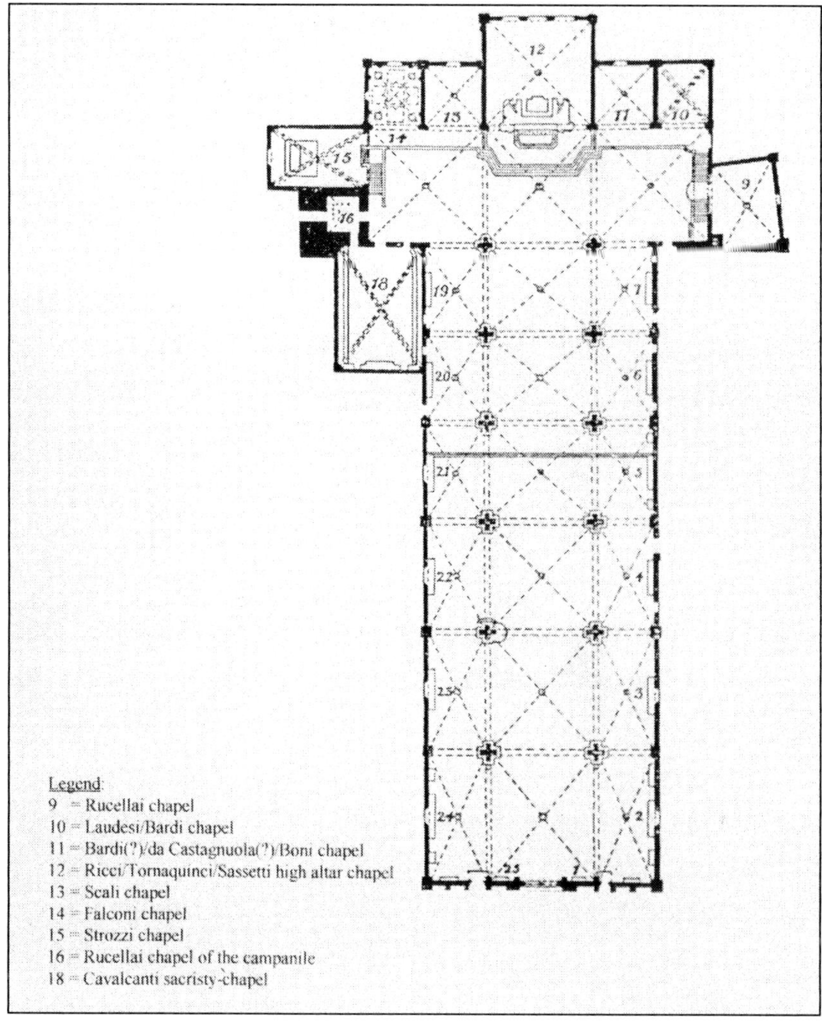


**Figure 6.2.** Santa Maria Novella, Florence, plan of the church in the fourteenth century. After James Wood Brown, *The Dominican Church of Santa Maria Novella of Florence* (Edinburgh, 1902).

with an altarpiece of the *Annunciation*, was originally placed below the window. Tomb slabs for various members of the family were on the floor before it, and the marble monument to the founder was placed against the west wall. Today very little of the *trecento* interior is preserved: in the late sixteenth century the altar and tombs were removed and replaced with a reliquary cabinet (figure 6.3). The painted archivolts articulating the upper walls and the trifora decorated with stained glass are today the only elements preserved from the original detailing, which may have also included frescoes.[5]

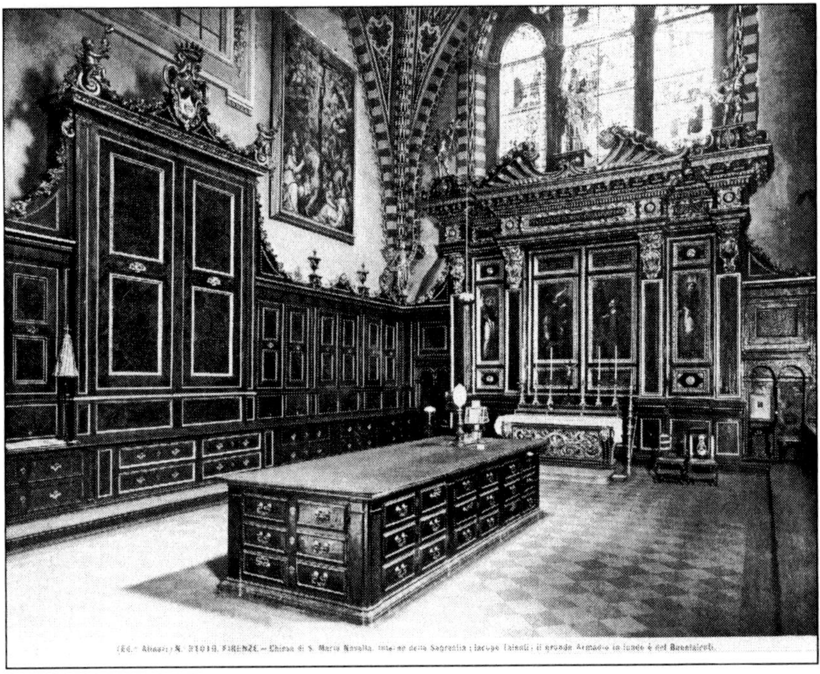

**Figure 6.3.** Sacristy, interior view, Santa Maria Novella, Florence. Alinai/Art Resource, N.Y.

The history of the space is well documented. Mainardo provided for the foundation, endowed it with a yearly fifteen florins for maintenance and votive masses and named his wife Monna Andrea (or Andreola), daughter of Jacopo di Donato Acciaiuoli, as executrix.[6] It was she who undertook the actual building of the sacristy/chapel and later added her own bequests to that of her husband, commissioning the altarpiece and stained glass window and possibly frescoes. Her active role as patron of the family chapel is recorded by all contemporary documents pertaining to the decoration and functioning of the space.

The extant contract for the stained glass, dated 16 November 1386, informs us that the subject matter of the window was yet to be established, but the glazier, Don Leonardo di Simone, a Vallombrosian monk, had already acquired some glass, for which he received ninety florins. Monna Andrea's role is unequivocally expressed in the terms of the contract, which specifies that the iconography was to comprise "quelle storie che piaceranno alla detta madonna Andrea."[7] In actuality, Monna Andrea could hardly have had such freedom in deciding the subject matter of the stained glass; indeed, fourteenth-century patrons had very little say in iconographic matters, which were at least supervised, and most often wholly controlled, by the Dominicans.[8] The contract, however, makes it clear that she was in charge of the commission.

The window depicts the *Annunciation* at the top of the central lancet (the prominence of its placement consistent with the dedication of the chapel), with the *Birth and Naming of St. John the Baptist* and the *Nativity of Christ* below; scenes from *The Life of St.John the Baptist* in the flanking lancets (the *Annunciation to Zacchariah* and *St. John presenting Christ to the people* on the left; and the *Young Baptist in the Desert* and *St. John before Herod* on the right); and the prophets *Elias* and *Isaiah* in the roundels.[9] The iconography thus focuses on the legend of the precursor but includes also those episodes from the Life of Christ related to the Incarnation. Since the altarpiece, originally situated directly below the window, represented the Annunciation, an intentional iconographic connection between the two was likely.[10] This cohesion of the decorative program of the space may indicate the existence of a learned advisor supervising Monna Andrea's patronage.[11]

The altarpiece for the chapel, a large triptych of the *Annunciation to the Virgin* by Giovanni del Biondo and his workshop (figure 6.4), seems to have

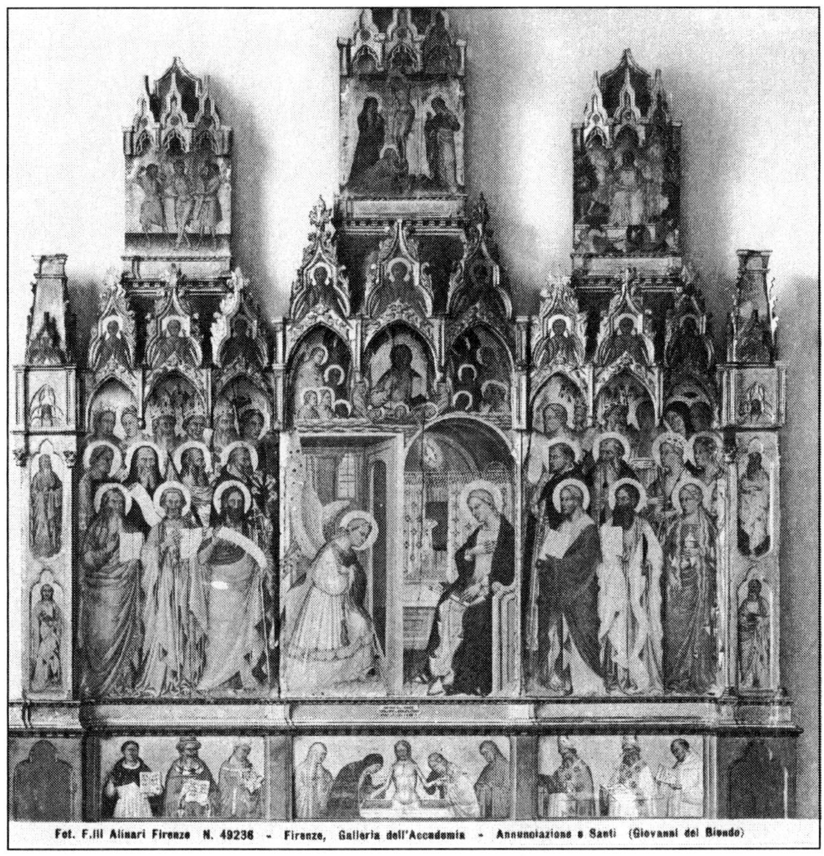


**Figure 6.4.** Giovanni del Biondo, *Annunciation and Saints*. ca. 1385, tempera on panel, Accademia, Florence. Alinai/Art Resource, N.Y.

been commissioned by Monna Andrea around the same time. The contract has not survived, but the work has been dated on stylistic grounds to around 1385. The central panel portrays the archangel Gabriel reverently kneeling in front of a Madonna caught by surprise while reading. They are flanked by three rows of standing saints, holding books, scrolls, or their attributes, and half-figures of saints in the pinnacles above. Each of the three wings is crowned by another, larger pinnacle, depicting scenes from the Passion of Christ: *Flagellation* on the left, the *Resurrection* on the right, and the *Crucifixion* in the center, directly above the *Annunciation*. The corresponding scene in the *predella* is the *Man of Sorrows* with the Three Marys and St. John the Evangelist, flanked by half-figures of clerical saints below the lateral wings.[12] The iconography thus centers on the dedication of the chapel but weaves in themes related to Christ's Passion and the implicit hope for redemption. The prayer and hope were certainly the patron's: the arms of the Cavalcanti are displayed in all three pinnacles, in close proximity to the Passion scenes. On the outer side of the frame pilasters, Monna Andrea also included the arms of her own family, the Acciaiuoli, next to those of her husband. The same shields had also decorated the frontal base of the pilasters, now blank: documentary sources indicate that the arms of the Cavalcanti were on the (proper) right, with those of the Acciaiuoli on the left.[13] It is probably not coincidental that Andrea's patron saint, Andrew, and that of her father, James, figure prominently in the first row of saints flanking the *Annunciation*.[14] St. John the Baptist, whose legend is the main subject of the stained glass, is seen in the foreground of the left wing, next to the archangel Gabriel. Reciprocity is thus created between the altarpiece and stained glass. The window displays the *Annunciation* in its uppermost panel, introducing the central theme of the altarpiece; the altarpiece points back to the Life of St. John the Baptist narrated in the stained glass. The cohesiveness of the iconographic program is manifest, its different elements complementing each other and contributing to the overall message. Although the earliest mention of the altarpiece in the sacristy dates only from 1586, there seems to be little doubt that it was indeed commissioned for this space.[15]

By the end of the 1380s the sacristy/chapel and its furnishings must have been completed, since authorization was sought to hire a chaplain. The authorization, granted to Monna Andrea in 1390, recognizes her as de facto patron of the structure, "quam ipsa domina uxor domini Mainardi de Cavalcantibus construxit."[16] It seems likely that in the years to follow, Andrea continued to be actively involved with the family chapel, insuring its upkeep. At the end of her life, she requested to be buried in the chapel, alongside Mainardo and two of her sons. In her will, drawn up in 1411, she also made a final bequest of two hundred florins for the painting of the space.[17] Since no trace other than decoratively painted ribs and archivolts has survived, it is unclear whether the chapel was frescoed. Fineschi recorded in the eighteenth century that the chapel had been "in antico dipinta, ma essendo perdute, e smarrite le figure, fu restaurata, e lasciati solamente gli ornati agli spigoli della gran volta."[18] Whether the frescoes were executed or not, it is noteworthy that Monna Andrea provided for them in her will, so the decorative program of the chapel could be completed.

As recounted so far, the history of Santa Maria Novella's sacristy seems remarkably straightforward. Mainardo Cavalcanti founded it through testamentary bequest, and his widow and executrix took charge of the project and saw to its completion, decoration, and functioning. She thus fulfilled her husband's last wishes and assured him a proper resting place, near the altar where frequent votive masses and prayers for his soul were said. Why, then, is a reassessment of the patronage history necessary? Indeed, if the recorded story of the sacristy ended with the hiring of its chaplain, this study would be unnecessary. Since then, however, much has intervened.

Our perception of the past is inevitably influenced by a large array of factors and constructs (our own as well as those of previous centuries). First, primary sources are joined, explained, detailed, and often contradicted by later documents and interpretations. The historiography of a building (or any other work of art, as well as of an event or place) becomes an essential component of how we understand it. At the same time, we cannot fully assess any one event (in this case, act of patronage) unless we place it within the more comprehensive context of the society whose norms, rules, laws, and customs prompted and governed it. The analysis of the mainly female patronage of Santa Maria Novella's sacristy in the context of late fourteenth- and early fifteenth-century Florence sheds light on women's status and place. Women assumed a subordinate position even when actively involved in an act of patronage, which implies power of decision and personal disposable wealth. Monna Andrea's own testimony stands witness: in her 1411 will she regards the chapel as belonging to Mainardo and his sons, and not her.[19] At the same time, despite Andrea being effectively in charge after her husband's passing (including additional bequests of her own money); despite her arms on the altarpiece witnessing her contribution; and despite her being recognized as builder and de facto patron in 1390, her tomb did not even come close to the magnificent wall monument in which her husband was buried, and her funeral could in no way have rivaled the luxury and pomp about which documents marvel when describing Mainardo's. This role of subordination was picked up by later sources, even more to the detriment of Monna Andrea's contribution. If late fourteenth- and early fifteenth-century documents recognize her active patronage of the sacristy and chapel, later texts completely erase her name and give sole credit to Mainardo. Possibly an attempt to resolve, or rather not bother with, the apparent contradiction of female initiatives in a rigid patrilineal society, these new histories of patronage also reflect the later centuries' own male-oriented view of history. The remainder of this study will investigate both the fourteenth-century view of Andrea's contribution, including her own testimony, and history's rewriting of the events.

Late medieval Florence was a patriarchal society in which men created the rules and controlled the rights, power of decision, and wealth of its members. Women were legally dependent on their fathers or husbands; as contemporary documents point out so clearly, they were always somebody's daughter or wife and continued to be referred to as such even after the death of their male guardian.[20] Women had no right to guild membership or communal offices and were barred even from public ceremonies associated with the government; in general, their participation of any kind in the public life of Florence was discouraged and strictly regulated.[21] The low status of women affected even infants: the *Catasto* of 1427 indicates that girls were much more likely to not be registered at birth than boys, clearly a reflection of negligence and/or indifference for female offspring.[22] Giovanni di Pagolo Morelli (1371–1444) included in his *Ricordi* a long list of the qualities for which a woman should strive, and the aspects of behavior (focused on better serving the husband) she should constantly improve. Should a woman always behave according to his advice, she had a better chance of having sons, while a rebellious attitude would lead to having daughters, clearly an unwelcome turn of events in Morelli's opinion.[23] Girls grew up as isolated as possible, shielded from—and instructed to avoid at any cost—contact with strangers and taught to obey their fathers, and later their husbands, in all matters. Indeed, the most important decisions in a woman's life were not her own. If her family had enough money for a desirable dowry, it would seek to marry her when extremely young and make an advantageous alliance. When the family could not afford a dowry, for a much smaller amount it could send the daughter to a convent. What had to be avoided was a woman living on her own, since women were not, in the view of society (i.e., of their male contemporaries), capable of resisting sin and making the right decisions.

Widows and even recluses were no exceptions to this rule: a woman's place, in medieval Florence, was in a household whose male head could keep an eye on her, prevent her from dangerous contact, and of course control her wealth.[24] Although a woman's dowry was in theory hers, it was unlikely she would ever come into actual possession of the money. When a girl married, the dowry went to her husband, who used and controlled it during their marriage. In the event of his death, the widow could reclaim her money and live independently: widowhood (providing the dowry was sufficient) was the only time when a woman was allowed some freedom in choosing the path of her future. Theoretically true, this course of action was hardly ever an actual choice for widowed Florentines.[25] If she were still very young, the widow's family would get involved trying to remarry her as fast as possible; if she were older and consequently had slim chances of remarrying, it was up to the husband's family to convince her to continue living in their household and not reclaim her dowry, that is, be an "honorable widow."

Either scenario insured that she continued to be dependent; situations in which women could make their own decisions were to be avoided at any cost. Revealing, in this context, is the example of Madonna Isabetta Sassetti, whose husband died in 1389 leaving her with three small children. Although she had been named guardian and coadministrator of the boys' inheritance in her husband's will, her family made her renounce these rights and promptly remarried her.[26] Thus even in the rare instance when the husband gave his widow rights over part of his legacy and trusted her with the raising of their children, the widow's family could still disregard these last wishes and dictate differently for the young woman. It seems that custom and tradition ruled supreme, and very few widows actually came in possession of their money and/or property. In other words, wealthy Florentine women were wealthy for their male relatives but never for themselves: the vast majority could not spend, donate, or enjoy their money. This of course explains the limited scope of women's artistic commissions, for which disposable wealth was necessary. At the same time, active patronage also implied personal decisions—another extremely limited prerogative of a woman living in fourteenth-century Florence.

The only time women could use their money according to their wishes (providing it had not been already spent by then) was on their deathbed: the archives of Florence are rich in female wills donating to churches, charitable institutions, or their relatives.[27] Bequests made specifically in connection with a funerary chapel fall under two different categories. The first category consists of women who contributed to the chapels founded by their families: some, like Monna Andrea, in order to fulfill the last wishes of their deceased husbands; others to complete the decoration or provide the maintenance of the space, especially if they also chose to be buried there. Most of these women get little credit in documents regarding the respective chapels, which as a rule mention only the founder. The second, less numerous, category comprises women who took the initiative and built or acquired a chapel for themselves and their descendants.

Such is the case of Monna Gemma Velluti, patron of the St. Michael Chapel in Santa Croce.[28] Donato di Berto Velluti, who wrote a *cronica* of the family between 1367 and 1370, records that Monna Gemma, the second wife of his grandfather Filippo di Bonaccorso, "fece compiere la cappella, ch'è in Santa Croce allato all'uscio della sagrestia, ch'è sotto in nome di San Michele: la quale cominciata per altrui, e peró vi sono dipinte l'arme nostre e di quello coale; ed io feci compiere le graticole del ferro dopo la mortalità del 1348, essendo ella morta per la mortalità del 1340."[29] Gemma, daughter of Scolaio de'Pulci, married Filippo in 1296 and was widowed sometime before 1321, when her son Alessandro also met an untimely death. After her son's death, Gemma rented out the houses she had inherited from him and retired to live at Santa Croce as a Franciscan tertiary.[30] She belonged therefore to that minority of widows who late in life (after the death of all male heirs) gained control of their personal wealth, part of which she used to acquire the Chapel of St. Michael in memory of her dead son and complete its frescoed decoration.[31] Even if Gemma's name had not been preserved in the family *cronica* (or had been later omitted and/or forgotten, as appears to have been the fate of Andrea Acciaiuoli), the frescoes still extant in the chapel tell their own story of patronage and personal message of salvation. The inclusion in the iconographic scheme of the rarely depicted St. Alessandro of Fiesole, the patron saint of Gemma's dead son, cannot be coincidental.[32] The other walls depict episodes from the legend of the archangel Michael, to whom the chapel is dedicated: *St. Michael Fighting the Dragon* on the south wall, and *The Miracle at Mount Gargano* on the north.[33] In the latter scene, a young woman with a small child is given special prominence in the group of adoring figures on the right. She may represent Gemma with her son, Alessandro, at the time when she was widowed, perhaps the time of her acquiring the chapel in Santa Croce (figure 6.5).[34] Gemma's patronage is not unique in *trecento* Florence, but as a widow who had access to her assets and could use them freely, she belongs to a minority. One cannot help but wonder, however, if she would have considered, under different circumstances, to set up such a memorial for herself, instead of her son.

Indeed, evidence found elsewhere sheds light on the way women themselves perceived their role and position in the society of the time. Monna

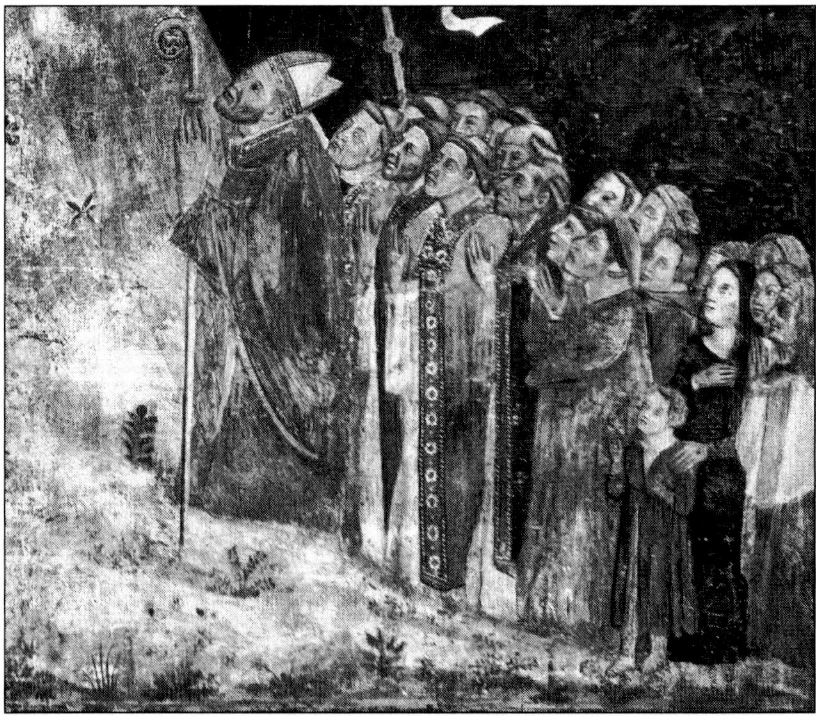

**Figure 6.5.** Italian School, *Apparition of St. Michael* (detail), 1330s, fresco, Velluti Chapel, Santa Croce, Florence. Alinai/Art Resource, N.Y.

Andrea Acciaiuoli's will is a case in point. As mentioned already, she requested burial in the sacristy/chapel, in one of the tombs located at the foot of the altar. Excavations executed in the late 1970s and early 1980s at Santa Maria Novella verified the existence of vaults underneath the chapel, and the early seventeenth-century *sepoltuario* of the church mentions two slabs in front of the altar, "due avelli con chiusine di macigno senza iscrizione fatti dal medesimo Mainardo per se e per li suoi descndenti, cioè l'uno; e l'altro per le donne maritate in quella linea, come dalle scritture de'Cavalcanti si trova."[35] The *sepoltuario* is however mistaken in assuming that Mainardo was buried alongside his sons in one of the tombs. He had received a far more elaborate monument.[36] The tomb, which has not survived, is recorded by textual sources as a marble sarcophagus and inscription praising Mainardo's achievements, situated on the altar wall, and probably set within an architectural frame.[37] This funerary monument would have been a most unusual presence in Santa Maria Novella in the fourteenth century, when only members of the ecclesiastic hierarchy seem to have been given the honor of raised sarcophagi or wall tombs.[38] Mainardo's privileged position as founder of the sacristy, perhaps enhanced by virtue of his kinship with Fra Aldobrandino Cavalcanti, bishop of Orvieto and supposed founder of the new Santa Maria Novella, was thus highlighted.[39] Indeed, for a layman to have such an elaborate funerary monument was perceived as unusual even by later centuries: the above-mentioned *sepoltuario* records it in the chapel but mistakes it for a bishop's tomb—hence the assumption that Mainardo was buried below the altar.[40] Equally lavish was his funeral, described by a contemporary as "onorevolissime quanto si pote."[41] The entire church of Santa Maria Novella was lit up and embellished for the ceremony: numerous candles and torches (at least twenty-four of which were "grande onorevoli") illuminated the interior, especially the chancel and the Strozzi and Rucellai chapels situated at the ends of the transept—thus symmetrically framing the *cappella maggiore* where the funeral Mass was in all likelihood said.[42] The *campanile* itself was lit throughout, as if letting the rest of Florence know about the magnificence of Cavalcanti's funeral. Mainardo's bier, draped in gold and carried by knights of the Republic, was accompanied by five caparisoned horses and a populous cortege. As documented for other *trecento* funerals, standards and flags (of the Republic, guilds, or other groups paying homage to the deceased), and family or individual insignia would have been carried in the procession and then left on the tomb, together with the rich textiles that had covered the bier.[43] The poor of Florence mourned the sad passing, while the Dominicans of Santa Maria Novella remembered Mainardo's soul in their prayers, on the day of the funeral and in perpetuity.

A magnificent tomb and an expensive, visible funeral seem to be honors reserved for Florentine men. Their wives and daughters passed on with much less pomp and were buried in segregated—and, for the most part, inconspicuous—tombs.[44] Monna Andrea Acciaiuoli, whose contribution to the building and embellishment of the family chapel is acknowledged in contemporary documents, was no exception to this rule. She was buried in the tomb designated for the women of the family at the foot of the altar, and not even a special inscription singled her out as patron of the space. Moreover, her funeral did not attract her contemporaries' attention; to the best of my knowledge, no documents mentioning it have come down to us.

Although Monna Andrea had contributed at least as much money as Mainardo, and certainly more time and energy, to Santa Maria Novella's sacristy, the visible marks of her contribution were always kept in the shadow of her husband's. She herself maintained this subordination when in her will she referred to the chapel as "Mainardo's and his sons," thereby excluding herself. The wording of the will illustrates the way in which society influenced women's own perception of their place and role; however, our interpretation of it should be qualified, since it was written (and its content, as well as official language, surely influenced) by a male notary and possibly other male members of the family, who advised and "helped" her in matters of which she would have been (considered) ignorant. Whether the will reflects Monna Andrea's convictions, or those accepted (and acceptable) at the time, her contribution is defined as merely having fulfilled her deceased husband's wishes: the credit of having built a new, spacious sacristy for the Dominicans, lavishly decorated with a modern altarpiece and stained-glass window, went entirely to Mainardo. Furthermore, ownership of the chapel and its burial places was passed on from him to his male heirs; the women of the family, should they choose to be buried there, had a separate tomb but no lawful claim over the space.

Moreover, although Monna Andrea did not commission a tomb as lavish as her husband's and was not buried with equal pomp and ceremony, she made sure that her soul would be properly remembered in prayer. In her will she requested one thousand votive masses to be said within two months of her death at the altar of the sacristy (and therefore above her tomb).[45] This was an incredibly demanding request, which would have meant no less than thirty-three masses daily! Moreover, in order to assure its fulfillment, she made it a precondition to the above-mentioned bequest of two hundred florins for the painting of the chapel. There seem to have been no restrictions for women as regards the number and frequency of votive masses and prayers: male or female, a donor was entitled to as many masses as his/her purse could afford. In actuality however, this meant that most women would have been indirectly restricted, since their personal wealth (i.e., of which they could dispose freely) was negligible compared to that of men. Yet women such as Monna Andrea who had enough assets at the time of death could be prayed for as often as their husbands and fathers; her contribution to the family chapel may not have been acknowledged by their contemporaries and future generations, yet her atonement and piety would have been remembered by the Dominicans of Santa Maria Novella.

Let us now turn to later accounts of the building, embellishment, and patronage of Santa Maria Novella's sacristy/chapel. A chronological survey of extant documentation is revealing from the perspective of women's studies: *all* sources postdating Monna Andrea's will and until the 1950s either totally ignore her contribution and mention only Mainardo, or noncommittally record the patronage of the "Cavalcanti family." Following in the footsteps of fourteenth-century female dependence and subordination, and adding their own centuries' preconceptions, later texts gradually make Andrea Acciaiuoli's name disappear from the record. The acknowledgement of her efforts and expenditure diminished with time, to be retrieved only by modern scholarship.

The series of documents regarding the sacristy as Mainardo's achievement starts with the 1586 *cronaca* of Santa Maria Novella written by Modesto Biliotti. According to Biliotti, Mainardo Cavalcanti, a praiseworthy Florentine citizen honored with high dignities such as being named marshall of the queen of Naples, founded the chapel as a gesture of great benevolence and in memory of his ancestor Aldobrandino, bishop of Orvieto. He dedicated the chapel to the Virgin Annunciate and subsequently had a large panel of the *Annunciation* displayed on the wall above the altar. At his death in 1379, he was buried in the chapel in a marble sarcophagus adorned with a laudatory inscription. Another inscription on the altar wall (which Biliotti claims to have read many times before the reliquary cabinet covered it) recorded the fact that the window of the chapel, depicting stories from the Life of St. John the Baptist, had been commissioned by Mainardo's widow.[46] Biliotti's story thus reads as if Mainardo Cavalcanti's chapel was built during his lifetime (and presumably under his supervision), dedicated and outfitted with a lavish altarpiece, and finished just in time to receive his body. Monna Andrea's contribution, while acknowledged, is reduced to the stained-glass window, and the altarpiece (for which no documentation is mentioned) is specifically given to Mainardo.[47] Later manuscripts follow Biliotti's lead. The entry for the sacristy in Sermartelli's 1617 *sepoltuario* of Santa Maria Novella reads: "fu fatta da Mainardo Cavalcanti Maliscalco della Regina Giovanna di Napoli; il quale a perpetua memoria di frate Aldobrandino Vescovo d'Orvieto suo consanguineo l'eretta da fondamenti, secondo il disegno di fra Jacopo da Nipozzano."[48] When describing the altarpiece, the same manuscript mentions the arms painted on its frame, "a mano dritta del proprio padrone (sic!), quella a mano manca delli Acciaiuoli."[49] Another century later, Borghigiani in his *cronaca* of the Convent of Santa Maria Novella goes back to Biliotti's assumption and gives credit for the altarpiece to Mainardo.[50] Around the same time, Giuseppe Richa simply states that Mainardo Cavalcanti built the structure and was buried in a splendid tomb whose inscription he duly records; there is no mention of altarpiece, stained glass, or Monna Andrea Acciaiuoli.[51]

Two main factors need to be pointed out in defense of all early writers. First is the already mentioned fact that the physical evidence of Mainardo's patronage in the sacristy/chapel was much more obvious than that of his wife. Second, the traditional dating of the building in the 1360s—during Jacopo de Nipozzano's tenure as architect of Santa Maria Novella—placed it during Mainardo's life and therefore gave no reason to doubt his active patronage. Moreover, the authors in question may not have seen the documents mentioning Andrea's role in commissioning the stained glass and certainly would not have studied the altarpiece contextually, investigating her imprint on the iconography and choice of armorial devices. One could thus argue that in virtue of the accepted tradition, through the repetition of fragmentary or inaccurate information, the story of Mainardo Cavalcanti's full-fledged patronage was transmitted through the centuries. However, whereas in the sixteenth-century *cronaca* she was at least credited for the stained glass window, in later accounts her patronage is completely omitted. Similarly, the early seventeenth-century *sepoltuario* mentions Andrea's family's arms alongside those of the Cavalcanti on the altarpiece yet gives emphasis to the fact that the latter were the arms of the "rightful patron." This trend continued well into the twentieth century: Brown's 1902 monograph of Santa Maria Novella and even the otherwise remarkably reliable compendium of Florentine churches by Paatz in the 1950s maintain the 1360s dating of the sacristy and give full credit for its building to Mainardo. Neither scholar even mentions Monna Andrea's name.[52]

Throughout the historiography of the sacristy, from the seventeenth-century *sepoltuario* of Florentine churches by Rosselli to the early twentieth-century one by Cirri, some sources adopted a noncommittal approach, giving its patronage to the "Cavalcanti family," without singling out any one member.[53] While this approach did not openly discredit Monna Andrea as a patron, it contributed nothing to our knowledge of her contribution. It was only in the 1950s that she was rehabilitated, as it were, as rightful patron. Father Stefano Orlandi published the document recording the authorization to hire a chaplain, granted to Andrea in 1390.[54] Correlating it on one hand with her will and the previously published commission for the stained glass and on the other hand, with the absence of Mainardo's name from all these documents, he concluded that Monna Andrea Acciaiuoli should be credited with the building of the chapel, which had most likely taken place after her husband's passing.[55]

Not all fourteenth-century female patrons, however, had Monna Andrea's fate in later texts. A converse example is Guardina Tornaquinci, daughter of Neri di Piero Guardi and widow of Cardinale Tornaquinci, whose will of 17 February 1303 left two hundred gold florins to Santa Maria Novella for a family chapel.[56] Of interest in the context of this study is the fact that Guardina's act of patronage was not connected with the wish of a deceased husband. Nor did it fulfill some other family obligation. Hers was an independent commission, in which she used part of her dowry to found a chapel for herself and her descendants. The will specifies that all the possessions (liquid assets as well as property) she had received from her father, Neri di Piero Guardi, were to be given to the poor of the city of Florence. The Dominicans of Santa Maria Novella would receive a significant part. The amount of two hundred gold florins was to be set aside for the building of a chapel dedicated to St. Catherine in the Church of Santa Maria Novella, on the side of the street that led to the *piazza vecchia*.[57] The prior, a certain Fra Bartolommeo d'Ugone Aldobrandino of the third order, and Guardina's daughter, Donna Margherita (Ghita), were named executors. However, the actual receipt of the bequest by the Dominicans was delayed for over two decades. It was only in 1325 that Margherita, wife of Branca degli Scali, was granted a chapel in exchange for the two hundred florins left by her mother.[58] Since by that time the Chapel of St. Catherine already had a patron, Margherita was given the chapel dedicated to St. Luke in the west transept.[59]

Guardina's role as patron of the chapel of St. Luke was never questioned. The documents that ignored Andrea Acciaiuoli's contribution never fail to mention Guardina, "nobil matrona e già moglie de Cardinale Tornaquinci."[60] Andrea's misfortune seems to have been that the initial bequest was her husband's: he thus took, in the eyes of contemporaries and later chroniclers, the foremost role of founder, while she merely fulfilled his wishes. In so doing, however, she actively supervised the building and decoration of the space and became its de facto patron. That this was overlooked by later documents reflects not only the preeminence given to the initial bequest but also Andrea's status as a woman. Conversely, if male heirs assumed an important role in the patronage of a space founded or acquired by a previous generation, they were sure to be remembered. In the case of the St. Gregory Chapel in the east transept of Santa Maria Novella, for instance, the three sons of the founder, Riccardo di Ricco Bardi, are expressly mentioned in documents. Riccardo had left in his 1334 will two hundred gold florins for a family chapel in the Dominican church, and a deed of the convent dated 15 February 1335 (Florentine style) granted the chapel dedicated to St. Gregory to his sons Piero, Alessandro, and Tommaso.[61] It is noteworthy that the same early seventeenth century *sepoltuario* that did not even record Monna Andrea's name in conjunction with the chapel founded by her deceased husband reads for the chapel of St. Gregory: "fu eretta nel 1336 da figlioli di Riccardo de Bardi come per il testamento di esso."[62] In this case, therefore, not only are the executors mentioned by name, but they are considered "builders" (i.e., patrons), despite the fact that they had contributed nothing to the acquisition of the space for their family but merely made sure that their father's donation was passed on to the Dominicans.[63] In view of this and other similar examples, it seems that Monna Andrea's name may also have appeared more frequently in later documents, had she not been a woman.

The study of Monna Andrea's prominent role as patron of the sacristy/chapel also raises the issue of access to transept chapels in the fourteenth century. Santa Maria Novella, like all mendicant churches, was divided by the presence of a rood screen spanning the entire width of the three aisles.[64] Functionally maintaining *clausura*, it symbolically separated the "upper church," restricted to the use of the friars, from the "lower church" accessible to everybody, a topic addressed in this volume by Virginia Chieffo Raguin. The traditional view holds that the laity was forbidden access beyond the rood screen, and its solid mass and locked gates obscured even the view of the main altar and flanking chapels.[65] Elsewhere, I have argued, based upon documents regarding both Santa Maria Novella and Santa Croce, that access into the "friars' church" was less restricted than previously thought and that at the least the patrons of chapels located in the transepts would have had to be able to congregate in their own private spaces.[66] Yet all documents that spell out or hint at the presence of men beyond the rood screens indicate that the said privilege was not extended to their wives and daughters. One of the most explicit references to this sex separation is found in the 4 July 1385 will of Francesco Bruni, requesting burial in Santa Croce, in the family grave located near the door of the choir "which divides the place of the men from the place of the women."[67] Bruni further made a bequest of three hundred gold florins to the friars minor in order to insure the burial of all his male descendants in the said grave on one side of the door, and the female members of his family on the other side.

How do we reconcile the recorded facts about access beyond the rood screen with the reality of female burials in the transepts? Was it only in the repose of death that women transcended the limitations of gender? Were women, then, unable to use their family chapels, take part in funerals, pray by their husbands' tombs, be present at votive masses for the souls of their loved ones? Not likely. Although most documents imply or even spell out that women were not to enter the friars' church, others testify to the fact that the rules of segregation were not always respected. The *statuti* drawn in 1414, for example, specified that women were to be fined five soldi every time they ventured through the grilles of the rood screen of the church of San Cristofano during Mass.[68] Women whose families had chapels beyond the rood screens may have enjoyed a special—albeit unwritten, and so far undocumented—status. It is difficult to imagine that Monna Andrea never saw the space where she requested burial, her husband's exceptional tomb, or the altarpiece and stained-glass window she commissioned.

In a larger context, the seeming contradiction of the records on regulation of access reveals the difficulty of reading and interpreting the evidence. From the perspective of the twenty-first century, the assessment of women's place in the society of *trecento* Florence is full of contradictions. First, the very act of cultural patronage by women defies their position of subordination and limited access to personal assets. Yet extant works of art and documents reveal numerous such acts. Second, our knowledge of women's patronage is quite limited, especially in comparison with similar male efforts. Yet contemporary documents record donations by women and their active role as patrons. The sacristy/chapel of Santa Maria Novella is a case in point. The study of its history and historiography reveals the difficulty of reading the evidence, as well as the contradictory nature of evidence itself. The rules and regulations of *trecento* Florence were often caused by the existence of contrary practices. Strict fines had to be imposed on women who ventured beyond the rood screens precisely because they did it too often, or in large numbers. The insistence of families on controlling the freedom and wealth of their widows could be read in a similar manner. At the same time, the historical record between the *trecento* and the twenty-first century offers a series of interpretations, each anchored in its own time period and colored by its own biases. The historian's task is to find that delicate balance between law and common practice, between the history created and written by men and the ways is which women crafted their own niche. In *trecento* Florence, women such as Andrea Acciaiuoli, Guardina Tornaquinci, or Gemma Velluti demonstrated that they knew how to create and maintain that balance.

## NOTES

1. On the private chapels of fourteenth-century Florence, see Annegret Hoger, "Studien zur Entstehung der Familienkapelle und zu Familienkapellen und -Altaren des Trecento in Florentiner Kirchen," Ph.D. diss., University of Bonn, 1976; Giurescu, "Trecento Family Chapels."

2. See for instance Catherine King, "Women as Patrons: Nuns, Widows, and Rulers," in *Siena, Florence, and Padua: Art, Society and Religion 1280–1400*, ed. Diana Norman (New Haven: Yale University Press, 1995), vol. 2, 243–66.

3. The sacristy was a result of the conversion of the chancel of the first Santa Maria Novella, which abutted the nave of the new, differently oriented, basilica. The architecture was traditionally attributed to Fra Jacopo Talenti (see Orlandi, *Necrologio*, vol. 1, 525), and consequently the structure was dated to ca. 1360; see Borghigiani, "Cronica Annalistica," vol. 2, 76, and later James Wood Brown, *The Dominican Church of Santa Maria Novella of Florence* (Edinburgh: Schulze, 1902), 136, and Walter Paatz, *Die Kirchen von Florenz* (Frankfurt am Main: V. Klostermann, 1952), vol. 3, 691; Haines, "Sacristy of Santa Maria Novella," 577, clarifies the chronology. For Mainardo's will see note 6 below.

4. The sacristy measures approximately 8.70 meters in width and 14.60 meters in length; the standard chapels flanking the chancel are 5.64 meters wide and 6.94 meters deep.

5. On the remodeling of the sacristy, see Haines, "Sacristy of Santa Maria Novella," 598f.

6. Orlandi, *Necrologio*, 1: 547–48; also Haines, "Sacristy of Santa Maria Novella," 578, who cites the passages regarding the founding of the sacristy.

7. "those stories that would please the said madonna Andrea." The contract was published in Cesare Guasti, ed., *Lettere di un notario a un mercante del secolo XIV con altre lettere e documenti* (Florence: Le Monnier, 1880), vol. 2, 387; it is a rare fourteenth-century document that defines the role of the patron in deciding the iconography.

8. See Jane Collins Long, "Bardi Patronage at Santa Croce in Florence, ca.1320–1343," Ph.D. diss., Columbia University, 1988, 197; in a larger context, John Larner, *Culture and Society in Italy 1290–1420* (NewYork: Scribner, 1971); Giurescu, "Trecento Family Chapels," esp. 250–67.

9. On the stained glass, see Giuseppe Marchini, *Le vetrate italiene* (Milan: Electa, 1955), 219, where he attributes it to Niccolo di Pietro Gerini; Marchini, "Le vetrate," in Umberto Baldini, ed., *Santa Maria Novella: La Basilica, il convento, I chiostri monumentali* (Florence: Nardini, 1981), 268–69; Haines, "Sacristy of Santa Maria Novella," 588–90.

10. A point made by Haines, "Sacristy of Santa Maria Novella," 589. Many chapels had unified decorative programs in the fourteenth century (including frescoes, altarpiece, and stained glass), often executed by the same artist or workshop; see Giurescu, "Trecento Family Chapels," 215–18.

11. A certain fra Benedetto da Poggiolo, cf. Marchini, "Le vetrate," 268–69; also Haines, "Sacristy of Santa Maria Novella," 588.

12. For a detailed analysis of the altarpiece, see Offner and Steinweg, *Corpus of Florentine Painting*, 107–12.

13. ASF, MS 621, fol. 30; see, in the context of the gendering of pictorial space, the chapter by Corine Schleif in this volume. The arms were effaced at a later date, probably at the time when the patronage inscription located below the main panel of the altarpiece also disappeared, see Offner and Steinweg, *Corpus of Florentine Painting*, 107.

14. A point made by Offner and Steinweg, *Corpus of Florentine Painting*, 107, as support for Monna Andrea's patronage.

15. The first mention is found in Biliotti, "Chronica," 49, who notes that the altarpiece hung on the rear wall of the chapel until the erection of the large reliquary cupboard in 1582. Offner and Steinweg, *Corpus of Florentine Painting*, 111–12, recounts the later history of the altarpiece: first moved to the east wall of the chapel; then in the eighteenth century to one of the dormitories. At the1810 suppression of the convent it was placed in storage at S.Marco and then given to the Accademia Museum.

16. "built by Mainardo Cavalcanti's widow." Cf. Orlandi, *Necrologio*, vol. 1, 549.

17. Passages of Monna Andrea's will were transcribed by Haines, "Sacristy of Santa Maria Novella," 578 and 587. The will is preserved in ASF, Notarile antecosimiano, C–705, Ser Cristofano d'Andrea da Laterina, Testamenti 1385–1425, fol. 229.

18. "in ancient times painted, but since the figures were damaged, and lost, it was restaured, and only the ornaments on the vault were left." See Vincenzo Fineschi, *Il forestiero istruito in Santa Maria Novella*, rev. ed. (Rome: Multigrafica Editrice, 1977), 35; elsewhere, however, he suggests that the money mentioned in Andrea's will must have been used for the altarpiece instead, as cited by Orlandi, *Necrologio*, vol. 1, 550. This latter possibility was however ruled out by the recent dating of the altarpiece; see also Haines, "Sacristy of Santa Maria Novella," 590–91.

19. A similar contemporary view is expressed in Alessandra Macinghi Strozzi's letters, which show her accepting the patrilineal and patriarchal system of fifteenth-century Florence; see Ann Morton Crabb, "How Typical Was Alessandra Macinghi Strozzi of Fifteenth-Century Florentine Widows?" in *Upon My Husband's Death: Widows in the Literature and Histories of Medieval Europe*, ed. Louise Mirrer (Ann Arbor: University of Michigan Press, 1992), 47–68.

20. On women in late medieval and early Renaissance Italy see, among others, Christiane Klapisch-Zuber, *Women, Family, and Ritual in Renaissance Italy* (Chicago: University of Chicago Press, 1985); Stanley Chojnacki, "The Power of Love: Wives and Husbands in Late Medieval Venice," in *Women and Power in the Middle Ages*, ed. Mary Erler and Maryanne Kiowaleski (Athens: University of Georgia Press, 1988), 126–48; *Women and Religion in Medieval and Renaissance Italy*, ed. Daniel Bornstein and Roberto Rusconi, trans. Margery J. Schneider (Chicago: University of Chicago Press, 1996).

21. David Herlihy, *Women, Family and Society in Medieval Europe: Historical Essays, 1978–1991* (Providence and Oxford: Berghahn Books, 1995), 15–16; Richard Trexler, *Public Life in Renaissance Florence* (Ithaca: Cornell University Press, 1980), 15–17.

22. David Herlihy and Christiane Klapisch-Zuber, *Tuscans and Their Families. A Study of the Catasto of 1427* (New Haven: Yale University Press, 1985), 135–36, who also note that girls were much more likely to be sent away for nursing than their brothers.

23. Passages from Morelli's "Ricordi" published in Maria Consiglia de Matteis, ed., *Donna nel medioevo: Aspetti culturali e di vitta quotidiana* (Bologna: Pàtron Editore, 1986), 299–305.

24. Christiane Klapisch-Zuber, "The 'Cruel Mother': Maternity, Widowhood, and Dowry in Florence in the Fourteenth and Fifteenth Centuries," in *Women, Family, and Ritual in Renaissance Italy*, esp. 119.

25. Ibid., 120–21f; Crabb, "How Typical Was Alessandra Macinghi Strozzi," 50.

26. Klapisch-Zuber, "The 'Cruel Mother,' " 124.

27. For Santa Maria Novella, see the collections of wills in ASF, Conv. Soppr. 102, 105 (Testamenti 1299–1400), 102, 97–99 and 102, 106, as well as individual wills preserved in *Diplomatico Santa Maria Novella.*

28. On the Velluti chapel, see Giurescu, "Trecento Family Chapels," 39–46, with references.

29. "completed the chapel dedicated to St. Michael in Santa Croce, located next to the door leading to the sacristy; the chapel had been begun by others, and thus their arms are painted alongside ours; and I commissioned the iron railing after the plague of 1348, Monna Gemma having died in the plague of 1340." See Isidoro del Lungo and Guglielmo Volpi, eds., *La Cronica domestica di Messer Donato Velluti, scritta fra il 1367 e il 1370, con le addizioni di Paolo Velluti scritte fra il 1555 e il 1560* (Florence: Sansoni, 1914), 76.

30. Ibid., 106; Gemma had become a tertiary after her husband's death.

31. On the controversy regarding the dating and patronage of the chapel's frescoes, see Giurescu, "Trecento Family Chapels," 40–44, with references to its historiography.

32. Andrew Ladis, "The Velluti Chapel in Santa Croce, Florence," *Apollo* 120 (October 1980): 243. The male donor at his feet could be Alessandro himself; however,

both figures are too damaged to permit any more precise identification. Conversely, these figures have been considered later; see Julian Gardner, "The Early Decoration of Santa Croce in Florence," *The Burlington Magazine* 113 (1971): 392, who believes that these figures were added at a later date. For the sixth-century bishop of Fiesole, S. Alessandro, see George Kaftal, *Iconography of the Saints in Tuscan Painting* (Florence: Sansoni, 1952), cols. 17–18.

33. For the legend of St. Michael, see *The Golden Legend of Jacobus de Voragine*, trans. Granger Ryan and Helmut Ripperger (NewYork: Arno, 1969), 578–86; on its iconography, Kaftal, *Iconography of the Saints*, cols. 737–42.

34. Richard Offner, *A Critical and Historical Corpus of Florentine Painting*, new edition by Miklos Boskovits, section 3, vol. 9 (Florence: Giunti Barbera, 1984), 23.

35. "two tombs with sandstone slabs without inscription made by the same Mainardo, one for himself and his descendants, the other for the women married into the family, according to old books of the Cavalcanti family." ASF, MS 621, fol. 30; Haines, "Sacristy of Santa Maria Novella," 586.

36. On Mainardo's tomb, see Haines, "Sacristy of Santa Maria Novella," 582–86. A prototype for it may have been the tomb of Niccolo Acciaiuoli in the Carthusian monastery of Florence, dated to the second half of the fourteenth century and attributed to the circle of Andrea Orcagna. See Goffredo Viti, *The Chartreuse of Florence* (Florence: M.S. Grafica, 1994), 15–18, and fig. 22.

37. The inscription is transcribed in BNCF, II. 1316–18, Ferdinando Leopoldo Del Migliore, "Notizie istoriche di varie chiese di Firenze," vol. 2, 1657, unpaginated; Orlandi, *Necrologio*, vol. 1, 548, and Haines, "Sacristy of Santa Maria Novella," 586; a copy can be seen in the 1734 marble plaque above the entrance to the sacristy.

38. Another exception to this rule may have been the tomb commissioned by Tommaso di Michele Falconi in 1383 for the chapel of St. Dominic, which has not survived. See Kathleen Alden Giles, "The Strozzi Chapel in Santa Maria Novella: Florentine Painting and Patronage 1340–1355," Ph.D. diss., Institute of Fine Arts, 1977, 39.

39. See Borghigiani, "Cronica Annalistica," 1: 162–63f on Aldobrandino's contribution to the new campaign at Santa Maria Novella starting in 1278. The Cavalcanti also had patronage over the so-called Sala dei Beati (the old sacristy of the church) situated beyond the west transept (see Orlandi, *Necrologio*, vol. 1, 549; Haines, "Sacristy of Santa Maria Novella," 576) and owned another chapel on the rood screen; see Orlandi, *Necrologio*, vol. 2, 403; Marcia B. Hall, "The *Ponte* in Santa Maria Novella: The Problem of the Rood Screen in Italy," *Journal of the Warburg and Courtauld Institutes* 37 (1974), 164; Giurescu, "Trecento Family Chapels," 192–93.

40. ASF, MS 621, fol. 30v.

41. "most honorable." The description of the funeral is in BNCF.II, I, 139, fol. 46; also Antonio Maria Biscioni, ed., *Istorie pistolesi ovvero delle cose avvenute in Toscana dall'anno* MCCC *al* MCCXLVIII (Milan: Silvestri, 1845), 462.

42. The building of the Cavalcanti sacristy/chapel had at the most only started by Mainardo's death. At the same time, other cases are documented where at least part of the funerary Mass was held in the chancel rather than the chapel of the defunct's family; see for example the 1429 burial of Matteo Castellani as described by his descendant Francesco di Matteo. See *Francesco di Matteo Castellani, Ricordanze*, ed. Giovanni Ciappelli (Florence: Olschi, 1992), 8–9.

43. See, among others, the 1377 funeral of Niccolaio di Jacopo degli Alberti, described in BNCF.II.I, 139, fol. 19, and partly transcribed in Filippo Moise, *Santa Croce di Firenze: Illustrazione storico-artistica* (Florence, 1845), 114–15; also in Luigi Passerini, *Gli Alberti di Firenze: Genealogia, storia e documenti* (Florence: Cellini, 1869), 77.

44. To the best of my knowledge, the only elaborate fourteenth-century female tomb is that in the St. Sylvester chapel in Santa Croce (an *avello* tomb with a sculptured sarcophagus set in a painted niche depicting the Entombment with a female donor); even there, however, a clear distinction is made between it and the other, larger and more lavish tomb intended for the men of the family; see Giurescu, "Trecento Family Chapels," 71–73. On the chapel of St. Sylvester, see Long, "Bardi Patronage"; Long, "Salvation through Meditation: The Tomb Frescoes in the Holy Confessors Chapel at Santa Croce in Florence," *Gesta* 34 (1995): 77–88.

45. Haines, "Sacristy of Santa Maria Novella," 587.

46. Biliotti, "Chronica," 48–49.

47. This very acknowledgment of her contribution was likely due to the existence of the inscription on the wall, later covered by the reliquary cabinet commissioned in 1583. On the cabinet, see Haines, "Sacristy of Santa Maria Novella," 599–603.

48. "was founded by Mainardo Cavalcanti, Marshall of the Queen Giovanna of Naples, who built it anew in memory of his relative fra Aldorbandino, bishop of Orvieto, after the design of fra Jacopo da Nipozzano." ASF, MS 621, fol. 30.

49. "on the right those of the patron, on the left those of the Acciaiuoli."

50. Borghigiani, "Cronica Annalistica,"quoted in Orlandi, *Necrologio*, vol. 2, 400–01.

51. Giuseppe Richa, *Notizie istoriche delle chiese fiorentine*, 10 vols. (Florence: Viviani, 1754–62), vol. 3, 43–45.

52. Brown, *The Dominican Church*, 136; Paatz, *Die Kirchen von Florenz*, vol. 3, 691, on the dating of sacristy, 715 on the stained glass.

53. BNCF II, IV, 534–36: Stefano Rosselli, "Sepoltuario fiorentino, ovvero Descrizione delle chiese, cappelle e sepolture, loro armi e inscrizioni della città di Firenze e suoi contorni" (1657), fol. 714; BNCF, Cirri, "Sepoltuario (Chiese di Firenze e dintorni)," vol. 8, fol. 3392.

54. MOPH, v. XIX, Reg. Litt. Fr. Raym. Capuani, 97, quoted by Orlandi, *Necrologio*, vol. 1, 549.

55. Orlandi, *Necrologio*, vol. 1, 550; Monna Andrea's contribution was reviewed and detailed by Haines, "Sacristy of Santa Maria Novella," 577–91.

56. The original testament has, to my knowledge, not survived; a copy dated 16 April 1325 is preserved in ASF, Conv. Soppr. 102, 105, fols. 12–13v.

57. The donation referred to the chapel (later of the Ruccellai family) that at the time was being added to the end of the east transept.

58. To the best of my knowledge, the specific reasons for this delay are not mentioned in any of the documents regarding the chapel. A first payment is recorded on 23 August 1325, when a certain Fra Taddeo Compagni received twenty florins out of the two hundred, to be used for the reconstruction of the facade (ASF, Conv. Soppr. 102, 105, fol. 14v); another forty florins were received by him on 23 November of the same year (fol. 15).

59. The act of the convent, dated 3 August 1325, is preserved in ASF, Conv. Soppr. 102, 105, fols. 13v–14v. For a detailed building and patronage history of both chapels, see Giurescu, "Trecento Family Chapels," 29–31, 103–12.

60. "Guardina, noble lady and widow of Cardinale Tornaquinci." ASF, MS 621, fol. 35v; Borghigiani, "Cronica Annalistica," 246–47; Biliotti, "Chronica," 56.

61. Riccardo's will is, to the best of my knowledge, not extant, but it is mentioned in BNCF, Passerini 45, 149; and ASF, MS 621, fol. 18v. The 1335 document is preserved in ASF, Notarile antecosimiano B 1951, fols. 36v–37r, and was transcribed by Irene Hueck, "Stifter und Patronachtsrecht: Dokumente zu zwei Kapellen der Bardi," *Mitteilungen des Kunsthistorischen Institutes Florenz* 20 (1976): 268–69. On the patronage history of the chapel, see Giurescu, "Trecento Family Chapels," 23–28.

62. "was built in 1336 by the sons of Riccardo de Bardi in accordance with his testament." ASF, MS 621, fol. 18v.

63. Later, however, they did provide for the frescoed decoration of the space, which dates from the second half of the century; see Biliotti, "Chronica," 54; BNCF, Cirri, "Sepoltuario," 3977. On the frescoes, see David Wilkins, "Early Florentine Frescoes in Santa Maria Novella," *Art Quarterly* 1 (1978): 154; James Stubblebine, "Cimabue and Duccio in Santa Maria Novella," *Pantheon* 31 (1973): 17.

64. Borghigiani, "Cronica Annalistica," quoted in Orlandi, *Necrologio*, 2: 398–99; Hall, "The *Ponte*"; Hall, *Renovation and Counter-Reformation: Vasari and Duke Cosimo in Santa Maria Novella and Santa Croce 1565–1577* (Oxford: Clarendon, 1979), 2–4.

65. Hall, "The *Ponte*," 163–64; Leon Satkowski, *Giorgio Vasari: Architect and Courtier* (Princeton: Princeton University Press, 1993), 93.

66. Giurescu, "Trecento Family Chapels," 205–11. See also Jacqueline E. Jung, "Beyond the Barrier: The Unifying Role of the Choir Screen in Gothic Churches," *The Art Bulletin* 82 (December 2000), 622–57.

67. ASF, *Diplomatico Santa Croce*, 4 July 1385: "portam que este propinqua coro et dividit locum hominum a loco mulierum."

68. Statuti di Braga 1414, rubrica 36, quoted in Richa, *Notizie*, vol. 1, 72.

## Abbreviations

ASF = Archivio di Stato Firenze
BNCF = Biblioteca Nazionale Centrale Firenze

## Frequently Cited Sources

Biliotti, Modesto. "Chronica Pulcherrimae Aedis Magnique Coenobii S. Mariae Cognomento Novellae Florentinae Civitatis," *Analecta Sacri Ordinis Fratrum Praedicatorum* 1 (1893–94); 2 (1895–96); 3 (1897–98); 12 (1915–16); 13 (1917–18).

Borghigiani, Vincenzo. "Cronica Annalistica del Venerabile Convento di Santa Maria Novella di Firenze dell'Ordine de Predicatori dal Primo anno di Sua Fondazione fino al 155 dal qual principia la Cronica di Fra Modesto Biliotti," 3 vols., MS Archivio di Santa Maria Novella, 1457–60.

Giurescu, Ena. "Trecento Family Chapels in Santa Maria Novella and Santa Croce: Architecture, Patronage, and Competition." Ph.D. diss., Institute of Fine Arts, 1997.

Haines, Margaret. "The Sacristy of Santa Maria Novella in Florence: The History of Its Functions and Furnishings." *Memorie domenicane* 11 (1980): 575–626.

Offner, Richard, and Klara Steinweg. *A Critical and Historical Corpus of Florentine Painting*. Section 4, vol. 5. Published under the auspices of the Institute of Fine Arts, New York University. New York: Augustin, 1969.

Orlandi, Stefano, ed. *"Necrologio" di Santa Maria Novella: Testo integrale dall'inizio al MDIV corredato di note biografiche tratte da documenti coevi*. 2 vols. Florence: Olschki, 1955.

## FURTHER READING

Cohn, Samuel K., Jr. *The Cult of Remembrance and the Black Death: Six Renaissance Cities in Central Italy*. Baltimore: Johns Hopkins University Press, 1992.

Goldthwaite, Richard A. *Wealth and the Demand for Art in Italy 1300–1600*. Baltimore: Johns Hopkins University Press, 1993.

Haines, Margaret. "The Sacristy of Santa Maria Novella in Florence: The History of Its Functions and Furnishings." *Memorie domenicane* 11 (1980): 575–626.

King, Catherine. "Women as Patrons: Nuns, Widows, and Rulers," in *Siena, Florence, and Padua: Art, Society and Religion 1280–1400*. Ed. Diana Norman. New Haven: Yale University Press, 1995, vol. 2, 243–66.

Klapisch-Zuber, Christiane. *Women, Family, and Ritual in Renaissance Italy*. Chicago: University of Chicago Press, 1985.

Mirrer, Louise, ed. *Upon My Husband's Death: Widows in the Literature and Histories of Medieval Europe*. Ann Arbor: University of Michigan Press, 1992.

SEVEN

# GENDER, CELIBACY, AND PROSCRIPTIONS OF SACRED SPACE: SYMBOL AND PRACTICE

JANE TIBBETTS SCHULENBURG

SPACE IS NEITHER INERT nor neutral, nor is its organization, articulation, or the formulation of its boundaries a natural phenomenon. Rather, spatial constructs are the historical and cultural products of an age. As metaphors and symbolic systems, they embody the most basic values and meaning of a culture. Operating as a mechanism for classification, spatial arrangements attempt to demarcate and reinforce the hierarchical ordering of society, to define and clarify social roles and relations, to maintain prevailing patterns of privilege or advantage, and to regulate social behavior. Spatial constructions are therefore fundamental statements of power, authority, and privilege, and over time they have been used to serve a wide range of special interests. Once space has been ordered or constituted—with its establishment of boundaries and restrictions—it, in turn, exerts its own influence on society and gender stratification. Moreover, long after the original purpose of spatial arrangements/exclusionary policies had been forgotten and their usefulness had run its course, they frequently remained an important force in the collective memory.[1]

Medieval churchmen had more than a passing interest in the construction of sacred space. On one level, the medieval church as ritual center was much more than a mere building. It was seen as a symbolic code: a "model" of the cosmos and image of the Celestial City, imbued with divine order and harmony as were the heavenly spheres.[2] In their attempts to reflect the symbolic interconnection between the Celestial City and the church as its earthly representation, churchmen throughout the Middle Ages were concerned with the "divine" ordering as well as the necessary protection of sacred space.

Central to many of the church's most holy beliefs and rituals, sacred space was seen as a type of privileged, efficacious space set apart from that which was profane or desacralized.[3] Cathedrals, churches, chapels, and monasteries, along with their precincts and cemeteries, were consecrated in formal religious ceremonies and were perceived as occupying special sacralized space. According to Peter of Celle, abbot of St. Remi (twelfth century), "the cloister lies on the border of angelic purity and earthly contamination."[4] Thus in order to maintain the sacred quality of this privileged and ordered space, and to avoid desecration or pollution from outside forces, certain symbolic or physical boundaries were established. Moreover, beliefs in explicit dangers or divine punishment were formulated and circulated by churchmen to deter or threaten potential transgressors (especially women) who might plot to defy these policies and cross the forbidden thresholds.[5]

Although deeply affected by spatial policies, women have historically been denied the opportunity to exercise a direct role in determining or controlling religious or sacred space. Furthermore, women have been particularly vulnerable to changes or reforms in the articulation of space. Thus the adoption of gender-based spatial proscriptions can be seen as an indirect index of ecclesiastical authority over women: they embody underlying values/attitudes and fears of the church hierarchy toward female sexuality and the perceived disruptive nature and "uncontainability" of women.[6]

During the past several decades scholars in a number of disciplines have explored the various aspects of space, place, and symbolic classification.[7] However, the phenomenon of gender as the determinant in the formulation of proscriptions of sacred space in the medieval world seems to have been taken for granted; and perhaps for that reason, the gender-based ordering of sacred space has not received the kind of attention it deserves. Through a study of several thousand saints' lives, canons of church councils, cartularies, liturgical collections, handbooks of ecclesiastical offices, penitentials, chronicles, correspondence, architectural and archeological data, enough evidence is available to provide a rough index of the various attempts at ordering and negotiating sacred space, and particularly the development of exclusionary policies as practiced by the medieval church. This study will survey one aspect of the sexual division of sacred space, the placement and displacement and the general exclusion of women from male monastic churches from around 500 through 1200.

## THE EXCLUSION OF WOMEN FROM MONASTIC CHURCHES

In general, parish churches and cathedrals, as public centers of worship and pilgrimage, encouraged the participation of women in various religious activities and rituals. Although within these churches space was heavily inflected by gender—for example, the clergy attempted to strictly segregate the sexes, provide preferential space to the male laity, and severely limit female participation within sacred spaces (i.e., the altar area, etc.)—women still assumed essential functions and were valued for their contributions to the faith.[8] However, in contrast to these public centers of worship, many major medieval churches and chapels, even cemeteries and holy wells, were designated as strictly off limits to all members of the female sex. Women were prohibited from entering these sacred spaces and therefore found themselves at a distinct disadvantage in their need to practice their religion, that is, to hear Mass, make confession, or personally visit the tombs of relatives or saints located in these churches. This gender-based discriminatory policy appears to have been particularly difficult for women during the period from the ninth through the twelfth centuries, an era that witnessed a growing popularity of the cult of relics as well as the proliferation of male monastic foundations, which also served as major cult centers.

Influenced by ancient Greek, Jewish, and early Christian practices, the origins of these gender-based exclusionary policies are found in the early eremitic and monastic milieu and pertained particularly to male monastic churches and their precincts. With their emphasis on leading the life of "impatient angels" with strict asceticism and celibacy and their exaggerated fear of female sexuality, one of the major monastic characteristics was the rigorous avoidance of women. Many of these holy men/founders of monastic communities had espoused the eremitic life, fleeing to the "desert," to escape from the distractions of the "fleshy" world, which included the myriad dangers traditionally associated with women. Therefore the *vitae* of these hermit saints frequently provide us with vivid descriptions of "brash" female intruders who allegedly attempted to seduce these holy men. The negative hagiographic portrayals of extreme female behavior marginalized women as the dangerous "other." The lives, however, recounted in glowing detail the heroics of these spiritual athletes, that is their personal or private struggles with female distractions, temptation, concupiscence, the creative "ruses of Satan," and their ultimate success at "becoming dead to the world."[9] Over time this blatant fear of female sanctity, which often assumed the dimensions of a full-blown misogynism, became spatialized in the institutionalization of strict codes of female avoidance adopted by male monastic communities.

Monastic *regulae* and canons of church councils were especially concerned with the strict prohibition of female entry into monastic cloisters and churches. St. Caesarius of Arles notes in his *Regula ad Monachos* that women were forbidden to enter the monastery; the *Regula S. Ferreoli* warns that no women, including nuns and young women, were to be allowed within the monastery.[10] The Carolingian reformer, St. Benedict of Aniane, notes that under no circumstances were women to enter the basilica of the monastery of Aniane.[11] The Camaldolese Benedictines not only forbid women entry into their churches but, according to a sermon by St. Romuald (d. 1027), prohibited them (under penalty of excommunication) from setting foot in the forests in which the monks' cells and churches were located.[12] The Cistercians were equally severe in forbidding all women entry into their monasteries.[13]

A number of canons of church councils, for example, warned that the abbot must not allow any female to come into his monastery, not even to attend a solemn religious service. The severity of this policy is underscored by the fact that if the abbot disobeyed this injunction, he would be excommunicated or sent to another monastery where he would be condemned to bread and water for three months.[14] Many other records (e.g., cartularies, chronicles, saints' lives, etc.), especially those relating to individual monastic houses, underscored the importance of these exclusionary policies for these communities and their reputations.

Sources of the period, however, seem to indirectly reflect the fact that despite their strict policies, churchmen often experienced difficulties putting them into practice: problems resulted in policing their restrictive barriers and keeping women from disturbing their sacred space. They therefore tried to enforce their authority and exclusionary policies by threats of divine wrath or supernatural punishment. Thus the popular saints' lives and chronicles of the period record a series of fascinating yet gruesome cautionary tales intended to serve as strong deterrents to potential female transgressors. They describe, for example, brazen women, who, daring to overstep these forbidden thresholds or boundaries of sacred space, found themselves subject to swift visible punishments by the "wronged" saints. Frequently these retaliatory acts were recorded as posthumous miracles of the saints whose church or sacred space had been violated by these female intruders. When St. Siviard was abbot of the monastery of Anisole(?) (Maine) and wrote the *vita* of its founder St. Calais (d. 545), a woman named Gunda attempted to enter the monastery and its church, which had always been strictly off limits to all women. She was interested in discovering, if, after some one hundred years, St. Calais still enforced this gender-based restriction. According to the saint's life, she therefore cut off her hair and disguised herself as a man in order to enter the cloister without being noticed. She coordinated her entry with that of the monks going to divine office, namely, when the doors of the church were open. Gunda then went into the oratory where the body of their patron Saint Calais, was located. Suddenly, according to the *vita*, she was miraculously struck down by God—she lost her sight, and black blood flowed from her breast. She also let out such a horrible scream that she attracted the attention of all of those who were present in the church. When interrogated by the monks, Gunda admitted her crime. The author then notes that this punishment had in fact a salutary effect in that it prevented other women, who might have been tempted, from trying a similar stunt.[15]

According to tradition, the hermit saint Goeznou had such a fear of women that he erected a huge stone as a marker beyond which no female was to tread under penalty of death. (Here the concept of the 'threshold' was seen not simply as a metaphor but as a point of maximum tension. It was at this spot that special vigilance was demanded against infiltration.) As noted in the saint's *vita*, in order to test this policy, a woman was said to have pushed another past this barrier, whereupon the assailant fell dead, and the woman who had reluctantly transgressed remained unharmed.[16] The tradition associated with the oratory of St. Goulven warned that all female transgressors would be struck blind by the saint. Those female trespassers of St. Fiacre's chapel, through the posthumous intervention of the angry saint, were said to have gone mad on the spot.[17] Similarly, we are told that in 1091, Queen-Saint Margaret of Scotland was prohibited from entering the Church of St. Lawrence from which all members of the female sex were rejected. When she attempted to ignore this policy and enter the church with her offerings, she was said to have been suddenly smitten and repelled. Fortunately, she was restored to health by the prayers of the clergy and was then able to present them with her offerings.[18]

Further cautionary examples derive from Symeon of Durham's defense of the exclusionary reform policies adopted at the Cathedral of Durham (twelfth century). Briefly, the proscriptive policy at Durham was tied to the post-Conquest reform and the replacement in 1083 of the married clergy/canons by reformed Benedictine monks. It appears that with the reform initiated by William of St. Calais, who had previously been a monk at the monastery of St. Carileph (St. Calais) in Maine, the famous seventh-century patron St. Cuthbert was conveniently provided with a posthumous abhorrence of females (in the tradition of St. Calais).[19] Thus the reform writings of Symeon of Durham served to reshape the patron saint of Durham according to the blatant prejudices of the period. Although this new reform type clearly conflicted with the historical Cuthbert, who was known to have befriended many women during his lifetime, this "historical inaccuracy" or creative reconstruction was apparently not problematic for the reformers. Symeon contended that Cuthbert had in fact been a blatant misogynist all of his life, and because of his great aversion toward women it was well known that women were unable to enter any of the churches with which the saint had been associated. He also noted, "This custom is so diligently observed, even unto the present day, that it is unlawful for women to set foot even within the cemeteries of those churches in which his body obtained a temporary resting-place, unless, indeed, compelled to do so by the approach of any enemy or the dread of fire."[20] Moreover, with the reformers' emphasis on celibacy and cultic purity, as well as the need to control or contain and segregate women from the monks/male clergy and sacred space, they established in the name of St. Cuthbert's alleged misogynism a line of local blue frosterly marble in the floor of the second bay of the nave of Durham Cathedral. This line can still be seen today, stretching across the pavement from north to south, approximately one foot wide with a cross at its center.

Beyond this "holy barrier," or impenetrable threshold, women were forbidden to pass. Moreover, according to the sixteenth-century *Rites of Durham*, if by chance any woman crossed it into the body of the church she would be taken straightaway and punished for some days![21]

Symeon of Durham then provides a lively description of a number of frightening punishments inflicted posthumously by the wrathful saint (from his feretory) on "shameless" women who dared to test the sacrosanct space of the cathedral, churchyard, or cemetery of Durham. He tells of a certain Sungeova who defied this sacred space by venturing across the churchyard. She immediately lost her senses and died the same evening.[22] Another disrespectful woman who dared to pass through the cemetery of Durham became mad and ended her life by cutting her own throat.[23] Symeon also relates in some detail the story of Judith, wife of Earl Tostig:

> An honorable and devout woman [who] exceedingly loved St. Cuthbert, and contributed many ornaments to his church; and promised that she would add yet more together with landed possessions, if permission were granted her to enter within its walls, and to pray at his sepulcher. Not venturing to do such a thing as this in her own person, she had planned to send one of her waiting-maids before her, concluding that if the girl could do this in safety, she herself, the mistress, who was to follow after her, would incur no danger.

However, when the maid secretly attempted to enter the sacred churchyard, she was struck by a violent gust of wind and suddenly became ill. She had scarcely returned home when she died. Symeon adds that the countess was terrified by this turn of events, and to make amends, she and her husband commissioned a crucifix and images of Mary and St. John the Evangelist, covered in gold and silver, which they presented along with a number of other ornaments for the decoration of the church.[24] Thus after introducing a number of cautionary examples, Symeon notes, "Many other instances might easily be added to these, showing how the audacity of women was punished from heaven; but let these suffice, since we must proceed to other matters."[25]

Reginald, monk of Durham (twelfth century), relates another case in which a woman dared to defy the sacred spatial barriers of Durham. Here Helisend, the chambermaid of the queen of Scotland, disguised in a black cope and hood, secretly entered the cathedral. However the sacristan, Bernard, intercepted her with the objurgations of the coarsest kind, and she was forcibly ejected from the church.[26]

Later sources that describe the building of the Lady Chapel at Durham in the early twelfth century further reinforce these popular antifeminist reform attitudes and the apparent need to rationalize and protect the cathedral's exclusionary policies of sacred space. During the construction of the Lady Chapel, originally located at the far east end of the church behind St.

Cuthbert's shrine, the foundations and lower walls began to shrink and crack. This basic structural problem was attributed by churchmen to supernatural causes, namely, Cuthbert's great hatred of women. They believed or contended that the saint was simply objecting in his own subtle way to having a chapel of the Virgin (which would attract hordes of women) built so uncomfortably close to his own tomb. The historian Geoffrey of Coldingham, in his famous early account (ca. 1214) of the problems Bishop Hugh du Puiset experienced in the building of the Galilee or Lady Chapel writes: "[W]henever the walls were built to any great height cracks appeared in them to the peril of the workmen; which was enough to indicate to him that God and his servant Cuthbert disapproved. The work was stopped and transferred to the west where women would be allowed to enter; so those who had not access to the secret and holy places might again gain solace from the contemplation of them."[27]

Thus, contrary to the traditional spatial arrangements, which placed the Lady Chapel at the east end of the church, the Lady Chapel at Durham came to be situated in a unique location outside the west wall of the cathedral, thus keeping women physically as far as possible from the sacred east end of the church and the feretory or shrine of the holy St. Cuthbert.[28]

Similar cautionary tales can be found in other sources of the period. The contemporary *vita* of St. Bartholomew of Farne (d. 1193) recounts, for example, the story of a Flemish woman who had been a close friend of the saint in his early years. Later, after he had adopted the eremitic life, she came to visit him on the island of the Inner Farne, which had been made famous by St. Cuthbert. When St. Bartholomew forbid her to enter his chapel, she became enraged. She complained angrily to her former friend that she was being treated like a dog. Attempting to defy this sacred boundary or threshold established by the saint, and to set foot in his chapel, this female trespasser was suddenly thrown down on her back "as if by a whirlwind." According to tradition, it was only through St. Bartholomew's intervention that she recovered.[29]

Perhaps one of the most marvelous examples of these didactic tales can be found in Goscelin of Canterbury's *Life of St. Augustine.*[30] In describing Augustine and his missionary companions' trip from Rome to England, he relates their adventures during their overnight stay at Sai on the Loire. Here the missionaries were attacked by the inhabitants. Goscelin stresses that the women were particularly violent and that they attempted to drive them out of the area. As described by Goscelin:

> But the women gathered together at the same time and rampaged against God's Saints not just with irreverence but with so much madness, wailing, contempt, mockery, and derision, that men seemed in some sense harmless in comparison with them. It was not enough to cast them out, but they ran them down, dragged and pushed

> them along, exhausted them, and drove them out with mocking impudence.

After some time, the newly converted at Sai, inspired by miracles, established a church on the very site where Augustine had spent the night. In recounting or rationalizing its gender-based exclusionary policy (in contrast to the policy of Canterbury where the saint's tomb was located and women could enter "freely and legitimately"), Goscelin relates that a "perpetual miracle endures whereby no woman is ever able to enter that church or to draw water from the fountain, to the end that the world may know how greatly this gender offended God in the injury shown his servants."[31]

Goscelin then provides in some detail a marvelously frightening example of a woman who dared to defy this policy established at the church of Sai and her "just" punishment, namely, an exploding womb followed by death! According to Goscelin:

> A prestigious matron attempted to enter here with a large wax candle, as if the saint would be flattered by her power and wealth. To those who stood by and attempted to frighten her off she responded that she had not sinned against the saint but desired to do him honor, and she pressed on in her presumptuous intention. And so she had scarcely reached the forbidden boundary and sacred threshold when her entrails suddenly burst out; the secret parts of her womb flowed upon the earth, and she fell down miserably and died. The dead woman was dragged outside and taught everyone in horrific fashion what she herself had believed of no one. By such a rebuke all women have been instructed that they should fear touching open doors more than closed ones.[32]

Although the expressed purpose of these cautionary tales was to serve as a deterrent to others contemplating similar actions, their repetition might also provide us with an indirect index of oblique strategies actually adopted by women who resented these discriminatory policies and thus attempted to test or challenge the boundaries of ecclesiastical/patriarchal authority. These stories might also have been designed as propaganda or subtle advertisement for these exclusive male monasteries whose famous churches housed the tombs of popular saints and important collections of relics. Thus they were used to call attention to the overwhelming attraction or fame of the individual saint or church and to make the monastery or pilgrimage site all the more valued.

However, in general, these sources taken together underscore the church's enduring concern (sometimes more exaggerated than others) with the "necessary" segregation, containment, and exclusion of women from sacred space. With the emphasis on celibacy and cultic purity and the underlying fear of female sexuality and threat of moral contagion, the church was highly suspicious of women assuming the privilege of entering monastic churches and their precincts. This was seen as a dangerous precedent, one that could only have a ruinous effect on the moral tenor of the monastery and its life of celibacy. It was seen also as a source of rumor and scandal that could destroy their hard-won reputations. Moreover, on a practical level, some monks clearly did not see any need for women or a female presence (except for that of the Virgin Mary and female saints) in their monasteries. In fact, many felt they were better off without any women within miles of their monasteries as they would only provide a source of distraction and temptation. The churchmen therefore had the luxury (at least in theory) to cultivate a totally masculine religious milieu or a "world without women."[33]

Although female monasteries frequently adopted policies of strict active and passive enclosure, they were unable to get along without a male presence, since they required a priest for at least sacramental functions and confession. Therefore their rules stipulate, for example, that with the exception of bishops, provisors, suppliers, priests, deacons, aged lectors, builders, and so on, men were forbidden entry into the secret parts of the monastery and in the oratory.[34] In addition it appears that, at least in many of the early female monasteries, there is a basic difference in the ordering of sacred space; for in contrast to the male communities, women's houses made provision for the laity (male and female) to be allowed into their main ecclesia and burial churches. This is the case, for example, at La Balme, discussed later in this study, and this arrangement can be further corroborated by a variety of evidence from other female foundations of the period.[35] It also appears that many of the early Merovingian and Carolingian female monasteries had several churches: a separate church for the abbess and nuns (the abbatial church), a funerary church, one for the laity, and another for churchmen. If the community had a major church, it would frequently be divided so as to have separate space partitioned off for nuns in order to remove them from the distractions of the outside world; however, it would allow the laity, pilgrims, and others entrance into the nave and chapels as well as access to the saints' tombs.[36] It therefore appears that the more inclusive spatial policies of the women's communities in regard to access into their churches did not have the same effect on men as the male policies of exclusion had on women. I have not found, for example, parallel cases of alleged spiritual deprivations for men or male attempts to break into convents to worship or to venerate relics found in female monastic churches. Rather these exclusionary policies adopted by male communities seem to have placed a disproportionate burden or special hardship on women who wished to visit male monastic or pilgrimage churches for prayer and religious services, to visit the tombs of their male relatives, and particularly to receive the special benefits of the holy dead—the saints and their relics.

## POLICIES OF NEGOTIATION AND ACCOMMODATION OF SACRED SPACE

Although we find a proliferation of monastic churches that were officially designated as strictly off limits to women, there is also some evidence of perhaps a certain awareness in regard to the special problems that these policies might create for women. There appears to have been a flexibility on the part of some churchmen to make provisions for female worshippers who would otherwise find themselves shut out from the church without opportunities for worship, Communion, or direct access to the saints and holy relics.

One solution to the problem of the exclusion of women from sacred space was to provide a separate or alternative sacred space, namely, a special chapel or small church, built just outside of the monastery's walls, to accommodate female worshippers. According to Symeon of Durham, a small church of this type was built by St. Cuthbert on Lindisfarne Island. Inhabitants called it the "grene cyrice" because it was situated upon a green plain. Cuthbert directed "that the women who wished to hear masses and the word of God should assemble there and that they should never approach the church frequented by himself and the monks."[37] This special chapel was therefore built to serve the religious needs of women; however, it was also to keep them from attempting to enter the monastery's main church. The *Regula* of the monastery of Tarnatensis notes that women are forbidden to enter into the monastery; however they could go into the oratory or guest house.[38] According to a description of the impressive Carolingian abbey of Farfa, written by Abbot Hugo at the end of the tenth century: "There were five other basilicas besides the main one. . . . The fifth church, small but marvelously built, was set up outside the walls of the monastery in honor of the Virgin Mary, where women gathered for prayer and visitations in accordance with an old rule prohibiting women from entering the monastery."[39] Similar arrangements were made in the tenth century at the great reform center of Cluny. As noted in *The Life of St. Odo of Cluny*, "Now, not far from it [the monastery of Cluny] there was an oratory to which women were admitted to pray."[40] The Cistercians also made special provisions for female worshippers who were denied access to their churches. According to their *Consuetudines*, in many of their abbeys they built near the porterage a chapel for women that opened to the outside of the monastery's wall. (This location also allowed the porter to dispense bread and nourishment to women travelers without allowing them within the monastic precinct.)[41]

Other sources record special concessions made to accommodate female worshippers. The *vita* of St. Theofroi (d. ca. 728) explains that although women were not permitted to enter his monastery's church, the abbot allowed them to come near to the church doors ("haberent sedem circa templi januam"), and there they might receive special instructions on the merits of salvation.[42] Similarly, Goscelin of Canterbury notes in regard to the exclusionary policy of the monastic church of Sai: "But lest women there should seem entirely deprived of the holy father's grace, the inhabitants built a suitable holding-area for them before the doors of the church (pro foribus ecclesiae receptaculum illis congruum aedificavere) where they would be able to gather, pray, pay their offerings and vows, and approach the holy mysteries."[43]

However, in general, these exclusionary policies must have been particularly onerous for those women who personally sought cures and miracles from a particular saint whose tomb was located within a male monastery. A moving description of the special hardships that these spatial prohibitions could cause for women can be found in the *vita* of the abbot saint Leutfridus (d. ca. 738). The life notes that Leutfridus' church contained the relics of a number of saints, but its access was strictly forbidden to women. One day a blind woman on pilgrimage approached the monastery searching for a cure. When she learned that no women were admitted into the church and that she would be unable to approach the saint's relics for a cure, she was forced to give a candle in memory of God to a man. He then (serving as the woman's proxy) placed the candle before the tomb of St. Leutfridus. According to Leutfridus' miracles, only in this "indirect" way did the blind woman receive an immediate cure.[44]

Our sources also provide a few exceptional examples of perhaps a certain sympathy and enlightened sensitivity toward women and the special difficulties they experienced because of regulations of exclusionary space. They also recognized their need for equal access to the tombs of saints and their intercessory powers. One early case can be found in Gregory of Tours' (d. ca. 594) *Life of the Fathers*. In this work he relates a discussion between the aged brother abbots Lupicinus and Romanus making preparations for their burials. Romanus said to his brother:

> "I do not want to have my tomb in a monastery which women are forbidden to enter. As you know, the Lord has given me the grace of bringing cures, although I am unworthy and do not deserve it, and many have been snatched from various illnesses by the imposition of my hands and the power of the Lord's cross. Thus many people will gather at my tomb when I leave the light of this life. That is why I ask to rest far from the monastery." For that reason, when he died he was buried ten miles from the monastery, on a small hill. At length a great church was built over the tomb, and large crowds came there every day. Many miracles are now accomplished there in the name of God: the blind find light, the deaf their hearing, the paralysed the use of their limbs.[45]

Thus according to Gregory of Tours, Romanus chose not to be buried in his own monastery (which would have excluded female pilgrims) but rather at a site located at a safe distance from his monastery. It is interesting to note that the church in which the saint's tomb found its resting place was La Balme, a large convent where Romanus' sister held the office of abbess. Therefore, in contrast to his own monastic church, this church that belonged to nuns was then open to both female and male pilgrims.[46]

The case of the monastic church of Elnone is also of interest. According to the *Life of St. Amand* (d. ca. 679), sixteen years after the saint's death a new church was built. The explanation for this new building was that the old one was too inadequate or small and that it was inaccessible to women.[47]

The formulation of policies of exclusion and an awareness of the special difficulties they might cause for women are also recorded in the *vita* of St. Alto, abbot of Altomünster (d. ca. 760). Here Alto is described as strongly objecting to the plans of his superior, the missionary reformer St. Boniface, who insisted that women be forbidden entry into Alto's new church. Boniface finally consented to the Abbot's petition and consecrated this new monastic church, thus allowing women as well as men to worship there in common. Perhaps reflecting a compromise in their negotiations, the sacred fountain located next to the church was consecrated with the proviso that no woman be permitted to approach it or drink from it.[48]

An interesting case concerns the Monastery of Castres. During the translation of the relics of St. Vincent of Saragossa to the Monastery of Castres, we learn that the martyr's body was not immediately brought into the monastic church (which was closed to women) but rather placed in the church of the Genitricis Dei—located outside of the cloister's gate. Here many devoted women flocked to see the relics. It was determined that later, near the monastery, a new church would be built in the saint's honor which would allow access to both sexes. However, with the decline in the number of women pilgrims interested in the saint, the monks of Castres changed their building plans. They finally decided to place these relics within the exclusionary space of the main church of the monastery, which then remained off limits to women.[49]

A unique and fascinating case of special concessions made in response to women's insistence on access to holy relics is found in the monastery of Fleury/St.-Benoît-sur-Loire. According to the *Miracles of St. Benedict*, when the popular relics of Sts. Denis and Sebastian were brought to the Monastery of Fleury in the ninth century, a large crowd of men and women followed the saints' relics because of certain miracles that occurred. Ancient authority had forbidden women's admittance within the outer gates of the monastery; thus, entreaties were made so that women would be permitted to enter the church where the relics were in order to pray and carry out their vows. But since this went against monastic discipline, the women were refused. The women persisted in their request, complaining that they had come from a long distance to see the holy relics; they therefore caused an impressive disturbance that could not be ignored. Others joined them, and with great difficulty they were able to persuade the abbot to have a tent set up outside the monastery gates on the eastern side where the relics would be displayed for twenty-four hours, beginning at the vigil of Sunday, after which time they were then taken back inside the monastic church. When this arrangement was carried out, crowds of people from nearby and distant places flocked to Fleury to secure healing for the soul and body.[50] It then appears from this account that the women did not quietly or passively accept the restrictive spatial policies of the monastery; rather, they staged an angry protest. And it was only in response to this pressure that the abbot and monks of Fleury begrudgingly granted these women this rather limited privilege.

Other sources note special concessions made by churchmen or religious communities to individual noblewomen or abbesses, who under unique circumstances were allowed entrance into their monastic churches. The *vita* of St. Lioba (friend and kinswoman of St. Boniface) relates: "Sometimes Lioba came to the monastery of Fulda [St. Boniface's monastery] to say her prayers, a privilege never granted any women either before or since, because from the day that monks began to dwell there, entrance was forbidden to women. Permission was only granted to her for the simple reason that the holy martyr St. Boniface had commended her to the seniors of the monastery and because he had ordered her remains to be buried there."[51]

Similarly we learn that the monastery of St. Bertin made special concessions to allow a noblewoman to enter the monastery's church.[52] Thus in 938, despite the strict prohibitions against female entry, Adela, Countess of Flanders was allowed to enter the church. Apparently in a state of extreme illness, the countess had petitioned the bishop and monastery for a special exemption to allow her to pray for a cure before the altar of their patron, St. Bertin. Although we are assured that in the entire history of the monastery no woman had ever crossed its threshold, the countess was given special permission to enter the church by the advocatus of the bishop, the treasurer of the monastery (who no doubt exercised an important role in this decision), and the monks. She was brought into the monastery during Easter week by the bishop "not without great trembling." She prostrated herself before the altar of St. Bertin where she prayed and her "body received health." The saint's life adds that after the countess' miraculous cure, she brought them many ornaments, and as long as she lived she never ceased to make generous donations to the monastery. Thus at least from an economic standpoint, the granting of this unique privilege proved beneficial to the monastery. Moreover, perhaps in light of her own difficulty in gaining access to the church of St. Bertin, the sources note that after Countess Adela was restored to health she had a special church for women built close to the monastery.

*The Chronicle of Hugh of Flavigny* refers to another exceptional case in which a woman was allowed within a male monastery. Apparently, in order to learn more about the reform practices of monasticism, Ava, abbess of St. Maur of Verdun, was permitted to observe monastic life at the great reform center of Cluny. Although St. Odo and the rules of the monastery apparently forbade any woman entrance into the cloister of the great church, out of friendship for Abbot Richard, founder of Ava's community of St. Maur, Abbot Odilo of Cluny not only brought Ava into the cloister but also brought her into the chapter. In addition, on Sunday she was received in the procession of brothers. The chronicler, Hugh of Flavigny, however, underscores the exceptional character of this event, "for continually up until today" (ca. 1100) he writes, "the memory of this visit still remains at Cluny."[53]

Other sources note special adjustments or a relaxation of these strict policies that excluded women from male monastic space. One concession made at the General Chapter of the Cistercians in 1157, for example, allowed women to visit a new church of the Order during the nine days following its dedication. It also stressed that this period of time could not under any circumstances be extended and that women guests were not allowed to remain in the church over night.[54] (This limited provision that permitted women to visit newly constructed Cistercian churches appears to have been based on economic expediency with the intent that in the enthusiasm of the "open houses" the female visitors would be moved to make generous contributions to the community.) A number of cases, however, reveal the punishments imposed upon Cistercian abbots for their "excessive" hospitality to female religious and other women. The abbot of Savigny, for example, was severely punished for inviting a group of nuns to sing in his monastery's new choir and to eat in their refectory on the day of the dedication of his church.[55]

Similarly, economic motivation appears to have provided the rationale for the manipulation or relaxation of the gender-based exclusionary policies at the Abbey of Ottobeuren. Here we learn that the late medieval reform abbot "nevertheless . . . admitted noble women to parts of the monastery; and since these were wealthy, they abundantly endowed the monastery."[56]

Perhaps one of the most dramatic public challenges to the gender-based proscriptions of sacred space is described in the *Miracles of Robert of Arbrissel*. Upon learning that women were prohibited from entering the abbey church of Menelay (where he was slated to preach), Robert of Arbrissel publicly defied their policies and brought many women along with him into the church. He thus blatantly provoked those in charge of guarding the church doors (whose job it was to turn women away); they then loudly invoked their patron saint Menelay to avenge this insult. As described in the *Miracles*, Robert of Arbrissel responded to their threats with a stirring defense of women and their nature, arguing that in fact the saints are not enemies of the Brides of Christ. He then demanded: "[W]ho is it who dared to say that there would be any church in which women would not be permitted to enter because of their transgressions and guilt. Which is more important, the material temple of God or the spiritual temple in which God lives? If the woman takes and eats the body and blood of Christ, think what folly it is to believe that she must not enter the church!" And according to the *Miracles*, "In this manner, after he had publicly demonstrated the truth, this error stopped and became totally extinct."[57]

Thus although many of the institutional sources from this period describe strict ideals and policies of women's exclusion from monastic churches, cloisters, and their precincts, at the same time and under certain conditions, they also reveal negotiations and a flexibility on the part of some churchmen. Special provisions of alternate space and adjustments in the boundaries of sacred space were therefore made for women with religious leanings. In some cases these concessions were forced upon reluctant churchmen by determined women who were intent on having equal opportunities in their access to the tombs of saints and holy relics. Frequently these manipulations of sacred space appear to have been the result of rather crass economic considerations; other cases, however, seem to reveal a sensitivity and sympathy toward women, an awareness of the special difficulties brought about by these proscriptive policies.

While there is a continuity of these gender-based exclusionary policies from around 500 through 1200, it appears that they became especially problematic for women from the ninth through the twelfth centuries. For it was during this period that there emerged a growing popularity of the cult of the saints, pilgrimages, along with the establishment of many new or reformed male monasteries which housed famous collections of relics. Women were strongly attracted to the cults of saints; they needed direct access to the saints' tombs, their special intercessory powers and miraculous cures.[58] At the same time the reform movements of the period, for example, the Carolingian, Cluniac, and Gregorian reforms, placed an increased emphasis on the regularization of monastic life, ritual purity, and celibacy with its exaggerated fear of female sexuality and the threat of moral contagion. Taken together these fears and beliefs stressed the need to reemphasize and attempt to implement severe policies of exclusion from male monasteries. Thus during this period the sources frequently focus on exacting codes that defined and limited sacred space; they also underscored the various threats, challenges, and negotiations in regard to women and their limited access to sacred space, especially admission to the tombs of the holy dead.

Despite harsh, uncompromising policies and threats of divine intervention, it appears that during this period churchmen frequently experienced difficulties in their attempts to enforce their agendas of exclusion. Women did not acquiesce or accept quietly, without protesting, these spatial restrictions. This is underscored by the repeated warnings of canons to ecclesiastics that they must use their authority to stop women from threatening their special prerogatives or from encroaching on sacred space. In addition, many of the sources, especially male saints' lives, frequently condemn "imprudent," disruptive females who dared to test, challenge, or ignore the "sacred" prohibitions and who refused to be scared off by the "divine deterrents." These defiant women perhaps saw these discriminatory measures for exactly what they were—not divinely inspired, natural, inevitable, or static, but rather culturally determined man-made proscriptions of sacred space used to exercise control, regulate social behavior, or accommodate financial gain. In their acts of "insubordination," in overstepping the arbitrary thresholds or boundaries and pushing aside the man-made barriers that were designed to cordon off sacred space, these medieval women dared to protest publicly the inequities of these policies for themselves and their sex.

## NOTES

The essay is reprinted from *Medieval Purity and Piety: Essays on Medieval Clerical Celibacy and Religious Reform*, ed. Michael Frassetto (New York: Garland 1998), 353–76.

1. There has been a great deal of recent interest in the topics of sacred and gendered spaces. See especially the classic study by Mircea Eliade, *The Sacred and the Profane: The Nature of Religion*, trans. Willard R. Trask (1959, San Diego: Harcourt Brace, reprint 1987); Mary Douglas, *Purity and Danger: An Analysis of the Concepts of Pollution and Taboo* (1966, reprint New York: Praeger, 1984); Daphne Spain, *Gendered Spaces* (Chapel Hill: University of North Carolina Press, 1992); and Shirley Ardener, ed., *Women and Space: Ground Rules and Social Maps: Cross-Cultural Perspectives on Women*, rev. ed. (1981, reprint Oxford: Berg, 1993); Beatriz Colomina, ed., *Sexuality and Space*, Princeton Papers on Architecture (Princeton: Princeton University Press, 1992); Jane Rendell, Barbara Penner and Iain Borden, *Gender Space Architecture: An Interdisciplinary Introduction* (London and New York: Routledge, 2000); Yi-Fu Tuan, *Space and Place: The Perspective of Experience* (Minneapolis: Minnesota University Press, 1977); Yi-Fu Tuan, *Topophilia: A Study of Environmental Perception, Attitudes, and Values* (1974, reprint New York: Columbia University Press, 1990). See also note 7 for medieval studies on space.

2. See especially Otto von Simson, *The Gothic Cathedral: Origins of Gothic Architecture and the Medieval Concept of Order*, 2nd ed. (New York: Pantheon Books, 1962), 8, 35–38.

3. See especially Eliade, *The Sacred and the Profane*, and Douglas, *Purity and Danger*.

4. Peter of Celle, "The School and the Cloister," in *Selected Works*, trans. Hugh Feiss (Kalamazoo, Mich.: Cistercian, 1987), 79.

5. Douglas, *Purity and Danger*, 1–22, 121–39.

6. Carol J. Clover notes the "uncontainability" of the independent women of early Scandinavia in "The Politics of Scarcity: Notes on the Sex Ratio in Early Scandinavia," in *New Readings on Women in Old English Literature*, ed. Helen Damico and Alexandra Hennessey Olson (Bloomington: Indiana University Press, 1990), 128.

7. See note 1. Also for the study of sacred space in the Middle Ages see Sofia Goesch Gajano and Lucetta Scaraffia, *Luoghi sacri et spàzi délla santità* (Turin: Rosenberg and Sellier, 1990) (I would like to thank Mary Martin McLaughlin for this reference); Margaret Aston, "Segregation in Church," in *Women in the Church*, ed. W. J. Sheils and Diana Wood, *Studies in Church History*, vol. 27 (Oxford: Blackwell, 1990), 237–94; *Gesta* (The International Center of Medieval Art) 31/2 (1992) (this issue is devoted to medieval women religious and sacred space); Roberta Gilchrist, *Gender and Material Culture: The Archaeology of Religious Women* (London and New York:

Routledge, 1994); Barbara H. Rosenwein, *Negotiating Space: Power, Restraint, and Privileges of Immunity in Early Medieval Europe* (Ithaca: Cornell University Press, 1999); and Barbara A. Hanawalt and Michal Kobialka, *Medieval Practices of Space:* Medieval Cultures, vol. 23 (Minneapolis: University of Minnnesota Press, 2000).

8. See Aston, "Segregation in Church"; Schulenburg, "Medieval Women and Sacred Space: Symbol and Practice," paper delivered at the Seventh Berkshire Conference on the History of Women, Wellesley College, June 21, 1987. I am presently working on a major book project on the medieval construction of gender and sacred space, from "womb to tomb," ca. 500–1200.

9. See Schulenburg, *Forgetful of Their Sex: Female Sanctity and Society, ca. 500–1100* (Chicago: University of Chicago Press, 1998), 286–96, 307–48. See also Schulenburg, "Saints and Sex, ca. 500–1100: Striding Down the Nettled Path of Life," in *Sex in the Middle Ages: A Book of Essays*, ed. Joyce E. Salisbury (New York: Garland, 1991), 203–31.

10. *Patrologiae cursus completes, Series latina*, ed. J.-P. Migne (Paris, 1844–64); hereafter cited as *PL*. *PL* 66, ch. 154, col. 337.

11. *PL*, 66, ch. 159, col. 341.

12. *PL*, 66, ch. 164, col. 345.

13. *PL*, 66, ch. 155, cols. 338–39.

14. Charles Joseph Hefele and Dom H. Leclercq, *Histoire des conciles* 3, 1 (Paris: Letouzey, 1909), Council of Auxerre (587), 220.

15. *Acta Sanctorum*, hereafter cited as AASS, Julii I (July 1), 87.

16. AASS, Oct. XI (Oct. 25), 691.

17. AASS, Aug. VI (Aug. 30), 598–620.

18. Johanne Mabillon, *Acta Ordinis S. Benedicti* (Luca, 1740), vol. 5, 269.

19. See Joan Nicholson, "*Feminae Gloriosae:* Women in the Age of Bede," in *Medieval Women: Studies in Church History*, Subsidia, no. 1, ed. Derek Baker (Oxford: Blackwell, 1978), esp. 28, where she notes this posthumous antifeminism; Victoria Tudor, "The Misogyny of Saint Cuthbert," *Archaeologia Aeliana*, 5th series, 12 (1984): 157–67; Victoria Tudor, "The Cult of St. Cuthbert in the Twelfth Century: The Evidence of Reginald of Durham," in *Saint Cuthbert: His Cult and His Community to AD 1200*, ed. Gerald Bonner, David Rollason, and Clare Stancliffe (Woodbridge, Suffolk, and Rochester, N.Y.: Boydell, 1989), 447–67; Schulenburg, *Forgetful of Their Sex*, 345–48.

20. *The Historical Works of Simeon of Durham: The Church Historians of England*, trans. Joseph Stevenson (London: Seeleys, 1855), 3, pt. 2, ch. 22, 657–58.

21. *Rites of Durham* (1593), Publication of the Surtees Society: CVII (Durham and Edinburgh: Andrews, 1902), ch. 17, 35.

22. *The Historical Works of Simeon of Durham*, ch. 23, 658.

23. Ibid., ch. 24, 658–59.

24. Ibid., ch. 46, 682–83.

25. Ibid., ch. 24, 659.

26. Reginald of Durham, *Libellus de Admirandis Beati Cuthberti Virtutibus, Publication of the Surtees Society: I* (London: Nichols and Son,1835), ch. 74, 151–54.

27. *Historia Dunelmensis Scriptores Tres*, ed. J. Raine, Surtees Society: 9, 1839, 11, cited and translated by David Park in "The Wall Paintings in the Galilee Chapel of Durham Cathedral," *Friends of Durham Cathedral*, Fifty-seventh Annual Report, 1990, 21. I would like to thank Miriam Cill for her kindness in providing me with this interesting study.

28. *Rites of Durham*, ch. 22, 43.

29. David Hugh Farmer, *The Oxford Dictionary of Saints* (Oxford: Oxford University Press, 1978/82), 30; also AASS, Iun. V (June 24), 714–21.

30. I would like to express my extreme gratitude to David Townsend for sharing this wonderful source with me. This is also David Townsend's translation of Goscelin's *Life of St. Augustine Bishop of Canterbury*, AASS, Maii VI (May 26), 377. See Townsend's interesting study, along with his translation of this incident, "Omissions, Emissions, Missionaries, and Master Signifiers in Norman Canterbury," *Exemplaria* 7/2 (1995): 291–315.

31. AASS, Maii VI (May 26), 377, trans. Townsend.

32. Ibid.

33. See, for example, David F. Noble, *A World without Women: The Christian Clerical Culture of Western Science* (New York: Knopf, 1992).

34. For a general survey of various policies of active and passive enclosure during this early period, see Schulenburg, "Strict Active Enclosure and Its Effects on the Female Monastic Experience (ca. 500–1100)," in *Distant Echoes: Medieval Religious Women*, ed. John A. Nichols and Lillian Thomas Shank (Kalamazoo, Mich.: Cistercian, 1984), vol. 1, 51–86; see also Sarah Foot's major study, *Veiled Women*, Studies in Early Medieval Britain (Aldershot, Hants, and Burlington, Vt.: Ashgate, 2000), vols. 1 and 2; Shari Horner, *The Discourse of Enclosure: Representing Women in Old English Literature* (Albany: State University of New York Press, 2001). See also Césaire d'Arles, *Oeuvres Monastiques: Oeuvres pour les Moniales, I, Sources Chrétiennes*, no. 345, ed./trans. Adalbert de Vogüé and Joel Correau (Paris: Editions du Cerf, 1988), especially 35–273; Sr. Maria Caritas McCarthy, *The Rule for Nuns of St. Caesarius of Arles: A Translation with a Critical Introduction* (Washington, D.C.: Catholic University of America Press, 1960); R. Naz, "Césaire d'Arles (règles de saint)" in *Dictionnaire de droit canonique* 3 (Paris: Letouzey et Ané, 1938), 260–78; William E. Klingshirn, *Caesarius of Arles: The Making of a Christian Community in Late Antique Gaul* (Cambridge and New York: Cambridge University Press, 1994); *The Ordeal of Community: Rule of Donatus of Besançon*, Peregrina Translation Series no. 5, 2nd ed., trans. Jo Ann McNamara and John Halborg (Toronto: Peregrina, 1993), ch. 55, 62. For the late Middle Ages, see the important study by Elizabeth M. Makowski, *Canon Law and Cloistered Women: Periculoso and Its Commentators, 1298–1545*, Studies in Medieval and Early Modern Canon Law, vol. 5 (Washington, D.C.: Catholic University Press, 1997).

35. See Césaire d'Arles, *Oeuvres Monastiques: Oeuvres pour les moniales*, 98–113; Marquise de Maille, "Les monastères colombaniens des femmes," in *Les Cryptes des Jouarre* (Paris: Picard, 1971), 26ff; Yvonne Labande-Mailfert, "Les débuts de Sainte-Croix," in *Histoire de l'Abbaye Sainte-Croix de Poitiers: Quatorze siècles de vie monastique, in Mémoires de la Sociétés des Antiquaires de l'Ouest*, 4th série, 19 (1986–1987), 25–116.

36. See note 35; also for the later period see *Gesta* 31/2 (1992).

37. *Historical Works of Simeon of Durham*, ch. 22, 657–58.

38. *PL*, 66, ch. 154, col. 337.

39. "A Description of the Monastery in the Ninth Century as Recounted ca. A.D. 1000 by Abbot Hugo in the *Destructio Monasterii Farfensis*" in Charles B. McClendon, *The Imperial Abbey of Farfa: Architectural Currents of the Early Middle Ages* (New Haven and London: Yale University Press, 1987), Document 6, 131,

translation 64. I would like to thank Roberta Magnusson for bringing this interesting source to my attention.

40. John of Salerno, *The Life of St. Odo of Cluny* in *St. Odo of Cluny: The Makers of Christendom*, ed. Dom Gerard Sitwell (New York: Sheed and Ward, 1958), ch. 36, 37.

41. Marcel Aubert, *L'Architecture Cistercienne en France* (Paris: Editions d'art et d'histoire, 1947), vol. 1, 47.

42. *Acta Sanctorum Ordinis S. Benedicti*, vol. 3, 481.

43. *AASS*, Maii VI (May 26), 377, trans. David Townsend.

44. *Acta Sanctorum Ordinis S. Benedicti*, vol. 3, 593.

45. Gregory of Tours, *Life of the Fathers*, Translated Texts for Historians, Latin Series 1, trans. Edward James (Liverpool: Liverpool University Press, 1985), bk. 1, ch. 6, 34.

46. Ibid., 34, 137, no. 11.

47. *PL*, 66, ch. 161, col. 343; see also Maille, *Les Cryptes de Jouarre*, 27.

48. *PL*, 66, ch. 163, cols. 344–45.

49. *PL*, 66, ch. 159, col. 341; *PL* 126, bk. 2, ch. 4, col. 1020C; bk. 2, ch. 16, col. 1023D, and ch. 17, col. 1024A. "Consuetudo (ut meminimus) praefatae congregationis fuit, ut feminae omnes ab ingressu monasterii arcerentur. Idcirco ejusdem coenobii fratres prudenter providerant, ut corpus beati Vincenti levitae et martyris in basilica Dei genitricis Mariae poneretur, ad quam liber erat mulierum accessus. At vero successu temporis, conventu hujusmodi per dies cessante, intulerunt illud in seniorem monasterii ecclesiam, atque retro altare beati Benedicti (donec ejus templum consummaretur) posuerunt." I would like to thank Thomas Head for his comments on these events, which he treated in a fascinating paper, "Opposition to Pilgrims and Miracles: The Rhetoric and Practice of Monastic Reform."

50. *Les miracles de Saint Benoît écrits par Adrevald, Aimoin, André, Raoul Tortaire et Hugues de Sainte Marie, moines de Fleury*, ed. Eugène de Certain (Paris: Renouard, 1858), vol. 1, 64–65. See also Thomas F. Head, *Hagiography and the Cult of Saints: The Diocese of Orléans, 800–1200*, Cambridge Studies in Medieval Life and Thought, fourth series, no. 14 (Cambridge and New York: Cambridge University Press, 1990), 138–52; Janet Nelson, "Les femmes et l'évangelisation," *Revue du Nord* 68 (1968): 480–81; and Janet Nelson, "Women and the Word in the Earlier Middle Ages," in *Women in the Church*, ed. W. J. Sheils and Diana Wood, *Studies in Church History*, vol. 27 (Oxford: Blackwell, 1990), 68.

51. Rudolf, *The Life of St. Leoba in the Anglo-Saxon Missionaries in Germany*, trans. and ed. Charles H. Talbot (New York: Sheed and Ward, 1954), 233.

52. *Acta Sanctorum Ordinis S. Benedicti*, 3, 139.

53. *Chronicon Hugonis*, *PL*, 154, col. 239.

54. Aubert, *L'Architecture Cistercienne*, 47.

55. Ibid.

56. George G. Coulton, *Five Centuries of Religion: The Friars and the Dead Weight of Tradition, 1200–1400 A.D.* (Cambridge: Cambridge University Press, 1927), 649.

57. Jacques Dalarun, "Robert d'Arbrissel et les femmes," *Annales ESC* 39, no. 6 (1984): 152–53. I would like to thank André Vauchez for bringing this study to my attention.

58. See Pierre-André Sigal, *L'Homme et les miracles dans la France médiévale (XI–XII siècle)* (Paris: Cerf, 1985); Ronald C. Finucane, *Miracles and Pilgrims: Popular Beliefs in Medieval England* (Totowa, N.J.: Rowman and Littlefield, 1977); Bat-Sheva Albert, *Le Pèlerinage à l'époque Carolingienne*, Bibliothèque de la revue d'histoire ecclésiastique, fascicule 82 (Louvain-la-Neuve: College Erasme, 1999); Jonathan Sumption, *Pilgrimage: An Image of Mediaeval Religion* (London: Faber and Faber, 1975); Tudor, "The Cult of St. Cuthbert in the Twelfth Century," 447–67; Susan Signe Morrison, *Women Pilgrims in Late Medieval England: Private Piety as Public Performance* (London and New York: Routledge, 2000); Diana Webb, *Pilgrims and Pilgrimage in the Medieval West*, International Library of Historical Studies, 12 (London and New York: Tauris, 1999); Debra J. Birch, *Pilgrimage to Rome in the Middle Ages: Continuity and Change*, Studies in the History of Medieval Religion (Woodbridge, Suffolk, and Rochester, N.Y.: Boydell, 1998). See also Schulenburg, "Saints, Gender and the Production of Miracles in Medieval Europe," paper presented at the Ninth Berkshire Conference on the History of Women, Vassar College, June 1992; "Negotiating Sacred Space: Women, the Holy Dead, and Miracles," paper presented at the International Medieval Congress, University of Leeds, Leeds, England, 11 July 1995; "Economics and the Cult of Relics: Considerations of Gender and Space," paper presented at the Thirty-second International Congress on Medieval Studies, Western Michigan University, Kalamazoo, Michigan, 9 May 1997; "Women, Pilgrimage, Exclusionary Policies and Space: 'Forgive Us Our Trespasses!' " paper presented at the Thirty-sixth International Congress on Medieval Studies, Western Michigan University, Kalamazoo, Michigan, 3 May 2001.

## FURTHER READING


Ardener, Shirley, ed. *Women and Space: Ground Rules and Social Maps: Cross-Cultural Perspectives on Women*. Rev. ed. 1981; Oxford: Berg, 1993.

Aston, Margaret. "Segregation in Church." In *Women in the Church. Studies in Church History* 27. Ed. W. J. Sheils and Diana Wood. Oxford: Blackwell, 1990: 237–94.

Douglas, Mary. *Purity and Danger: An Analysis of the Concepts of Pollution and Taboo*. 1966; New York: Praeger, 1984.

Eliade, Mircea. *The Sacred and the Profane: The Nature of Religion*. Trans. Willard R. Trask. 1959; San Diego: Harcourt Brace, 1987.

*Gesta* (The International Center of Medieval Art) 31/2 (1992).

Gilchrist, Roberta. *Gender and Material Culture: The Archaeology of Religious Women*. London and New York: Routledge, 1994.

Schulenburg, Jane T. *Forgetful of Their Sex: Female Sanctity and Society*. Chicago: University of Chicago Press, 1998.

———. "Strict Active Enclosure and Its Effects on the Female Monastic Experience (ca. 500–1100)." In *Distant Echoes. Medieval Religious Women*, vol. 1, Ed. John A. Nichols and Lillian Thomas Shank. Kalamazoo, Mich.: Cistercian, 1984: 51–86.

Simeon of Durham. *The Historical Works of Simeon of Durham: The Church Historians of England*. Trans. Joseph Stevenson. London: Seeleys, 1855.

Spain, Daphne. *Gendered Spaces*. Chapel Hill: University of North Carolina Press, 1992.

Tuan, Yi-Fu. *Space and Place: The Perspective of Experience*. Minneapolis: Minnesota University Press, 1977.

Tudor, Victoria. "The Cult of St. Cuthbert in the Twelfth Century: The Evidence of Reginald of Durham." In *Saint Cuthbert: His Cult and His Community to AD 1200*. Ed. Gerald Bonner, David Rollason, and Clare Stancliffe. Woodbridge, Suffolk, and Rochester, N.Y.: Boydell, 1989: 447–67.

———. "The Misogyny of Saint Cuthbert." *Archaeologia Aeliana*, 5th series, 12 (1984): 156–67.

Von Simson, Otto. *The Gothic Cathedral: Origins of Gothic Architecture and the Medieval Concept of Order*. 2nd ed. New York: Pantheon, 1962.

EIGHT

# MEN ON THE RIGHT—WOMEN ON THE LEFT: (A)SYMMETRICAL SPACES AND GENDERED PLACES

CORINE SCHLEIF

*In memory of Elfriede Michler*

THE DOORBELL RANG, and I opened the door. "Do you want him on the right or on the left?" The question, uttered hesitatingly in a local Westerwald dialect of German, came from the young man in slightly muddied work clothes who was standing outside. It was September 1995, and my father-in-law had just died. When I asked what was customary the workman replied politely that one is buried just as one stands before the altar when one is married. After conferring with my mother-in-law I told him to prepare the grave in the family plot in the village cemetery in this customary way. Thus my father-in-law assumed his last resting place on the right, just as he had stood before the altar fifty-six years before. Innumerable Christian couples have positioned themselves in this manner in countless European and American churches and cemeteries. Marriage portraits and diptychs, which first became common in the Renaissance, have likewise followed this positioning.[1] The arrangement is governed by convention and not by law.

In the Middle Ages such placement was already ubiquitous. Throughout medieval and early modern times, men and women situated themselves according to these conventions when represented on sacred objects and in religious images: contemporary male venerators knelt on the right, and female venerators, on the left. For example, the couple that commissioned the *Ghent Altarpiece*, Jodocus Vijd and Isabel Borlout, saw to it that Jan van Eyck painted their pictures respectively on the exteriors of the right and left shutters (figures 8.1, 8.2), and the donors of the *Beaune Altarpiece*, Nicolas Rolin and Guigone des Salins, had Rogier van der Weyden include their portraits similarly on the right and left wings, visible when the altar was closed (figures 8.3, 8.4).

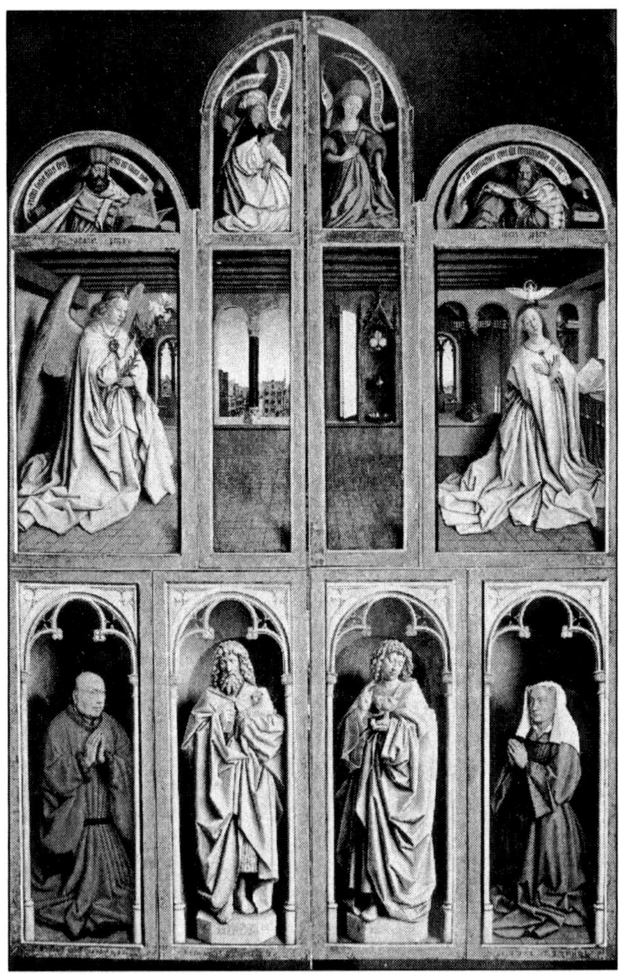

**Figure 8.1.** Jan van Eyck, *Altarpiece of the Lamb*, closed, 1432, Cathedral of St. Bavo, Ghent. After Hermann Beenken, Hubert und Jan Van Eyck (Munich: Bruckmann, 1941).

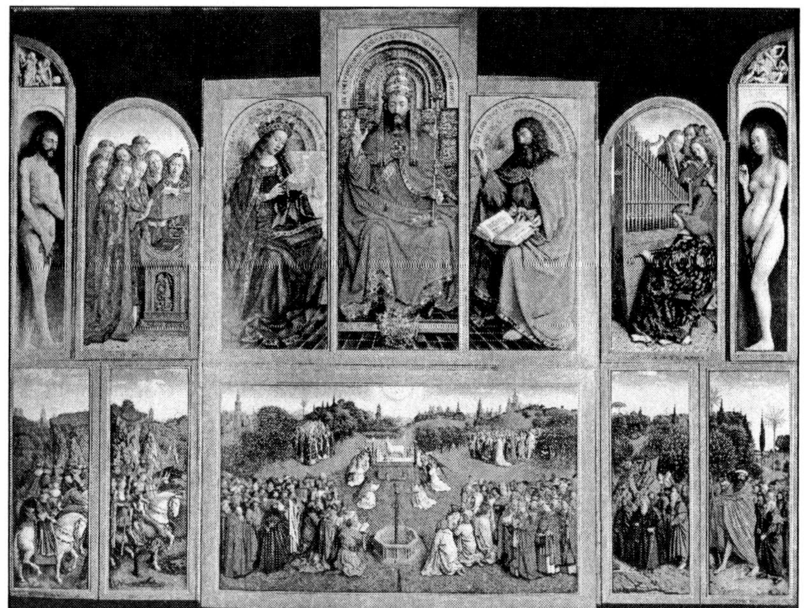

**Figure 8.2.** Jan van Eyck, *Altarpiece of the Lamb*, open, 1432, Cathedral of St. Bavo, Ghent. Foto Marburg.

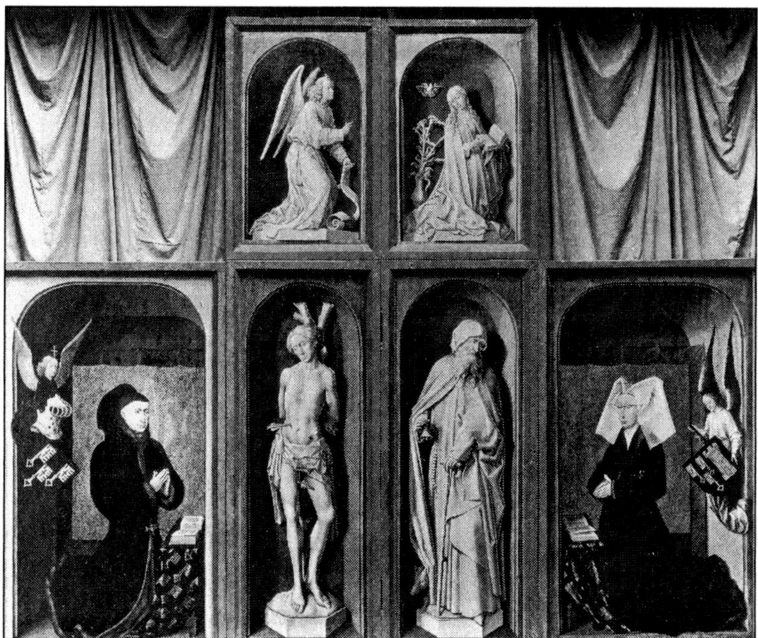

**Figure 8.3.** Rogier van der Weyden, *Last Judgment Altarpiece*, closed, after 1433, Musée de l'Hôtel Dieu, Beaune. Foto Marburg.

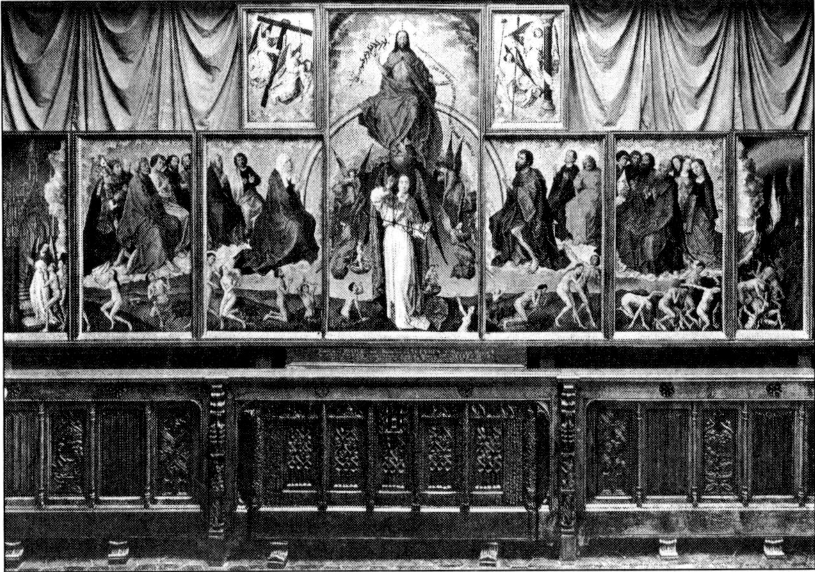

**Figure 8.4.** Rogier van der Weyden, *Last Judgment Altarpiece*, open, after 1433, Musée de l'Hôtel Dieu, Beaune. Foto Marburg.

The individuals in these works, and in many others like them, are represented separated from each other. Thus it is not their connection to each other that is paramount but rather the attachment between the venerators and those they venerate, in these cases, Christ as ruler of the world, the Lamb of God, and judge at the end of time. The kneeling figures are both marginal and liminal. Worthy only to stand in the wings, they direct their anatomies toward Christ. Located on the picture plane, they mark the threshold between the space/time of salvation history and that of other pious viewers who come and go outside the picture.

To my knowledge this commonplace of gendered left and right positioning within Christian imagery has gone unscrutinized. The literature on the meaning and function of left and right focuses on other contexts. Social psychologists and neurologists have investigated viewing patterns and paths of vision that derive from Western customs of reading from left to right, experiences of right-handedness, and the acquisition of spatial orientation.[2] A few art historians—among them Heinrich Wölfflin—have formally analyzed pictorial compositions with respect to left and right.[3] Structural anthropologists have inquired into the meanings of right and left, primarily in ancient and non-European cultures. Of these investigations, the anthology initiated and edited by Rodney Needham is particularly rich in insights.[4] However, several medievalists have explored notions associated with right and left in early medieval religious texts. Of these articles, which were quite useful for the preparation of this chapter, most fundamental are the studies by Otto Nussbaum on the values of right and left in the Roman liturgy and Ursula Deitmaring on the meanings of right and left in theological and literary texts before 1200.[5] Likewise the architectural historian Friedrich Möbius has studied the sociology of ecclesiastical architecture during the early Middle Ages, including the gendering of right and left spaces.[6]

## AN EMBODIED SUBJECT POSITION

How does one define left and right? Where is left and right? According to the *Oxford English Dictionary*, the matter is not so simple. "Left" refers to that side of the body which "is usually the weaker of the two and which is in the position of west if one is facing north, its individual parts, and their clothing, designating the corresponding side of any other body or object." Thus, where left and right are changes when you face another direction, or if you are prostrate and not upright. Obviously then, "left and right" always presupposes an embodied subject position. Already Aristotle addressed this matter of implicit self-referentiality with respect to left-right orientation: "It is in relation to ourselves that we speak of above and below, or right and left.[. . .] We name them either as they correspond with our own right hands (as in augury), or by analogy with our own (as in the right hand of a statue)."[7]

The matter of left and right seems to pose particular problems for teachers and students of art history. When standing at a podium facing an audience and confronted with two sets of buttons to operate two slide projectors simultaneously, the art historian must first know whether the buttons on his/her left operate the project on the viewer's left or the speaker's left. Similarly it is not unusual for a student taking an art history exam for the first time to ask innocently, "What do you mean by 'left' and 'right'?" Precisely phrased, the question becomes "Whose left or right?"

Generally, during the Middle Ages and continuing into the modern period, left and right were referenced according to a subject position of the work itself. Parenthetically it may be added that theater conventions for referencing stage right and left still follow these older practices. Only recently has usage changed in art history so that today left and right refer to the embodied subject position of the viewing audience. One might speculate that the change was wrought through the increasing self-consciousness of beholders and the decreasing assumption of the authoritative agency of the image. To avoid confusion, the older conventions are now labeled "heraldic left and right" since they linger on in the traditions governing descriptions of heraldic devices that were defined with respect to the subject position of the objects they emblazon. The man's coat of arms always appears on the right (viewer's left) and the woman's on the left (viewer's right).[8] When escutcheons are mounted, as they usually are, at the margins or edges of a doorway, altar retable, reliquary, and so on, the depictions that comprise the armorial bearings—whether rampant dogs, shoes, fish, human faces, or hybrid creatures—are always oriented so that they face the center of the object. Arms, after all, stand for families and/or individuals, and it would indeed be impolite to turn one's backside toward the object being adorned and/or adored.

Returning to the two altarpieces, we note that here the men, Jodocus Vijd and Nicolas Rolin, kneel to the right of Christ, while the women, Isabel Borlout and Guigone des Salins, kneel to his left. Thus they positioned themselves within a world ordered according to divine plan, conceived from within the sacred picture rather than from the vantage point of contemporary or latter-day viewers. In a sense then, these donors belong more to the picture than to the world outside of it. It can safely be assumed that Jodocus Vijd and Nicolas Rolin saw themselves occupying positions on the right, and Isabel Borlout and Guigone des Salins perceived themselves experiencing salvation history from their embodied positions to the left.

## DEXTER VERSUS SINISTER

The augury to which Aristotle referred was the ancient custom of divination or reading omens. For example, flocks of birds were observed to see if they flew to the left or to the right of the beholder. Already in the poems of Homer positive and negative values are assigned to these directions. Birds flying left were a bad omen, and birds flying right were a portent of good things to come. The etymological vestiges of these ancient associations are still present in the meanings that cluster around the English word *sinister*, which, derived from the Latin, not only denotes the left-hand side, but that which is evil and threatening; or the English term *dexter*, which likewise springs from the Latin and signifies not only the right-hand side but also someone who is skillful, and although far less frequently, that which is auspicious. Before the time of Aristotle, the Greeks subscribed to an anatomical model that gendered the left and right sides of the body, believing that female offspring developed from semen produced by the left testicle or in the left side of the womb, both thought to be weaker, and male offspring from the right side(s) of the parents, considered to be stronger.[9] Similarly, according to common belief, changes in the right side of a pregnant woman's body indicated that she would bear a son and deviations in the left, a daughter.[10] If we place the systems of soothsaying and physiology atop each other as transparent overlays we see that good portents, strength, and male children are inscribed on the right, bad omens, weakness, and girl children on the left. Certainly the ancient Greeks did not always regard female babies as "bad luck," but in times of adversity and scarcity it was primarily girl infants that, unwanted, were set out to die of exposure.

Indeed, throughout Western cultural history the positive and superior seems to be drawn like a magnet to the right pole and the negative and inferior appears to be pulled to the left. Even today notions of inferiority associated with the left side remain in our collective consciousness as evidenced by such idioms as *way out in left field* or *a left-handed compliment*.

## RIGHT AND LEFT AS GOOD AND EVIL

Before donor images can be examined, attention must be drawn to yet another set of meanings attached to left and right in the Middle Ages. When mapping the history of salvation onto a bilaterally arranged picture plane or representational field, the meanings were in some cases more drastic, expressing absolute oppositions of good and evil.

A good versus evil right-left polarity that originated in the New Testament is that of the Last Judgment. The Gospel of Matthew tells that "he shall set the sheep at his right hand, but the goats on the left" (31:6). During the Middle Ages, this metaphoric description was translated into more literal imagery with Christ typically enthroned in the center, judging the blessed to his right and the damned to his left. The *Beaune Altarpiece* provides one of the many examples (figure 8.4).

According to the accounts of the Crucifixion in Matthew 27, Mark 15, and Luke 23, Christ was crucified along with two malefactors, one on the right, and the other on the left. One repented and was saved, and the other scorned Christ and was damned. The apocryphal Acts of Pontius Pilatus, dating from the early fifth century, place the "good thief," Dismas, on Christ's right and the "bad thief," Gestas, to his left.[11] In the first Crucifixion scenes, dating from the same period, this good-bad polarity is codified visually in the representation of Gestas placed at Christ's left, turning his face downward, away from Christ.[12]

Similarly, very early on, other iconographic motifs were inscribed within this bipolar Crucifixion schema. "Longinus," as the spear-bearer (John 19: 34) at the Crucifixion came to be called, who became conflated with the converted centurion mentioned in the accounts given by Matthew and Mark, was represented on Christ's right, whereas Stephaton, as the sponge-bearer (Mark 15: 36; John 19: 29) came to be known, was inscribed as the unbelieving negative pendant on Christ's left.[13] In diagrammatic representations, notions of type and antitype were likewise projected onto the image and ordered with respect to the vertical axis. For example, in the *Hortus Deliciarum of Herrad of Hohenbourg* (or Landsberg) dating from around 1175 (figure 8.5), the personification of Ecclesia, here shown filling her chalice with blood issuing from the wound in Christ's side, represents the New Covenant and joins Dismas and Longinus at Christ's right. The corresponding blindfolded figure of Synagoga, symbolizing the Old Covenant, aligns herself with Gestas and Stephaton on Christ's left.[14]

In the late Middle Ages the polemics of left and right find renewed expression in veristically rendered gestures and facial features. In the *Crucifixion* from the Collegiate Church in Tübingen, attributed to Hans Schäufelein

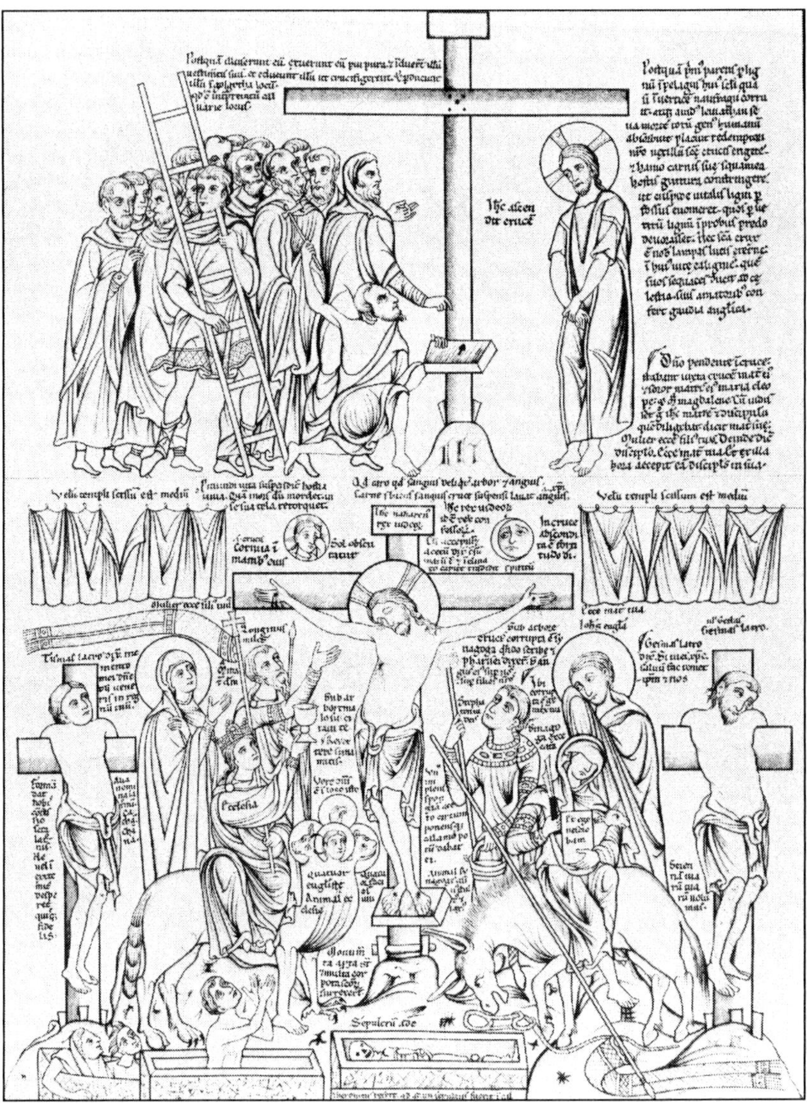

**Figure 8.5.** *Crucifixion*, Herrad of Hohenbourg's *Hortus deliciarum*. Nineteenth-century copy of destroyed original, ca.1180–95. After A. Straub and G. Keller, *Herrade de Landsberg, Hortvs Deliciarvm*. Schlesier and Schweikhardt: Strasbourg, 1879–99.

and dating from 1520, yet another "heavy" joins the crowd on Christ's left—the smith's wife who agreed to make the nails when her husband refused (figure 8.6). This painting also exhibits contorted figures, grotesque faces, and unflattering views of the negative characters on Christ's left—all the

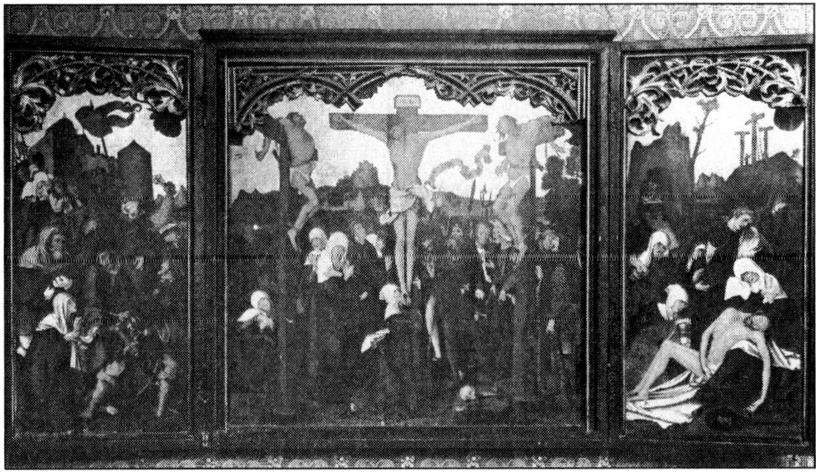

**Figure 8.6.** Attributed to Hans Schäufelein, *Crucifixion*, 1520, oil on panel, Collegiate Church, Tübingen. Foto Marburg.

attributes of "otherness" that Ruth Mellinkoff has so aptly described and illustrated in her volumes on outcasts.[15] Thus through representations of this central event in the history of salvation, the spaces to Christ's right and left came to be labeled as "good" and "evil" places, filled and populated by that which was respectively good or evil. What had begun as a dynamic biblical narrative, with variants and loose ends, had become a static mental diagram, strictly ordered and categorized.

Other linear stories likewise were presented visually as codified symmetrical designs. For example, frescoes representing Abel, with his acceptable sacrifice of a lamb, and Cain with his unacceptable offering of grain, were painted, around 1200, on the respective right and left sides of the triumphal arch in the church of St. Jakob in Grissian (South Tyrol).[16] These same events represented in grisaille, making them appear as sculpted decoration, fill the respective spaces in what resembles the two halves of a tympanum over the heads of Adam and Eve in the *Ghent Altarpiece* (figure 8.2).

Similarly, Christ's parable of the Wise and Foolish Virgins provides the figural decoration of numerous late medieval church portals, including but not limited to the late medieval German brides' portals that served as a backdrop for countless weddings held outside the churches. Already in the sculptural decoration at Saint-Pierre in Aulnay, dating from around 1130, a row of virgins holding their oil lamps upright and burning adorn the archivolts to the right of the central figure of Christ, and corresponding carved figures, their lamps overturned because they had failed to prepare themselves by bringing enough oil, comprise the carved voussoirs to his left (figure 8.7). Thus many stories were represented through geometric patterns that made

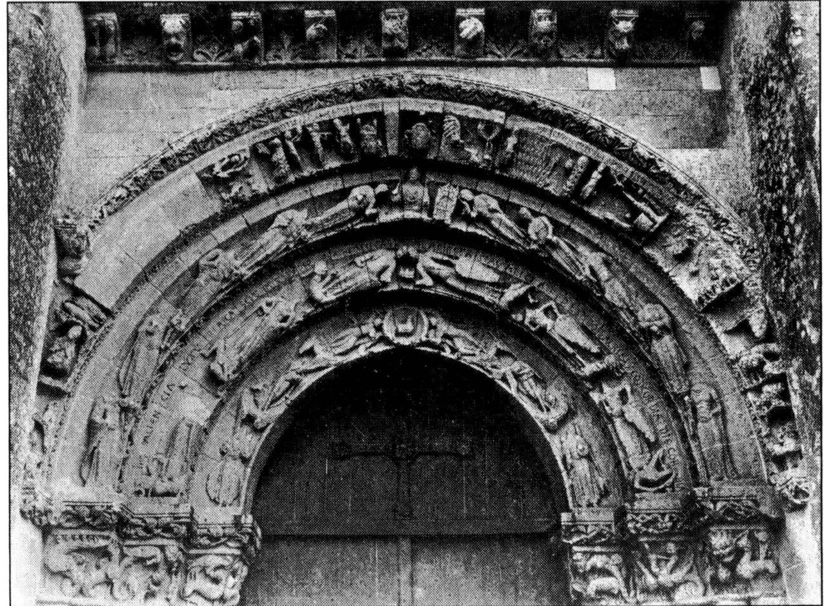

**Figure 8.7.** *Wise and Foolish Virgins*, ca. 1130, stone sculpture, archivolts over the central west portal, Saint-Pierre, Aulnay. Foto Marburg.

use of the natural symmetry of the body, an all-encompassing aesthetic that carried intrinsic formal qualities suggestive of functionality or purposiveness.

## AT THE RIGHT HAND OF GOD THE FATHER

Of course, not only the polarities of good and evil were viewed as part of this universal design. In other contexts, to be close to God—even on his left side—was very prestigious. Biblical and patristic references to the favored position at the right hand of God the Father abound. The Apostles' Creed describes Christ as sitting on the right hand of the Father. This follows Ephesians 1:20, "Which he wrought in Christ, when he raised him from the dead, and set him at his own right hand in the heavenly places," as well as Matthew 22: 44, "The Lord said unto my Lord, Sit thou on my right hand until I make thine enemies thy footstool," a quote from the beginning of Psalm 109, which thereby became a reference to God the Father and Christ. The church fathers elaborated on these passages in their speculations on the godhead and the nature of the Trinity, and these abstractions subsequently developed through visual diagrams of doctrine in the Middle Ages. In the ninth century, an illuminator of the Utrecht Psalter, for example, illustrated "Dixit dominus domino meo sede a dextris meis," with two nimbed figures seated within a mandorla.[17] In the late Middle Ages all three persons of the

Trinity were represented enthroned next to each other, frequently all of the same age. With God the Father in the center and Christ to his right, the Holy Spirit could only assume the place to his left (figure 8.8). Thus although the doctrine of the Trinity, so clearly articulated by Augustine, asserted that all three were equal, their representation as bodies, each taking up separate spaces on a broad throne, necessitated an implicit hierarchy of position that compromised the iconography of the three coequal beings. Representations of Christ and the Virgin interceding before the throne of God the Father on behalf of mankind were likewise arranged so that Christ was on the right hand of the Father, and Mary was consequently on his left.

A similar conception drove the arrangement of figures that adorned the walls erected during the Romanesque and early Gothic periods to enclose choirs. Christ, flanked by six apostles, was placed to the right of the choir

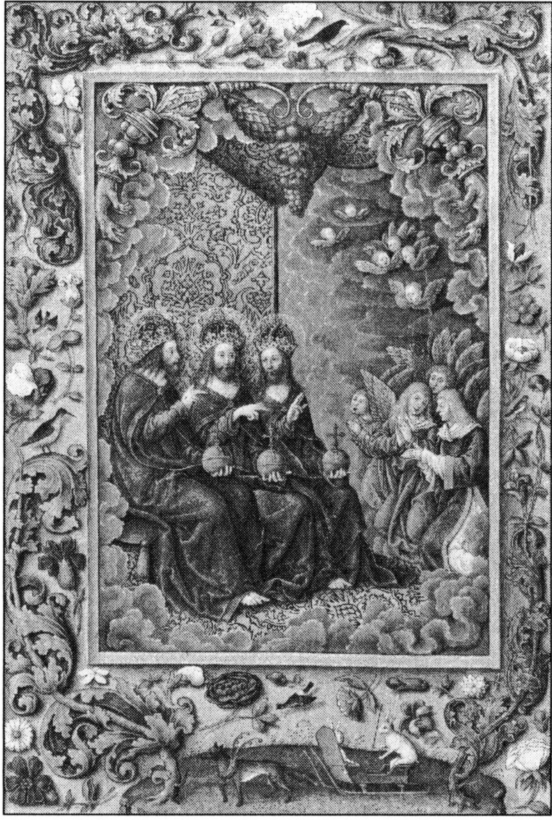

**Figure 8.8.** Jakob Elsner, miniature showing the Synthronoi Trinity, Kreß Missal, 1513. Germanisches Nationalmuseum, Nuremberg, Hs 113264, fol. 2v. Germanisches Nationalmuseum.

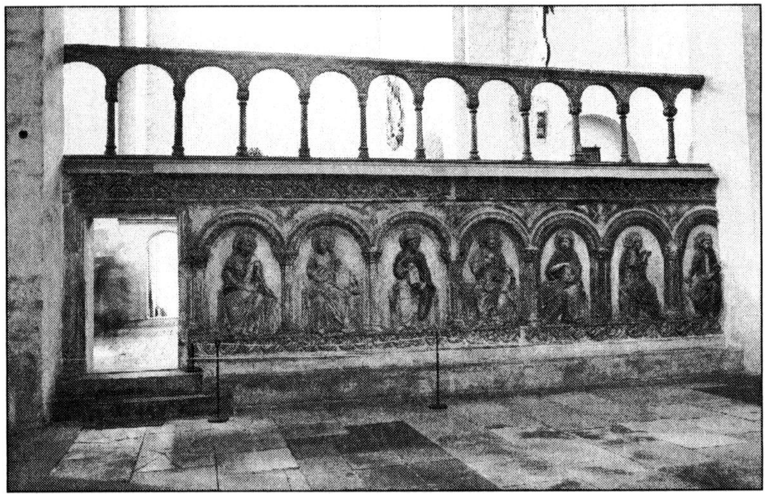

**Figure 8.9.** *Christ and Six Apostles*, north choir enclosure, ca. 1200, stucco, Liebfrauenkirche, Halberstadt. Foto Marburg.

(figure 8.9), and the Virgin, flanked by the other six, to the left (figure 8.10). Thus, on the enclosure of the east choir in the Liebfrauenkirche at Halberstadt (ca. 1200), the Virgin addresses viewers from her side on the left, looking out into the south transept. In the relief in the church of St. Michael's in Hildesheim of approximately the same date, the Virgin likewise addressed

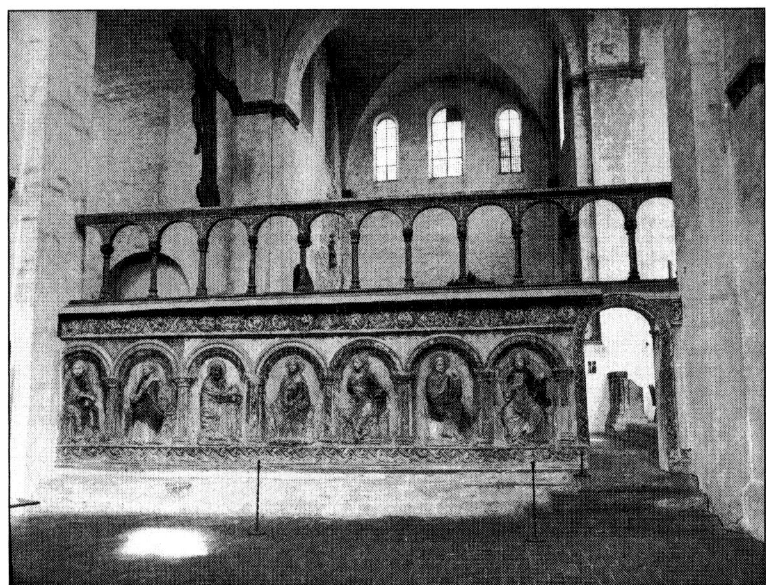

**Figure 8.10.** *Virgin and Six Apostles*, south choir enclosure, ca. 1200, stucco, Liebfrauenkirche, Halberstadt. Foto Marburg.

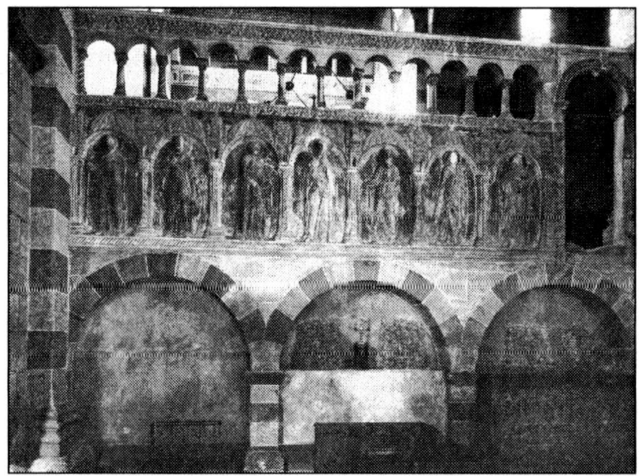

**Figure 8.11.** *Virgin and Apostles with St. Benedict*, north choir enclosure, ca. 1200, stucco, St. Michaelskirche, Hildesheim. Foto Marburg.

the audience from her place on the left but facing the north transept, since the imagery is located on the enclosure of a west choir (figure 8.11).[18] Thus the iconography of the heavenly hierarchy was aesthetically ordered and superimposed onto the hierarchy of places of the church interior, which included positioning according to relative left and right valences.

## GENDERING SPACES ON THE RIGHT AND LEFT

One of the oldest and perhaps the most expansive depictions of venerators ordered according to a gendered left/right polarity are the so-called Virgins and Martyrs rendered in mosaics dating from the third quarter of the sixth century in the church of Sant' Apollinare Nuovo in Ravenna (figure 8.12).

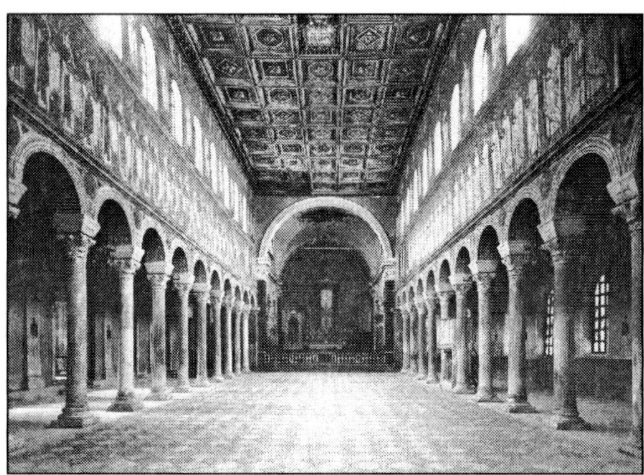

**Figure 8.12.** Male and Female Martyrs, ca. 490, mosaic, Sant' Apollinare Nuovo, Ravenna. Foto Marburg.

High above the nave on the left wall of the center aisle (from the standpoint of those entering the building), holy women in a long line, each named and holding a crown, process toward the chancel; opposite them, on the right wall, holy men in a lengthy row, likewise each named and grasping a crown, assume the same directional strides toward the altar. Richard Krautheimer pointed out that, according to the writings of Procopius and others, the central aisle of the early Byzantine church was generally reserved for liturgical processions of the clergy, and the laity looked on from the side aisles and galleries with the men separated from the women across the nave.[19] Bishop Agnellus wrote that the depictions of male martyrs were located on the side of the men ("parte virorum").[20] The mosaics thus would have provided permanent gender labels for the side aisles in which the congregation of the faithful assumed their places. Gazing up at the opposite side of the nave each gender would have been able to define itself against its other. Just as these holy martyrs had gone before, approaching the throne of God in two separate lines, so the contemporary faithful followed in their train, filing into their preordained gendered spaces. Through these elaborate mosaic labels the spaces became places.[21] According to some documents, the spaces occupied may have been even more particularized in some cases. During the early Christian era, the faithful frequently attended Mass in groups that were not only homosocial in structure but also composed of individuals of like age and marital status, groups distinguished as, for example, girls, boys, virgins, or widows.[22] As people entered the church they separated from their families and moved into their appropriate same-sex places, following the examples of the martyrs above. This performance gendered all ecclesiastical rituals for the participants, and in another sense it ritualized gender, placing it in the realm of things that are enacted automatically, according to social rules and outside of conscious individual decision-making processes.

In several other ecclesiastical buildings of the Middle Ages and the Renaissance, architectural spaces have been gendered by grouping images of male and female saints. At Orsanmichele in Florence, images of the forefathers of Christ appear in the vaulting over the right aisle and those of the foremothers over the left aisle, from the vantage point of the congregation.[23] It is not known if living women and men gathered respectively in the aisles under the vaulted canopy inhabited by their holy counterparts. Perhaps the male and female saints served more generally to suggest an intrinsic binary order. Here reciprocal referentiality also becomes apparent: not only can "left" be the signifier for women and "right" for men, but the relationship of signifier and signified can be reversed and "women" can signify left and "men" right.[24] Thus Christendom was fashioned as a bilateral organism with different but complementary parts comprising a harmonious whole.

This also can be observed on the smaller scale of diagrammatic images, such as the late medieval Madonna Misericordia, in which the Virgin extends her cloak to protect the faithful huddled underneath. In the figure sculpted by Gregor Erhart for the pilgrimage church in Frauenstein in Austria, three men representing various stations in life and rungs of society kneel on the Virgin's right, and three women likewise standing for diverse types kneel on her left (figure 8.13).[25]

Returning to the *Ghent Altarpiece* and the *Beaune Altarpiece*, certain additional segments are likewise ordered with respect to gender. In the *Ghent Altarpiece*, the throng of male martyrs approaches the Agnus Dei from its right and the female martyrs from its left (figure 8.2). In the *Beaune Altarpiece*, the Apostle Collegium is joined at their far right by three male saints and at their left by three female saints (figure 8.4).

Early on, this likewise became the conventional arrangement for donors and sponsors of monuments who wished to attach themselves piously and pictorially to their donations. One of the oldest and best known examples of figures rendered as a sponsoring couple is that of Justinian and Theodora in the chancel mosaics of San Vitale in Ravenna, dating from the 540s. Here, it was actually Julianus Argentarius who financed the building and its decoration; and it was two successive archbishops as well as others present locally who initiated the undertaking. High above the main altar, images of Emperor Justinian and Empress Theodora face each other

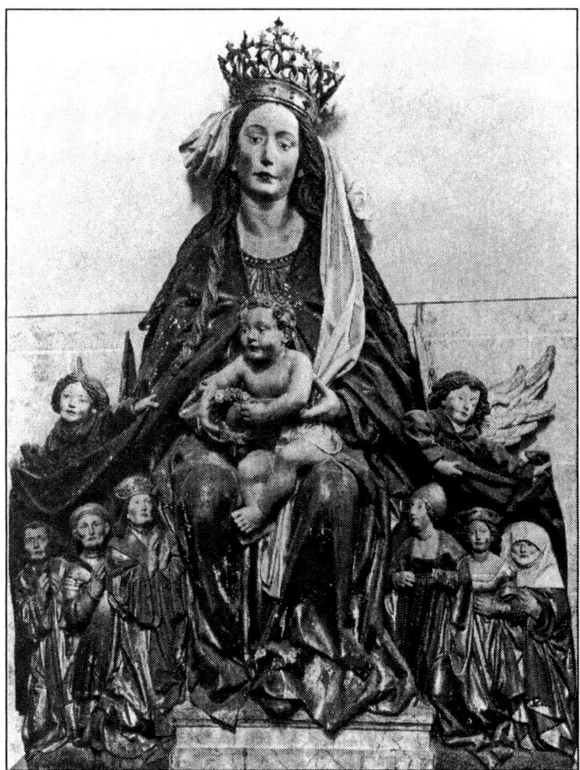

**Figure 8.13.** Gregor Erhart, *Madonna Misericordia*, 1501–14, stone sculpture, Wallfahrtskirche, Frauenstein (Austria). Foto Marburg.

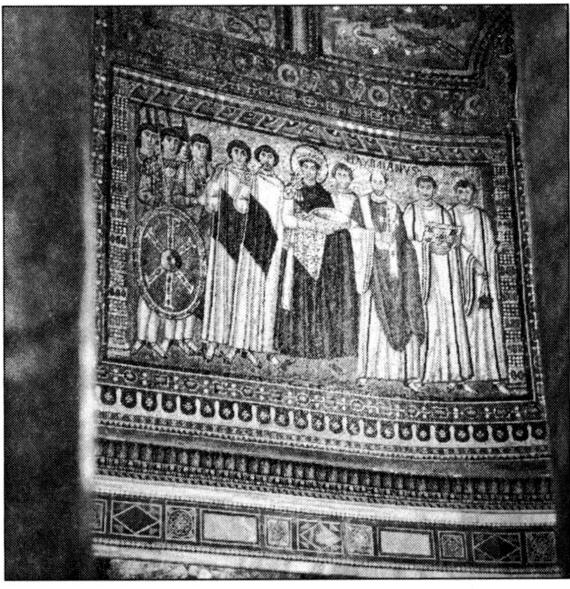

**Figure 8.14.** *Emperor Justinian with Entourage*, ca. 547, mosaic, north side of choir, San Vitale, Ravenna. Foto Marburg.

across the choir. Christ represented above, enthroned in the dome of the apse, looks down to his right on Justinian and his retinue (figure 8.14) and to his left on Theodora and her courtiers (figure 8.15). Otto von Simson and others have suggested that the mosaics may represent the imperial roles within the offertory procession at the Mass. Justinian brings, as his oblation, the eucharistic bread, in a gold paten; Theodora carries the wine in a jeweled chalice.[26] But a careful look reveals that not all aspects of these mosaics form perfect parallels to each other. Justinian's entourage is all male, comprised of military and ecclesiastical leaders; Theodora's companions are female and male, including not only women from her court but also apparently high-ranking eunuchs.[27] Von Simson also drew attention to subtler differences. The location of Justinian and his court is nonspecific, indicating that he could be understood to stand within the chancel in which he is represented. Theodora's ambience is, however, defined by an architectural conch and a cloth baldachin, and the strongly implied movement toward an open portal may show that she and her retinue have been "displaced" to the prothesis or the narthex that adjoined the apse. These distinctions may have alluded to the emperor's right to be in the choir with the clergy, a privilege not shared by the empress. Thus the mosaics exude the notion of parity through their parallel placement in the chancel, while

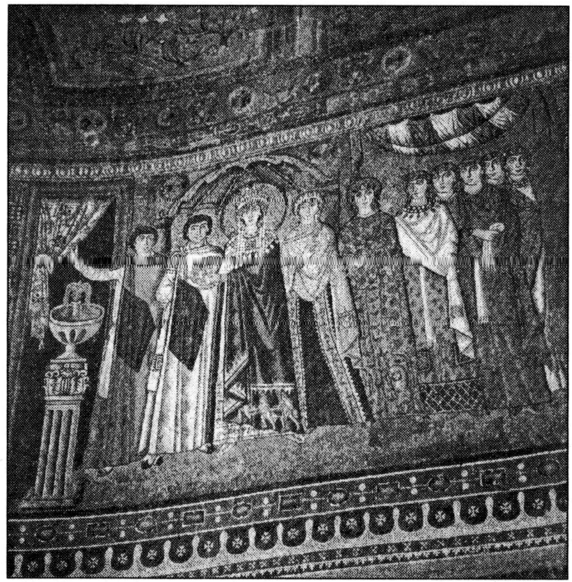

**Figure 8.15.** *Empress Theodora with Entourage*, ca. 547, mosaic, south side of choir, San Vitale, Ravenna. Foto Marburg.

they deny equal privilege through the unequal significance of left and right as well as through the differences in represented locations. The presence of eunuchs—a third gender—on the women's side also destabilizes the notion of perfect bilateral gender symmetry.

Lest we read these mosaics all too concretely, it must be remembered that the imperial couple never entered the church after its completion or saw the mosaics. Probably Archbishop Victor and his successor, Maximianus, wished to devise a program that linked them visually to Justinian and Theodora.[28] Clearly the mosaics established an ongoing presence of protecting patrons, one that was particularly important since it stressed allegiances to the new orthodox rulers after reclaiming hegemony from the Arian Ostrogoths who had ruled the city.[29] The mosaics likewise construct the imperial couple as particularly pious. Perhaps the representations were less a reflection of the "real" than necessary promotional fashionings in the light of the allegations of Procopius that the imperial couple was widely reviled and that Theodora's dubious background connected her with the low life of the circus and with prostitution.[30] Perhaps also the gender distinctions here functioned less to mark access to real space than to provide a vicarious but enduring map of abstract gender positioning, together with hints of tolerated territorial trespassing.

Medieval patrons did nonetheless commission gendered compartments within sacred structures that were meant to be inhabited by specific lay men or lay women. When Louis IX commissioned the building of the Ste. Chapelle in Paris in the middle of the thirteenth century in order to house his prized relics of the holy blood, thorns, wood from the cross, and other precious physical remains from the Passion, he included separate loggia for himself and Queen Blanche on the upper level of the chapel. The relics were kept on the tribune where they were protected in the *chaise* and on feast days displayed to an elite audience. Louis established his own space on the right of the relics and the queen's in the corresponding space on the left.[31]

In the late Middle Ages gendered positions could likewise be labeled through subtle and very particularized conflations of sponsors with their saintly patrons. In 1420, the wealthy merchant couple Konrad and Afra Hirn initiated a donation complex for the so-called Goldschmiedekapelle in the St. Annakirche in Augsburg. Afra Hirn chose St. Helena as her patron and commissioned a fresco cycle of the finding of the true cross for the north wall; Konrad, a member of the confraternity of St. James, had scenes from this saint's legend painted on the south wall. Thus from the standpoint of the donors and other laity who gathered in the chapel and faced the choir in the east, James, the male patron, was on the right and Helena, the female patron, on the left.[32]

## NORTH/SOUTH, DARK/LIGHT, AND OTHER OVERLYING POLARITIES

As is apparent from many of the above examples, other binary constructions had worked their way into notions of left and right, either as previous semantic associations such as *pentimenti* still visible beneath the surface, or as metonymies connected like the links of a chain. The gendered rhetoric of left and right had become fortified in the all-encompassing yet complex and sometimes extremely differentiated endeavor of mapping the cosmos onto the church building.[33] This practice of rendering the church and the church building a spatial and temporal microcosm of the universe and of eternity was a commonplace of the Middle Ages and the Renaissance. East versus West polarities localized judgment, the end of time, hell, sin, death, and devils in the West, and placed the resurrection, heaven, celestial hierarchies, eternal bliss, and holiness in the East.[34] Corresponding events were staged and enacted in respective parts of the buildings. The area outside the west portal sometimes became a place of civil judgment; impenitent sinners or individuals designated to represent all transgressors were at times driven out of the west door; or, in other cases, those doing penance for public crimes were not allowed any farther than the west narthex during Lent.[35] Moreover, the clergy inhabited the choir in the east end, and, even in churches with double choirs, the most important altar or the "high altar," as it came to be called, was located in the east.[36] It was of course not only rituals but also pictures that served to produce meanings of place. Frescoes in the dome of the apse, such as those from the twelfth century at Prüfening near Regensburg[37] and at Mittelzell on the island of Reichenau, often display members of the heavenly hierarchy; while frescoes in the west end, such as that from around 800 at Mustair, or the numerous and more famous sculpture programs on west facades, such as those in Autun and Conques from the twelfth century, show the Last Judgment. Thus these spaces too became places.

Concomitant associations bifurcated the church along the longitudinal axis. At this nexus, the meanings of left and right became mingled with those of north and south, dark and light. Here, as is still apparent from the mosaic place markers at Sant' Apollinare Nuovo in Ravenna and the painted pictorial labels in Orsanmichele in Florence, left and right were referenced from the standpoint of the faithful themselves, as they stood facing the choir. From this vantage point, women were associated with the left or northern and darker portion of the church and men with the right or southern and lighter side of the building.

Again it is not evident that always or in every case actual practices of occupying space followed these abstract linkages.[38] Most of the sources that address physical use of space within the church interior are from the early Middle Ages. The Carolingian liturgical apologist Amalarius states clearly that laymen were on the south and laywomen on the north: "Masculi stant in australi parte, et feminae in boreali." Other sources confirm this practice at least on feast days.[39] In Denmark there is evidence of separate entrances for men and women respectively, on the south and north sides of Romanesque parish churches. At Ejby, the tympanum from the south portal is adorned with a figure of Christ enthroned, and that from the north is decorated with a five-tailed dragon.[40]

Another source may allude obliquely to a perceived necessity of gender separation. In his well-known and curious justification of the need to enlarge the abbey church of St. Denis in the middle of the twelfth century, Abbot Suger comments that the building was so crowded, particularly on feast days, that it was unpleasant for women, who sometimes screamed or fainted or had to be carried aloft by men because of the press of the crowd.[41] Such circumstances would have been particularly troublesome when decorum dictated distance between men and women when in church. Apparently, however, this gender divide was not always and in every case longitudinal. At Durham, the floor pavement is still marked at the edge of the westernmost bay, delineating the easternmost limits for women. It must also be noted that in many Catholic and Protestant parishes in the United

States and Canada a longitudinal separation of the genders was practiced well into the twentieth century. In fact, in rural areas in some parts of Europe it is still practiced today. But to maintain that this is a simple matter of a custom surviving intact since the early Christian period may be in error. Certainly before the advent of stationary seating for the ordinary parishioners, much more mobility would have been possible and even expected. In processions, front/back dichotomies would have dictated positioning, with women lining up behind the men.[42] Further it was the demands of the occasion that would have determined if the laity, or some of them, gathered before a privately donated altar to be present at a mass celebrated for "their" dead or to observe the feast day of one of "their" saints. Clearly, along with the more pervasive conventions, each church would have had its own spatial associations, named and otherwise, as well as its own history of changes. Generally, the introduction of privately donated choir stalls for important families would also have imposed conflicting social hierarchies that created new and more immobile places within the hierarchy of a church interior during the later Middle Ages. In such cases social spaces are not merely superimposed, but because their boundaries are not mutually limiting, they interpenetrate each other.[43]

The most disruptive force in any uniform north/south gender division in oriented churches may have been the advent of long sermons in the later Middle Ages. During the High Middle Ages, the structure known variously as a rood screen or choir screen in English, *jubé* in French, *Lettner* in German, and *tramezzo* or *ponte* in Italian formed the single most prominent visual focus for the laity when they gathered in the nave.[44] This high, narrow partition that traversed the width of the nave, closing off the choir to the west, often provided a platform for lections, liturgical drama, and short sermons. It usually supported a monumental crucifix or Crucifixion group, and altars were frequently built into it on the west side at the floor level. By the fourteenth century, however, a pulpit—mounted on a pier on the side of the central aisle in the nave—began to impose another focus of attention.

Perhaps the left/right polarity continued to take precedence over that of north/south even with the new emphasis on preaching. A woodcut showing Savonarola preaching from a pulpit on the side of the nave in the Duomo in Florence shows the public gathered before him—men on the(ir) right, and women on the(ir) left (figure 8.16). In this particular case, laymen occupied the space to the east and laywomen that to the west, thus superimposing other binary associations of direction with those of anatomy. Pictorial documents from the fifteenth century indicate that the genders were separated in Italy even when people attended sermons held outdoors. Panel paintings by Sano di Pietro showing San Bernardino preaching in Siena show a curtain separating the audience longitudinally into two groups: men and women. It is interesting that the positions of the listeners in the Piazza San Francesco appear

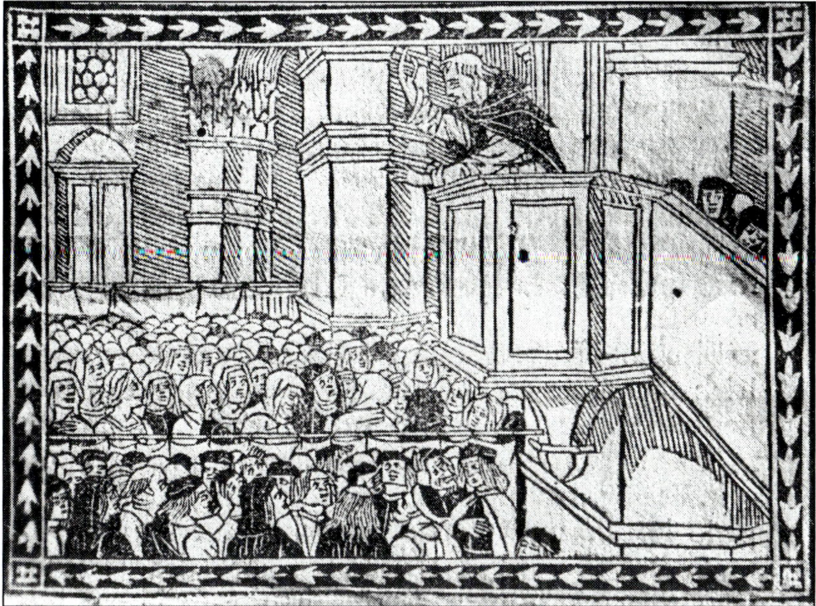

**Figure 8.16.** *Savonarola Preaching in Florence Cathedral*, 1496, woodcut illustration from *Compendio di Revelatione dello inutile servo di Iesu Cristo Frate Hieronymo da Ferrara*. Foto Marburg.

reversed (figure 8.17), whereas the figures depicted in the Piazza del Campo assume their expected gender positions with respect to left and right (figure 8.18). Another painting of the latter event, by Neroccio di Bartolomeo, housed in the Palazzo Pubblico, confirms this conformity to normal gendered placement.[45] Thus also in these illustrations from Tuscany most often the women are on the(ir) left, but the only true common denominator appears to be that the women always are positioned to the west of the men.

Retreating from the complexities of allocations of "real" space and returning once again to the exegesis of the early and High Middle Ages, we find an abundance of verbal rhetoric that collapses the distinctions between signifiers and signifieds, often making them interchangeable. With their hunger for an all-encompassing tropological hermeneutic, theologians explicated the men's side as symbolic of the strong and steadfast saints who must struggle against intense passions and the women's side as a figure of those weak souls whom God protects from major trials. In his collection of references to the symbolism of the church building, Josef Sauer has found corresponding expressions from Amalarius in the ninth century, as well as from Sicardus, Durandus, and Honorius Augustodunensis in the twelfth.[46] Exegetes were likewise faced with the dilemma of the changing place of left

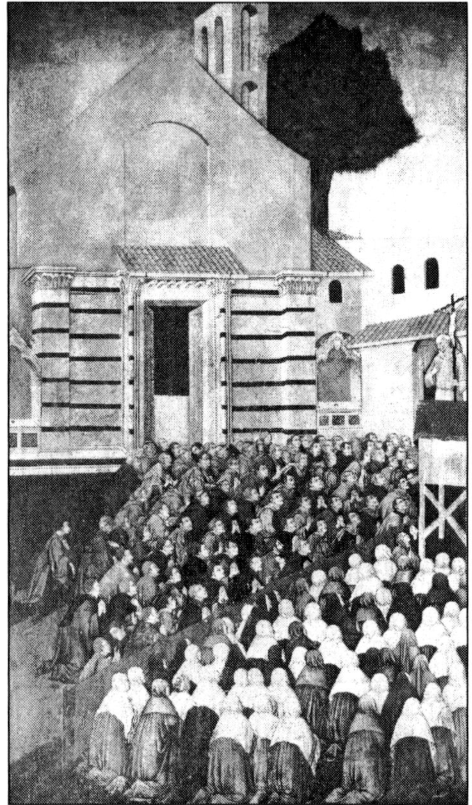

**Figure 8.17.** Sano di Pietro, *San Bernardino Preaching in Piazza San Francesco in Siena*, 1444–50, tempera on panel, Siena Cathedral. Alinari/Art Resource, N.Y.

and right relative to the body from which it was perceived to be referenced. The Gospel was read from the right side of the *jubé*, referenced from the standpoint of the deacon who was facing the lay listeners while reading. which was, in oriented sanctuaries, the north side. The less important reading of the Epistle occurred on the south side, or left side, as referenced from the clergyman responsible for the lection. Honorius solved the exegetical dilemma when he asserted that it was fitting and proper that the Gospel be read with the deacon standing in front of the women, on the north side, "which was characterized by the things of the flesh" in order to call them to a life of the spirit. The north side likewise represented the devil, with whom the Gospel was in combat. Medieval theologians also placed Jews and pagans into this scheme. Jews, as the children of God, were located on the south; heathens, as children of Satan, were located on the north. Already in the fifth century, Saint Augustine had associated the

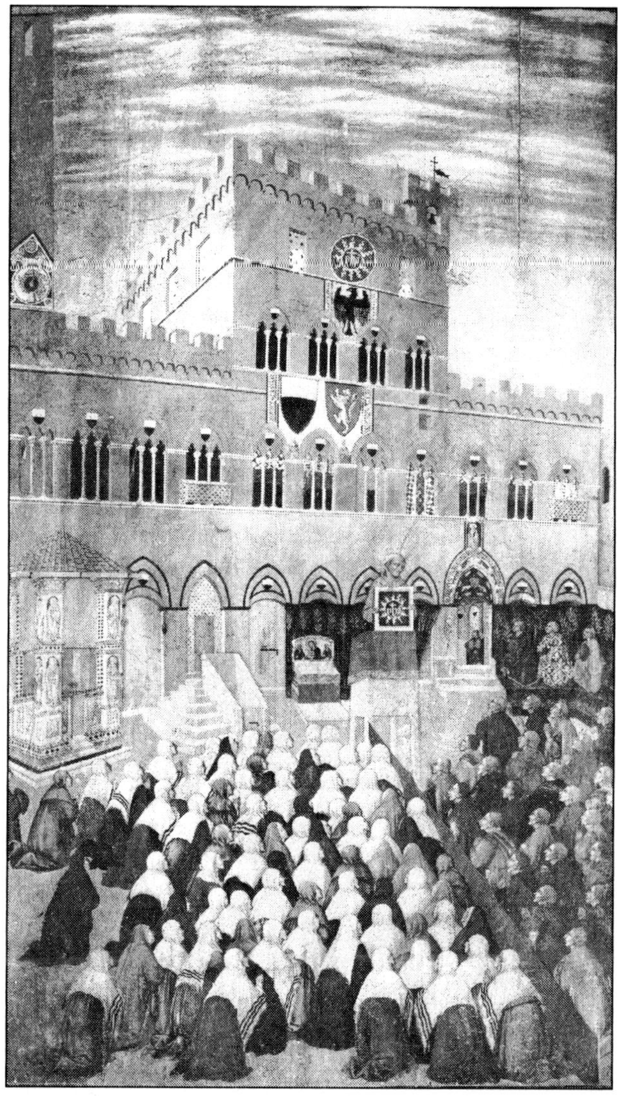

**Figure 8.18.** Sano di Pietro, *San Bernardino Preaching in the Piazza del Campo*, 1477, tempera on panel, Siena Cathedral. Alinari/Art Resource, N.Y.

right with the *vita aeterna* and the left with the *vita praesens*. Honorius similarly termed the left an image of the present life and earthly sensitivities, whereas the right represented the next world and spiritual proclivities. Durandus associated the left with mortality and humanity, the right with immortality and the divine. Thus metonymic chains discursively connected right, south, light, Jews, the contemplative life, eternity, divinity, and men and joined left, north, darkness, heathens, the active life, the present, humanity, and women. Implicitly then, the spatial hierarchy of the church building employed two mutually inflected models: the orientations of the microcosm of the body (up/down, front/back, left/right) and the directions of the macrocosm of the universe (east/west, north/south). The one served to naturalize and the other to divinize.

## WOMEN ON THE RIGHT

Nonetheless the woman was not always displaced to the left. The matter depended first and foremost on the pendant figure. In Crucifixion groups in which figures of the Virgin and St. John the Evangelist were juxtaposed flanking Christ, it was the Virgin who assumed the favored position on Christ's right. The same was true when the Virgin was paired with John the Baptist in the so-called Deësis, that motif in which the two flank a central image of Christ, as in both the *Ghent Altarpiece* and the *Beaune* altarpiece (figures 8.2, 8.4). Clearly the Virgin assumed a place higher than all of *man*kind. The large expanded Crucifixion Group carved by Bernd Notke and mounted on the triumphal arch of Lübeck Cathedral in 1477 (figure 8.19) complicates the matter, because additional figures participate in the diagram: the Virgin on Christ's right and St. John on his left; the saint, Mary Magdalen, on Christ's right and the donor, Bishop Albert II Kummedick, on Christ's left; Adam on Christ's right and Eve on his left.[47] The *Ghent Altarpiece* likewise assigns these positions respectively to Adam and Eve (figure 8.2).[48] It is then the status of the two pendant persons relative to each other within the heavenly hierarchy that determined the appropriate positions of left and right. The *Wipplar Epitaph* in the church of St. Lorenz in Nuremberg, dating from around 1420, presents the paradigm in its simplest form (figure 8.20). In the upper register, the Virgin and St. John attend compassionately to the Man of Sorrows as he emerges somewhat anachronistically from the tomb. Below, the couple—husband from the Wipplar family, wife from the von Balcke family—kneel in contemplation of the Sacred Face of Christ. Mary and the male venerator are to Christ's right, St. John and the female orant to his left. Indeed, gender appears nearly always to have been the determinant when a contemporary venerating couple was depicted.

Exceptions were fairly rare and explanations even rarer. Madeline Caviness has called attention to the miniature showing Queen Aelfgifu on the dexter side and King Cnut on the sinister side of the cross they are presenting to Christ and thereby to the New Minster at Winchester (figure 8.21). She has suggested that the queen may have chosen to commission the work while she had control of the treasury in the absence of her husband and thus placed herself in the dominant position.[49]

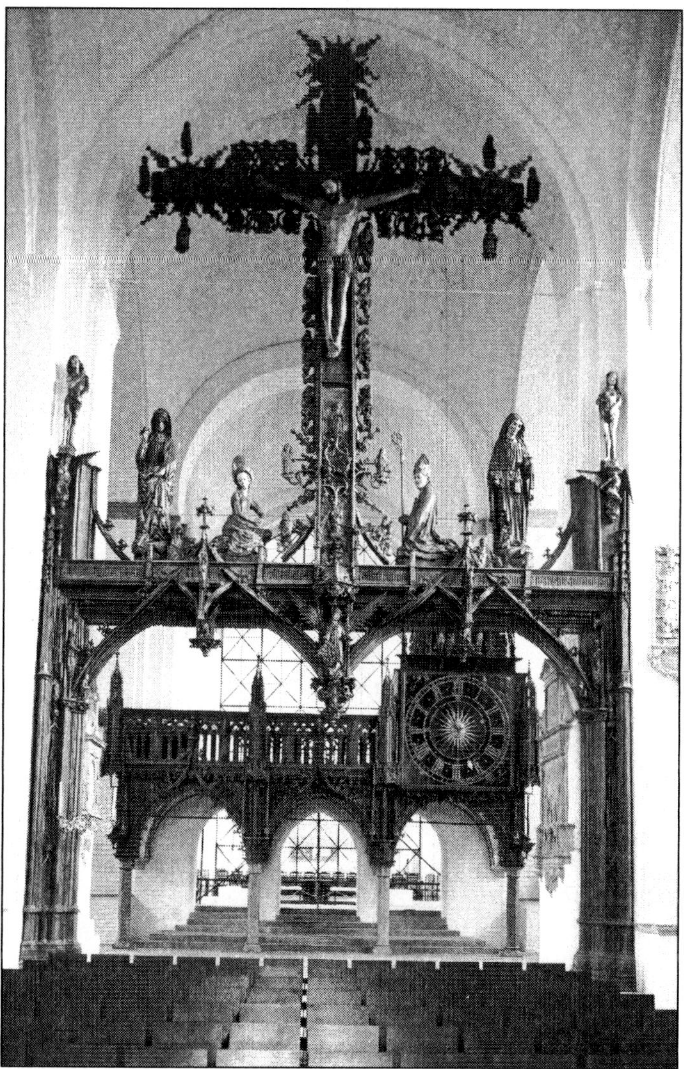

**Figure 8.19.** Bernd Notke, Crucifixion Group, 1477, wood sculpture, Lübeck Cathedral. Foto Marburg.

In a sandstone relief from the chapel of the first residence of Emperor Louis the Bavarian in Munich, today housed in the Bayerischen National-museum, Louis kneels to the Virgin's left and his wife Margarete of Holland kneels to her right, giving the chapel that is being received by the Christ Child perched on the Virgin's knee (figure 8.22). The relief appears to date from the building campaigns that enlarged the old residence between 1321

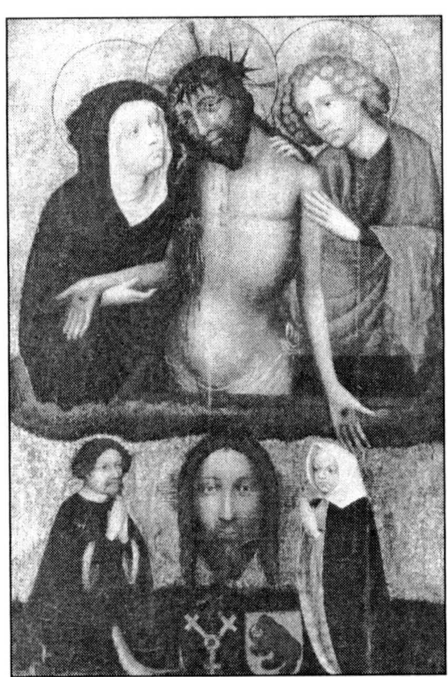

**Figure 8.20.** Wipplar Epitaph, ca. 1420, tempera on panel, St. Lorenzkirche, Nuremberg. Bild- und Tonarchiv, Stadt Nuremberg.

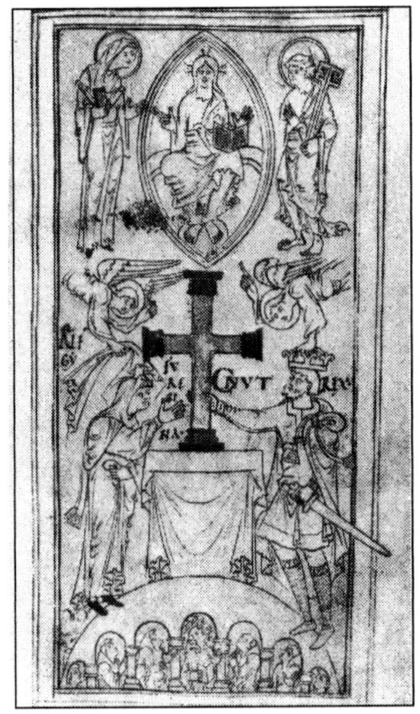

**Figure 8.21.** *Queen Aelfgifu (Emma) and King Cnut Presenting a Cross to New Minster*, 1031, Winchester, *Liber vitae*, London, British Library, Stowe MS 944, fol. 6r. Foto Marburg.

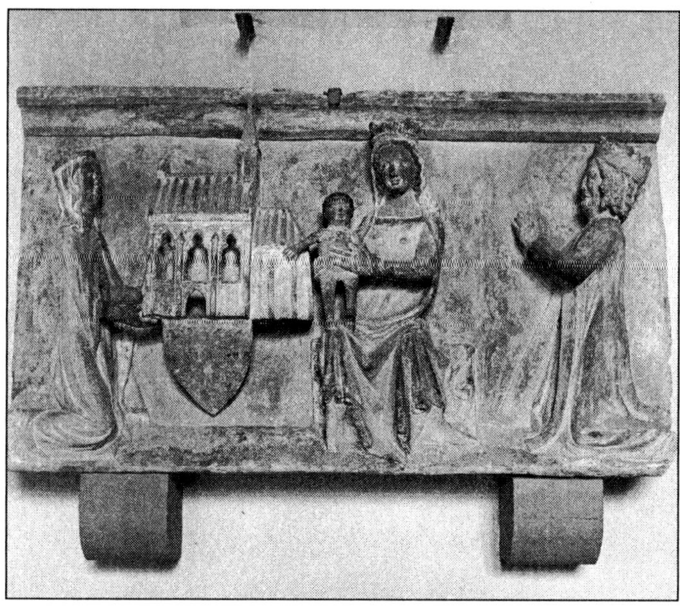

**Figure 8.22.** *Margarete of Holland and Louis the Bavarian with the Virgin and Child,* 1321–24, stone relief, Bayerisches Nationalmusem, Munich. Foto Marburg.

and 1324. At this date the chapel was dedicated to St. Margaret.[50] Thus the relief with its atypical composition may have been made especially to underscore the fact that the chapel had been donated by the Empress Margarete or that it was to be credited to her as a memorial, that is, for the purpose of her soul's salvation.

In a fresco in the tiny private oratory that Emperor Charles IV built for himself in the fortress Karlstein in 1355, in which he is said to have spent hours alone in prayer, Charles had himself placed to the left of the Virgin and Child and his wife Anna von Schweidnitz to the right (figure 8.23). Since women were not allowed in this portion of the castle it is unlikely that Anna was the party responsible for putting herself in this favorable position and thus displacing Charles. More likely, Charles wished to place himself in the position of humility, which he conveniently offset in that the Christ child bends down to him and clasps his praying hands between his own tiny palms in the gesture of vassalage and fealty.[51] As Charles turned to leave his oratory he would have seen the other fresco he commissioned over the door lintel, showing himself and Anna holding the reliquary of the true cross. Here he saw himself on the right side, which was *right* for his gender.

In his famed portraits of the Duke and Duchess of Urbino, probably executed shortly after 1472 and today in the Uffizi (figures 8.24, 8.25), Piero della Francesca provides us with an example of a marriage diptych that

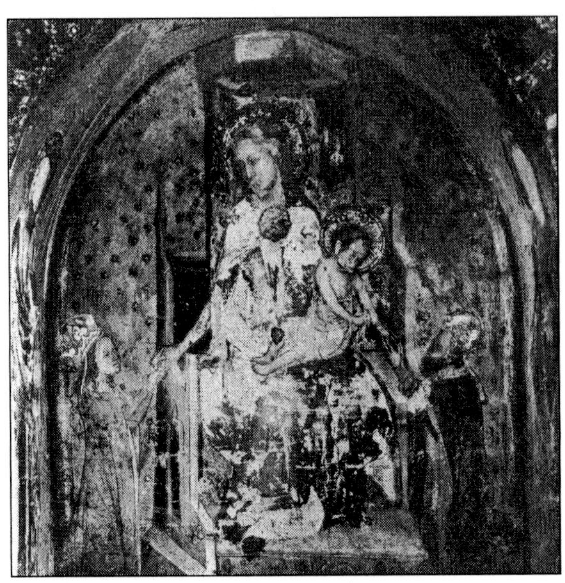

**Figure 8.23.** *Emperor Charles IV and Anna von Schweidnitz Venerating the Virgin and Child*, 1355, fresco, Karlstein. Foto Marburg.

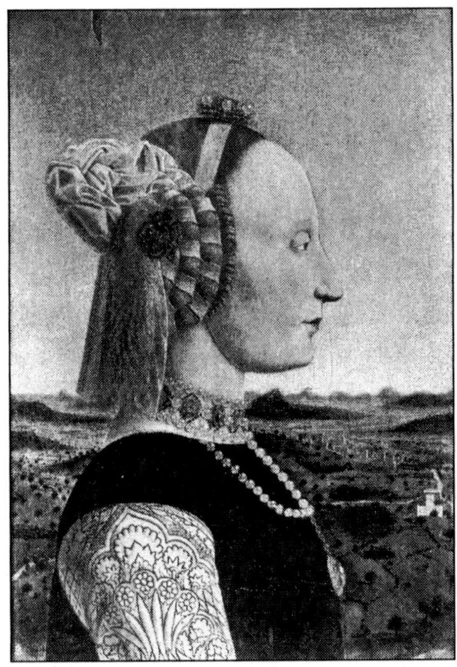

**Figure 8.24.** Piero della Francesca, Portrait of Battista Sforza, after 1472, oil on panel, Uffizi Gallery, Florence. Alinari/Art Resource, N.Y.

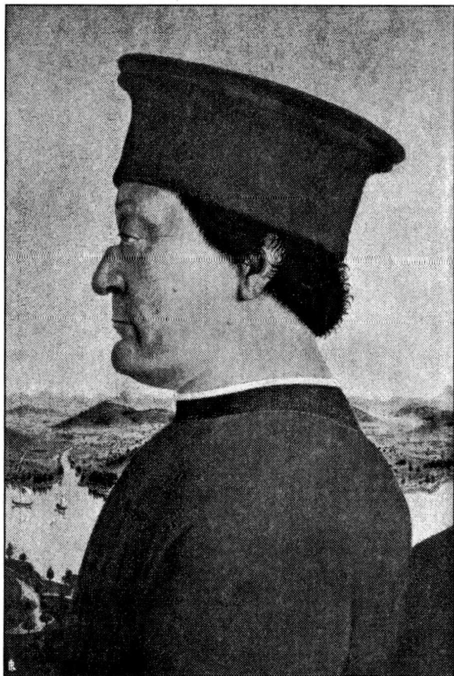

**Figure 8.25.** Piero della Francesca, Portrait of Federico da Montefeltro, after 1472, oil on panel, Uffizi Gallery, Florence. Alinari/Art Resource, N.Y.

reverses the normative gendered positions. In this case, history provides a clear rationale for the anomaly. Federico da Montefeltro had lost an eye in a joust and therefore could only be portrayed from the left side. Consequently Piero portrayed him in profile, as was customary in Italy, but from the left, rendering only the deformation on the bridge of his nose as evidence of the facial disfiguration.[52] This position necessitated the placement of Federico's visage on the heraldic left, facing the image of his widow, Battista Sforza, on the heraldic right.

For the donor figures Francesco Sassetti and his wife Nera Corsi, whom Dominico del Ghirlandaio has reversed from the gendered norm in his fresco for the Sassetti Chapel in the Church of Santa Trìnita in Florence (ca. 1480), no such easy justification presents itself.[53] Certainly other digressions from the norm can likewise be identified, for which satisfactory explanations can no longer be found.

In cases in which the woman was the sole donor, she could achieve emplacement by showing herself on the favorable side. During the Ottonian era, Abbess Hitda (978–1042) had herself shown on the "good" side of St. Walburga, as she presented her saintly patron with the Gospel codex she had commissioned (figure 8.26). In this case there was no contest over space and no one to displace the woman to the less favorable side.

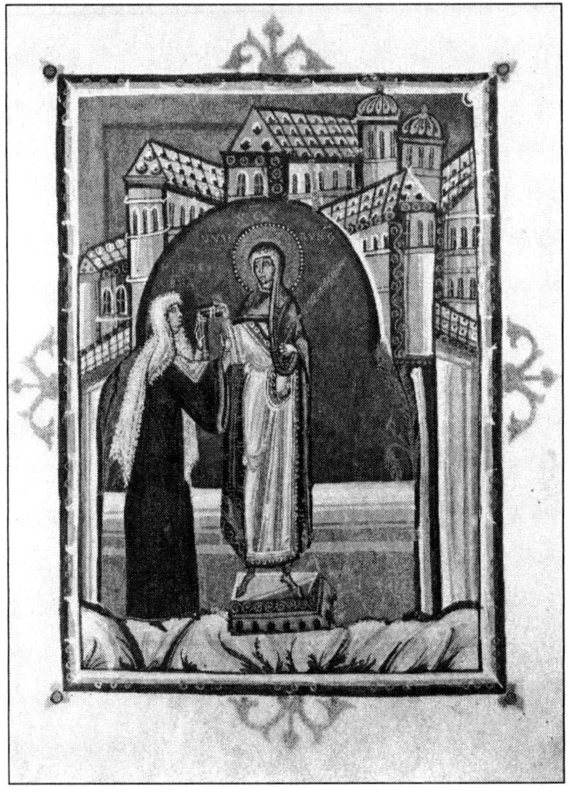

**Figure 8.26.** *Abbess Hitda Presenting Gospel Book to Saint Walburga*, ca. 1000, Hitda Codex, Darmstadt, Landesbibliothek, cod. 1640, fol. 6r. Foto Marburg.

In cases in which there were multiple female venerators with no male orant figures, they could be represented to the left and the right, as in the illumination in an antiphonal from the convent of Heilig Kreuz in Regensburg, completed in 1491 (figure 8.27).[54] The miniature shows the scene of the mystical marriage of St. Catherine within the *hortus conclusus*. A row of six women kneeling spans the width of the foreground space. Each is accompanied by a named female saint, who, standing behind, gently recommends her charge by placing a hand lightly on the head or shoulder. On the basis of information gleaned from the colophon and associated sources, we can assume the largest figure, depicted in secular dress and to the Virgin's right, must represent the Nuremberg donor Agnes Volckamer, who had sponsored the book by sending forty gilders to her niece Magdalena Holzschuher, a novice at Heilig Kreuz. Magdalena appears at the center right, wearing a white veil. The other women, identified as Kunigund Ortleib, Sofia von Wolfskel, Barbara Hegner, and Brigitte Stromer, were nuns from Nuremberg who had been sent to Heilig Kreuz when the convent was reformed.

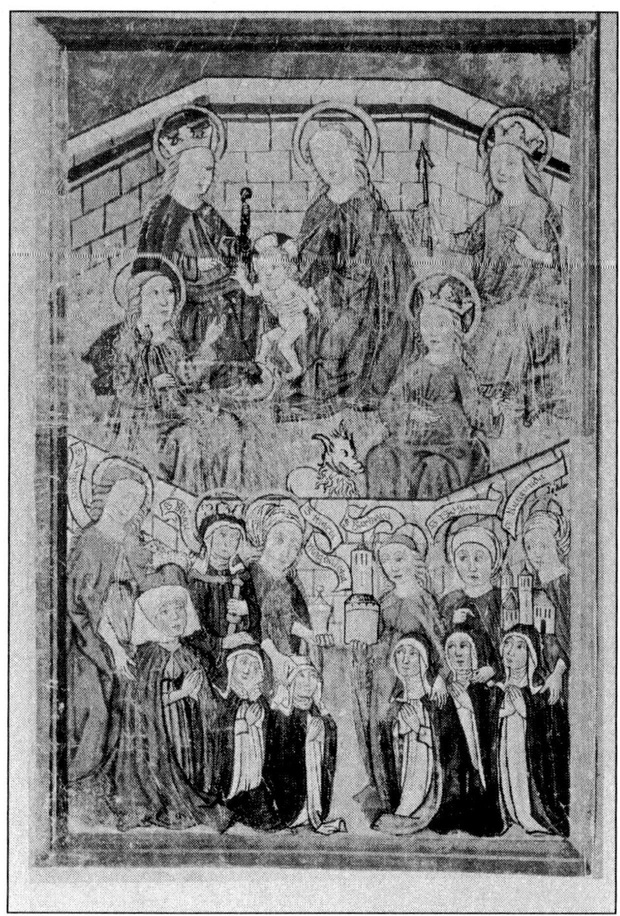

**Figure 8.27.** *Mystical Marriage of St. Catherine*, 1491, Antiphonal, Regensburg, Bischöfliche Zentralbibliothek. Bischöfliche Zentralbibliothek.

## THE POLITICS OF LEFT AND RIGHT

At the most basic level the politics and economics of marriage underlie the representations of couples and occasionally other family members as venerators or donors. Recent scholarship suggests, for example, that in the mosaics of San Vitale in Ravenna, very specific and intentional marriage politics may have motivated the inclusion of what are now thought to be portraits of Anastasius, Theodora's grandson, and Joannina, the daughter of Belisarius and his wife, Antonina, among the venerators (figures 8.14, 8.15).[55]

More general marriage politics were in fact evident in all the conventional donor couple representations of the late Middle Ages. In keeping with the prevailing decorum, wives or widows who commissioned works of art usually had themselves depicted on the heraldic left and their husbands on the favored right. The *St. Anne Altarpiece*, donated by Ottilia Mayer for the Church of St. Lorenz in Nuremberg, provides an interesting case for scrutiny (figure 8.28).[56] In 1510, three years after her husband's death, Ottilia Mayer began the process that led to the commission. Her name appears on all the documents as the sole donor. Her own image was painted on the predella, on the heraldic left of the relics; figures of her husband and their four sons appear in the corresponding position on the heraldic right. A comparison of the accompanying crests reveals that Ottilia had the privilege of a coat of arms, whereas Heinrich, who had been of more modest birth but had amassed wealth as a merchant, had only a house mark. Undoubtedly, Heinrich would not have been allowed to donate an altar, adorned only with his house mark, for such a prominent public place, had he married someone of his own social

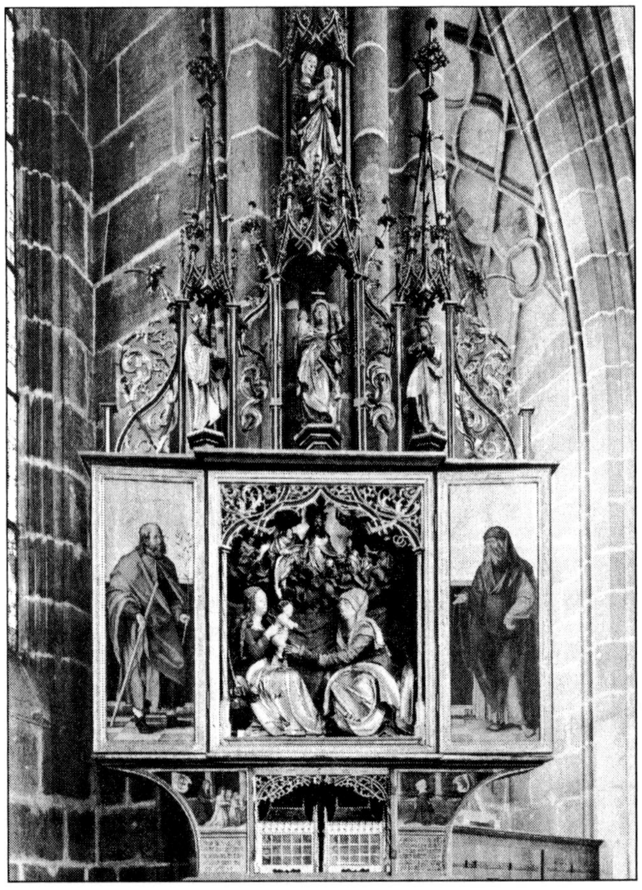

**Figure 8.28.** *St. Anne Altarpiece*, 1510–23, St. Lorenzkirche, Nuremberg. Photo Schier.

standing within the highly stratified society of early sixteenth-century Nuremberg. Through Ottilia Mayer's donation Heinrich Mayer's praying portrait took a permanent place in a very important church, and since the work was fashioned to subscribe to the gender codes of the left/right scheme, his image and house mark placed him on the favored right, displacing Ottila's image and coat of arms to the less favored left. Thus, Heinrich Mayer was able to reap the blessings of his wife's higher social status and his own dominant gender status. But the perfectly balanced symmetrical composition likewise allowed Ottilia Mayer to present herself, her sons, and her own family escutcheon in an important public place beside that of a financially successful husband. The name she uses in the painted inscription is her married name, which is somewhat exceptional. It was usually the wife's parental family name that was employed in Nuremberg inscriptions. The use of both names and arms from their wives' families could bring not only social prestige but also political rights to husbands. In some ways the donor credits on the *St. Anne Altarpiece* appear egalitarian indeed, compared to latter-day American counterparts, which might take the form of a bronze plaque acknowledging a gift by a "Mr. and Mrs. Henry Mayer," the kind of aggressively visual patronage that Sarah Stanbury discusses in her chapter on Margery Kempe. Here the wife is all but subsumed, having lost both first and last names and being allotted no more than the space necessary for the three letters in "Mrs."

In other medieval contexts, the kneeling male venerator on the right and the female on the left furthered a more ambitious political agenda. In 1370, Emperor Charles IV commissioned a mosaic of the Last Judgment for the Golden Portal of St. Vitus Cathedral in Prague. Separated from the scene, Charles and his fourth wife, Elizabeth of Pomerania, kneel in the spandrels (figure 8.29). Through his series of marriages Charles had carried out carefully calculated political maneuvers. His first marriage, to Blanche of Valois, solidified relations with France. The second, to Anna of the Palatinate, served to reconcile Charles with the house of Wittelsbach after years of strife with Louis the Bavarian, the other contender for the imperial throne. The third, to Anna von Schweidnitz, mentioned above (figure 8.23), brought a large portion of Silesia under Charles's control. With this last marriage to Elizabeth of Pomerania, Charles established hegemony over Lower Lusatia.[57] Including their images on the sacred monuments he commissioned allowed him to proclaim these various political and dynastic alliances in a subtle, pious, and discreetly traditional context. This mosaic, like other images of Charles with a wife or wives—or, for that matter, like countless similar representations of imperial, royal, and aristocratic couples—served to reinforce apparent gender symmetry, although real equality or shared power did not exist. In fact, the mosaic actually denies the true validity of the apparent gender symmetry through the inequity of the left/right positions of the figures. Elizabeth and the other three spouses were crowned empress, yet the power

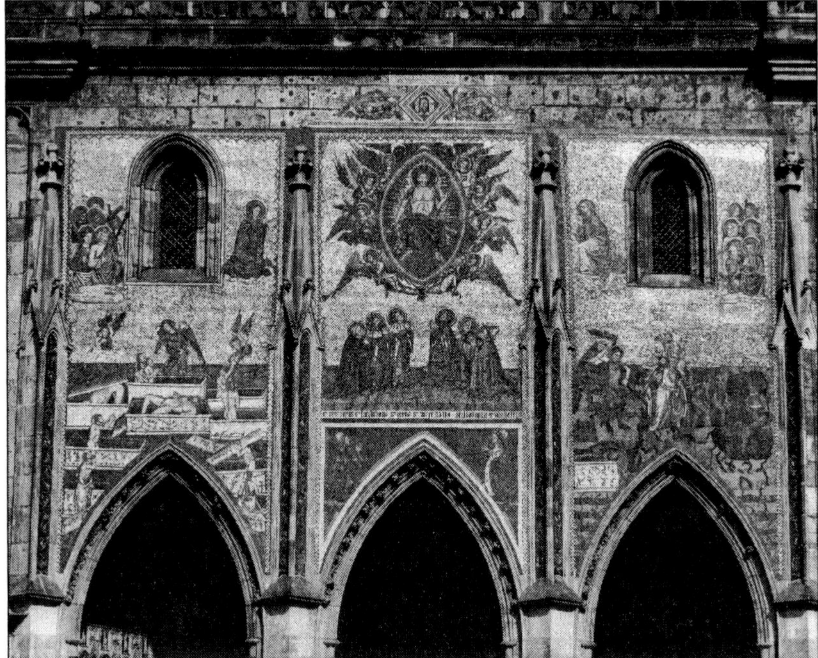

**Figure 8.29.** *Last Judgment with Charles IV and Elizabeth of Pomerania*, 1370, mosaic, Golden Portal, St. Vitus Cathedral, Prague. Foto Marburg.

was vested in the emperor. Along with the superficial illusion of gender symmetry and its actual denial came the polite pretense of dynastic equity together with its negation. One might ask how different viewers perceived such visual arrangements as that of the mosaic on the Golden Portal. Perhaps Elizabeth and her family saw with pride the symmetry of the composition, but Charles recognized primarily the iconological predominance of the right side.

Yi-Fu Tuan has pointed out that although people do not usually confuse orientations of up and down or front and back, they easily mistake right for left.[58] The reason lies in the overt symmetry of these designations, and their very minimal physical distinctions, suggesting the interchangeability of the positions. The relative valences of left and right resulted from projecting asymmetrical social values onto a geometrically symmetrical scheme, one that thus posits harmony and equity—separate and different, but equal. The simplicity of the arrangement likewise supports a claim for basic and universal truthfulness. Yet the positive and negative associations of right and left are not universally held. Among the Timucua of north Florida, for example, the word for right hand signifies "dislike, ruin, weak, sickly, scandal, and misfortune," whereas that for the left hand denotes "strong, healthy, lucky, and fortunate."[59] Likewise in Zuni culture, the left is personified by male gods who are older and wiser than their counterparts associated with the right.[60] In Chinese culture, yin is associated with the right but is inferior and linked with the female, whereas yang is connected with the left and is superior and associated with the male.[61] Observing this arbitrariness we might be reminded of the writings of Gregory Bateson, who has demonstrated how the models that have been put forward as universal for the natural world—including notions of innate symmetry, asymmetry, and harmony—belong to the cultural (i.e., political) production of knowledge.[62]

## THE POWER OF THE LEFT

Through these explorations an implicit power of the left begins to emerge. First of all, by the largely consistent assigning of positions to the right and left, these spaces became places, gendered places. These gendered places—both experienced and historical—are transported from one real space to another via mental maps that take the form of diagrams and designs that are often coupled with linguistic labels. Lefebvre uses the term "mental space."[63] Tuan speaks of "mythical spaces."[64] Juri Lotman considers "right-left" as one of the schemes for structuring the world that he includes as one of the "axiological hierarchies" comprising the categories of evaluation that belong to "metalanguage."[65] Returning once again to the *Ghent Altarpiece* and *Beaune Altarpieces* we notice that the donors—male and female—kneel in architectural niches (figures 8.1, 8.3). It would appear that these places were carved out for them before they came to occupy them. They thus merely assumed their rightful a priori places, places as legitimate as those of the saints in the neighboring niches. The stone niches and the spaces they define appear far more permanent than their transient inhabitants. We may observe with Lefebvre that such spaces conceal their contents by means of their overloaded meanings.[66] Again the spaces have become places.

Second, the man assumes the best place, and the woman is therefore displaced. She takes, quite literally, what is left. We may be reminded of the dialogue in Lewis Carroll's novel, in which it is unclear who will lead Alice through Wonderland. Tweedledee complains that if Tweedledum takes her right hand, "I will be left with her left!"[67] For venerators, his *place* and her *displace* exist discursively with each other.

This *displace* in the discourse also brings certain advantages. In those numerous medieval admonitions to follow female role models of spirituality, many of which have been explored in the last decade by Carolyn Walker Bynum, the metaphor of the topsy-turvy world and the rhetorical strategy of paradoxical logic, which goes back at least as far as the Pauline epistles, was utilized to demonstrate how God favors the weak and perfects his power in weakness.[68] Augustine and other church fathers advised the faithful to be metaphorically "ambidextrous."[69] The *Wipplar Epitaph* (figure 8.20) appears to make use of these sensitivities. In the upper register, the Virgin tenderly caresses Christ's arm as he places his drooping head close to her face. His left arm hangs down, transcending the cloudy border that separates the two realms, providing a diagonal connection between his mother and her female counterpart kneeling in the lower zone. This compositional design works against the aesthetics of bilateral symmetry. Christ's feminine vulnerability and the close physical as well as tight emotional bonds between Christ and the two women challenge any intrinsic binarism of left and right.

More generally we are thus reminded of the strength of argument from the standpoint of the disadvantaged. Psychoanalytically speaking, this positional disadvantage has been produced as a result of the fear of difference. As Jane Gallop has pointed out, "Polarization, which is the theatrical representation of difference, tames and binds that anxiety."[70] Lifting the veil of supposed symmetry to expose the asymmetry of being "left" empowered women and those who wished to be like women.

While writing this chapter, I ran across a German bumper sticker that I purchased and affixed to the file folder in which I carry the notes and correspondence for this project. In appropriating the slogan I make use of yet other semantic associations with nearly universal valances, those etymologically connected with the oppositional members of the French parliament, seated to the left of the president in the nineteenth century during the time of the Restoration. The sticker reads simply and paradoxically: "Links tut gut" (figure 8.30), which translates with a fortuitous ambivalence as "Left does well" and "Left feels good."

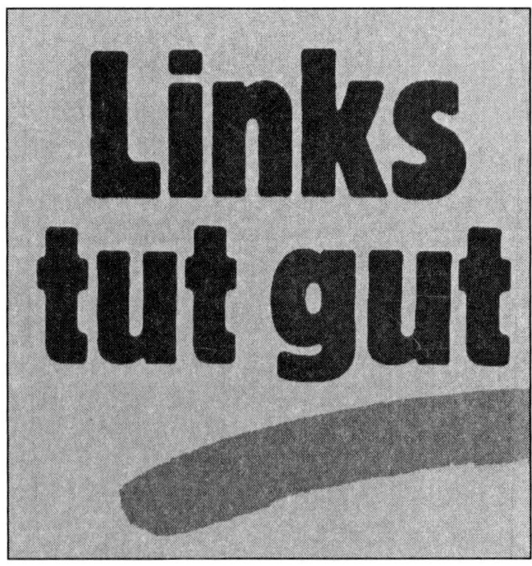


**Figure 8.30.** Bumper Sticker, *Links tut gut*, late 1990s, (Left feels good or Left does well). Photo Schier.

## NOTES

This chapter is the expanded version of a paper read at the conference Place and Displacement in the Renaissance, sponsored by the Center for Medieval and Early Renaissance Studies at Binghamton University in 1991. My late husband, Alfred Michler, helped in the preparation of that paper. The article has benefitted from supportive comments and helpful conversations with many individuals including Ann Matchette, the late Elfriede Michler, and Birgitta Bøggild Johannsen. I am grateful to Truus van Bueren and Lars Jones who perused their respective files and data bases with respect to left/right positioning of memorial images in the Low Countries and donor figures in Italy. Pia Cuneo and the members of an interdisciplinary reading group—Dhira Mahoney, Juliann Vitullo, and Diane Wolfthal—read this chapter in draft and made many helpful suggestions and corrections. Volker Schier put much effort into several new photographs. I am grateful to Yael Even for encouraging the publication of this chapter. For her own essay dealing with matters of left and right, see "Judith Leyster: An Unsuitable Place for a Woman," *Konsthistorisk tidskrift* 71 (2002): 115–124; see also Gabriela Signori, "Frauen links—Männer rechts. Bemerkungen zu einem wissenschaftlichen Gemeinplatz," ed. Rolf Ballof, *Geschichte des Mittelalters für unsere Zeit* (Stuttgart: Steiner, 2003): 179–198.

1. Berthold Hinz, "Studien zur Geschichte des Ehepaarbildnisses," *Marburger Jahrbuch für Kunstwissenschaft* 19 (1974): 139–218.

2. Wilfrid Ennenbach provides a critical overview of the existing literature in his recent examination of the interplay of various social-psychological factors. See "Über das Rechts und Links im Bilde," *Zeitschrift für Ästhetik und allgemeine Kunstwissenschaft* 41 (1996): 5–57.

3. "Über das Rechts und Links im Bilde," in *Gedanken zur Kunstgeschichte* (Basel: Schwabe, 1941), 82–90. Peter Parshall has recently considered left and right with regard to Albrecht Dürer's work as draftsman and printmaker. See "Albrecht Dürer and the Axis of Meaning," *Allen Memorial Art Museum Bulletin* 50, no. 2 (1997), 4–31.

4. Rodney Needham, ed., *Right and Left: Essays on Dual Symbolic Classification* (Chicago and London: University of Chicago Press, 1973), which includes an English translation of the seminal study by Robert Hertz, "La prééminence de la main droite: étude sur la polarité religieuse," originally published in 1909.

5. Otto Nussbaum, "Die Bewertung von Rechts und Links in der römischen Liturgie," *Jahrbuch für Antike und Christentum* 5 (1962): 158–71; Ursula Deitmaring, "Die Bedeutung von Rechts und Links in theologischen und literarischen Texten bis um 1200," *Zeitschrift für deutsches Altertum und deutsche Literatur* 128 (1969): 265–92. Deitmaring does not include gender implications.

6. See particularly Friedrich Möbius, "Basilikale Raumstruktur im Feudalisierungsprozess: Anmerkungen zu einer 'Ikonologie der Seitenschiffe,' " *Kritische Berichte* 7, no. 2/3 (1979): 5–17; Möbius, "Die Frühmittelalterliche Basilika: Zur Soziologie und Symbolik eines Architektonischen Typs," *Kritische Berichte* 9 (1981): 3–19.

7. *Aristotle on the Heavens*, trans. W. K. C. Guthrie (Cambridge and New York: Cambridge University Press, 1960), 141. Michael Camille cites this passage in his discussion of bodily orientation with respect to the body as the model for the cosmos as it inscribes vertical hierarchies in "The Image and the Self: Unwriting Late

Medieval Bodies," in *Framing Medieval Bodies*, ed. Sarah Kay and Miri Rubin (Manchester: Manchester University Press, 1994), 64.

8. The women's side is also termed the "spindle or distaff side" and the men's the "sword side." See "Spindelseite," and "Schwertseite," in Gert Oswald, *Lexikon der Heraldik* (Leipzig: Bibliographisches Institut, 1985).

9. Gregory Vincent Leftwich, "Ancient Conceptions of the Body and the Canon of Polykleitos," Ph.D. diss., Princeton University, 1987, 305–10. I wish to thank Nancy Serwint for providing this information and the reference. See also Geoffrey Lloyd, "Right and Left in Greek Philosophy," in Needham, *Right and Left*, 167–86.

10. Nussbaum, "Bewertung von Rechts und Links," 160; Following this general scheme, Galen aligned the right side with maleness and warmth, the left with femaleness and cold. See *Galen on the Usefulness of the Parts of the Body*, ed. and trans. Margaret Tallmadge May, (Ithaca: Cornell University Press, 1968), vol. 2, 626–28. Such notions lingered long and spread into many fields including early modern hippology. Sixteenth-century veterinarian texts assert that after mating with the mare, if the stallion dismounts to the right, the foal will be a colt and if to the left, a filly. Some treatises also advise the breeder to bind the stallion's left testicle in order to assure the birth of a colt. I am grateful to Pia Cuneo for sharing this research from her forthcoming book, *The Horse in Renaissance Art*.

11. Edgar Hennecke and Wilhelm Schneemelcher, eds., *Evangelien*, in *Neutestamentliche Apokryphen in deutscher Übersetzung* (Tübingen: Mohr, 1968), vol. 1, 340.

12. Elisabeth Lucchesi Palli, "Schächer," in *Lexikon der christlichen Ikonographie* (Rome: Herder, 1971); E. Lucchesi Palli, "Kreuzigung," in *Lexikon der christlichen Ikonographie*.

13. Ibid.

14. Deitmaring, "Bedeutung von Rechts und Links," 291; The image is from fol. 150r of this no longer extant manuscript. See Herrad of Hohenbourg, *Hortus Deliciarum*, ed. Rosalie Green (London and Leiden: Warburg Institute and Brill, 1979), vol. 2, 266–67; *Ecclesia und Synagoga*, ed. Herbert Jochum (exh. cat. Alte Synagoge Essen, Regionalgeschichtliches Museum, Saarbrücken 1993); Heinz Schreckenberg, *Die Juden in der Kunst Europas* (Göttingen: Vandenhoeck und Ruprecht, 1996), 31–72.

15. Ruth Mellinkoff, *Outcasts: Signs of Otherness in Northern European Art of the Late Middle Ages*, 2 vols. (Berkeley and Los Angeles: University of California Press, 1993).

16. Erika Dinkler-v. Schubert, "Rechts und Links," in *Lexikon der christlichen Ikonographie* (Rome: Herder, 1971).

17. Koert van der Horst, William Noel, and Wilhelmina C. M. Wüstefeld, *The Utrecht Psalter in Medieval Art: Picturing the Psalms of David* (exh. cat. Museum Catharijneconvent, Utrecht, 1996), 252.

18. Christoph Schulz-Mons, *Die Chorschrankenreliefs der Michaelskirche zu Hildesheim* (Hildesheim: Bernward Verlag, 1979).

19. Richard Krautheimer, *Early Christian and Byzantine Architecture* (Hamondsworth: Penguin, 1986; first printing 1965), esp. 218–19. He refers specifically to sources on Hagia Sophia.

20. Liber Pontificalis, pars secunda, in Migne, *Patrologia Latina*, vol. 106 (Paris 1851), col. 620, as cited by Möbius, "Basilikale Raumstruktur," note 32.

21. Notions of how spaces become places have been explored by Yi-Fu Tuan, *Space and Place: The Perspective of Experience* (Minneapolis: University of Minnesota Press, 1977), and in several essays in the anthology *The Power of Place*, ed. John Agnew and James Duncan (London and Boston: Hyman, 1989). In their essay, "Social and Symbolic Places in Renaissance Venice and Florence," 81–100, Edward Muir and Ronald Weissman assert that "one might distinguish between 'place' seen primarily as a cultural artifact, embedded in a grid of other meaningful objects and locales, and 'space' understood as a physical location that related to other locations," 93. See also in the same volume M. Richardson, "Place and Culture: Two Disciplines, Two Concepts, Two Images of Christ, and a Single Goal," 140–56.

22. See especially Heinrich Selhorst, "Die Platzordnung im Gläubigenraum der altchristlichen Kirche," Ph.D. diss., University of Münster, 1931, who found and analyzed a wealth of early textual sources and thus provides the basis for later authors. See also Nussbaum, "Bewertung von Rechts und Links," 168–69; Möbius, "Basilikale Raumstruktur im Feudalisierungsprozess. Anmerkungen zu einer 'Ikonologie der Seitenschiffe,' " 8. To a degree such practices must have been maintained in various contexts even into the modern era. See the excellent collection of sources particularly from England in Margaret Aston, "Segregation in Church," *Women in the Church*, ed. W. J. Sheils and Diana Wood, *Studies in Church History*, vol. 27 (Oxford: Blackwell, 1990), 237–94. The connection drawn between women's place on the north side of the church and the veneration of the Virgin in this portion of the building is, nonetheless, problematic.

23. I wish to thank David Wilkens for calling this to my attention.

24. In their classic study *Sexual Meanings: The Cultural Construction of Gender and Sexuality* (Cambridge and New York: Cambridge University Press, 1981), Sherry Ortner and Harriet Whitehead discuss many similar instances in which gender constructions and other social constructs produce mutually inflected meanings resulting in reciprocally reinforcing systems.

25. Angela Mohr, *Die Schutzmantelmadonna von Frauenstein* (Steyr: Ennsthaler, 1983).

26. Otto von Simson, *Sacred Fortress: Byzantine Art and Statecraft in Ravenna* (Princeton: Princeton University Press, 1987; first printed in 1948), 30–31.

27. For an interesting discussion of eunuchs in patristic and medieval history and literature see Kathryn M. Ringrose, "Living in the Shadows: Eunuchs and Gender in Byzantium," in *Third Sex, Third Gender: Beyond Sexual Dimorphism in Culture and History*, ed. Gilbert H. Herdt (New York: Zone Books, 1994), 85–109.

28. For new findings based on conservation and historical data see Irina Andrescu-Treadgold and Warren Treadgold, "Procopius and the Imperial Panels of S. Vitale," *Art Bulletin* 79 (1997): 708–23.

29. For a recent discussion of the reinscription of orthodoxy in Ravenna see Annabel Jane Wharton, *Refiguring the Post Classical City: Dura Europos, Jerash, Jerusalem, and Ravanna* (Cambridge and New York: Cambridge University Press, 1995), 105–47.

30. Doubts have been raised concerning the factuality of the accusations made by Procopius. Perhaps Theodora was maligned because she was of common birth. For a recent discussion of Theodora and her patronage see Anne L. McClanan, "The Empress Theodora and the Tradition of Women's Patronage in the Early Byzantine Empire," in *The Cultural Patronage of Medieval Women*, ed. June Hall McCash (Athens: University of Georgia Press, 1996), 50–72.

31. I wish to thank Donna Sadler for calling this to my attention. See her publication "The King as Subject, the King as Author: Art and Politics of Louis IX," in *European Monarchy: Its Evolution and Practice from Roman Antiquity to Modern Times*, ed. Heinz Durchhardt, Richard A. Jackson, and David Sturdy (Stuttgart: Steiner, 1992), 53–68, esp. 63.

32. Elisabeth Vavra, "Pro remedio animae—Motivation oder leere Formel. Überlegungen zur Stiftung religiöser Kunstobjekte," in *Materielle Kultur und religiöse Stiftung im Spätmittelalter*, ed. Gerhard Jaritz (Vienna: Verlag der Österreichischen Akademie der Wissenschaften, 1990), 123–56, esp. 131–34.

33. Josef Sauer has collected the various textual sources that support these notions in his *Symbolik des Kirchengebäudes und seine Ausstattung in der Auffassung des Mittelalters* (Freiburg: Herder, 1942, reprinted Münster: Mehren und Hobbeling, 1964). See esp. 87–96.

34. See Franz Joseph Dölger, *Sonne der Gerechtigkeit und der Schwarze: Eine religionsgeschichtliche Studie zum Taufgelöbnis*, Liturgiegeschichtliche Forschungen 2, (Münster: Aschendorff, 1918), 1–150, esp. 37–48; Dölger, *Sol Salutis, Gebet und Gesang im christlichen Altertum*, Liturgiegeschichtliche Forschungen, 4–5 (Münster: Aschendorff, 1925), esp. 98ff, for discussions of the early liturgical meanings of the directions of East and West.

35. Peter Cornelius Claussen, *Chartres-Studien: Zu Vorgeschichte, Funktion und Skulptur der Vorhallen* (Wiesbaden: Steiner, 1975), 11–17.

36. On social and ritual emplacement see the chapter by Ruth Evans in this volume.

37. Heidrun Stein-Kecks, *Die romanischen Wandmalereien in der Klosterkirche Prüfening* (Regensburg: Mittelbayerische Druck- und Verlags-Gesellschaft, 1987).

38. Explorations of the uses of various parts of the medieval church building still remain a desideratum of art and architectural history. Unfortunately sociological analyses of liturgical spaces have been preempted by formal descriptions and stylistic comparisons. Notable exceptions are cited above in the work of Friedrich Möbius.

39. Möbius, "Basilikale Raumstruktur im Feudalisierungsprozess. Anmerkungen zu einer 'Ikonologie der Seitenschiffe,' " esp. 7; Möbius, "Die Frühmittelalterliche Basilika. Zur Soziologie und Symbolik eines Architektonischen Typs."

40. For photographs and descriptions see *Danmarks Kirker: Københavns Amt* 3, 2 (Copenhagen: Gads, 1944), 1208–11.

41. Suger writes that on feast days the church was so filled with people that no one could enter, exit, or move about, but only stand like a marble statue. He stresses, "The distress of the women, however, was so great and so intolerable that you could see with horror how they, squeezed in by the mass of strong men as in a winepress, exhibited bloodless faces as in imagined death; how they cried out horribly as though in labor; how several of them, miserably trodden underfoot [but then] lifted by the pious assistance of men above the heads of the crowd, marched forward as though upon a pavement, and how many others, gasping with their last breath, panted in the cloisters of the brethren to the despair of everyone." *Abbot Suger on the Abbey Church of St.-Denis and Its Art Treasures*, ed. Erwin Panofsky, second ed., Gerda Panofsky-Soergel (1946, Princeton: Princeton University Press, 1979), 86–89.

42. For insights on processions and processional hierarchies see Friedrich Möbius, "Die 'Ecclesia Maior' von Centula (790–799): Wanderliturgie im höfischen Kontext," *Kritische Berichte* 11 (1983): 42–58.

43. These terms are introduced by Henri Lefebvre. See his *Production of Space*, trans. Donald Nicholson-Smith, (Oxford: Blackwell, 1994; first published in 1974), 86–87. For discussions of other "places" or social spaces in church interiors—particularly those established by class structure in Lutheran churches at the time of the Reformation—see Reinhold Wex, "Oben und unten oder Martin Luthers Predigkunst angesichts der Torgauer Schloßkapelle," *Kritische Berichte* 11 (1983): 4–24; Aston, "Segregation in Church."

44. Erika Kirchner-Doberer, "Die deutsche Lettner bis 1300," Ph.D. diss., University of Vienna, 1946; Marcia Hall, "The *Ponte* in S. Maria Novella: The Problem of the Rood Screen in Italy," *Journal of the Warburg and Courtauld Institutes* 37 (1974): 157–73; Marcia Hall, "The *Tramezzo* in Santa Croce, Florence, Reconstructed," *Art Bulletin* 56 (1974): 325–41; Hall, "The Italian Rood Screen: Some Implications for Liturgy and Function," in *Essays Presented to Myron P Gilmore*, ed. Sergio Bertelli (History of Art / History of Music) (Florence: La Nuova Italia Ed., 1978), vol. 2, 213–18.

45. Reproduced by Aston, "Segregation in Church," 262.

46. Sauer, *Symbolik des Kirchengebäudes*, 93–95; Selhorst, *Die Platzordnung*, 36–37; Deitmaring, "Bedeutung von Rechts und Links," 270, 281, 285–86; Möbius, "Basilikale Raumstruktur im Feudalisierungsprozess: Anmerkungen zu einer 'Ikonologie der Seitenschiffe,' " 10–11.

47. *Triumphkreuz im Dom zu Lübeck*, with contributions by Karlheinz Stoll, Ewald Vetter, and Eike Oellermann (Wiesbaden: Reichert, 1977); Max Hasse, *Das Triumphkreuz des Bernt Notke im Lübecker Dom* (Hamburg: Ellermann, 1952).

48. Helga Sciurie has pointed to yet another, less common, system for hierarchical gendered ordering of couples. In the *Adam Portal* of Bamberg Cathedral, Adam and Eve as well as the imperial foundation saints Henry and Cunegund were among the figures in the jambs. Here the two men assumed the innermost positions and their wives the respective positions next to them to the outside. See "Vom Münzbild zum Standbild: Beobachtungen an Darstellungen deutscher Herrscherpaare des 12. und 13. Jahrhunderts," in *Auf der Suche nach der Frau im Mittelalter*, ed. Bea Lundt (Munich: Fink, 1991), 135–63.

49. Madeline Caviness, "Anchoress, Abbess, and Queen: Donors and Patrons or Intercessors and Matrons?" in *Cultural Patronage of Medieval Women*, 105–54.

50. Robert Suckale, *Die Hofkunst Kaiser Ludwigs des Bayern* (Munich: Hirmer, 1993), 22.

51. For a discussion of these gestures see Corine Schleif, "Hands That Appoint, Anoint, and Ally: Late-Medieval Donor Strategies for Appropriating Approbation through Painting," *Art History* 16 (1993): 1–33.

52. Kenneth Clark, *Piero della Francesca* (London and New York: Phaidon 1969), 56.

53. I am grateful to John Paoletti for calling the last two anomalous examples to my attention. For the documents on the Sassetti commission see Aby Warburg, "Francesco Sassettis letztwillige Verfügung," in A. Warburg, *Gesammelte Schriften* 1907, reprint (Leipzig: Teubner, 1932), vol. 1, 127–58.

54. Elisabeth Schraut, *Stifterinnen und Künstlerinnen im mittelalterlichen Nürnberg* (exh. cat. Nuremberg Stadtarchiv, 1987), 14.

55. Andrescu-Treadgold and Treadgold, "Procopius and the Imperial Panels of S. Vitale."

56. Hartmut Boockmann, "Kirche und Frömigkeit vor der Reformation," in *Martin Luther und die Reformation in Deutschland* (exh. cat. Germanisches National-museum, Nuremberg, 1983), 41–72.

57. Franz Machilek, "Anna von Schweidnitz (1338/39–1362)" in *Schweidnitz in Wandel der Zeiten*, ed. Werner Bein (exh. cat. Spitalhof Reutlingen) (Würzburg: Bergstadtverlag Korn, 1990), 317–22; Dieter Veldtrup, *Zwischen Eherecht und Familienpolitik: Studien zu den dynastischen Heiratsprojekten Karls IV* (Warendorf: Fallbusch, Hölscher, Rieger, 1988).

58. Tuan, *Space and Place*, 42.

59. Julian Granberry, "Eba/Fara: An Ethnolinguistic Note on Timucua Hand Use," *International Journal of American Linguistics* 62 (1996): 188–95.

60. Lloyd, "Right and Left in Greek Philosophy," 168.

61. Ibid; Tuan, *Space and Place*, 44.

62. Gregory Bateson, *Mind and Nature: A Necessary Unit* (New York: Dutton, 1979).

63. Lefebvre, *The Production of Space*, 11.

64. Tuan, *Space and Place*, 85–100.

65. Juri Lotman, "On the Metalanguage of a Typological Description of Culture," *Semiotica* 14 (1975): 97–123, esp. 102.

66. Lefebvre, *The Production of Space*, 92.

67. I wish to thank Virginia Chieffo Raguin for calling this passage to my attention.

68. Carolyn Walker Bynum, *Jesus as Mother* (Los Angeles and Berkeley: University of California Press, 1982); In the essay " ' . . . And Woman His Humanity': Female Imagery in the Religious Writing of the Later Middle Ages," in Bynum, *Fragmentation and Redemption* (New York: Zone Books, 1991), 151–79, Bynum stresses the complementarity of gender construction in medieval theology.

69. Deitmaring, "Bedeutung von Rechts und Links," 275.

70. *Feminism and Psychoanalysis* (London: Macmillan, 1982); Laura Mulvey cites this passage in *Visual and Other Pleasures* (Bloomington: Indiana University Press, 1989), 161, and discusses how the either/or binary pattern leaves the argument "trapped within its own conceptual frame," 162.

## SCHLEIF FURTHER READING

Agnew, John, and James Duncan, eds. *The Power of Place*. London and Boston: Unwin Hyman, 1989.

Aston, Margaret, "Segregation in Church," *Women in the Church*. Studies in Church History 27. Ed. W. J. Sheils and Diana Wood. Oxford: Blackwell, 1990, 237–94.

Deitmaring, Ursula. "Die Bedeutung von Rechts und Links in theologischen und literarischen Texten bis um 1200." *Zeitschrift für deutsches Altertum und deutsche Literatur* 128 (1969): 265–92.

Erika Dinkler-v. Schubert. "Rechts und Links." In *Lexikon der christlichen Ikonographie*. Rome: Herder, 1971.

Krautheimer, Richard. *Early Christian and Byzantine Architecture*. 1965; Hamondsworth: Penguin, 1986.

Lefebvre, Henri. *The Production of Space*. Trans. Donald Nicholson-Smith. 1974; Oxford: Blackwell, 1994.

McCash, June Hall, ed. *The Cultural Patronage of Medieval Women*. Athens: University of Georgia Press, 1996.

Möbius, Friedrich. "Basilikale Raumstruktur im Feudalisierungsprozess: Anmerkungen zu einer 'Ikonologie der Seitenschiffe.'" *Kritische Berichte* 7 (1979), no. 2/3: 5–17.

Möbius, Friedrich. "Die Frühmittelalterliche Basilika: Zur Soziologie und Symbolik eines Architektonischen Typs." *Kritische Berichte* 9 (1981): 3–19.

Needham, Rodney, ed. *Right and Left: Essays on Dual Symbolic Classification*. Chicago: University of Chicago Press, 1973.

Nussbaum, Otto. "Die Bewertung von Rechts und Links in der römischen Liturgie." *Jahrbuch für Antike und Christentum* 5 (1962): 158–71.

Ortner, Sherry, and Harriet Whitehead. *Sexual Meanings: The Cultural Construction of Gender and Sexuality*. Cambridge: Cambridge University Press, 1981.

Sauer, Josef. *Symbolik des Kirchengebäudes und seine Ausstattung in der Auffassung des Mittelalters*. 1942; Münster: Mehren und Hobbeling, 1964.

Selhorst, Heinrich. "Die Platzordnung im Gläubigenraum der altchristlichen Kirche." Diss. University of Münster, 1931.

Tuan, Yi-Fu. *Space and Place: The Perspective of Experience*. Minneapolis: University of Minnesota Press, 1977.

# CONTRIBUTORS

VIRGINIA BLANTON is Assistant Professor of English at the University of Missouri-Kansas City. Her publications include articles in *Studies in Iconography, The Journal of Medieval and Early Modern Studies,* and Historical *Reflections/Réflexions Historiques,* as well as a guide to films featuring medieval women, published as the first monograph in the *Medieval Feminist Forum* Subsidia series. She is currently writing a longitudinal study about the medieval cult of Æthelthryth, focusing on the various manifestations of devotion expressed to this saint over an 800 year period.

RUTH EVANS is senior lecturer in English Studies at the University of Stirling, Scotland, UK. She has published articles on English medieval drama, courtly literature, virginity literature, Margery Kempe, Chaucer, and translation theory. She has contributed to the *The Cambridge Guide to Women's Writing in English* (1999) and *The Cambridge Companion to Medieval Women's Writing* (2003). She is co-editor (with Jocelyn Wogan-Browne, Nicholas Watson and Andrew Taylor) of *The Idea of the Vernacular: An Anthology of Middle English Literary Theory,* 1280–1530 (1999), and (with Sarah Salih and Anke Bernau) of *Medieval Virginities* (2003). She is currently writing a book on Chaucer and memory.

KATHERINE FRENCH is an associate professor of History at SUNY-New Paltz. She is one of the co-editors of *The Parish in English Life* (1997) and the author of *The People of the Parish: Community Life in a Medieval English Diocese* (2001). Her full-length monograph on women in English parish life is forthcoming from University of Pennsylvania Press.

ENA GIURESCU HELLER is executive director, Museum of Biblical Art, New York City. Her most recent publications include *Reluctant Partners: Art and Religion in Dialogue* (The Gallery at the American Bible Society/The Henry Luce Foundation, 2004) and the exhibition catalog *Icons or Portraits? Images of Jesus and Mary from the Collection of Michael Hall* (The Gallery at the American Bible Society, 2002). She is a contributor to the forthcoming volume *The Art of Sandra Bowden* (Square Halo Books, 2005).

VIRGINIA CHIEFFO RAGUIN is professor of art history at the College of the Holy Cross. She has published on medieval art and architecture and also on stained glass from medieval through modern times and is co-editor of *Artistic Integration in Goth ic Buildings* (Toronto 1995). Her survey, *Stained Glass from its Origins to the Present*, was published by Harry Abrams in 2003. A member of the Corpus Vitrearum, she has co-authored with Helen Zakin *Stained Glass before 1700 in the Collections of the Midwest States* (London: Harvey Miller, 2001). With Sarah Stanbury, she maintains the website *Mapping Margery Kempe*, www.holycross.edu/kempe.

CORINE SCHLEIF teaches at Arzona State University. Her monograph *Donatio et Memoria* appeared in 1990. Recently she has authored two articles for the symposium volume *Adam Kraft* (Germanisches Nationalmuseum Nuremberg, 2002), an article on Tilman Riemenschneider (*Studies in the History of Art*, 2004), and another on Albrecht Dürer, Agnes Frey, and Willibald Pirckheimer, in a volume on Dürer, ed. Larry Silver, University of Pennsylvania Press, forthcoming. Together with Volker Schier she has written *Katerina's Windows: Donation and Devotion, Art and Music as Heard and Seen through the Writings of a Birgittine Nun*, forthcoming from the University of Chicago Press.

JANE TIBBETTS SCHULENBURG is professor of history in the Department of Liberal Studies and the Arts, Women's Studies and Medieval Studies, University of Wisconsin at Madison. Her major publication is *Forgetful of Their Sex: Female Sanctity and Society, ca. 500–1100* (1998). She has also published articles on medieval women and monasticism, enclosure, women saints and society, and is presently working on a major project on gender and proscriptions of sacred space in the medieval world ca. 500–1200.

SARAH STANBURY is associate professor of English at College of the Holy Cross. In addition to articles on Chaucer and late medieval visual culture, her publications include an edition of *Pearl* (TEAMS, Medieval Institute Publications, 2002) and *Seeing the Gawain-Poet: Description and the Act of Perception* (1991). She is also co-editor of *Feminist Approaches to the Body in Medieval Literature* (1993) and *Writing on the Body: Female Embodiment and Feminist Theory* (1997). With Virginia Raguin, she maintains the website *Mapping Margery Kempe*, www.holycross.edu/kempe.

# INDEX

Note to the Reader: Monuments are listed under the name of their location.


abbesses, 16. *See also* Æthelthryth, Hita, Sexburg, Whitburg
access. *See* space
Acciaiuoli, Jacopo di Donato, 164
Acciaiuoli, Monna Andrea, 15, 17, 161, 164, 166–67, 170–77
  arms of, 166
actors
  cross-dressing, 27–28
  female, 35
  male impersonators, 24, 35–36
*Ad Herennium*, 113
Adam and Eve, 24–27, 230
Adela, countess of Flanders, 16, 197
Aelfgifu, Queen, 230–32, fig. 8.21
Æthelthryth, St., 13, 47–56, 59–66, fig. 2.1
Æthelwold, Bishop, 49, 51
Agatha, St., 56
Agnellus, Bishop, 220
Alessandro of Fiesole, St., 170
altar, 7, 84, 94, 197
  of St. Cornelius, 146
  of St. Erasmus, 146
  of the Annunciation, 163
altarpiece, 92, 163,165, 208–10, 221, 238–39, fig. 6.4
Alto, St., abbot of Altomünster, 196
Amalarius, 225
anchoress, 7, 10
Andrew, St., 166
angel, 90
Anglo-Saxon nobles, 60
Anna of the Palatinate, 239
Annunciation. *See* Virgin Mary, Annunciation
Apocalypse manuscript, 7, 9
Apostles, 217–18, figs. 8.9, 8.10
  Creed, 216
Aquinas, Thomas, St., 113
Argentarius, Julianus, 221–22
Aristotle, 211–12
Ashley, Kathleen, 55–56
Ashton, Devon, parish church, 86
Assisi, 78
Aston, Margaret, 143
Attelath, Johanna and Robert, 129
Atwell, Mistress, 149
Augsburg, St. Annakirche, 224
Augustine, St., 25–28, 191–92, 217, 229
  *Concerning the City of God against the Pagans*, 25
Aulnay, church of Saint-Pierre, 215–16, fig. 8.7
Ava, abbess of St. Maur of Verdun, 197–98

Baret, John, of Bury St. Edmonds, 80, 123
barriers. *See* space
Bartholomew of Farne, St. *vita*, 191
Baynbrygge, Agnes, 149
Beaune, Musée de l'Hotel Dieu, *Last Judgment Altarpiece*, 208–10, 213, 221, 230, 241, figs. 8.3, 8.4
Beckwith, Sarah, 24, 27, 31, 48, 83
Bede, *Historia Ecclesiastica Gentis Anglorum*, 48–50, 56, 63
bedding, 38
*Belles Heures of Jean de Berry*, 123
Benedict of Aniane, St., 187
Benedictine monks, 49, 187
Bernardino, San, 227–28, fig. 8.17
Bernard, St., 130
Beverly, guild returns, 35
  Minster chapterhouse, 78, 97, n.7
Biliotti, Modesto, *cronaca* of Santa Maria Novella, 173
binary divisions. *See* polarities
Binski, Paul, 7–8
Blake, E. O., 51
Blanche of Castile, Queen 224
Blanche of Valois, 239
body, the, 4, 5, 10, 12–14, 17, 23–28, 30, 33, 36–37, 40, 47–53, 55, 58–60, 62–65, 83, 86, 88–90, 92, 115, 117, 123, 126–27, 198, 212, 216–17, 228, 230
Biondo, Giovanni, del, 165, fig. 6.4
Boniface, St., 196–97
*Book of Hours of James IV*, 100, n.26, 112–13, fig. 4.6
Book of Life (*liber vitae*), 90–92, 94–95
Borghigiani, *cronaca* of the Convent of Santa Maria Novella, 173
Borlout, Isabel, 208–10, 212, fig. 8.1
Boundaries. *See* space
Bourdieu, Pierre, 3–5, 11, 17
brasses, 123, 127–30, figs. 4.10, 4.11
Braunche, Leticia, Margaret and Robert, 127–29, fig. 4.11
Bridget of Sweden, St., *Revelations*, 109, 114
Bridgewater, Somerset, St. Mary's parish church, 144, 152–55
Britby, John, 29
Brose, Margaret, 62–63
Bruni, Francesco, 176
building campaigns, 152
burials, 127, 207. *See also* tombs
Bury St. Edmonds, St. Mary's church, 123
Butler, Judith 12–13, 50
Bynum, Carolyn Walker, 10, 241

Calais, St., 188–90
Cambridgeshire, Franciscan convent of Denny, 83, 117
candlestick, five-flame, 112, fig. 4.5
Cannon, Christopher, 58
Canterbury, Cathedral of Christ Church, 192
Carol, Lewis, *Alice in Wonderland*, 81
Carruthers, Mary, 121
Castres, monastery of Castres, 196
Catherine, St., 236–37, fig. 8.27. *See also* Katherine, St.
Cavalcanti, Aldobrandino, bishop of Orvieto, 171
Cavalcanti, Mainardo, 15, 17, 162, 164, 166–67, 171–74
  arms of, 166
Caviness, Madeline, 119, 230
Celestial City, 186
celibacy, 9, 187
Cesarius of Arles, St., *Regula ad Monachos*, 187
chapels
  funerary, 169
  of the Virgin (Lady Chapel), 191, 194
  private, 2, 85–86, 123, 152, 155
charity, 83
Charles IV, Emperor, 233, 239–40, figs. 8.23, 8.29
chastity, 48–49, 56–60, 83, 114, 116, 130
Chaucer, Geoffrey, *Book of the Duchess*, 38
childbirth, 114–15
choir. *See* church
Chrétien de Troyes, *Lancelot*, 38
Christ, 78–79, 56, 83, 86, 114, 117, 124, 143, 210, 215, 241
  Christ as lover, 86, 116

Christ Child, 231–33, fig. 8.22
Crucifixion, 213–15, 230–31, figs. 8.5, 8.6, 8.19
Good Shepherd, 117–18, fig. 4.7
Lamb of God, 208–10, fig. 8.2
parables of, 119–21, figs. 4.8, 4.9
Passion, 114, 116, 166
Resurrection of, 118
with Six Apostles, 217–18, fig. 8.9
*See also*, Last Judgment, Man of Sorrows
chronicles, monastic, 2, 13, 53. *See also* *Liber Eliensis*
as revisionist history, 13, 15, 53, 167
church
as cosmos, 224
as human body, 6
chancel, 4, 85
choir, 122–23
cloister, 186
nave, 4
*See also* chapels, oratory
churchwardens, 144–46, 149, 152, 155
Cirri, *sepoltuario*, 174
Cistercian Order, 198
civil judgment, 224–25
class, 1–2, 4, 85
Clasy, Mistress, 146
clergy, 122, 125, 141
clerical space, 84–85, 117, 225. *See also* church, choir
Clerk, John, wife of, 150
Clopton, John, 80–81, 88, 123
Clopton, William, 80–81
Cluny, abbey of Cluny, 194, 197–98
Cnut, King, 230–32, fig. 8.21
coats of arms, 79–80, 112, 126
arms of Burgundy, 111–12, fig. 4.5
Coldingham, royal monastery, 49, 56
Colomina, Beatriz, 26
Communion, 89. *See also* Eucharist
community, 3, 11, 125. *See also* polarities, public vs. private
Compostela, basilica of St. James, 109
Coney, Walter, 123
Conques, monastery of St. Foi, 109
Corpus Christi, feast, 25. *See also* York, Corpus Christi play cycle
Corsi, Nera, 235
cosmos, 224
cross-dressing, 12, 27–29, 35–37
Crucifixion. *See* Christ, Crucifixion
crying. *See* weeping
Cuthbert, St. 189–91, 194

da Firenze, Andrea, 161
de Certeau, Michel, 30–32
Deitmaring, Ursula, 211
Denny, convent of. *See* Cambridgeshire, Franciscan convent of Denny
devil, 228
Dobell, Giles, 142
Dominican Order, 162, 172, 175
donations, suppression of women's, 173
donor portraits, 109, 123
donors/patrons, 1, 33, 77–83, 169–76, fig. 3.3
right and left positions of, 33, 208–11, 219–24
Dorman, William, 142
Douglas, Mary, 58
dowry, 168, 174
dress/costume, 126, 130
Duffy, Eamon, *The Stripping of the Altars*, 5
Durandus, William, 229
Durham, Cathedral, 189–90, 225
Lady Chapel, 190–91

Eden, Garden of, 24–26, 28
Earth, 26, 28. *See also* Eden
East Anglia, churches, 79
Easter Sepulcher, 123
Ebsdorf, Benedictine convent, glazing program, 117–22, figs. 4.7, 4.9
*Ecclesia*, 6, 60, 213
Ecgfrith, king of Northumbria, 49, 56–57, 59–60, 63, 66, fig. 2.1
Edgar, King, 49
Edward the Confessor, 54, 145
Eldersham, Margaret, 149–50
Elias, Norbert, 38
Elizabeth of Pomerania, 239–40, fig. 2.29
Ellis, Deborah, 105
Elnone, monastic church, 196. *See* Saint-Amand-les-Eaux, monastery of Elnone

Elsner, Jakob, *Kress Missal*, 217, fig. 8.8
Ely, Cathedral and royal monastery, 12–13, 47–56, 58–62, 64–65
capitals, 59–60, fig. 2.1
"Liberty of Ely", 61
*See also Liber Eliensis*
enclosure. *See* space
Eormenild, queen of Mercia, 49, 64
Erhart, Gregor, 220–21, fig. 8.13
Eucharist, 84–85, 89
Eve, 24, 26, 230
exclusionary rules, 83, 85, 152–55, 175–76, 186, 188. *See also* space

Fall of Adam and Eve, 25
Farfa, abbey of Farfa, 194
Fell, Christine, 49
Ferris, Joan, 149
Fiacre, St., chapel of, 189
field, 3, 5
fig-leaf, 27
fines, 176. *See also* punishments
Fleury. *See* St.-Benoit-sur-Loire, monastery of Fleury
Florence of Worcester, 63
Florence, 161–83
Orsanmichele, 220, 225
Santa Maria Novella, 15, 17, 127, 161–69, 171–72, 175, figs. 6.1, 6.2, 6.3
Strozzi Chapel, 161
St. Gregory's chapel, 175
Santa Croce, 226–27, fig. 8.16
St. Michael's chapel, 16, 169–70, fig. 6.5
Peruzzi chapel, 161
forgeries, inventions. *See* chronicles
Foster, Master, 146
Foucault, Michel, 5, 25, 26, 32, *History of Sexuality*, 26
Foy, St. 55
Franciscan Order, 16; tertiary confraternity, 169
Frauenstein, Wallfahrtskirche, *Madonna Misericordia*, 220–21, fig. 8.13
fund raising, 146–49, 151–56
funeral, 171–72, 176, 207–8

Gabriel, Archangel, 166
Galilei, Galileo, , 32
Gallop, Jane, 241
gaze, 8–9, 52
gender, 9, 12, 28, 240
body vs. mind/soul, 6
male vs. female, 3, 6, 14–15, 17
restrictions and prohibitions, 2, 5, 15–16, 83–84, 122, 152, 176, 199–200. *See also* space
gender ambiguity, 28, 240
gendered organization, 11, 155, 219–25, 241–42
geography, feminist, 4
Gervase, Norman servant, 65
Ghent, Cathedral of St. Bavo, *Altarpiece of the Lamb*, 208–10, 215, 221, 230, 241, figs. 8.1, 8.2
Ghita, Dona Margherita, 175
Gregory of Tours, St., *Life of the Fathers*, 195–96
Gibson, Gail McMurray, 10, 77, 80
Gilchrist, Roberta, 10–11, 17, 59, 143
Ghirlandaio, Dominico del, 235
Giotto, 125, 161
God the Father, 86, 124, 216–19
Goeffrey of Coldingham, 191
Goeznou, St., 188–89
Goldberg, Jeremy, 35
good vs. evil, 213–16
*Gorleston Psalter*, 79
Goscelin of Canterbury, 191–95
*Life of St. Augustine*, 191–93
Goulven, St., 189
Gravdal, Kathryn, 66
Graves, C. Pamela, 5, 11, 85–86
Grayingham, Lincoln, parish church, 143
Gregory, St., vision of the Man of Sorrows, 86
guilds, 34–35, 151, 154, 156, 168
Gunda, challenger of St. Calais, 188–90

habitus, 3, 5, 17
hagiography, 54–56
Halberstadt, Liebfrauenkirche, 218, figs. 8.9, 8.10

Hanseatic League, 128–29
Harington, Mariot, 143
Harling, Ann of East Harling, 80
Helena, St., 224
Henry VII, King, 38, 112
Herbert, bishop of Norwich, 122
Hereward, 60, 62, 64, *Gesta Herewardi*, 62, 64
Hildesheim, St. Michaelskirche, 218–19, fig. 8.11
Hillen, Henry, 85
Hirn, Konrad and Afra, 224
Hitda, Abbess, 235–36, fig. 8.26
Hocktide, 151
Holzschuher, Magdalena, 236
Homer, 212
Honorius of Autun, 229
*hortus conclusus*, 119, 236
*Hortus Deliciarum of Herrad of Hohenbourg*, (Landsberg), 213, fig. 8.5
host, elevation of, 7. *See also* Eucharist
Houlbrooke, R. A., 144
*Hours of Mary of Burgundy*, 8, 109–11, 113, fig. 4.4
housekeeping, 114
housemark, 238
Hubberd, Mother, 146
Hudson, Anne, 93
Hugh du Puiset, Bishop, 191
Hugh of Flavigny, *Chronicle of Hugh of Flavigny*, 197–98
Hugo, abbot of Farfa, 194
husbands, 33

icons, 88
Ilminster, Somerset, parish church, 142
inclusion, 125–31. *See also* space
incorruptibility, 48–52, 61–62, 67
inscriptions/ texts, 80–82, 86, figs. 3.1, 3.3
intercessor, 16, 90, 96

Jacopo di Nipozzano, architect, 173–74
James, St., 166, 224
Jerusalem, 78, 115
  Tomb of the Holy Sepulcher, 114
Jews, 228
John the Baptist, St., life of, 165–66, 173
John the Evangelist, St., 7, 9
Jones, Sarah Rees, 31
jube. *See* screens
Judith, wife of Earl Tostig, 190
Justinian, Emperor, 221–23, fig. 8.14

Kabyle house, 3, 10
Karlstein, 233, fig. 8.23
Katherine, St., 91
Kemp, Margery, 13–14, 29, 75–103, 105–40
  Boke of Lyfe (Book of Life), 90–92, 94–95
  *Book of Margery Kemp*, 13, 77, 82
  *Meditation on the Life of Christ*, 77
King's Lynn. *See* Lynn
kiss of peace, 143
Krautheimer, Richard, 220

La Balme. *See* St. Cloud, convent of La Balme
Lady of Pity, 87, fig. 3.3
Last Judgment, 209–10, 213, 239–40, figs. 8.4, 8.29
Lavenham, parish church, 7, frontispiece
LeFebvre, Henri, 23, 24, 30
left side placement, 241–42, fig. 8.30
Leicester, All Saints parish church, 78
Lent, 224–25
  Lenten veils, 115
Leutfridus, St., *vita*, 195
*Liber Eliensis*, 13, 47–56, 58–60, 62–66
*Liber Vitae*, 91
*Life of St. Amand*, 196
*Life of St. Odo of Cluny*, 194, 197–98
Lioba, St., *vita*, 197
literacy, 109, 113, 130–31
liturgy. *See* ritual
Lollards, 93–94, 134, n.36
  *Twelve Conclusions of the Lollards*, 93
London, St. Martin Vintry, parish church, 143
Long Melford, Holy Trinity Church, 80–82, 87, 88, 92, 123, figs. 3.1, 3.2, 3.3, 3.4
Louis IX, King, 224

Louis the Bavarian, Emperor, 231–33, 239, fig. 8.22
Lübeck, 128
  Cathedral, 230–31, fig. 8.19
Lucas, Alice, 149–50
Lynn, 90, 105, 122, 125–26
  Chapel of St. Nicholas, 96, 122, 124, 129
  guildhall, 96
  Hospital of St. John, 115
  Lynn Priory, Chapel, 78
    St. Margaret's, 14, 29, 80, 83–85, 88, 90,107–8, 115, 122–24, figs. 4.1, 4.2, 4.3
    brasses, 80, 127–31, figs. 4.10, 4.11
    Chapel of the Gesine, 78, 106
    Chapel of St. John, 90
Magnus, Albertus, St. 113
Man of Sorrows, 86, 90, 92, 94, 166, 230–32, figs. 3.4, 3.6, 6.4, 8.20
Manning, Robert, *Handlying Synne*, 142–43
maps/mapping, 59. *See also* space
Margaret of Scotland, Queen St., 189
Margarete of Holland, 231–33, fig. 8.22
Marian chapel, English placement, 143
Marks, Richard, 80
Martyrs/victims, 52, 63, 219–20, fig. 8.12
Mary of Burgundy, 109–11, fig. 4.4
Mary. *See* Virgin Mary
Mass, 7, 9, 111–12, 115–16, 141, 176, fig.4.5. *See also* memorial masses
Massey, Doreen, 4
Master of Mary of Burgundy, 109–11, fig. 4.4
Matilda, Queen, 51, 53, 60
Maximilian of Hapsburg, 110
Mayer, Ottilia and Heinrich, 238–39
meals, 125–26
mediator. *See* intercessor
meditations. *See* prayers
memorial masses, 77, 172
memory aids, 113–14, 122
Michael, Archangel, 170
Middleton, Thomas and wife, 148
*miles Christi*, 65–66
Minehead, Somerset, parish church, 142
*Miracle of Aethelthyrth's Resistance*, 59–60, fig. 2.1
*Miracle of Mount Gargano*, 170, fig. 6.5
*Miracles of Robert of Arbrissel*, 198–99
*Miracles of St. Benedict*, 196
Mirk, John, 27
Moi, Toril, 4
Möibius, Friedrich, 211
monastic privileges, 51, 54–55, 61, 194–200
  rules, 11, 186–200
Montefeltro, Federico da, 233–35, fig. 8.25
Morelli, Giovanni di Pagolo, *Ricordi*, 168
Morley, Mistress, 150
Morrison, Susan Signe, 10
Mylner, James, 146
mystical marriage, 116, 124
  of St. Catherine, 236–37, fig. 8.27
mystical music, 116

narrative. *See* chronicle
Neroccio di Bartolomeo, painter, 227
Norman administration, 53, 62
Norman invasion, 51, 54, 60–61
north side, 141–42, 154. *See also* polarities, north vs. south
Norwich
  Norwich Cathedral, *Despenser Retable*, 79–80
  St. Peter Mancroft, 86
  St. Stephen's, 78, 116, 126
Notke, Bernd, *Crucifixion*, 230–31, fig. 8.13
Nowyk, Henry, 150
nunneries, East Anglian, 11,
Nuremberg, 15
  St. Lorenz, 8–9, 230, 238
    *Wipplar Epitaph*, 230–32, fig. 8.20
    *St. Anne Altarpiece*, 238–39, fig. 8.28
Nussbaum, Otto, 211

*Obsecro te*, prayer, 111
Odilo, abbot of Cluny, 197–98
oratory, 109, 113, figs 4.4, 4.6
Orcagna, Andrea, 161
Orgel, Stephen, 36
Orlandi, Father Stephano, 174
*Ormesby Psalter*, 92
Ostrogoths, 223
Otter, Monica, 51–52, 66
Ottobeuren, abbey of Ottobeuren, 198

Padua, Arena Chapel, 125
*Parable of the Vine-dressers*, 119–22, figs. 4.8, 4.9
Paris, Ste. Chapelle, 224
parish, 1–2, 5–6, 11, 15, 141–56
patronage, 75, 80
 men and women of York, 33–34
 *See also* donors and women, donations of
patronymic, 76
Peacock Feast, 128–29, fig. 4.11
Pen, Mistress, 150
Peter of Celle, 186
pews, 14–15, 141–56
 selling of, 142, 153
Phelan, Peggy, 5
Philip the Good, 111–12, fig. 4.5
Piero della Francesca, 233–35, figs. 8.24, 8.25
Piero di Cosimo, 125
Pilate's wife, Procula, 37–39
*Pilgrim's Guide to Santiago de Compostela*, 109
pilgrimage, 10, 78, 115, 125, 145, 199
play/performance, 13. *See also* York cycle
polarities, 224–30. *See also* space
polarities, directional
 north vs. south, 14, 141, 154, 225, 228
 east vs. west, 224–25
 left vs. right, 14, 17, 207–42
 front vs. back, 141, 154
Pomfriet, Elizabeth and John, 146, 150
Pontius Pilate, *Acts of*, 213
Prague, Cathedral of St. Vitus, 239–40, fig. 8.29
Procopius, 220, 223
prostitution, 29, 143, 223
public vs. private. *See* space
pulpit, 226
punishments, 16, 51, 65, 186, 188–90, 192, 198
purity, 52–53, 144

Raguin, Virginia, 29, 77, 80, 176
rape, 51–53, 56, 58, 63, 66
Ravenna
 Sant' Apollinare Nuovo, 219–20, 225, fig. 8.12
 San Vitale, 221–23, 237, figs. 8.14, 8.15
Regensburg, Heilig Kreuz convent, 236–37, fig. 8.27
Reginald of Durham, 190–91
Reims, abbey of St. Remi, 186
*Regula ad Monachos*, 187
Regula S. Ferreoli, 187
relics, 15, 127, 187, 196, 224
Ricco Bardi, Riccardo di, 175
Richa, Guiseppe, 173
Ridyard, Susan, 51–53
Ringland, parish church, 94
*Rites of Durham*, 190
ritual, 5, 13, 86, 89, 93, 124, 152
 Holy Week, 9, 115, 160
 initiation rites, 56
 processions, 35, 115, 160
 Purification of the Blessed Virgin Mary, 35
 *See also* Communion
Robert of Arbrissel, 198–99
Robertson, Elizabeth, 10
Rogationtide, 31
Rolin, Nicolas, 208–10, 212, fig. 8.3
Romanus, St., 16, 195–96
Rome, 88
 Church of the Holy Apostles, 124
 Santa Croce in Gerusalemme, 88
 Santa Maria Maggiore, 125
Romuald, St., 187–88
rood screens. *See* space
*Rosario della vita*, 114
rosary, 117
Rosselli, Stefano, *sepoltuario*, 174
Rubin, Gayle, 62
Russell, John, 145
Rykener, John/Eleanor, 29

sacraments, 2, 122, 126. *See also* Mass
Saint-Amand-les-Eaux, monastery of Elone, 196
Salins, Guigone des, 208–10, 212, fig. 8.3
Sano di Pietro, 226–27, *San Bernardino Preaching in Piazza San Francesco, Siena*, fig. 8.17, *San Bernardino Preaching in Piazza del Campo*, 8.18
sarcophagus, 50–52, 62, 173
Sassetti, Francesco, 235
Sassetti, Madonna Isabetta, 169
Savonarola, 226–27, fig. 8.16

Schäuffelein, Hans, *Crucifixion*, 213–15, fig. 8.6
Schleif, Corine, 33, 143, 155
Schulenburg, Jane Tibbetts, 51, 66
Screen. *See* space
Seating. *See* pews
Segregation. *See* space
sermons, 106
Sewenna and Sewara, 57, 59–60, 63, fig. 2.1
Sexburg, abbess, 49, 64–65
sexual ambiguity. *See* gender ambiguity
sexual discovery/knowledge, 24–26
  fig-leaf, 27
sexuality, erotic, 28–29, 37
Sforza, Battista, 233–35, fig. 8.24
Shakespearean drama, 36
Sheingorn, Pamela, 55–56
shields. *See* coats of arms
Siena, Cathedral of Siena, 227–29, fig. 8.18
Silver, Brenda, 58
Simone, Don Leonardo di, 164
Siviard, St., abbot of Anisole, 188
Smith, Simon, wife of, 150
sounds/vocalizations, 114–17. *See also* weeping
Space. *See also* polarities, directional
  access to, 7–8, 15, 85, 122–23, 175–76, 186, 194–200
  Eden vs. Earth, 28
  boundaries in, 6, 51, 59, 188–90, 192, 225
  enclosure within, 48, 50, 117–22
  public vs. private, 3–5, 76–77
  screens dividing, 3–6, 106, 141, 176, 226, 228
  segregation within, 142, 176, 186, 225–30
*Speculum humanae salvationis*, 117–19, fig. 4.8
Sponsler, Claire, 37
Spryngolde, Robert, 122
squint, 6–9, 115, frontispiece
St. Bertin. *See* St. Omer monastery of St. Bertin
St. Cloud, convent of La Balme, 193, 195–96
St. Margaret's. *See* Lynn, St. Margaret's; Westminster, St. Margaret's
St. Stephen's, Norwich. *See* Norwich, St. Stephen's
St.-Benoit-sur-Loire, monastery of Fleury, 196–97
St. Omer, monastery of St. Bertin, 16, 197
stained glass, 80, 117–22, 164–65, 176, figs. 4.7, 4.9
Stanbury, Sarah, 109, 113, 125
Star Court, 142
status, symbols of, 1, 54, 144, 146–47, 150. *See also* class
Stephen, King, 51, 53, 60, 67
Stevenson, Mistress, 149–50
stockfish, 89–90
Strohm, Paul, 30
Suger, abbot of St. Denis, 130
sumptuary laws, 16
Symeon of Durham, 189–90, 194
*Synagoga*, 213

Talbot, Elizabeth, 81–82, fig. 3.2
Tarnatensis, monastery of, *Regula*, 194
Tebbe, Agnes, 149
theater, public, 39
Theodora, Empress, 221–23, fig. 8.15
Theofroi, St., *Vita*, 194
Throne of Mercy, 86, 92, fig. 3.5
Tilney, Elizabeth, 81–82, fig. 3.2
Tolmie, Jane, 36
tombs, 2, 16, 85, 125, 127–29, 163, 172–73, 176, 187, 199
Tonbert, King, 55
Tornaquinci, Guardina, 161, 174–75, 176–77
*Traité sur l'oraison dominicale*, 111–12, fig. 4.5
transvestite, 29, 35–36
Tree of Knowledge, 25
Trinity, 90–95, 117, 123, 216–17, figs. 3.4, 3.5, 3.6, 8.8
  Trinity, guild of, 96, 123
Tübingen, Collegiate Church, *Crucifixion* Altarpiece, 213–15, fig. 8.6
Tudor, Margaret, 112–13, fig. 4.6

University of Paris, 113
Urbino, Duke and Duchess, 233–35, figs. 8.24, 8.25

van der Weyden, Rogier, *Beaune Altarpiece*, 208–10, 213, 221, 230, 241, figs. 8.3, 8.4
van Eyck, Jan, *Altarpiece of the Lamb*, (Ghent Altarpiece), 208–10, 215, 221, 230, 241, figs. 8.1, 8.2
Velluti, Monna Gemma, 16, 161, 169–70, 176–77
Vijd, Jodocus, 208–10, 212, fig. 8.1
Vincent of Saragosa, St., relics of, 196
virago, 64–66
Virgin and Child, 111–13, 231–33, figs. 4.4, 4.5, 4.6, 8.22
Virgin Mary, 56, 91, 110, 150, 162, 217–19, 241–42, figs. 8.10, 8.11
  Annunciation, 163, 165–66, 173, figs. 4.4, 6.4
  as *Madonna Misericordia*, 220–21, fig. 8.13
  with Six Apostles, 217–19, fig. 8.10
Virgins, Wise and Foolish, 215–16, fig. 8.7
virtues and vices, 114
visions, 77–79, 83, 90
Volckamer, Agnes, 236
von Schweidnitz, Anna, 233, 239, fig. 8.23
von Simpson, Otto, 3, 222

Walburga, St., 235–36, fig. 8.26
Walker, John, 94, fig. 3.6
Walker, Ralph (Rauff), 29–30
Walsoken, de, Adam and Margaret, 127–29, fig. 4.10
weeping, 78, 83–84, 114–15, 123, 125, 130
Werburg, nun of Ely, 49
Westminster
  abbey, 145
  St. Margaret's parish church, 144–49, 151–52
*What the Goodwife Taught Her Daughter*, 144
widows, 34, 149, 168–69, 177, 237–38
Wihtburg, abbess, 49–50, 64–65
Wilfred, bishop of York, 56
William of St. Calais, 189
William the Conqueror, 60–65
wills, 169, 171, 170–76
Winchester, Minster, *Liber vitae*, 230–32, fig. 8.21
*Wipplar Epitaph*, 230–31, 241, fig. 8.20
wives, 33, 117–19, 237–38. *See also* women, widows
Wogan-Brown, Jocelyn, 10
Wölfflin, Heinrich, 210
women, 168
  behavior, 143–44, 151–52, 190, 197
  female pollution, 142–43
  donations of, 33–34, 49, 75–77, 80–81, 94, 149, 151, 155, 161–75, 189–90, 192, 195, 197, 230, 235–39, *See also* pews
  segregation of, 176, 186–93, 230–37
  *See also*, gender, wives, widows
Woodforde, Christopher, 80
Woolf, Virginia, 1
Wyclif, John, 93

Yates, Francis, 113
York, 23
  Holy Trinity Goodramgate, 94, fig. 3.6
  Minster, 80
York Corpus Christi play cycle, 12, 23, 33, 35
  the Cardmakers' *The Creation of Adam and Eve*, 27
  the Coopers' *Fall of Man*, 26, 38
  the Skinners' *Entry into Jerusalem*, 30
  the Tapiters' and Couchers' *Christ before Pilate I*, 37–38
  the Barkers' *Fall of Lucifer*, 31–32
  pageant stations, 39
  pageant wagon, 32–33
  procession route, 24, 31, 34–35, 38–39
  *See also* Corpus Christi
*York House Book*, 38

Zika, Charles, 33

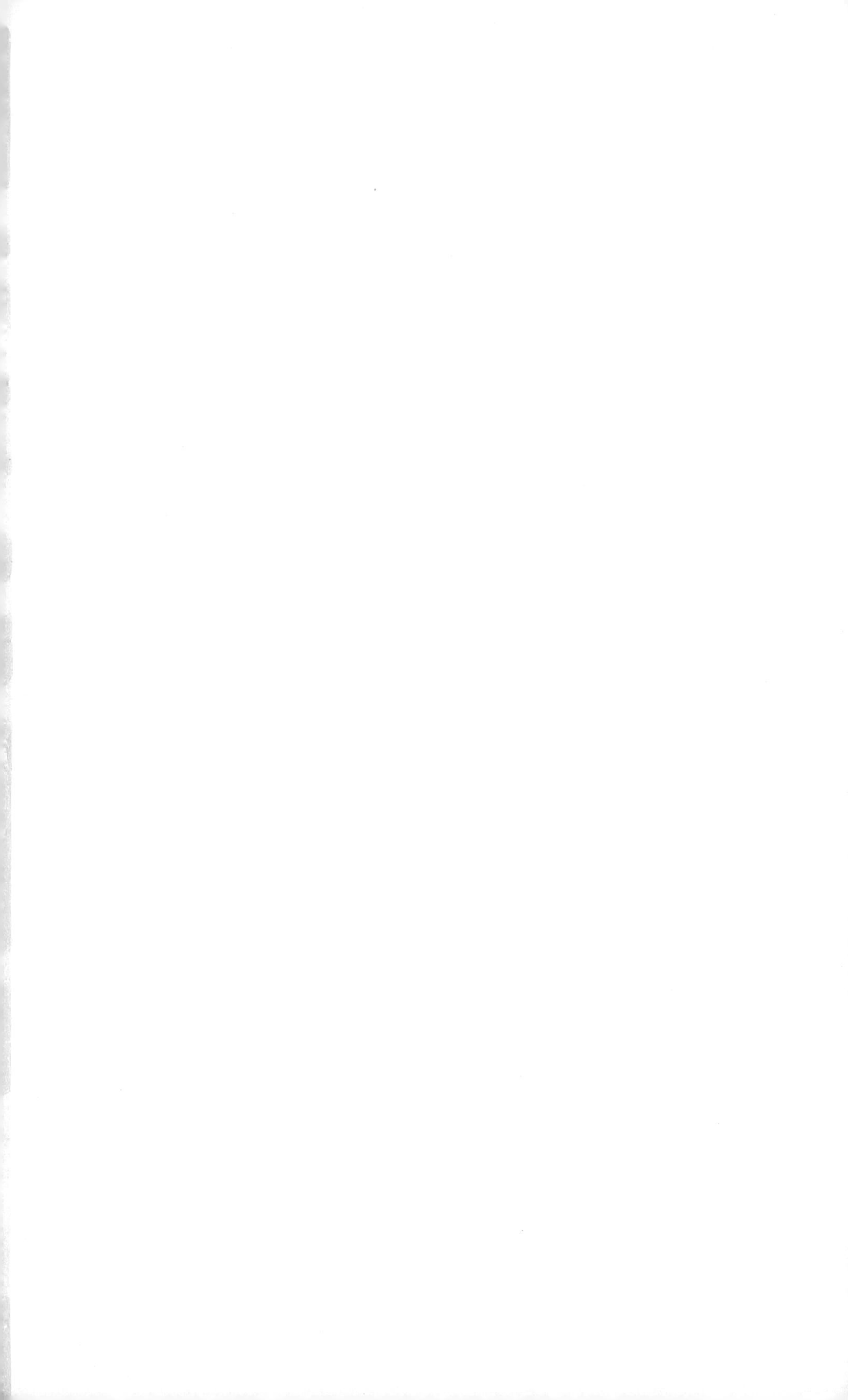